Praise for Volume I,
The DNA of Democracy

"As drawn here, the arc of world and American history is inspiring. The book's narrative about greater and greater equality and independence feels natural and works toward a conclusion that emphasizes increasing inclusion and equality in politics. **The DNA of Democracy** is a thorough and praise-filled history of democracy."

—*Foreword Reviews*

"Lyons has penned books of poetry, and it shows in his writing. **The DNA of Democracy** will engage readers interested in the deep history of democracy in America."

—*Indie Book Reviews*

SHADOWS *of the* Acropolis

Volume II

Shadows of the Acropolis

Richard C. Lyons

Shadows of the Acropolis: Volume II

Cover and Interior Design: Indigo Design, Inc.

designbyindigo.com

ISBN 978-0-9973462-9-9

Printed in the U.S.A.

This work is dedicated to those who have given their labors, their fortunes, their health, their hopes, their faith and their lives in sacrifice, throughout history's annals, to serve with their full devotion in the eternal war for human freedom.

Foreword

Over the entry door to the ancient temple city of Delphi, Greece, stood a lentil with one simple admonition" "Know Thyself." The godhead of the Temple of Delphi was the god of the sciences, the god of light, Apollo. Pilgrims from all over the Greek world sought out to find Delphi, as they sought the ultimate illumination to answer the question, "Who Am I?" It was the question which began the Greek expedition to know the Earth and its member humanity through the sciences. Thus, the demand began the studies of Thales, of Heraclitus, of Anaxagoras, of Pythagoras and Democritus. It was a question which consumed Socrates the Athenian, who was convinced and who showed to the various populous of the ancient city-state, that in fact, one of the most difficult things for humans to do in this world, seems the most simple – to know oneself. Socrates, in the full sunlight, on his beloved Acropolis, deemed it the first devotion of the true philosopher's soul to know oneself through a rigorous path of self-effacement, which was lighted by way of the continual discovery of the truth, which could only be fulfilled in a free society.

In "The DNA of Democracy," this author wrote a study hoping to illuminate the subject for the reader sufficiently that they might define what comprises the DNA of Democracy and what traits comprise its opposite: Tyranny. The work began with the Ten Commandments and ended with the Suffragette Movement, when the American system of federalism, in 1920, enjoyed at once the most direct democracy and the most representative government the world has ever produced. In America, at that time, there was a profound mixture of diffused powers societally with which "government" had nothing whatever to do, while Americans enjoyed direct democracy locally and representative democracy at the state and federal levels of governance.

However, just as Greece is no longer what it was in the days of Socrates, neither is the government of the United States the same today, as it was in 1920. Heraclitus was famous for saying one could never set foot in the same river twice. Neither can one stop time or the continuous change of our reality's circumstances. So, this second volume in the series, sets about to discover what has changed in this country's system of democracy since 1900, and asks why? So, that we may in America, in this day, at this hour in our history, best "Know Ourselves."

Do you wonder why, as a citizen, it seems that you are no longer represented? Do you wonder why half the nation is incensed no matter who is the President? Do you wonder why the nation feels so politically divided? Do you wonder why people in this country are polarized and enmity between each side is on the rise? Do you wonder why people in the media speak in many tongues providing different "truths?" Do you wonder why our politics have become a matter of name calling, closed-door maneuverings and political persecutions rather than a matter of respectful debate between parties of mutual respect and good intent? Do you wonder why we seem to be reaching for solutions, not through democratic processes, but through intrigue, hatred and violence? You have the right book in your hands right now - As we must set about to actually "know" our nation as she is... at this pivotally important moment.

Join me in a literary journey of discovery to find what has turned our one nation under God, into two nations that are at violent odds as we will travel through time and events from 1900 to today. You will read true histories, combined with some elucidating commentary which will help us define where we are today by defining what has changed... and why. As much as "The DNA of Democracy" explains from whence Democracy came to us up to 1920, the "Shadows of the Acropolis" will help explain where we are.

It is a part of the expedition that never ends...this eternal quest to "Know Thyself."

Table Contents

Preface

The freedom of humanity, observable in the annals of history, can be equated to the astronomical finding of a quasar, a rarity indeed, in the otherwise uniform darkness of its surroundings. Where quasars exist, they pour out an incomparable energy and an intermittent, brilliant light, more visible than any other stellar object in the universe as it is observed...and then vanishes. The intermittent light of human liberty has always been defined by its brilliance, and by the envelope of darkness that has surrounded it.

From the ashes of Athens, to the blood-soaked Roman Forum, to the castle keeps of England, history has noted how common the environments of enslavement have been, and how rare the occasions of humanity's transcendence above them—as with the Acropolis, the Twelve Tables, and the Magna Carta. It has been a human struggle against tyranny that humanity has seldom won, and only amid the constancy of tyrannical torments through interspersed sacrificial rebellions occurring over millennia.

Wherever, whenever mankind has won confronting tyranny, freedom has remained imperiled still. The existence of human liberty is rare, for it requires for its very life that all citizens agree that their liberty is the paramount common priority. Therefore, its foundations are always at hazard of fracturing from human weaknesses, and by the sometimes-beguiling appearance of tyranny. In humanities long story, the foundations of freedom have fractured everywhere they have been framed.

In America, the sacrifices of all the ages before us have been poured into the foundations of our freedom, atop which formed a beacon, like philosophical lightening striking through the ages, to land in the remarkable wilderness of the American colonies—home to the influence of the Iroquois and Cherokee Leagues, where freedom had space and could breathe.

Freedom took root in America in the form of humanity's "original powers" that grew out of nothing but the wilderness: that of the independent individual, the family, the associations of faiths, one's property, and one's enterprises. Each benefitted in their American birth from a centuries old system of common law which kept them secure.

Early on, the only "government" that existed was the township where, as in Athens, everyone represented themselves. Each entity of the original powers in America thrived based on and within a "Declaration of Independence" from intrusive governance. Our nation's freedom was founded on the very definition of "independence," whose synonyms are *self-reliance, self-subsistence, self-sufficiency, and self-support.*

Once the nation was born out of the immeasurable sacrifices of the Revolution, the Constitution of the United States created a blend of elements from constitutions going back to Athens, Rome, and England, with ideas of federalism that were actually unique to the Iroquois League. Each of the elements were carefully woven together to arrive at a government that, at once, diffused, separated, and contained power. As in the tradition of the Cherokee League, the central power was kept at a minimum so that each individual's power might be maintained at the maximum.

The Bill of Rights, comprising the first ten amendments to the Constitution, confers on each individual common rights for which humanity had fought for six thousand years to achieve—since the Ten Commandments were wrought atop Mount Zion, since Rome's Twelve Tables were hammered into brass by the Decemvirs, since the signing of the Magna Carta first brought a measure of common law, property rights, and freedom to England, and since the Declaration of Right ended the Divine Right of Kings.

Our constitution further demands that all our laws come from the single wellspring of authority: the people. And further dictates that the laws be faithfully and equally executed. Thereby, the people create a common law for all, which rules each individual. But our Constitutional Law rules the government as well—which is the inverse of the tyrannical design. Up to the point of our Constitution's framing, it took the length of human history for such a rebellious democracy to overcome the dominance of tyranny.

Democracies throughout history have had their failings. Democracy only has *being* as an eternal idea. In reality, it is either becoming more a reflection of the light of democracy's "ideal," or it is falling away, like the appearance of a quasar, emitting at one time the most brilliant light then pulsing with a lesser flame—more in keeping with the darkness of tyranny's surroundings. Democracy is always either becoming or falling away...it is an *idea* that must always be held to with faithful devotion—as it was by Themistocles, who while on his vagrant ships off the coasts of Salamis, watched his city state become wreathed in smoke, saw ascend a lurid flame and the billowing ash rise with the winds from a perishing Athens and said, "We have indeed left our houses and our walls...not thinking it fit to become slaves for the sake of things that have not life or soul...."

Our system, ideally of diffused and limited governance, is one whereby each citizen is endowed to be the sole author of themselves. It is a system that allows each citizen their own sacred pursuit of a personal grail of fulfillment in accordance with their gifts. Each citizen is, themselves, capable of engaging and igniting their own inner quasar to flood the world with light, which, on a national scale, becomes the mosaic of a constellation.

Such is the ideal. In reality, our freedom and structure of government are fragile and mortal owing to the nature of government power, and human nature when *in* power. The writer Somerset Maugham voiced this warning in 1941 that, "If a nation values anything more than freedom, it will lose its freedom; and the irony is that if it is comfort or money that it values more, it will lose that too."

In Volume I of this series, *The DNA of Democracy,* we traced the history of democracy until it landed in America. We chronicled the country's unique circumstances, its revolution, its original constitutional framework, equality's confirmation through the unprecedented crucible of the Civil War, and the broadest participation achieved through the Women's Suffrage movement, wherein our American form of democracy achieved its greatest outflowing of light.

In this, Volume II of the *Shadows of the Acropolis* series, we will discover how our federal government has failed to uphold the "ideals" of our original liberty. This failure has occurred over the past century, whereby fundamental freedoms inherent in our founding, in our Constitution, in our Free Enterprise system, in our Bill of Rights, in our Original Powers and in our Natural Rights as individuals have been steadily overshadowed by our federal government's assumption of ever-expanding powers, at the expense of the diffused intermediary powers which once stood between every individual citizen and the federal government. This volume will recount, with definition, the light of freedom which flowed out of our original principles, and the shadows that have fallen over that light. This work details what powers of ours have been levied from us by the federal government, in this very dramatic shift in the fundamental structure of our nation. A shift of powers which has brought us, in the present, to the very edge of tyranny's darkness.

I chose the title, *Shadows of the Acropolis,* for it was upon the Acropolis plateau of classical Athens that shown the most remarkable beacon of democracy's original light. It is to that original light that modern democracies, such as they are, owe their own. When from that original light we fall, it is indeed a falling, first into shadows, then into darkness.

So, let us begin, let us first define the characteristics of a modern tyranny, how we have differed historically, and why the nature of governmental power unrelentingly tends to tyranny, as this bears directly on the changes that have occurred in America and in other modern democracies over the past century.

Introduction

Beings of Modern Tyranny

Modern-day China occupies one fifth of the land surface of the globe, covering 9.6 million square kilometers. Within its physical area exists every kind of climate the earth expresses. Within her borders resides one-fifth of the world's population, or 1.4 billion people.

The country is organized into thirty-three administrative districts, each overseen by a centralized series of massive bureaucracies employing ten million people, a figure that does not include the military. These ten million functionaries are overseen by twenty ministers, who answer to one man and one man alone—Xi Jinping, the premier of the People's Republic of China and the general secretary of the Communist Party, or the CCP. The "one" man who, through a few, rules vast multitudes from the central city of Beijing—the center of the culture, the economy, the communications infrastructure, the police, the military, and all power over the vast reaches of China. Beijing is the center of the Chinese government, it is the center of the Communist Party, it is—as far as any of 1.4 billion people are concerned—the center of everything.

Whether any the of 1.4 billion people have a job, whether they have clothes, whether they have a car or a bicycle, whether they have a child, whether their child has an education, or the child's family even has a home, is directly up to one man who controls everyone in the nation through his twenty ministers. The government is the universal landlord.

The economy of China recorded a 2019 GDP of $14.3 trillion, employing one billion people, who produce millions of goods yet not one of these goods is produced without the approval of the "one" man and his ministers. If you are to "own" or produce anything in China, it takes the form of a "gift," which the government alone may grant and which the government alone can take away at any time. Only those who are approved are given such a "gift." The government has the sole power to raise anyone up, and the sole power to ruin anyone. The government is the universal employer.

From one's earliest days as a subject in China, they are educated through a controlled prism. The CCP dictates the only subjects and sole contents to be learned by every student, which ultimately determines their view of the world. The "faith" of the people of China is dictated: everyone's paramount "faith" must be given to the state. No CCP member, of its 95 million, can practice a religion—religion is considered monolithic. It is faith in the premier that is important. Outside of the CCP, no other subject may hold religious views or express religious thoughts that the state does not allow. If they do, they are subject to arrest.

China has a myriad of mass organizations, from youth clubs to women's groups to trade groups, which Americans would equate to our numerous associations based on occupations or interests. But, in China, the myriad organizations have one source and one end. They are each born of, and "associated" with, the CCP. They are the means whereby the Communist Party further indoctrinates every subject into right thinking, and into right performance, toward the "right" end of the party. If one attempts to criticize these organizations or tries to form a voluntary association outside those that are strictly permitted as a "gift" from government, they are subject to arrest.

Everything that a person sees and hears of the arts that are produced throughout their lives is only with the approval of the CCP. Every sport or game is approved by the CCP. Everything one consumes from the media, whether news or entertainment, is determined by the CCP. If one produces or plays or views or listens to anything that is not approved, they are subject to arrest.

So, you are a Chinese renegade and suffer an unapproved thought, have a misguided faith, or an unapproved friend; or, you engage in an unapproved club, listen to unapproved music or videos, or play an unapproved game. So what...right? A slap on the wrist? Wrong.

The state-sanctioned, CCP-approved telecom giant China Mobile has been tracking you for a very long time. They know who you have phoned, they know what you have read or watched or listened to. They know what apps you have and during what time you use them. Every bit of content you have accessed—they know "*what*" down to the kilobyte and "*when*" down to the second.

Combining that technology with the state-sanctioned, CCP-approved facial recognition firm Megvii, the state knows all of the above *plus* where you are right now. They know how you got there, they know where you were, and they'll know where you go from here and who you are travelling with. The state knows each and every person you have any kind of contact with. They even know your mood, even if you wear a mask—through artificial intelligence capabilities, they can see through it. The Chinese government knows your body temperature to within 0.3 degrees Celsius.

In a country that holds one-fifth of the people living on earth today, the state knows where everyone is and exactly what they are doing—and it is doing everything to determine what they are thinking. In a country that is the fifth largest on the globe, there is not a corner left anywhere for anyone to hide.

So, you suffered an unapproved thought and expressed it to a friend and discussed it at a family event. That shouldn't be a problem, right? Wrong. The government heard you. The government, the CCP, the military, the police, the court, and the penal system of China are all one united entity. Even if your thought was just a small one—you spoke it, and you cannot prove you did not think it. You can be arrested. You can be held indefinitely. Go ahead, plead your case—the verdict is determined. You can be imprisoned anywhere, exiled anyplace, executed any time, without having any recourse because you had the one thought and expressed it to a friend and to your family. And now, your friend and family will suffer the same party-approved, state-dictated fate with you, because you shared an unapproved thought. Your life, and theirs, is over—and what remains is likely to be excruciating pain.

This is what becomes of the rule of "the one through the few" who enslave multitudes. It is as old as the Pharaohs. In a nation of 1.4 billion, all of China is ruled by a single person. And for the 1.4 billion Chinese in the world, from the confinement of a Chinese cradle to the state-allotted container of a Chinese grave, all of life in China seems to be enchained. China has been a common keep of humanity for four thousand years. Today, with the help of technology, it has the means to be totalitarian. And it is, in the very modern sense of the word.

The European Model

The term and style of governance known as "*totalitarian*" comes to us from early and mid-20th century Russia and Germany. It refers to mechanized, omnipresent tyranny. Its definition has been enhanced since then by technology's every advance.

The National Socialist Party of Germany and the Socialist Bolshevik Party of Russia both had small beginnings. But each grew through an utter disregard for justice, democratic principles, or human life—a disregard which both Hitler and Lenin shared. Their parties, like the CCP, dedicated themselves to taking over every organ from governance, to education, to faith, to the economy, to the people's assemblies, to the justice system, to the electioneering system, to the police, to the military, to every aspect of society. In their societies, not a corner was free for any survivor. Every aspect of society in those totalitarian utopias was strangled by a single, dedicated party, ruled by "one." Only the speed of the takeovers differed, neither the means nor the ends, when all of society operated and became "one" entity. The Nazis demanded it be done for the good of the "Fatherland;" after all, the government was their "father." The Bolshevik's claimed absolute power for the good of "Mother Russia;" after all, government was everyone's "mother." Thus, Hitler and Lenin suffocated the life out of masses of their own populations and treated the whole of Europe like an innocent babe strangled in the crib by its parents.

America differs from these tyrannies of China and Europe—and there is a reason.

The American Difference

American society is made up of a dynamic cornucopia of constituent elements starting with each "individual" and spreading out to an area's individual families, its single's scenes, its churches and clubs, its schools and parks, its PTAs, its local sports, and its businesses. From a city or town's restaurants to its cinemas, art galleries, and concert halls, down to the bakeries, the book stores, and coffee shops, and the 331 million people that flow creatively through life across 50 states from the surfers of Hawaii to the snow skiers of Vermont, to each their own—individually.

Ideally, each teacher lends a distinct learning perspective, leading energetic minds in an individual direction. Ideally, each painter decides the canvass to paint on, the spectrum of color to determine the palette, the subject to paint, the message to convey. Ideally, each musician decides the key of their own melody, the instruments to accompany them, and the sentiment to send through the vibrant air. Ideally the government, our federal government, is supposed to be one small entity within the vast, creative, experiential society of the United States. Our government was originally built to stay that way...by the sensible controls of our Constitution...to stay *out* of everyone's way!

In America, our government is not referred to as a *father* or a *mother*—it is "Uncle Sam." An uncle does not live in your house. An uncle does not tell you or your kids what to do or what to eat or what to believe. An uncle does not control the local school or demand what your child can or cannot learn. An uncle does not know or own your business or determine what you do or what your salary is. An uncle is not your grocer or your priest or your teacher or your doctor or your landlord or your banker or anything other than an at-arms-length relation who you might call on now and then, who is kept out of doors and at a distance unless or until invited in. That is the "ideal" of American government. Government is a *part* of American society— it is not supposed to consume society into itself.

The difference in America is that we are supposed to invest in our federal government only those powers we choose to give it as individuals and citizens. And those powers are supposed to be kept at a minimum, and they are supposed to be controlled by the original fountain of authority: the people, through voting elections. Again, that is the ideal.

The Inherent Problem of Government

However, there is a constancy about all governments—from China to Russia to Germany to America. Once given birth and invested with power, governments become living beings with natural processes and instincts, and they are also subject to the ills ever present in the nature of humanity and the nature of power.

As Woodrow Wilson observed: "Government is not a machine; but a living being." A government consumes material and produces waste in proportion. A government will grow and seek to develop strength. A government will develop a distinct identity. A government develops a range of motion, defined by what it controls; it will range as far as possible and control all that it can. A government will react and adapt to its surroundings. A government will develop territoriality, staking claim over what it governs to the furthest possible expanse. These are natural processes and the habits of all governments within their habitats. If one trespasses into its claimed territory, a government, like a tiger, will respond aggressively. It is in the nature of powerful beings, it is in the nature of governments, it is the nature of a tiger.

The growth of such a being is controlled only by a lack of what it needs to consume to grow. In a government's case, that is all the money it can take. The range of such a being can only be controlled either by predators or by barricades emplaced to deny further range.

There are other natural processes in common with the life of a government: a government will reproduce itself in the form of departments and agencies, which it controls within its domain. Over time, like a living species, a government will mutate over generations. The instincts of the governmental beast stay the same but based on the surroundings, it becomes more efficient and expansive in its feeding, in assuming more range and control, and becomes more prolific in its procreation.

More than being a creature of nature, a government also resembles a being of *human* nature. Its ideas come of human passions and reasonings, its motives are outpourings of human motives. Not only do the instincts of nature apply—making government possessive, reactive, reproductive, territorial, and retaliatory—but human attributes apply too.

If it is in human nature to be kind, it is also in human nature to be cruel. What is human nature when invested with power? What is human nature when part of the animating force of governance over others? We can say what it is by the historical evidence supplied by tyranny: Human nature, when invested with the power of governance, is not kind. It is jealous, it is covetous, it is pompous, it is inflated, it is rude, it seeks its own interests, it is quick tempered, it recoils at unwelcome truths, it broods over injury. When human nature is supplied with governing power, it is cunning, it is controlling, it is injurious, and it is lethal.

A government is never a "mother" or a 'father" or a "friend." Governmental power is always a threat. The architect of the Constitution, James Madison, put it discreetly when he said, "The essence of Government is power; and power, lodged as it must be in human hands, will ever be liable to abuse."

Another hand-me-down from nature, and human nature, that makes governmental power dangerous are political parties. They are a derivative of herds in nature and tribes among humanity: parties have their own morality. A party parallels the social system of a wolf pack, with its own sense of a closed power structure, its own unique howling, its own sense of club loyalty, its own group defense system, its own will to further power at the expense of other packs as we witness today in members of the CCP versus those who are not "members." Or, as seen in the last century in the National Socialist and Bolshevik Parties, it can be said of the power within such parties, and the governments they control, as Shakespeare said of his character Coriolanus, "There is no more mercy in him than there is milk in a male tiger."

Such herds seek to serve the group alone, from elders to cubs and all their relatives, exclusive of those outside the club. As evidence, one may ask, "How were the Saxons treated by the Normans? How were the Liberal Democrats of Germany treated by the Nazis?" The instincts of a herd are always the same, only the names change.

The American Wh"Y" in the Road

America's founders, who stood at the precipice of having to construct a new system of government, with history's invariable examples of continuous and all-consuming tyrannies in view, acted with a healthy fear of the natural instincts of government to expand, to grow, and to assume control. They acted on a reasoned knowledge of what human nature could do when it assumed the power to dominate and punish "others," they knew it to be in the nature of political parties to protect and serve themselves— at the expense of "others."

The central question of the Constitutional Convention of 1787, given the natural earthbound instincts of government, was how much power a government should have, and how that power should be controlled. Befitting of a generation that grew up being educated with Plato's reverence of "ideals," and with Newton's physics masterpiece the *Magnificent Principia*, they turned their gaze skyward to the immutable spheres and their orbits based on the constancy of universal laws, and they were prayerful that the orbit of a federal government of their creation might be so constrained—by constitutional law. They fashioned the Constitution to be the celestial reins on our government's natural ambitions. The question that only time could answer was and is: would the reins of a constitution hold tame the will of the tiger?

That is why our nation was so uniquely devised as a system of federalism: a system of barricades to protect *against* the natural formation of a centralized concentration of power; whereby the government becomes the sole benefactor and punisher of every person within the government's bounds, where "the one and the few" maintain the populace as prisoners and themselves as gods...

America's founders could have created a style of governance like so many of those since history began, since Cain and Abel: a state wherein the "one"—the tiger—would exercise absolute power over everyone as it does this very day in China, in Russia, in Venezuela, and in Cuba. Instead, when the Founders came to the "Y" in the American road between tyranny and liberty, they decided that every "one" should own absolute power over themselves.

The first objective in the design of the American government was to shield every individual's original powers – the absolute power of the individual to govern themselves! This liberty extended to one's family, one's faith, one's associations, one's property, one's occupation, one's enterprises, one's town, one's state, and finally, to one's federal representation in lawmaking assemblies. That is American society—of which the federal government is supposed to be a cornered and barricaded part. At least, that is the ideal.

This road was taken so that the heirs of our founders' heroism and labor—that is, we "ourselves" —might never become the mute slaves of a totalitarian style of governance such as we see in China today.

The Problem of Federalism

Today, in addition to the natural and human problems inherent in any government, we see the problematic question that federalism poses around the world. How much power should a central government hold over member regions, states, or nations?

In the European Union, the city of Brussels has, in keeping with the nature of government, gone on the offensive since its inception in 2000, taking evermore legislative authority from the member nations. The power of the Euro bureaucracy has become evermore meddlesome in each member nation in every aspect of their societies through a system of ministerial law, dictated by unelected bureaucrats who no one ever saw, or heard of… or voted for. It is the emergence of an absolutism akin to that of Louis XIV, without the crown.

True to her history, Britain recently determined to free herself from this growing continental hegemony, and this new bureaucratic technocracy through Brexit. Because, as Joseph C. Sternberg *put* it, "First born in the 1950s at the high-water mark for faith in technocracy, the successive institutions that blossomed into today's EU were always premised on the notion that voters couldn't be trusted." Britons have had the vote over their own issues for a very long time and a legal independence that stretches back proudly to England's unique Magna Carta.

Let's look further at Britain: She herself is a type of "federation" of England, Scotland, Wales, and Northern Ireland. But Scotland, Wales, and Northern Ireland have each been having trouble with the arrangement of power being centered in, and overbearing from, London for centuries. Britain is a member of a wider federation, as well, in her loose arrangement of the Commonwealth—a body of former colonies wherein each member agrees on a set of governing laws for commercial purposes without attempting to dictate to each other how to behave internally.

The "federal" problem goes back as far as history. It is a continuous question: how much power does a central authority have over member states? The Persian Empire had the problem within their tyrannical system of satrapies. Athens experienced the problem with member city-state democracies of the Delian League (I would refer the reader to the *Melian Dialogue* for the details of those circumstances).

Returning to today, Beijing is struggling to exert her absolutism in Hong Kong, a semi-independent city-state operating outside China's strictly and centrally controlled federation of provinces, or *Shengs*. The problem with federalism is in full view for everyone to note - how bothered China's 20 ministers are, and how bothered the premier is, to not hold absolute control over every inch of that minute territory and every one of those businesses and subjects. In Beijing, there really is no question: Hong Kong will be consumed by the CCP's absolute rule.

There are other factors of nature to consider regarding federalism, factors that extend from Newton once again: that which has mass and is in motion - gathers mass. A government that is on the move everywhere will gather power wherever it goes, increasing its size, assuming control, gathering ever more.

Then, there is the physics problem of centrifugal force: a central governmental body of such size tends, by its very gravity, to pull to itself all surrounding objects of lesser gravity. Our own sun, were it not counterbalanced by the gaseous giants at the nether end of our solar system, would have collapsed into itself the inner planets of our system to the sphere of Mars. But because the planets of Jupiter, Saturn, and Neptune exist, the gravity of the solar system is balanced...and life here on Earth is blessed to exist.

Lastly comes the problem of polarity: the tendency of matter to form based on magnetically opposite poles. It tends to make political parties even more opposed and hostile to each other. Only a common law system that is central and mutually respected and equally executed can be the arbiter of peace between opposite parties, much as the Earth is kept balanced at the equator by her poles.

So, these are the dilemmas bearing on a central governance—and why barricades and balances are essential to liberty. The maintenance of individual liberty and a free society is entirely based on power's containment, and our right relations based on a common, constitutional law.

Now, let us see how well we have contained our tiger. Or shall we find that nature, human nature, and physics have turned our governance against us?

PART ONE

A Little Levy

Let us venture into this work, where we will juxtapose the "Light" in the principles of our original founding with the "Shadows" which have fallen over those principles since 1900. We will see how and why we have come to where we are today and what the implications are for our common liberty.

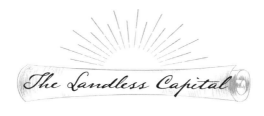

The Landless Capital

– Light –

DINNER AT JEFFERSON'S

A dinner was served on June 20, 1790, at the New York home of Thomas Jefferson, to his political rival Alexander Hamilton and his sometimes-political ally James Madison. The three were at odds concerning the relative strength that the national government was to have comparative to the states. Two major topics were on the agenda that evening, which were at a stalemate in Congress and needed compromise. On the one hand, the debts accruing from the Revolution were substantial and were held by each state in their respective budgets; and needed to be addressed. Secondly, the question as to where to place the capital of a new national, federal government was current on everyone's mind.

As Secretary of the Treasury, Hamilton wanted to create a national bank to assume the debts of all the states and for the future "adequate support of the public credit." To do so meant giving the national government more power than most of the states were comfortable with. Jefferson, the Secretary of State at the time, deeply distrusted the idea as being conducive toward creating a too-centralized financial power—which might lead to an upper class peopled solely by bankers, speculators, and politicians. Madison called it the possibility of "a corrupt mercantile minority." It would also provide a power to government that would, sooner or later, become invasive to the economy and might prove as coercive as the Bank of England had been toward the colonies before the Revolution.

Therefore, Jefferson and Madison, for their part, wanted to secure that the capital—the seat of a central government—was not misplaced to prove unbalancing to the states, either separately or collectively, or given to any other purpose or influence than popular rule. Certainly, it could not be influenced by financial interests, nor be dominant over them.

Many states made claims for being the best home for the new government. Hamilton wanted it to be in New York, in the banking and commercial center of the country. Pennsylvania's Philadelphia also made the same commercial claims, and she had the precedent of being the home of the Continental Congress. Putting the capital in either Philadelphia or New York made international sense. In London, Berlin, Paris, Rome, and Vienna, politics, finance, and culture were combined in one place so everyone knew where to go, who to entertain, and who to bribe.

Virginia made her claim: she was the largest, most populated, most influential state in the country's founding. Many of her residents thought that the state won most of the war alone, that she was first among equals, and therefore deserved the capital. Two of the men dining, Jefferson and Madison, were Virginians—yet they wanted the capital to be independent.

Massachusetts threw in her bid as being the starting place of the rebellion and the rock of the Revolution. Fisher Aimes, a representative of the state, wondered why the capital was even *considered* to be placed on the Potomac River, as though it were "a Euphrates flowing through paradise." Some congressional members preferred the capital to be on wheels, so it could be maneuvered as needed through the states and thus truly representative of everybody.

As the three men sat at table, the discussion led to a resolution. Jefferson and Madison were brought to agree that there should be a national bank: there had to be a mechanism to handle the debt, create a uniform currency, and keep government functioning. And Hamilton was given to agree that the capital would be built on the Potomac River, very deliberately outside the country's commercial centers and very deliberately outside of any state—ensuring no state would be supreme over others. Given the number of votes each man could persuade to confirm this resolution, the outcome in Congress was certain. But the Congress, on one matter—of the capital on the Potomac—was absolute: the capital was not to occupy or control more than ten square miles of land. A landless national government could not pose a threat to any state or anyone. The national government was to be land starved, with no assets of its own other than what the people provided it in the way of funds.

The concord is known historically as the Compromise of 1790, one of the most important in U.S. history, which resulted in both the Resident Act of 1790 (for Washington, DC) and the Assumption Bill of August 4, 1790 (for state debts).

— Shadow —

Executive Expansion

Theodore Roosevelt

Born in 1858, Theodore Roosevelt grew up in an age of political European empires, of industrial empires, and their builders in America.

Over his sixty years, Roosevelt was a venture capitalist and rancher in the Old West, an author of books and articles, a colonel and commander of a military organization that he raised himself called the Rough Riders, who expelled the Spanish Empire from Cuba. He was assistant Secretary of the Navy and prepared the U.S. Asiatic fleet for operations in the Philippines which expelled Spain from those islands. He was police commissioner of New York City and the governor of New York state. He was a visionary who oversaw the establishment of the Panama Canal connecting the Atlantic and Pacific oceans through Central America. And he was the 26th president of the United States. In his later years, he was still an adventurer who penetrated the previously impenetrable Amazon Basin.

In sum, Theodore Roosevelt might be the most unique character the United States ever produced.

In his life, Roosevelt witnessed Bismarck consolidate the ancient principalities and regions of Germany into a very formidable, centrally controlled empire. He witnessed Garibaldi and Vittorio Emanuel do the same in Italy. He witnessed Great Britain's commercial empire at its greatest strength, unifying 25 percent of the earth. Roosevelt's great ambition was to see America become a first-rate power in the world, the equal of the European powers. He saw a means of doing so through the creation of as muscular an executive office as he was a person, and the consolidation of power into the national government. Militarily and diplomatically, he flexed American muscle in Central and South America and the Pacific. But perhaps his greatest legacy occurred within the United States itself, through the "imperial" exercise of executive power.

Levying

A Monopoly

In the latter-day Industrial Age, the instincts of nature, and human nature, were on full display. Several titans emerged, such as J.P. Morgan in America and the Rothschilds of Europe. John D. Rockefeller epitomized the American model. He was a self-made man, the son of a con artist, whose scant education and apprenticeship as a bookkeeper was enough when allied with voracious ambition and very hard work. Rockefeller created the greatest business empire the world had ever seen. His business began as Clarke & Rockefeller in 1859, in the field of produce commission agents, putting together sellers and buyers of goods.

Abetted by the Civil War, Rockefeller made his first fortune. He made his second by growing into the oil business. In predictable manner, Rockefeller expanded his range of business activity to the nation and then to the world. Not content with controlling just his commercial empire, he sought to control the world oil market by buying or destroying his competition—to the ends of the earth—creating an American energy monopoly under the Standard Oil Trust.

Another product of the age was James J. Hill, another bookkeeper like Rockefeller, and another adventurer of the West like Roosevelt, who founded the Red River Transportation Company in steamboats, which soon expanded into the coal business, then into banking, and eventually into railroads, beginning with the St. Paul & Pacific Railroad. Hill became known as the "Empire Builder," who grew his business by adapting to every condition of the frontier and buying out or destroying the competition all along his rail lines throughout the West. He expanded his range by buying all the other rail lines in America, until he ran into the Union Pacific and William Rockefeller—John Rockefeller's brother. As is natural in human nature, they soon went to commercial war with one another. Hill, in partnership with J.P. Morgan, won the rail war, creating a monopoly known as the Northern Securities Company.

The amount of power held by these companies with their various integrated holdings in finance, real estate, manufacturing, and transportation were unprecedented. They had achieved what human nature could achieve when let loose in an environment where they could absorb or destroy all of their competition.

The Rough Rider, who had led the charge at San Juan Hill and blew the Spanish Empire out of Cuba and the Pacific, was no different. He set his sights on his competitors in power to create another kind of empire. Theodore Roosevelt brought forty-four antitrust lawsuits against Standard Oil and the Northern Securities Company, through his Justice Department, based on the little-used Sherman Antitrust Act of 1890; and broke them into pieces. He then created, under the executive branch, the Department of Commerce and Labor, and within that the Bureau of Corporations, through which to control the oil and rail industries and, thereafter and by the same means, hold power over the commerce of the United States. He famously referred to the U.S. Government's new title: "The Senior Partner" of industry.

Levying

The Lands Of The States

Roosevelt then determined on another path of assuming power to the national government and his executive office, particularly. Through a series of executive orders, without the consent of Congress, Roosevelt assumed from the public state domains the lands of thirty-one states into the federal government's balance sheet: 148 million acres of forests, 81 million acres of mineral lands, and 1.5 million acres of waterways—totaling over 360 thousand square miles of territory.

In the span of one presidency, Washington, DC, became the central locus of the economic activity of the country: the federal government and executive branch's superior power over the whole economy—became a monopoly.

In the span of one presidency, the national capital, which was designated at the nation's birth to never exceed ten square miles of territory, assumed lands that exceeded that of all the states that had petitioned to be the seat of the capital—Virginia, New York, Pennsylvania, and Massachusetts combined. The federal government, the "landless" government, became the largest landholder in the United States, dwarfing any state or combination of states.

And a new power emerged under the executive branch of government, the power of the regulatory agency. Despite the best laid plans of the Compromise of 1790, Roosevelt built his empire by levying power over the economy into the federal government, and into the executive branch, and by levying control of land in thirty-one states into the federal government and the executive branch. The federal government grew far beyond the ten-by-ten square miles agreed to by three of the nation's most important founders.

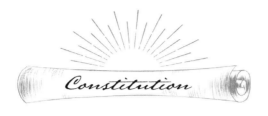

Constitution

– Light –

GEORGE WASHINGTON

After dutifully serving the new nation as its foremost soldier in casting off the chains of tyranny, having retired from that service, like only the Roman Cincinnatus had, by giving over the supreme power of the army to an assembly, our Continental Congress, George Washington was requested to fulfill a new service. He was invited to preside, as only he could, over the Constitutional Convention of 1787. It was an unprecedented role in the history of humanity, as fifty-five representatives of thirteen new states were to debate on the formation of a new nation, founded on the will of the people, not the will of a king, a conqueror or a dictator.

Washington had a unique fund of experience to draw upon. He had been educated in the classics, as were all his peers, and in the "natural rights" doctrine of John Locke; and upon this his revolutionary view of government was based. In keeping with that doctrine, he had lived his whole life within the bounds of material reality and common sense. So armed, he had faced every variety of fortune. He learned assiduously from every victory and defeat. He'd fought against the tyranny of the world's finest army and disabled its king in the colonies. He had dealt with continuous rebellions among his own underfunded soldiers. Among his staff, he'd had to deal with every kind of personality, most of whom thought they knew better than he, in order to form a cohesive force capable of winning a war. He had dealt with the assemblies of every renegade colony to secure funding for a starving army. He then had to hold the new states together, in a single hope that there was some light… at the end of everyone's sacrifice.

This convention was something new, yet his resolve never wavered. "It is not sufficient for a man to be a passive friend and well-wisher to the cause." Having done so much to win everyone's freedom, he had to do his part to secure it.

There were many who still doubted Washington. He still commanded in spirit, if not in form, his old army. He was the president of the veteran's association, The Society of the Cincinnati, who many believed had pretentions to create a new aristocracy. What many thought Washington might do was create a nation under "one" person. But that was exactly what Washington was determined not to do. It was up to every "one" at the convention to secure the right relationships between a national government, a series of various states, a multitude of localities, and each of four million individuals.

Could a right balance be found to answer the problem of federalism? An unprecedented balance had to be struck between a sovereign people and their government. If it was not found for everyone, every labor of Washington's life might be undone. "Thirteen sovereignties pulling at each other, and all tugging at the federal head will soon bring ruin to the whole," Washington had said. The individual had to be sovereign, all the forms of governance had to be responsive to the citizen, and the federal government had to be capable—but in keeping with the original principles of the Revolution. Meaning, the federal government had to govern as little as possible. What was most important, and unprecedented in history, the government had to govern itself.

As he ventured to Philadelphia, Washington knew he would be dealing with more than 50 personalities, each holding their own viewpoints on governance. In fact, with a sum of representation of over 50, it could be expected that every view in the political spectrum would be represented; some would be opposites, and half would likely be opposed to Washington's own views in some measure. In order for the convention to work, Washington could not dictate his view, he had to preside by listening to everyone else's. To conform everyone to his one view would be a tyranny equal to the tyranny the Revolution had just cast off.

Washington had another problem. Such was his reputation as the first among equals for having done so much to win everyone's victory that a nod, a wink, or a glance of his made during a debate might eclipse a perfectly reasoned argument, which covered a whole morning's discussions, and which made the best sense. So, upon arriving to Philadelphia, Washington made it his first resolve to invite his only rival in international fame to attend—he personally invited Benjamin Franklin, whose reputation for wisdom was equal to that of the oracle of universal law, Sir Isaac Newton. Washington personally went to Dr. Franklin's home, just off Market Street and Third, to ensure that the foremost citizen civilian might counterpoise the foremost citizen soldier at the convention among the fifty-odd various voices. Franklin complained that he was infirm at the age of eighty-one, but like his fellow citizens and representatives, he would do all that his age and his pains would allow.

Washington made another resolve through the spring and summer of 1787. He went to as many different churches as he could, whether Presbyterian, Quaker, or Anglican; he even attended a Roman Catholic service. No man was more knowledgeable than Washington on the value of mankind's spiritual counterpoise to civilian rule, that had once made the emperors of Rome tremble and had done so much to found America's freedoms. The people's churches and the people's assemblies influenced each other—neither ever ruled the other. This societal balance between the civil and the spiritual had proved an effective check of societal authorities that helped in the cultural rise of Europe. And this spiritual independence was elemental to the independence of America.

After the convention began on May 25, Washington spent most of the convention listening, always alert… always listening

He listened as the scope of the federal government was circumscribed to establishing justice, ensuring domestic tranquility, providing for the common defense, and securing the blessings of liberty. That was all.

Washington heard during the convention, time and again, that the greatest concern was the problem of federalism—the relative power of the federal government comparative to the states. He listened as the debates engaged: what were the barricades to be erected along a vertical plane between the federal government and the states? How were the states to defend the prerogatives of their independent localities, and defend their citizenry in the individual prerogatives that they had enjoyed for generations?

He listened as the roles in the federal system of the states were laid out as bulwarks against the encroachment of federal power. He listened to the proposed 10th amendment: "The powers not delegated to the United States by the Constitution, nor prohibited by it to the States, are reserved to the States respectively, or to the people." This amendment served to prohibit the federal government from exercising any tyranny vertically through the states, through their localities and through society's "original powers"—those within the American arch of independence: individuals, families, faiths, associations, properties, occupations, and enterprises. It took the form of powers not defined in the Constitution as being reserved to the states and the people.

He listened as the role of Congress was debated. The people's House and the Senate were to be the sole federal legislature, the "original fountain of authority," the formulators of every federal governing law. The federal assembly House was deemed closest to the people's explicit will. The people's House was to have the sole power of the federal purse and be the keepers of the common laws of interstate commerce.

The Senate was to be a check on the House pertaining to law, as its consent was necessary to every law—those which the Senate itself proposed or any that the House proposed. The Senate was also a check on the executive branch, as the persons to be appointed to form the executive needed the consent of the Senate. Washington, as a general and soldier, knew better than anyone in the room what these articles meant. Were he president, the Senate would have to approve his staff, or cabinet, and the House controlled the money; without which an executive can do nothing.

He listened as it was proposed that every meaningful office in government having to do with making law would be subject to frequent elections, and thereby answerable to the people's explicit will. The House offices, those closest to the people, were to be elected every two years to keep the house answerable to the people's will. The executive branch was to be elected every four years (a thing unheard of in an age of hereditary monarchy), and the senators were to be elected every six years to keep government ever answerable, ever rejuvenating, and ever stable. Washington said of the Congress: "Are they not the creatures of the people, amenable to them for their conduct, and dependent from day to day on their breath? Where then can be the danger of giving them such powers as are adequate to the great ends of government...."

He listened as a third and equally independent branch of government was proposed in the form of a federal judiciary. The people's will would be expressed through Congress, the laws arising therefrom were to be agreed to by the executive. The judiciary was to independently guarantee the sanctity of the law as being in keeping with the original law of the Constitution. Lastly, the executive was to enforce the "common law" of the United States.

The judiciary was further conceived as the critical balance point, with its mandate to ensure that no branch of government imposed its will monolithically or assumed the offices of the other branches, not even the judiciary could do so as that, too, would be tyranny. Washington listened as legal barricades were laid along a horizontal plane, precluding each branch of the federal government from overtaking the functions of the others.

Throughout the summer, as the executive office was conceived, everyone knew that only one person could fill the office. He was the one who listened continuously, as the powers that he well knew were required to lay the groundwork for tyranny, as shown throughout history, were denied to the executive office and the executive branch of federal governance. And he, before all the persons there convened, fully consented to every barricade—as necessary to everyone's freedom. For every "one" to be free, for everyone's rights to be secure, no "one" could rule tyrannically, not even he. The fifty-odd members, Washington among them, consented that the Constitution would be that highest law and barricade, protecting each and every individual's power—in and of themselves.

Further, in accordance with the Constitution, if he were to take office, he would have to swear an oath to the Constitution as being the social pact that was paramount, and above any other civil law. He had to swear not to be a law unto himself, but the faithful executor of the "common law" uniformly over all citizens, who were forever, by law, to be his equals.

There was still concern about the executive office branch as written in a letter by Pierce Butler to his son, that the powers of the office were still too great, that the members made it too powerful because of the greatness of the person who would first occupy it. "So that the man, who by his patriotism and virtue, contributed largely to the emancipation of his country, may be the innocent means of its being, when he is laid low, oppressed."

After the long spring and summer, on September 17th 1787, the final form of the Constitution took its shape and the members of the convention signed it—over fifty persons of independent will and viewpoints came to an agreement, one based on reason and natural rights. Washington watched and listened as Benjamin Franklin overcame his pains and was helped from his chair to the desk. The man deemed one of the wisest in the world signed the document, his eyes overcome with tears, saying, "I consent Sir, to this Constitution, because I expect no better and because I am not sure, that it is not the best."

The document was subsequently sent to the president of the Continental Congress, with a letter accompanying signed by Washington which began, "Sir, We have now the honor to submit to the consideration of the United States in Congress assembled, that Constitution which has appeared to us the most advisable."

In so doing, one of our nation's founders, rather than consuming all power to himself or into a single, central government, left the power of each citizen to themselves...

It was called a miracle because it was the final fruit of every member's agreement, and every member's disagreement, as debated in an open forum over six months which guaranteed that every member had brought their best argument, leading to the highest outcome of their collective reason. As Plato had written long before in Athens:

> *"The friction of the two [opposing views], when rubbed together, may possibly strike a light in which justice will shine forth, and the vision which is then revealed we will fix in our souls."*

Of those who had opposed some elements of the proposed Constitution, Washington praised their opposition as having helped to form a greater Constitution: "Upon the whole," he wrote, "I doubt whether the opposition to the Constitution will not ultimately be productive of more good than evil; it has called forth, in its defense, abilities which would not perhaps have been otherwise exerted that have thrown new light upon the science of Government."

Indeed, the members of the convention built a masterpiece, of a kind like the Athenian Acropolis, they built a level plateau, the housing of a nation in which, as upon the Acropolis, everyone could share a common light enshrined in law and share the individual light that issues from themselves. Benjamin Franklin was asked by a citizen after the Convention what form of government the Constitution created. Franklin answered, "A republic, if you can keep it." That was and is the wisest answer.

They termed the Constitution of 1787, "A New Order of the Ages." The answer to the multitudes of ages of tyrannical rule that has dominated history since humanities beginnings.

— Shadow —

Wilson's Will

Woodrow Wilson was a president whose background was entirely academic, save for a short two-year stint as governor of New Jersey. His adult life was spent on the paradisiacal university campuses of the northeast. He went to Johns Hopkins and was taught by esteemed scholars, such as Herbert Adams and Richard Ely, who were steeped in German "Ideal State" ideology, which was sweeping the intellectual world at the time.

During his studies, Wilson became enamored with the philosopher Friedrich Hegel of Germany, whose belief in historicism became embedded in Wilson's mindset. Hegel proposed that history was "progressing" through an evolution based on periods of *thesis*, which give birth to *anti-thesis*, its opposite. Arriving at a higher synthesis time and again, each age is superior to the last until an "Ideal State" is achieved, created by "world historical figures" who may be called the "one(s)."

In the Ideal State, the individual plays a small role. An individual only realizes freedom when they commit to "union" with the ideal state. As Hegel put it: "It is the moral Whole, the State, which is that form of reality in which the individual has and enjoys his freedom. All the worth which the human being possesses—all spiritual reality, he possesses only through the state."

In the Ideal State, the will of the state is seen as the "objective" will of the people, which is best known and best served by the one world historical figure and the few who serve the ideal state in a bureaucracy which best understands the people by being removed from them and the disputatious mess of politics. The philosophy of Hegel was immensely popular in nineteenth century Germany. He was a dominant figure in American academic circles, and he was the favorite philosopher of Karl Marx. In the twentieth century, Hegel was remarkably effective in laying the intellectual foundations that brought the world Vladimir Lenin, Adolf Hitler, and Mao Tso Tung. The conception of an Ideal State and a world historical figure just redressed the tyrant, the Pharaoh, in intellectual garb, and subsumed the individual (by the hundreds of millions) into another "ideal state" of slavery.

After achieving a PhD. in History and Government, Wilson went on to be a professor and writer. He taught in the ivory halls of Bryn Mawr, of Wesleyan, and then Princeton University, where he became its president in 1902. His literary works included *Congressional Government* and *The State*, which centered on the necessity of remaking the constitutional system of American government. Wilson's works were largely based on the works of Herbert Spencer and Walter Bagehot. Spencer believed (as this work concedes) that governments are biological animals, given to growth, change, and adaptation. Bagehot believed that all law is shaped and has to change based on the environment. As the environment changes—so must the law. The belief systems of Hegel, Spencer, and Bagehot greatly affected Wilson's philosophy of government.

Wilson's Belief System

The first key to Wilson's thinking is that he believed there is no law that is perfectible. He equally thought that mankind and government *are* perfectible—which conveniently stands the entire practical experience of humanity going back to the Ten Commandments on its head. History has been an invariable demonstration that no human government has ever achieved perfection. Unless, of course, you were the Pharaoh or a Caesar, in which case you were a god, above mankind, and you deemed your own government to be perfect; and all the slaves beneath you, worthy of their chains.

In *The State,* Wilson directly stated that there is no such thing as "universal" law that transcends time and place—including the Ten Commandments and the United States Constitution. Wilson believed that God uses history so that "the battle of life progresses, and the army of the Saints ever gains ground under divine leadership.... History will progress to bring a unity of sentiment...which would overcome particularism with an increasing unity of mind." In other words: political dilemmas will become less contentious as we progress to when we all "agree" on what we want.

I ask the reader—any reader—whether you have ever been in a room of twenty people, or ten people or five, wherein "everyone" agreed on anything? The United States Constitution, the highest law in the land, was conceived and written based on the nature of people to disagree, and the reason necessary in assembly, which comes to bear to bring light to a subject and compromise on a solution. Wilson believed in a unique "unity" of view unexampled in history outside the company of a tyrant who demands it.

Wilson had faith in another assumption: that history had overcome the basic character of human nature. Humanity was becoming more perfect all the time! It was the conception of natural rights, and law based on natural rights, that had to change accordingly with the time; for they are neither "natural" nor "unalienable." Human rights, any rights individuals have, are contingent on the times. Wilson wrote: "We are not bound to adhere to the doctrines held by the signers of the Declaration of Independence; we are as free as they were to make and unmake governments!" Wilson thought that real liberty did not mean each individual has natural rights unto themselves; real liberty means the people must be left free to make government whatever they want it to be...for they will all agree with him.

Wilson had faith in government progress too, that governments would overcome the millennia of tyranny and oppression and would not be a threat to anyone again—forever. Government could be trusted, therefore, there should be no barricades upon the state;

the state has rights that the state itself should determine with the time! In Wilson's view, the *government* had rights, but the citizens had no dependable natural rights—there was no such thing as a law that could not be changed. And it made no sense to put limits on the power of a highly centralized state.

This view of human nature, the nature of government, and natural rights-based law was diametrically opposed to the views and work done by the founders of our country to create and protect our individual rights and freedoms, everything they fought for, and the constitution they produced.

Woodrow Wilson was an academic who spent his whole life in ivory hallways and on perfectly manicured lawns, who believed in a utopia and thought he was God's chosen "one" to bring it. But his utopia was and is backwards with regard to human nature, with regard to the nature of government, and with regard to the necessity of continuous laws based on the defense of the individual's natural rights. It is a utopia unmoored from earthly reality, from common sense, and from common reason. This, Wilson's mindset, had a lot to do with how he viewed the practical system of governance in the United States and the things he did as President to change it.

Wilson on Government

Wilson advocated for a powerful, centralized state; he thought the country was at the right stage of historical development that centralization posed no threat. The modern democracy's politics needed to change to embody and be guided by "the unified will of the people." The new democratic rule would not be the "*rule of the many*," but the "*rule of the whole.*" Therefore, the foundations of the American government had to be radically transformed. Constitutional limitations on the state could be abandoned once the people had fully attained their "new freedom" in a modern democracy. The country's foundation would no longer be based on individual rights and representative rule. The country's foundation would be based on the *real* sovereign: the "underlying" will of society. And the supremacy of a modern presidency would answer the desire to have political leadership represent the nation's new "oneness of personality."

Rule in Wilson's "modern democracy" is based on the "underlying" or "implicit" common will of the nation, not the explicit citizen's will, as expressed through voting. The primary condition of the modern democratic state is unity of implicit will. A state can be said to have unity when it begins to think on a national, rather than local, scale.

How does one know the "implicit will" of so vast a nation? "The elite Universities should take it as their primary mission to train those who will objectively administer the state," wrote Wilson. An elite few become educated through a core curriculum on the history of the state and the current historical spirit. Since the underlying "spirit" is unified, one must approach understanding it from a common perspective. This study must find a way to discern the true *implicit will* or spirit of the people. Institutions then have to implement that will.

Sovereignty is not found in God, or in nature, or in the individual, but in the implicit will of the people and therefore in the single, unified will of the state, which "One" leader and an elite few determine.

As Wilson noted, this "science of administration" based on implicit will is a "foreign science, speaking very little of the language of English or American principle. It has been developed by French and German professors." Wilson thought the American tradition needed to be corrected by German State theory.

Wilson's New Democracy

In Wilson's view, the new governance of the nation had to be split between government that was subject to the people's representatives and politics, and government that was not. In this divorce of authorities, administrative agencies would have to make many decisions based on their esoteric, scientific expertise.

Such governance had to be shifted out of the way of politics—and the people. The administrators had to be insulated from political influence in order to make decisions that reflect the true general interest. Because of this independence from political accountability, the administrative agencies would, of course, remain politically neutral. Wilson believed that an unelected, unaccountable bureaucracy, based on the efficiencies found in Germany, would better represent the people's true "implicit will."

Wilson distrusted the people's representatives because they represented "the many, the people, who are sovereign, [and] have no single ear which one can approach and are selfish, ignorant, timid, stubborn or foolish with the selfishness of ignorance... in their thousands, while there are hundreds [the few] who are wise." Wilson, throughout his career, opined that the Congress, the people's house, would do better to abandon its legislative function.

As to the Senate, Wilson thought it a "very sorry, unseemly thing" to give senators the authority to reward political supporters through its appointment powers, which might veto the executive's will.

Along with a weaker Congress, Wilson wanted the executive branch to exercise a far greater authority. The executive should be one of the world historical individuals who are devoted to "one aim." Such a leader has to have been educated in the means of seeing the future; and knowing better than the people do themselves—the people's will. The executive administration must be composed of similar elite persons who possess an esoteric knowledge of the "spirit" of their age and the future course of history. Wilson's example of such a leader was Frederick the Great of Prussia, who best understood the "unified public will." Wilson was not alone; Hitler thought the same of Frederick the Great.

It is then the leader's role to show the people that his will is actually the people's own implicit will, through propaganda. The leader should engage in rhetoric that is ardently populist and democratic, while taking political power and putting it in the hands of the executive power and the administration. While from these few, the elite civil servants, the wider population will have nothing to fear;

they will not be given to any particular interest because they will have lifetime appointments. They will certainly not act in their own interests—that would be mere human nature. These angels will progress beyond human nature and will think only of the public good. Because they are insulated from any accountability, they will be politically neutral. Therefore, the government will never pose any threat. With this "new democracy," the expanded executive branch and the new administration, there comes the new idea of law: administrative law, which the new democracy adherents judge to be essential law even if it has no constitutional sanction. According to the new democracy, administrative law ought to be a primary source of public law—just as international law, constitutional law, state law, criminal and civil law, and administrative law should hold an equal place; though the laws are actually the dictates of executive agencies controlled by the executive branch of government. Further, the administrative "rules" are enforceable nationally, in every state, in every county, in every locality—without anyone voting. Unanswerable, unelected persons dictating "rules" which have the effect of laws enforceable everywhere, upon us all.

For the Administrative State to acquire the necessary powers to impose the people's "implicit will" (translation: "the leader's own will"), the administration must have a breadth of authority that may undo the limits prescribed as law in the Constitution. After all, as Wilson wrote in his *Notes on Lectures*: "Administration need not rely for its jurisdiction upon a specific constitutional or statutory grant authority—administration may do anything not expressly *forbidden* by law. Administration authority is as wide as the sphere in which it may move without infringing the laws!" According to Wilson's own words, "Liberty fixed in unalterable law" (such as our Constitutional Law) "would be no liberty at all!"

As to administrative law, again from *Notes on Lectures:* "Administration cannot wait upon legislation, but must be given leave, or take it, to proceed without specific warrant in giving effect to the characteristic life of the state." Wilson further contended that "even political liberties and privileges are not immune from the exercise of state power if the [implicit] will of the people endorses state action." That is, "his state's" will and action, not the "people's will" through direct or representative elections.

This is the road map America has taken away from a representative democracy to an Administrative State; the road from individual liberty to "national will." So, what is to become of the individual?

As the state becomes the implicit will of the whole society, the state must oversee individual self-development. Wilson, like Hegel, thought of the state as "the eternal, natural embodiment and expression of a higher form of life than the individual, namely, that common life which *gives leave* to individual life—and opportunity for completeness." An individual is only fulfilled through the aid and with the consent of the state.

This, again, is opposite to the founders' will that each individual is supreme, and the federal government is a distant, uninvolved, subservient entity responsive to the individuals' "explicit" will delivered through the vote and representation.

This, then, is Woodrow Wilson's vision of how to disorder our constitution and bring into America the same old order of the ages, humanity's common keep, by using new language to reintroduce the millennial, universal rule of the Pharaohs and "the few," into America by way of German philosophy—which launched every twentieth century career in tyranny. The leader's will *is* the hidden will of everybody; they just need educating...by the government.

Laws, old or new, are only useful if the leader and the few say they are... Individuals have no rights themselves, only those that the state—in its higher being—says they have. This is the DNA of tyranny, and it has been spliced into the DNA of our democracy. This is Wilson's vision of what government should be—a vision which one American political party has been working ever since to achieve. *Shadows of the Acropolis* will catalogue the ever-widening expansion of the "Administrative State" that Wilson began.

Wilson did even more to change America's way of thinking away from our unique founding. He destroyed some basics in our constitutional organization of government, particularly in reference to the states and local governments, and the federal house of our representatives.

The Wilson Presidency

Levying

Taxation

Two amendments came into effect early in Wilson's presidency, which fell in line with his will to create a strong, centralized government. The Sixteenth Amendment to the Constitution allowed for a federal income tax. Previously, the states were obligated to deliver national taxes to the federal government based on their population. It was therefore conceivable that states could band together as a defensive measure to control federal spending; at least, they had a capacity to negotiate federal spending and object to arbitrary increases. The federal income tax took that power away from the states and guaranteed the federal government an inexhaustible food supply. It also put into the hands of the federal government every person's name, where they live, how many kids they have, what they do for an occupation, what property they own, what enterprises they are involved in, what investments they have, and how they like to spend their money. All of which let the government know how much money they could take.

Levying

States' Independence

The Seventeenth Amendment to the Constitution concerned the election of senators to Congress. Per the Constitution, senators were representatives of the persons of their states, and of the states themselves, because they were elected by state legislatures. By allowing direct elections of senators, their function as representatives of their states and the majority will of their legislatures was taken away. Senators have not since had the same authority as representatives of independent states and have done little to defend the states as political entities in and of themselves.

On this debilitation of the states, Wilson levied more power into the federal state. Based on the new income tax, the federal government began redistribution operations immediately. It also began to take control of powers and prerogatives that were previously in the hands of the states alone.

The Road Construction Assistance Laws of 1916 are a case in point. They created the Federal Aid Road Act, and thereby, the Federal Highway Administration, which in turn created a "grant-in-aid" program instituted by this new federal agency of the U.S. government. Programs of the kind work this way: the federal government takes the income tax from every working citizen of every state. Then, the federal government determines what money to give back, to which states, in the form of grants. Then, the money is not given to the legislature of an awarded state for that state to spend based on its own prerogatives; rather, the federal agency propagates a smaller agency, or commission, within each receiving state, and distributes funds based on the "federal will" of the executive branch—thereby bypassing the state governments entirely. It is the federal government extending its reach, its control, and its power into every single state through the spawning of little agencies, which are children of the federal agency that directly control it.

The federal income tax, the direct election of senators, and the creation of agencies and grants-in-aid programs effectively reversed the relationship between the states and the federal government. The federal government was no longer dependent on the states for its income. The senators no longer represented their states effectively enough to object to any federal policy affecting state powers. Then the government took and controlled the money as it went back into states—which only the federal government chose. The federal government then chose *how* that money was spent within the states. Ever since, the states have become subsidiaries of the federal government's will. And senators no longer represent their state's interest at the federal level, they represent the federal will to the states. It is the direct inverse of our Constitution's design

Wilson took it further. The Smith Hughes Act of 1917 created the Federal Board of Vocational Education. It has been a model ever since on how the federal government can control education. The board was given the power to establish uniform standards for vocational education. In each state, an administrative commission (a child of the federal board) was built to enforce the standards. Non-compliant states (though their citizens fund *education*) did not get their education money back—instead, it went to another state that was "compliant" with the federal will.

Levying

States' Power to Agencies

The agencies described are a part of the executive branch of the federal government, a part of the Administrative State creating and executing administrative law. The House of Representatives holds the purse strings but funds all agency budgets as a part the overall federal budget; most agency budgets are on automatic, with automatic rises in revenues based on budgets the agencies submit. Therefore, the people's money goes into the federal government, and the people's representatives have little or nothing to do with how it is spent within an agency. It is decided by persons who often have lifetime appointments within a given agency, by persons whose importance and salaries increase with any increase in their budget, it is akin to a cost of living increase.

Over the next two decades, these levies of powers once held by localities and the states were assumed across horizontal barricades by the federal government. As swiftly, these levies of powers shifted across vertical barricades from the once co-equal branches of the House of Representatives and the Senate to the executive branch of government.

Another vertical barricade was bounded during Wilson's tenure, to the most minute local levels of government, because of his use of the party (or herd) system. Wilson determined to use the political party system to unite every local level assembly, no matter how small, to the federal level. "Party will" was exercised through party discipline, in a manner like the Russian Bolsheviks exercised their party's will to spread the Russian revolution. Initiatives of the executive branch became "the party line," those that did not tow that line into county and town assemblies would no longer be in the party. So, the federal government (or one party thereof) finds its authoritarian way into every town in America from Bangor, Maine to Baja, California whether the local citizens know it, and regardless of whether they like it or not.

Lastly, these shifts of power across horizontal and vertical barricades, supposedly laid down as sacrosanct by the founders, needed more reason than just one branch of government could provide in order to make them seem legitimate. Hence: Wilson's new role for the judiciary in his "new democracy."

Levying

The Judiciary

Wilson believed in an activist judiciary, one that would re-evaluate the law continuously based on the changing times. This is important to note because the judiciary is the arbiter of which governmental power is legitimate under the Constitution. Therefore, as Wilson noted: "The federal government is through its courts the final judge of its own powers. The whole balance of our federal system, therefore, lies in the federal courts...with them must lie the final statesmanship of control." Therefore, the courts had to become political.

Wilson's view of an ideal justice was John Marshall, ; the Chief Justice of the Supreme Court from 1801 to 1835. Marshall saw in the Constitution not *barriers* to federal power but *grants* of federal power. He had to—in his time, 14 years after the Constitutional

Convention, the role and power of the new federal government had to be defined in law; based in case precedent, and by addition. Wilson sought in the early 1900's and beyond, to have the powers of the federal government and the executive branch expanded, through the judiciary, by multiplication! Such a judiciary, he thought, becomes an invested partner with the executive branch on the road of progress to utopia—the unified "ideal state." This partnership effectively levied the separation of powers from the Constitution's Legislative–Judiciary–Executive design; to administration acts of lawmaking in the Executive branch, with the judiciary's partnering acts of a rubber-stamped approval of administrative law.

Wilson achieved his purpose, starting in motion a mutation away from the founding principles of the nation. He mutated the Constitution in a way that would create a path of centralization of our government vertically up to the federal level by removing power from local and state authorities, and horizontally into the executive and judicial branches by levying power from as Hamilton put it, the "original fountain of authority"—the people's houses of Congress to the new Administrative State.

With regard to the economy, Wilson passed The Federal Reserve Act of 1913, establishing a national central authority over the money supply and federal governance over inter-bank lending rates, thereby taking authority over the free marketplace in the determination how much liquidity was allowed in the system of free enterprise and setting up a national system to govern the banking and investment sector of the economy.

After suffering years of hardship and every variety of fortune for our freedom, George Washington had listened to every member of the Constitutional Convention. He had done all he could, with that great company gathered, to prevent a concentration of power at the federal level and particularly in the executive office, in what he, Benjamin Franklin, and the Constitutional Convention members considered unassailable constitutional law.

Woodrow Wilson never thought much of the Constitution; to Wilson the Constitution's fundamental and highest laws were infinitely changeable depending on the time, and him—the "one" executive.

Wilson thought there was no discernable difference in the futures of America and Bolshevik Russia, only the means differed on the way of each country to the same Ideal State of utopian socialism. Russia was wrong; it had chosen revolution. America would be different and choose *evolution* to the same end. He even predicted in *The State* that, "Concern for individual liberty can never permanently limit or define the role of government: Government does now whatever experience permits or the times demand."

Woodrow Wilson never thought much of the natural rights of the individual. His new State made each individual's natural rights infinitely changeable: into being whatever the State says they are at the time.

In America, Wilson's philosophy and works began a stark movement away from the Constitution, away from the individual, and away from a representative republic—a grotesque backward movement to the seemingly eternal, universal rule of the "one and the few" over the mute multitudes. It began then and has been moving America ever since to the common keep of tyranny's dismal entrance.

Such was Wilson's role in disordering our founders' constitutional "New Order of the Ages"—in one presidency. His works became another splicing of the DNA of tyranny onto our founding DNA, mutating our representative democracy.

And to be clear on who Woodrow Wilson was, the Ideal State—his utopian vision—could only happen in a nation that was as racially homogenized as it was homogenized in thought and "will." He segregated Washington, DC, for the first time. He fired most of the African Americans who worked in the government. His favorite movie was *The Birth of a Nation.*

And here is an irony: women were given the franchise (thank heaven and Wyoming), during the term of Woodrow Wilson, doubling the American franchise, but only after he personally made the franchise worth half of what it had been with the creation of the unrepresentative, unanswerable Administrative State.

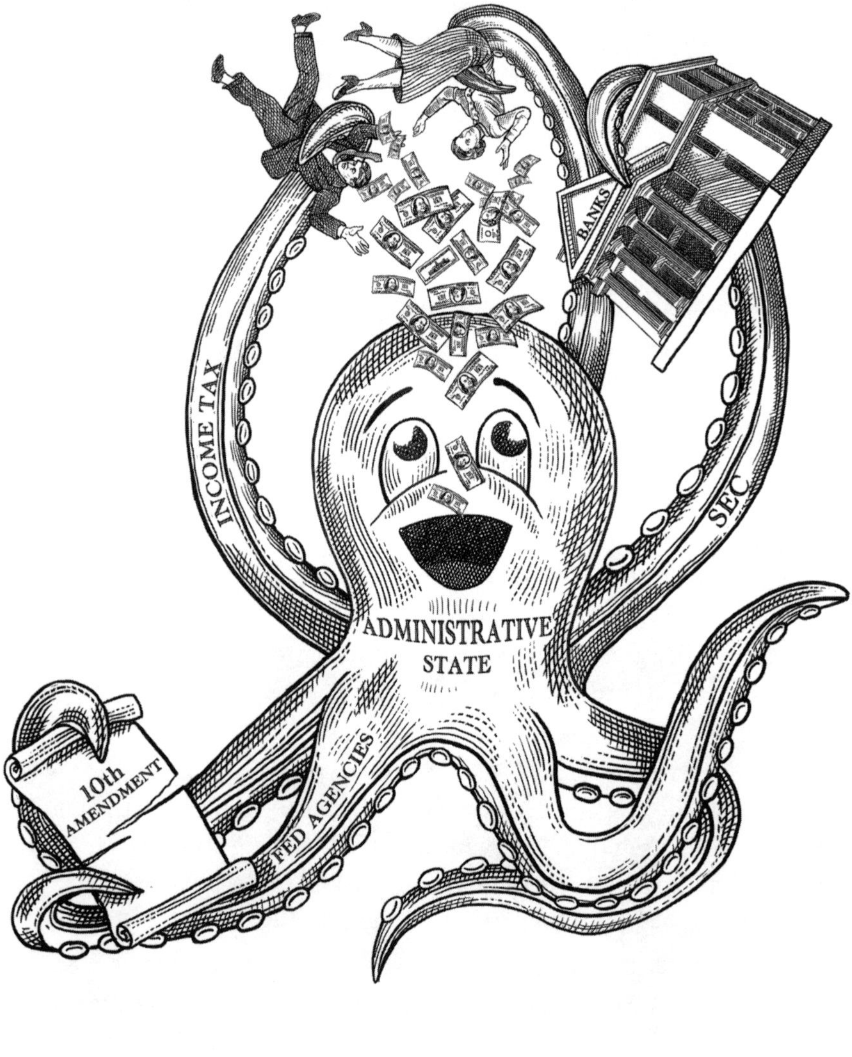

— *Along the American Road* —

In 1919, Captain Dwight D. Eisenhower was one of the leaders of a convoy that had been commissioned to seek out the best roadways in America that could be traversable in a state of military emergency by the machinery of the new century. The captain became part of the Transcontinental Motor Convoy. The convoy was made up of two travelling groups: a northern group was ordered to drive north and west, via US 30 for Oregon. While a southern group was to drive to Atlanta and then embark west for Sacramento. A military operation, it was comprised of eighty-one military vehicles including a tank, thirty-seven officers, and a total of several hundred enlisted soldiers.

The vehicles utilized were many of the new trucks, cars, and motorcycles then being produced in the Midwest. The favorites were the Harley-Davidson and Indian motorcycles, which were used as a type of outrider scout cavalry unit in order to discover what perils lay on the road ahead. The main body of the convoy stretched over two miles long, front-to-back.

It was a self-sufficient caravan that included water and gasoline trucks, a wrecker, and a blacksmith shop, along with an army medical staff with a dentist, a surgeon, and a medical officer.

The convoy was the news of the day through every town it went, inspiring the locals to come out and see the parade moving along at a slow to middlin' speed over hill and dale roads that got steadily worse as the caravan made its way west. There was entertainment at nearly every town—big banquets, music, and dances in some places, to simple outdoor picnics and melon eating contests in others.

The roads became increasingly worse until they reached Wyoming, where there was no road at all. Moving through Utah's majestic mountains and canyons proved just as hard. Despite the Harley and Indian outriders marking the trail ahead, the convoy suffered many accidents in the difficult terrain for a lack of sufficient roads and bridges rated for the modern-day vehicles. The group finally reached Carson City, Nevada, where the trekkers enjoyed the hot springs before the most difficult part of the journey—over the King's Grade Pass of the Sierra Nevada.

After two months of intense heat, drenching rain, regular washouts, and holes in what passed for roads at about every half-mile—that conspired to leave a liver in the rear-view mirror—the convoy finally reached Sacramento, California, on September 3, 1919. The state fair was on, and Governor William Stephens was there to welcome the travelers and veterans of the long road across a continent. There were bands and singers and dancers, and enough food to feed the masses. A mechanized equivalent of the Lewis and Clark expedition had reached its destination.

It was estimated that the convoys had passed through 350 towns and were seen by 3.5 million people along the way. At the end of it all, Eisenhower was convinced that the United States needed a new system of roadways to allow for trucks, cars, motorcycles, and a tank every now and then. His experience would come to bear in later years.

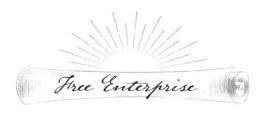

Free Enterprise

— Light —

ADAM SMITH

In politics, as in house building, the best judge of what works is the user, not the maker.

Adam Smith was born a contemporary of America's founding generation. He became a professor and a writer, known best for authoring *The Theory of Moral Sentiments*, a work on moral philosophy, and *An Inquiry into the Nature and Causes of the Wealth of Nations,* his masterpiece on economics. He socialized with some of the greatest minds of his time (who were not colonists), such as David Hume, Edward Gibbon, Samuel Johnson, James Boswell, and Edmund Burke. As a tutor, he toured Europe for a time and met Benjamin Franklin in Paris and Voltaire in Geneva. He became affectionately known by his students as the absent-minded professor, for having been, in one example, so involved in a problem that he walked for miles in a nightgown through a snowstorm, before he emerged from the problem that consumed him, to note that he was unhoused, in a driving winter gale.

Like most of his contemporaries, Smith was inspired by the scientific achievements of his age and particularly by the achievements of Isaac Newton, who mapped the movements of the stars through the universe with unexampled accuracy. Adam Smith embarked to map out something of his own—how humanity interacts within the universe of an economy, and how the economy effects and is affected by everyone under the sun.

Prior to Smith's time, the European economy had been of two kinds. There was the economy that was planned by monarchs and aristocrats through a patronage system that included grants of protection for monopolies, awards of patents for inventions, outlays of subsidies and protective tariffs for persons loyal to the crown, and secured guilds for craftsmen. This atop an agrarian society, which was one of landlords and those who tilled the soil and produced its fruits. Smith wrote an anecdote that became famous: "Landlords, like all other men, love to reap where they have never sown." This, Smith and his contemporaries deemed unjust. The second kind of economy was that of the Church, which managed the tillage of its own lands, control of its own village markets, and functioned as the interchange of charity between those who could and could not afford to be charitable.

The basis of wealth in monarchies may be added up thusly: land plus precious metals and jewels equals wealth. In the revolutionary age, there was revolution in every sense as the old economy gave way to industrialization—and to its human explorer, Adam Smith, who witnessed and detailed a whole new way of looking at the wealth of nations.

Smith considered that wealth in a society was not found solely in the coffers of a king but consisted in the standard of living enjoyed by its households; that all "wealth" should be measured from the viewpoint, not of a king, but of the common consumer. And that monarchical "gifts" toward creating a "planned economy" actually strangles an economy. Such a planned marketplace stifles an individual's natural ambition and capacity for invention, and a society's wider talent for innovation—both of which are the underpinnings of prosperity.

Smith noted: "All humans want to live better than they do," as we each have "a desire of bettering our condition, a desire which… comes with us from the womb, and never leaves us till we go to the grave." Smith argued that society should tap into this aspect of human nature, rather than imprison it within the will of a monarch.

Smith noticed something else about we fellow humans: that the love "to truck, barter and exchange one thing for another, is common to all." In order to advance the wealth of all households, Smith advised unleashing this natural ambition and inclination to unbridle everyone's "self-interest."

The genius of discovery made by Smith was that, when each person in a society acts out of enlightened self-interest, it benefits that society as a whole in greater measure than any monarch's planned market...even in greater measure than one governed by a church and said to be given to pure altruism.

This holds true because, in order for a person to act in their self-interest and profit for themselves, they must engage in an inverse relationship. One needs to invent not what one wants oneself, but what others want or need, for "the best judge of what works is the user, not the maker." In order to sell one's product, it cannot be at a price that the seller wants for oneself, but one that the consumer can best afford. Also, one cannot produce masses of products planning to sell them all—but must produce at the right equilibrium between supply and demand, which is found at the best market price for the consumer! One must produce to the will, taste, and capacity of the marketplace. And, thereby, a consumer may be able to purchase from the marketplace a bounty of things according to one's own tastes.

No inventor knows better than their customer what the customer wants, or what is better suited to their taste among many alternative creations. It is the *buyer* that becomes the inspiration of the inventor! And it is entirely free and voluntary, on all hands, that the inventor invents, that the investor invests, that the producer manufactures, that the retailer sells, and that the consumer purchases--each according to one's "natural liberty," as Smith coined it in *Wealth of Nations.*

In Smith's philosophy, all of this creative activity in the economy is not managed and caged within the iron grip of a tyrant, but rather expands and lifts the whole of society as by "an invisible hand," which no one notices is there, and which is formed by the individual aspirations of a people. Each individual has their own vision of success. Much like the myth of the *Iliad*, we each have our own vision of Helen's beauty, and what better than one's own vision to inspire an infinitude of aspirers on paths of imagination to ascend the limitless towers of invention?

One does not ascend such heights by wishes alone, but by arduous climbing from one strata of labor to the next. In industrialized societies, there is a division of labor as between the level plains, the foothills, and the mountains beyond: to achieve a height, one must endure the journey and commit to the climb. The division of labors yields many benefits, according to Smith. Firstly, each worker performing his own task makes that person most skillful and adept at that task performed over time. Secondly, not having to change tasks repeatedly brings greater efficiency. Lastly, those who specialize in their tasks are often the first inventors making their own manual labors obsolete and replacing themselves with machinery at a greater profit...and so they move up.

And this "diversity" of labor is a fundamental matter in a free society and is beneficial to its government as being representative of the people, as a free society:

> *"Necessarily requires a difference of capacities among its members, which enables them to serve as complements to one another, and to attain a higher and better life by the mutual exchange of their different services."*
>
> *Aristotle*

As long as an economy is not invaded by a governmental power, the movement from plain to foothills to mountaintop is unimpeded and open to all who faithfully aspire and labor. Even the poor and the politically averse can prosper in a free market, in contrast to a centrally guided system wherein everyone's position is politically determined; wherein those who know and are akin to persons of political power are alone benefitted. In contrast, in a free-market society, the whole of society combines to create and enjoy an ever-expanding higher standard of living.

Finally, Smith put forth that: "Little else is requisite to carry a state to the highest degree of opulence from the lowest barbarism but peace, easy taxes, and a tolerable administration of justice: all the rest being brought about in the natural course of things."

After ten years of hard labor, Adam Smith published his economically revolutionary and liberating *Wealth of Nations* in 1776, in the same year as our politically revolutionary and liberating Declaration of Independence. Smith charted America's economic independence, whose same principles have witnessed America's world leadership in manufacturing and technology and invention and production efficiency—far surpassing the "command and control" economies... unless they are copyists of our attainments.

Today, our *somewhat* free market is the economical ambient that is responsible for the achievements of Bill Gates and IBM, Steve Jobs and Apple, and Mark Zuckerberg and Facebook to name a few. Free Enterprise affords the innovator, the industrious, and the artist a vista that is open to endless advance, just as it did a century ago in the 1920s. In America, Adam Smith's free-market philosophy, coupled with the freedom of democracy, created the ambient whereby countless Americans could succeed in their personal visions.

Thomas Edison was born to an unwealthy family and was given his early education by his mother. He educated himself to pursue his interest in scientific experimentation. He began his career by selling newspapers and food on the rail lines between Port Huron and Detroit, Michigan. He earned $50 a week, saved what he could, and devoted that money to his experiments involving electricity and chemistry. He also took a job as a telegraph operator and, after having mastered that job, invented the Quadruplex Telegraph, secured the patent, then sold the patent to Western Union for $10,000. It was a vast sum at the time, which Edison invested in the Industrial Research Laboratory in Menlo Park, New Jersey— the first of its kind. Through decades of hard work, during which he became the master inventor to a community of inventors, Edison made discoveries and produced products carrying 1,093 patents in his name alone, not to mention those of his staff. During his career, he founded fourteen companies, among them General Electric, which is traded to this day as one of the largest components of the Dow Industrial Exchange.

Edison invented, and perfected for manufacturing, technologies that changed the world: the phonograph and the motion picture camera, which spawned the music and film industries. The microphone system of the telephone, a device used in all phones into the 1980s. And his premier invention that literally brought light into the darkness, the incandescent lightbulb—which he did not invent himself, but did perfect and manufacture en masse, making it so affordable that, as Edison said, "We will make electricity so cheap that only the rich will burn candles."

While running his Detroit Edison Illuminating Company, Edison found a young man working there who was much like himself. Henry Ford was born just outside Detroit and was raised as a farmer by a penniless father who had emigrated from Ireland during the Potato Famine. Henry had attended a one-room schoolhouse but learned the most after school from assembling and disassembling watches.

At seventeen, Henry gave up farming and took an apprentice job at the Dry Dock Engine Company, which was doing work on his dream—the internal combustion engine. While there, he earned his education in the trade. After work, Ford would go home and go to work again in his own machine shop, dedicating himself to the idea of creating a car that the average person could afford. In Germany, Karl Benz had created a car based on internal combustion that, as Ford noted, "none but a monarch" could afford. Ford's first effort produced the Quadracycle, which he proudly drove out of his garage. But it, too, proved unaffordable.

To earn the money necessary to work on further experimental models, Ford took a job at the Edison Illuminating Company of Detroit. There he met Edison, who had heard of Ford's after-work dedication. Edison sat with Ford, telling him, "Young man, you have it! A self-contained unit carrying its own fuel—keep at it!" This encounter led Henry to a fork in the road. He was soon offered a senior position, which would have secured his future for a lifetime with the Edison company. Or he could leave the firm—with all the financial insecurity that brought. Ford left the foothills of job security for the mountain of invention beyond.

In 1903, Henry founded the Ford Motor Company after raising $28,000 from the ordinary folks that his life was surrounded by. He experimented and experimented and experimented again. On the ninth model, in 1908, he did it. He built the "Model T," which he called a car "for the great multitude." Between 1908 and 1927, through his invention of an assembly line manufacturing process, Ford drove the cost of the Model T down from $950 to $280 per car—a price his own employees could afford from their wages. The Ford Company became the "model" for an industrial revolution in manufacturing processes, based on Ford's invention of the assembly line.

Andrew Mellon's father, Thomas, was also born to a poor immigrant family from Ireland. But he did well in Pittsburgh, Pennsylvania, in the steel and banking industries, enough so that his sons, Richard and Andrew, could use their instincts and talents to become what we call today "venture capitalists." One of their great successes occurred when the owners of the struggling Aluminum Company of America came to them for help and expertise; they needed a loan. Andrew Mellon believed in the company, so he financed it. He believed in it so much that, later, he decided to purchase a controlling interest and run the business. With his astute leadership, ALCOA became the largest aluminum company in America.

With Henry Frick, an associate of his father, Andrew Mellon also founded Union Steel, which later merged with United States Steel. And again, Mellon's influence through capital and management led to US Steel becoming the largest steel producer in the world.

On yet another occasion, a Texas oil company came to Andrew Mellon. It was, again, a struggling company badly in need of the capital necessary to keep its oil rigs in the Southwest in operation. Mellon studied the business and its chances, and decided it was a worthy investment. He later purchased a controlling interest and ran the business. Through Mellon's genius in the investment of capital and business management, the company grew into the petroleum juggernaut Gulf Oil.

In 1914, Mellon acquired Koppers Gas and Coke, a company that was dedicated to the brightest, most exciting investment of the time—the transmission of electricity through collections of utility companies, which were then newly operating and extending the advantage of light and warmth to every household throughout the Northeast.

Now, for the reader, just consider all the inventions and manufactures of just these three persons—Edison, Ford, and Mellon—and all the ancillary inventions and productions later spawned through their original efforts in what may be termed "chains of creations." From Edison's efforts alone came all the household appliances we use around us every day, from toasters to washing machines, to music transmission to television, to simple bedside lamps. From original inventions spring ancillary inventions, and from innovation springs even greater innovation.

In the 1920s, it was a brave new American world, it was the fruition of Adam Smith's free market philosophy. One can view, in the mind's eye, a group of friends—couples—driving through a life they could finally afford in one of Henry Ford's new mint model Ts, through Thomas Edison's newly illuminated streets powered by Andrew Mellon's Oklahoma gasoline, on their way to an area culturally bursting at the seams during what was termed the "Harlem Renaissance." Where, in any of the many privately-owned neighborhood Jazz clubs, the public could listen to the magnificent, artistic jazz virtuosos of Eubie Blake or Fats Waller playing the Harlem Stride-style of piano, or take in a band performance by Duke Ellington or Louis Armstrong, or venture down the street to hear the "Queen of Happiness," Florence Mills, sing. Yet further, one could stroll to a book shop and hear Claude McKay reading his poetry, or have a conversation with Langston Hughes about his latest novel. It was a period when "natural liberty" fully unleashed the power of the individual and the individuality that springs from every note of artistry.

In America, Adam Smith's vision in the *Wealth of Nations* rang perfectly true.

> "*The great multiplication of the production of all the different arts, in consequence of the division of labor, which occasions, in a well governed society, that universal opulence extends to the lowest ranks of the people [and] supplies them abundantly with what they have occasion for...and a general plenty diffuses itself through the different ranks of society.*"

When one looked above and around, the whole atmosphere was of new light. On Wall Street, the biggest opportunity appeared to be in the new utility companies, like those of Edison and Mellon. Only 50 percent of American homes had power at the time, mostly in the Northeast, leaving the bright growth opportunities of the South and West to consider for inventors and captains of industry, and as an investment for everybody.

With all of this life teeming in all directions, the federal government was an unthought of, insignificant being, hardly noticed in the corner of everyone's life. The notable people of the period were the industrialists, the builders, the artists, and the folks you met in every distinctive hometown and neighborhood. In the 1920s, the size of the federal government of the United States was smaller than that of many states, smaller than New York City's. It comprised less than 2 percent of the national economy...and that with a military that had just won a world war. The federal government had next to nothing to do with Adam Smith's idea of the American free market. It only had to govern, with steady justice, over the new markets.

In a free market system, there is always a new frontier, a vista of endless advance to measureless horizons, throught the avenues of free enterprise.

There was another invention of the era—not really "invented" but something that was newly available to the masses, based on everyone's participation in the steady rise of society's standard of living: credit. One could go to the local bank and take out a loan for the home, the farm, the car, the business. Something else new to the masses was the idea of "investment" that came along with the surplus wealth which the dynamism of a free market created. One could now take their wealth and invest it in one of the new corporations springing up everywhere and supplying everyone with a better life. Owing to this new wealth, the stock market began rising steadily through the 1920s.

In accordance with Smith's philosophy, everything has a price based on its desirability and relative supply to demand. This valuation ratio is prone to being warped from strict valuations when a money supply is too easily come by, and when persons—who are too clever—attempt to "earn where they never sowed."

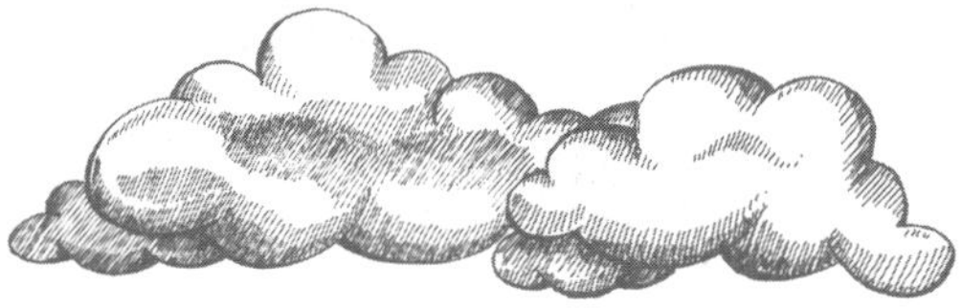

— Shadows —

Crash And Aftermath

The fruits of free enterprise were so bountiful in the 1920s that they were thought to be limitless, and people began believing that any investment in the stock market would only go up. It became a fad, a fashion, and a matter of faith. One in three people in America were invested in the market. And it was true, as Smith said, that like the landlords of old, "all other(s), love to reap where they never sowed." In an age that flowed with so much new wealth, where nothing seemed wanting, where the horizon promised endless prosperity, some folks, as is predictable of human nature, wanted one more thing...more.

As one example of how the market system became manipulated to overly profit a few, some persons became parts of large investment pools, arranged by investment firms, which invested "on margin," meaning the pool could put up 10 percent in cash in exchange for 100 percent of the paper value of a stock. Further, an individual belonging to the same investment pool could then go to a bank, present their portfolio, and take out a loan based on the fully recorded value of one's participation in the investment pool, and go away with ten times the value of their portfolio to invest again. "On margin" created a value on paper that was again ten times the value of the loan. Thus, the value of the portfolio could be exaggerated above its real value by one hundred times. This sort of unjust dealing grossly inflated the values of every stock on the market and vastly overextended every lending institution and brokerage that hazarded such loans. It has been estimated that the shadow value of all the borrowed money in the stock market grew to equal 18 percent of the national gross domestic product.

This situation was further fueled by the new national agency founded by Woodrow Wilson, the Federal Reserve, which set about to centrally control the economy by setting national rates for lending at an unnaturally low rate, given the inflation which followed the stock market's unnatural rise. Between 1924 and 1929, so much "cash" flooded into the stock market that it rose 300 percent, from 100 to 400 points in five years. During which time, there was another example of market manipulation: consortiums of investors would collude to "hike a price" of a stock and then sell out their interests collectively in the stock in one day, at the height of its perceived value. One practitioner of such price manipulation was Joseph Kennedy. It helped create his fortune. Such practiced wolves were at work among the novice herds of new investors.

Adam Smith was prophetic when, in the *Wealth of Nations*, he warned of such persons who might band together in a "conspiracy against the public or in some other contrivance to raise prices."

He strongly cautioned that a free market must be "overseen by a steady sense of justice." Wall Street in the 1920s, with the masses of new investors, and in the sprawling new credit markets intermixed with speculators, was the Wild West of the East—without a sheriff. It was no longer a rightly balanced, rightly valued free market; it was an overinflated, falsely valued paper market where everything seemed to be free. As Adam Smith also noted, in a balanced free market attended to with steady justice, there may be boundless prosperity—but nothing whatsoever is "free."

In the last great economic downturn, a recession occurred in 1923 during the Harding administration. The solution was simple: let the "invisible hand" work to adjust valuations to a true level, and let the excess growth of production be adjusted through industry making itself more efficient—which benefits shareholders and then the workforce, and the customer makes way for new expansion.

This downturn was different. There was excess industrial growth beyond market demand, and a severe valuation bubble. Then that bubble burst.

On October 24,1929, in the span of three hours, thirteen million stocks were dumped on the market and the panic gave way to a domino effect. In six days, the market lost $30 billion—or 50 percent of its value—and continued the avalanche for six more weeks, until it reached 20 percent of its former value.

The treasury secretary of the time, our same Andrew Mellon, recommended that the free market be allowed to adjust itself: that in order to right the economy, farmers, banks, and stockholders should liquidate their holdings so that stocks, prices, and wages might be "marked to market" and find their bottom. The free market value of equities would be reestablished, the balance sheets of banks would be recalibrated and the economy would stabilize... as it had always done before... and begin to rise again.

— Shadow —

Government's Hand

HERBERT HOOVER

Instead, President Herbert Hoover believed in applying a "benevolent hand" of government intervention and went to work instituting policies that made the downturn infinitely worse and spread it through the economic universe.

The government started selling bonds, removing the money supply from the markets when the economy desperately needed liquidity. The money supply declined 4 percent by the end of 1930, as citizens fled to the safety of government-issued bonds. Hoover also intervened through the media, to engage in a campaign to blame Wall Street as a whole rather than its bad actors, which further panicked investors away from the markets. Hoover then signed into law the protectionist Smoot-Hawley tariff bill, which began a trade war principally with European markets—which accounted for 25 percent of the sales of US farm products—effectively closing those markets.

Everywhere Hoover turned to control the markets with government, matters worsened. Eventually, in a paroxysm of panic, he went where no US government had gone before—he demanded that wages and hours be frozen by all companies at the levels realized before the crash. But business owners could not pay the wage rates demanded, because businesses could not sell their goods at their former prices. And most businesses lacked the liquidity necessary to bear the loss of continuing payrolls—so multitudes of businesses went out of business.

Then, to increase the crater created by government interference, Hoover instituted the largest tax hike since the new income tax had gone into effect: the Revenue Act of 1932 raised the top rates from 24 to 63 percent, taking whatever money was left for re-investment in the economy and raking it into the government. The stock market moved in one direction—down. Farmers could not sell their crops, businesses could not sell their products, employees could not get paid, home mortgages could not be repaid, so the housing market collapsed as did the value of property nationwide. Therefore, the banks themselves had no money, let alone any money to lend. The US government's interventions in the free market were a disaster, all from Hoover's "benevolent hand."

Hoover was defeated in the election of November 1932 by Franklin Delano Roosevelt. Hoover's successor was preparing to deal with the once-free market of America with a governmental "fist"—and our economy has never been a free enterprise market since.

Between the election and inauguration day, Hoover attempted to work with President-elect Roosevelt to assure that the economy's housing collapse did not lead to a banking system collapse. His pleas, both official and personal, were repulsed while Roosevelt cruised on his yacht off the coast of Florida, contemplating his agenda that could only be aided by a crisis that deepened. And the more the crisis deepened, the more people would turn to government as a people in abject need. Thus, there would be more room for government maneuvering to empower itself. A crisis suffered in a democracy is the perfect medium for a central government's exponential growth.

FRANKLIN ROOSEVELT

Franklin Delano Roosevelt had been Woodrow Wilson's secretary of the navy. He was a great admirer of Wilson, of his political writings, and his philosophical vision of the Administrative State. He had viewed the possibilities up close during World War I, when the executive branch of government made use of all its power as the seat of the commander to achieve national hegemony during an emergency. Roosevelt, while he was governor of New York and running for the presidency, spoke his fears of the growing concentration of wealth and power in the business sector of America. Roosevelt's aim as president was to use the "emergency" in the economy to grow and concentrate wealth and power in the Administrative State. And what better time than during a state of crisis, when the normal powers that would array against such an agenda were confused and defenseless—and left open the economy and every stratum of governance beneath the federal government open to a "benevolent" invasion.

– Shadow –

The New Deal

Roosevelt's First Inaugural

Roosevelt's inaugural of March 4, 1933 announced his intent. Midway through the Inaugural address, he declared an attack on the free market: "The money changers have fled from their high seats in the temple of our civilization. We may now restore that temple to the ancient truths. The measure of the restoration lies in the extent to which we apply social values more noble than mere monetary profit." Translation: *The federal government will be the high priests of ancient truths and noble values—and the new overlords of the economy.*

The speech announced a new power of federal government. "Our greatest primary task is to put people to work.... It can be accomplished in part by direct recruiting by the Government itself, treating the task as we would treat the emergency of war... accomplishing greatly needed projects to stimulate and reorganize the use of our natural resources." *The federal government will determine the right use of natural resources.*

Roosevelt continues, "Hand in hand with this we must frankly recognize the overbalance of population in our industrial centers and, by engaging on a national scale in a redistribution, endeavor to provide a better use of the land for those best fitted for the land." *Exercising federal power over individuals to remove them and their property rights when not at war.*

The address moved on to address what sectors of the economy would be nationalized and what others would be controlled by the federal government: "[Recovery] can be helped by national planning for and supervision of all forms of transportation and of communications and other utilities which have a definitely public character.... There must be a strict supervision of all banking and credits and investments." *The federal government will take over control of transportation, communication, energy distribution, banking and finance.* Added to this was the imperative: "We must act and act quickly."

Again, there was a plea to individuals for "sacrifice" of individual and property rights, which were previously prone to government claims solely when the country was at war. "We are, I know, ready and willing to submit our lives and property to such discipline, because it makes leadership which aims at a larger good...the larger purposes will bind upon us all a sacred obligation with a unity of duty hitherto evoked only in time of armed strife." *The multitudes' individual rights and property rights were to be sacrificed to government's single purpose of a "larger good"—a higher morality that the government will define.*

Roosevelt praised the Constitution: "Our constitutional system has proved itself the most superbly enduring political mechanism the modern world has produced." *And then, he proposes he will act outside of it.* "It is to be hoped that the normal balance of executive and legislative authority may be wholly adequate to meet the unprecedented task before us. But it may be that an unprecedented demand and need for undelayed action may call for temporary departure from the normal balance of public procedure."

Roosevelt then invoked the exercise of executive wartime powers: "But in the event that the Congress shall fail to take one of these two courses...I shall ask Congress for the one remaining instrument to meet the crisis—broad executive power to wage a war against the emergency, as great as the power that would be given me if we were in fact invaded by a foreign foe." *If the legislature does not agree with what the executive will propose, the executive will assume a greater-than-constitutional domestic power.*

The Brain Trust

Previous US administrations had formed their cabinets from a broad mix of persons who came from practical backgrounds, which were proven by their success in business, or militarily, or in previous experience of governance in the states. Roosevelt determined to break from this precedent and formed a cabinet almost exclusively from the Ivy League's professorial ranks.

The majority of the American intelligentsia of the 1920s, whether they strode university campuses or the planks of Broadway's theaters or sat in the salons of northeastern writers or in the offices of the popular press, were fascinated by two events: the progress of the Bolshevik Party in creating a utopian socialist state in Russia, and the real time consolidation of power by Benito

Mussolini's fascist party in Italy. Writers such as Lincoln Steffens wrote glowingly after a visit to the new Russia: "I have been over to the future and it works...I would like to spend the evening of my life watching the morning of the new world."

The social theorist and writer, Stuart Chase, pronounced against free enterprise: "Laissez-faire rides well on covered wagons, not so well on conveyor belts and cement roads." And he wrote in favor of socialism that there had to be a change, and that the necessary change was "going in the direction of more collectivism." He continued, "Russia, I am convinced, will solve for all practical purposes the economic problem.... Sixteen men in Moscow today are attempting one of the most audacious economic experiments in history, laying down the industrial future of 146 million people... for (the next) fifteen years."

On campuses such as Columbia University, people like George Counts began to teach that competition in school, though it was preparation for a system of free enterprise and individualism, was morally wrong, that universities had to start looking for models of "collectivism" to create a new society. The professor at the head of this new vanguard for socialism was Harvard's Felix Frankfurter, who pushed for radical change in America through an activist agenda in American law and government. Of his many followers, Rex Tugwell was most representative when he wrote: "Growth would not provide for the poor, only redistribution could," and that the "princes of property" would have to "share their resources." Comparing the US and the new Russian economic models, he stated, "With us, prices are a result; in Russia they are agents of social purpose."

Socialist periodicals like the *New Republic* and the *Nation* sprang up, advertising the virtues of socialism. The *New York Times* gave continuously glowing reviews of Russian Bolshevism through its writer, Walter Duranty. And Benito Mussolini graced the cover of *Time Magazine* for his achievements in taking political control over every intermediary power that lay between himself and absolute power in Italy.

This enthusiasm of the intelligentsia for a new society based in socialism and dictatorship—in complete departure from America's democratic basis and belief in individualism, property rights, and free enterprise—had a problem: in the 1928 election, the communist and socialist parties together gathered less than 1 percent of the vote. It was determined, by the practical, political socialists among the intelligentsia, that for socialism to have any practical success in America, it was necessary to attach the socialist cause and its collective goals to one of the dominant parties in America. They choose the Democratic Party. And they had a champion—Franklin Delano Roosevelt.

To prepare for his presidency, Roosevelt chose from among the professorial ranks what became the foundation of his "brain trust," a small group of scholars who would write position papers on everything concerning the economy. Among them were Raymond Moley, Adolf Berle, Samuel Rosenman, and Rex Tugwell. At Roosevelt's elbow and ear was advisor Felix Frankfurter.

Levying Wealth

To The Administrative State

The "New Deal," a term coined by Raymond Moley, demonstrated right from the start what the deal was: it was a new power emanating from the new administration which recognized few of the constitutional barriers between the federal government and the free market economy, private enterprise, and private property.

Franklin Delano Roosevelt took office on March 4, 1933, and the first act of the new administration was the uniform closing of all the banks in the country. The new congress, populated by one hundred new Democrats, pushed through the Emergency Banking Act, and the Federal Reserve was ordered to suffuse the banking system with cash into its twelve branches. Only those banks that Roosevelt and the Federal Reserve *allowed* to be reopened, received the cash inflows. The authority and power of the Federal Reserve, though it was very much the *cause* of the economic crisis owing to its setting of unnaturally low interest rates, was now expanded to govern, in detail, the entire national banking system. Every bank that reopened had to comply with every regulation that came from the Federal Reserve office—in Washington.

Then, on April 5, 1933, by an executive order of the president, all persons were required to deliver all gold coin, gold bullion, and gold certificates to the Federal Reserve Bank, through its twelve branches, or face a fine of up to $10,000 and up to ten years imprisonment. Roosevelt thereby nationalized the gold supply. The price paid in promissory notes for the gold was set at $20.67 per ounce.

On April 18, 1933, Roosevelt then single-handedly abandoned the gold standard, the common standard for all business and personal property valuations. This was of particular importance with regard to private property rights—as almost all contracts written between individuals and institutions were based on payments to be made based on the value of gold at the time of the transaction "payable in principle and interest in United States gold coin of the present standard of value." With the wave of a pen, that valuation no longer applied to $200 million worth of private contracts. It was a backhanded way of redistributing wealth across the country from creditor to debtor. Further, the Treasury of the United States would no longer honor the gold clauses of its own public contracts; anyone owed money by the treasury was now to be paid less in real terms. Then, the Thomas Amendment was passed through Congress to address the new value of gold in the United States. It stipulated that, henceforth, the president alone would determine the price of gold.

Through FDR's nationalization of the gold supply and his abandonment of the gold standard, he was personally negating every individual and every enterprise's property rights in America, which were dependent on that value. And everything was—gold was the central hub of the economic wheel around which everything, however great or small, was valued.

It became the habit of FDR to consider gold's price point over breakfast. What should gold cost today? Fifteen cents more seven cents less? It was not determined by balances of values in a free economy any longer, nor by international standards, but by one citizen among 130 million in America. One morning, while breakfasting with his adviser, Henry Morgenthau, Roosevelt came up with the notion to fix the gold price that day by increasing it twenty-one cents! Morgenthau looked at FDR curiously, and asked how he came up with that figure; by what analysis? Roosevelt responded, "It's a lucky number...because it's three times seven!" The entire value of the U.S economy and everything in it was determined by one man's idea of a lucky number that particular morning—over breakfast.

On May 27, 1933, Roosevelt's team pushed through another act whereby the administration could further seize federal control of the economy: the Securities Act of 1933 created the Securities and Exchange Commission. From that point forward, publicly traded companies had to report periodically and lay open their books before a federal authority. The SEC was also provided a stable of investigators who could investigate anyone, anywhere, involved with any company... and prosecute them.

FDR determined that the first head of the SEC should be Joseph Kennedy. When asked why a man who was one of the original "wolves of Wall Street" should be trusted with the SEC, Roosevelt advisor, Harold Ickes, answered, "He has made his pile...has invested his money in government securities...and he knows all the tricks of the trade.... Kennedy would like to make a name for himself and his family." On assuming the head office of the SEC, the pending investigations and indictments into Joe Kennedy's business practices disappeared. And Joe Kennedy, with the SEC and its hungry investigators and prosecutors, opened 2,300 investigations into his former colleagues.

In 1934, in hopes of stabilizing the marketplace from a period of chaos, Roosevelt decided the nation had go back onto the gold standard. So, of course, it was his decision as to the price of gold, which he set at $35 per ounce. The government profited $14.33 per ounce of gold seized, or 35%, by having confiscated the national gold supply the year before. What a lucky number.

With the new powers given the Federal Reserve and the SEC to control the banking and investment institutions in America, it inter-positioned the executive branch between every bank and its shareholders, every bank and its customers, every investment firm and its clients, and every publicly traded company and its shareholders. It also moved the geographical center of the economy, for the first time since Alexander Hamilton had founded the first American bank, out of New York and levitated it into Washington, DC; and concentrated control of the economy into the office of one person occupying one branch of government—the executive.

Levying Taxation

to Build the Administrative State

Abraham Lincoln, in his wisdom, said that America would never have a problem of friction or envy between classes because he was the perfect example of America: he went from splitting railroad ties to the presidency in one lifetime, which meant anybody could. During the campaign and the early stages of the new Roosevelt administration, American citizens were hearing something new, which was at odds with the idea of America being the only classless society in the world. Roosevelt the candidate, and his incoming administration, began vilifying the very persons who had built the American economy and established its prosperity. The economic leaders of America were termed selfish players, "Bourbons," unscrupulous money changers, self-seekers, persons of no vision, moneyed aristocrats, and economic royalists. There was another oddity with the language—it was coming from one of the wealthiest persons of one of the wealthiest families in the world. In addition, the Roosevelt's were *the* most powerful political family in America and quasi-royalty themselves.

The castigation of the free market and its leaders served, for the first time, to divide America's social conscious along economic lines. And it did have a purpose: it served as a type of saturation bombing to soften society up for dramatic changes in the American tax system. Roosevelt proclaimed that he would create a tax structure that would transform American society—and he did.

Through the Revenue Acts of 1934 and 1935, the top income tax rate was raised to 75 percent on any person making $50,000 or more, while at the same time all of the tax thresholds for those earning below $50,000 were dramatically lowered, so more and more families would pay more and more income taxes across the whole country. A new "death tax" was instituted to further seize wealth from the family structure, and it was doubly effective: persons who died paid a tax on their wealth for dying, while their survivors paid another tax on what was left over. The federal government became, and has since remained, the foremost profiteer of death.

Business taxes were changed from a 7 percent flat rate for all businesses of all kinds to a progressive tax rate that demanded more taxes the more that business was successful. The effective rate became so high that a person who invested in one's own business as a new venture paid 75 percent of all profits earned to the government, while bearing 100 percent of the burden of any prospective losses. The tax ended up taking away the ability one might have to reinvest in their own business during critical periods of growth, and during the depression. And the larger a business grew, the more liability to taxation the government demanded.

When the administration determined, in 1935, that the new taxes did not bring in enough revenue, there emerged in the professorial brain trust a new idea: why not tax the rest of the business profit not already seized through an undistributed profit tax? They then passed it through Congress as the Revenue Act of 1936. In effect, any business that wanted to save some of its profits after taxation, for prudent savings or for business development, was taxed again on what they did not spend, thereby dictating the fiscal policy of every enterprise in America: spend every penny earned or be taxed again.

When one discusses taxation, a common synonym applies, *levy*. The word *levy* applied to the states for the first 150 years of our country's history. When they delivered taxes from the people to the federal government, it was termed the state's levy. Levy shares a word root with *leverage* for a reason. By centralizing and levying taxes directly through the income tax, the federal government assumed all the leverage over America's citizens and their states. The federal government, at its sole discretion, exercises leverage over those from whom the government takes, in that it, alone, decides whether to take more… or less. And, in the case of redistribution, the government's leverage works in the other direction: To whom does the government give of what it has taken? Will it give more or less… and to whom?

Through centralized redistribution, citizens, localities, and states become attached to parties of government based on what may or may not be taken, or based on what may or may not be given. Beyond the obvious exercise of such power over individuals, the federal government also levied to itself a preeminent power over localities and states. The federal government took all of the nation's wealth and then determined how much it would give back, and to which localities or states it would give more… or less. As part of the New Deal, the Democratic Party, through the federal government, began to maximize its leverage: from whom would it take, to whom it would give. The states had to become submissive or be given - less. This is the ultimate fulcrum of power, the ultimate leverage that a central government can possess short of arbitrary judicial persecution. It was a power that was rejected during the nation's founding as granting too great a power to any central federal authority.

These unprecedented changes in the tax policy of our federal government—by taking most of the nation's wealth into itself—had one objective: to levy power from the citizens and states and eternize the prerogatives of power into one place—Washington, DC—and into one party—the Democratic Party. Wealth and power, previously distributed among individuals, localities, enterprises, associations, and states based on wealth that was earned and theirs, was moved to one central government in order to concentrate and wield all the power and wealth through a vastly expanded, unelected Administrative State and its agencies, which still exist in one branch of the government to this day—the executive.

Levying Power

to the Administrative State

The federal government went into the Administrative State-building business with a gusto, creating the Public Works Administration, which assumed a $5 billion budget newly wrested from the countryside, the equivalent of $103,711,940,298.51 today, and hired eight million people for building roads, dams, schools, and bridges where the government dictated they should be built—from funds which were normally used by states and localities to determine their own building and infrastructure needs.

This system of redistribution made every state and locality benefitted by the federal government beholden to the party of distribution—the Democratic Party. It made every business benefitted by government contracts beholden to the political party that bestowed the benefit—the Democratic Party. It made every laborer hired a Democratic Party union laborer. It was a reciprocal favor system, exercised through one party of government, that was adapted from the example of Benito Mussolini's fascist party and its concentration of the power structure of Italy. Republican Senator Arthur Vandenburg, from Michigan, said Roosevelt was leading "a government by executive decree...rejecting the old federalism and making the states his pawns." It would get worse.

The National Recovery Act empowered the new national recovery administration to regulate the minutiae of every business in every industry in every state across the country. If it sounds ambitious, it was. The NRA set out to centrally plan the production levels of, to name a few, the lumber, oil, and poultry industries—down to the wages they paid and the prices they were *allowed* to charge their customers. The central planning brain trust in Washington,

DC, hoped to raise prices to offset deflation. While doing so, the brain trust attempted to tell lumber companies how to harvest lumber and mill; they decided to dictate to oil companies how to drill for oil and refine it; they told poulterers how to pluck their chickens and what to charge for them. When Robert Jackson, a government lawyer and one of the brain trust members, was asked by a businessperson why government seemed suddenly to be everywhere at once in *everyone's* business, Jackson pontificated, "The man who is in government is brought in contact with the problems of all kinds and conditions of men: *Everybody's business is his business*!"

No business operation was too small that the government could not regulate it—they were "THE" experts. What the "experts" did was create regulations that drove small businesses out of business. The small mom-and-pop family shops that were all over America could not afford to adapt their businesses to meet every regulation pouring out of Washington. They could not afford to defend themselves from the regulations in court. Larger enterprises could afford to shake hands with the government man's regulating authority—and they profited by doing what they were told, while their competition was destroyed.

A sister agency was created to the NRA, the Agricultural Adjustment Administration, which set about to dictate farm production—*all* farm production. Again, it was an attempt to raise prices to levels realized before World War I. The government actually dictated to some farmers that they had to destroy their crops where they stood—to burn them—and then not grow certain foods again; during a time when many in the country were literally starving. The government did so as part of the "Ever Normal Granary Plan," which was conceived in Washington to keep surplus grains off the market. It worked to keep the nation's bounty off the market, and off everyone's table. It did not work to raise prices. The government, at one point, considered the price of pork too low in the marketplace. So, to "fix" a price, it was decided, in an office in Washington, to slaughter three million baby pigs nationally - in order to raise the price of pork.

The NRA, in one year alone, established 727 legal codes and 95 supplements to those codes, which were approved directly by the president himself or through the NRA administration head, producing ten thousand pages of new laws that were implemented even though never voted on by Congress. The NRA, just one agency, created in one year alone more "administrative law" than all the "legislative law" that had been created since the nation's founding 150 years before. And the NRA was just one of thirty new agencies under the direct control of the executive branch, which were busily writing volumes of administrative law as fast as they could push their pens and pound their typewriters.

The arrogance of these agencies was so pervasive, and their "expertise" so offensively dictated, that lawsuits sprang up against the unprecedented assumption of powers to centrally control every enterprise in America. Americans did not like the centralized planning that was based on the Russian Bolshevik model as much as the brain trust and the Democratic Party did.

Another idea was tried straight out of the Joseph Stalin centralized planning guidebook: collectivized farming. A prototype was organized by the brain truster Rex Tugwell, and the new resettlement administration. It was called "Casa Grande" in Arizona. Numbers of persons were relocated to this new conception of a socialist utopia. Everyone recruited would work together and share in the collected fruits of the common farm. No one would own anything. There would be no rights of property. There was "one tractor for all." The idea worked out as well as the hippie communes of the 1960s, which is to say it didn't. It happened almost immediately that people were arguing over what was whose and who owed the community more work, and who needed to pull more of their own load. It turned out that no one deserved what they had—compared to "me." The idea that *I alone should determine what is mine* still pervaded.

But Rex Tugwell had weightier things on his mind than the community's bickering over who owned most of the scarcity. He was concerned about how houses were to be arranged in

Casa Grande. He wanted them to be built according to certain architectural styles and painted with certain pastel colors. After all, "A community does not consist of houses alone. You cannot just build houses and tell people to go and live in them! They have to be taught how to live!" Rex should know—he operated a staff of six thousand, had a discretionary war chest of $91 million, and ten million acres of land to put people in—and they still didn't like it.

The farmers grew exasperated of being treated like shift workers, like tenant labor. They toiled all day, every day, and did not own the fruits of their labor. The contented feeling of working their own land did not exist. Eventually, most of the folks on the common farm became very angry. One day, one of the managers, Robert Faul, walked out in a rage saying Casa Grande was too much "like the Soviets." But there was good news, after years of toil and a bumper crop—each family of settlers was going to receive $65 per month from then on in wages.

Back in Washington, the Roosevelt administration was still on their mission of agency creation. There was even one created to make everyone feel better--or worse, depending on how the government wanted you to feel and about whom. The Workers Progress Administration was created by Roosevelt and his friend Harry Hopkins, and was administrated by Roy Stryker, who had been a co-writer of a socialist tome in vogue in northeastern universities called *American Economic Life*, which contained the famous line: "No individual ever built a skyscraper."

This new "artistic" agency was funded by every taxpayer in the nation. The administration hired 26,000 writers, actors, actresses, musicians, singers, dancers, painters, photographers, and others in order to, as Stryker put it, show that "federal money was desperately needed for relief programs" and to "show what a good job the agencies were doing in the field." A funny thing happened, though—neither the Workers Progress Administration, nor any of its artists, ever had a bad thing to say about the Democratic Party. They had glorious things to say and portray about one party of government—the Democratic Party—while having only deplorable things to say and portray about anyone who dared question these government policies. How is it possible that, among a free people, there was no second opinion?

This idea of party propaganda, paid for at taxpayer expense in the new era of mass media, was taken from Joseph Goebbels who was at that time active in Berlin. It was and is fundamental to the creation and execution of modern totalitarianism.

Levying

An Industrial Invasion

To take another idea from Rome, Berlin, and Moscow in the 1930s, there was a manner by which to take government control over an industry—you threatened it with bankruptcy and its owners with imprisonment. In America, taking over an industry would not be that easy; the country was vast, its industries many, and the courts in the various states surely full of objection.

In the 1920s, utilities were *the* industry, the one lighting up every house and street, every town and every city the electricity reached. The utility industry was *the* employer, and it was *the* investment that might lead to the country's enrichment and recovery while delivering power that was priced by the consumer, dependent on what they would and could afford.

Before the crash, the foremost exemplar of the possibilities in energy utilities was Sam Insull, an immigrant who came to America with nothing and worked his way up the ladder under Thomas Edison. He built Commonwealth Edison of Illinois, which literally lit up the city of Chicago and provided warmth to its citizens during their frigid winters. His holding company also raised the famous elevated train system, and his philanthropy built Chicago's Civic Opera, where tenors can be heard singing to this day.

When another such opportunity presented itself to light up the south, Henry Ford himself proposed to develop the Tennessee River Valley at no cost to taxpayers. He would effectively act as a proconsul, dedicating himself and his personal resources to bringing light, heat, and prosperity to a region. But the opportunity was rejected by Nebraska Senator George Norris and FDR. Roosevelt, as the governor of New York, had once rejected similar offers to develop the utility opportunities along the St. Lawrence River proffered by General Electric, DuPont, and Alcoa—preferring to set up the state-owned Power Authority of New York. To Roosevelt and the brain trust, the opportunity in the Tennessee River Valley was an ideal invasion route for government intervention and centralization of federal control over the economy's energy sector and the utility markets.

The Tennessee River basin spans seven states: from Virginia south to Kentucky, Tennessee, and North Carolina, then further down to Georgia, Alabama, and Mississippi. This presented a unique opportunity to create an unprecedented regional political authority that would exist above any state government's authority and could be controlled by the executive branch of the federal government alone. Being a newly conceived political entity, not covered by the barriers to power in the Constitution, the Tennessee Valley Authority could define its own powers—to the delight of the central planning brain trust.

The rationale for setting up the TVA was that the government had built two dams on the Tennessee River—the Muscle Shoals and Woodrow Wilson dams were built by the Defense Department to stabilize navigation on the rivers, but they also produced hydroelectric power. Up until the Roosevelt administration, dams constructed in the United States sold the excess power they produced to private utility companies, like Commonwealth & Southern, a utility holding company that set up stations for sales and distribution of power to their naturally expanding customer base throughout the Tennessee region and beyond.

Then an administration campaign of vilification began—again. According to the administration, the utility companies were solely responsible for the stock market crash; they were "demons" responsible for "destroying the world." The brain trust vowed that utility's chiefs would be called to account, and a post-depression utopia would be built "on the bones of Wall Street" and the utilities companies. The whole industry awoke to find themselves the likely target of federal sanctions as though they were foreign saboteurs.

The TVA was established by the Tennessee Valley Act on May18, 1933, and was assigned three directors who would report directly to Roosevelt—not to any state authority, nor to the Congress. Arthur Morgan, from Antioch College, would head up the directorate and oversee forestry, engineering, construction, and social and economic planning. Harcourt Morgan, from the University of Tennessee, would oversee fertilizer production and rural life planning. And a Felix Frankfurter protégé, thirty-three-year-old David Lilienthal, would be charged with the power program and legal disputes. Lilienthal's view of government was summed up in the following quote: "You see, I have a very strong feeling that if we cannot *control* our basic industries, and certainly nothing is more basic than the utilities industry, then we have no government in fact, merely a pathetic fiction of government."

If the range of the control given to the directors seems of a broad breadth, it had to be. It proposed to flood 153,000 arable acres of land to remake the entire Tennessee Valley, creating nine dams and multitudes of reservoirs and lakes. The new authority proposed to destroy three thousand family farms and displace fifteen thousand families from their homes and livelihoods by an act of eminent domain. The government was going to "relocate" them all. It would also relocate centuries-old cemeteries. What was left to be smothered by the flood waters were sacred Native American burial grounds and the teeming natural inhabitants of the Tennessee—every living thing with nowhere left to breathe.

But there was another inhabitant of the valley left to contend with: an assortment of power companies headed by Commonwealth & Southern and its president Wendell Wilke, one of the economy's so-called "malefactors" that the brain trust vowed to destroy. C&S had eleven operating companies controlling six power systems in two groups. The northern group reached up to Michigan and the southern group as far south as Florida. C&S had 200,000 shareholders holding $400 million in equity: a valuation that had been battered by the vilification campaign of the federal government. The company, nonetheless, reported gross annual earnings of $100 million as of May 1933. C&S was a healthy American company, even with what government intervention had done to destroy the economy since the crash.

Arthur Morgan and Wendell Wilke met in New York to discuss their relative positions. Wilke told Morgan that he understood the new law to mean that the TVA could produce power and transmit it as a government entity, but could not sell or distribute the power, as it would make the government a competitor in the energy market—a market that was "free" of government. Morgan did not say he agreed with Wilke's interpretation of the law, but something would be worked out between the TVA and the private sector C&S. Wilke recommended a five-year contract, whereby C&S would pay $500 million for the power generated by the government dams, thereby allowing the government to break even on its limited TVA program budget. What Wilke did not know, and Morgan did not tell him, was that the government's ambitions were not that small.

David Lilienthal was displeased that Morgan had tried to get along with Wilke at all. Lilienthal took over the negotiations with the idea of stringing C&S along with a five-year contract, while growing TVA to be a public sector energy company that could annihilate every private power company in the region. But he had to wait for the government distribution system to be up and running. At Lilienthal's first meeting with Wilke at the Cosmo Club in Washington, Wilke naively asked, "What could the TVA want with the sale of power? That is the private sector's job." Lilienthal returned a smile, while playing a role Felix Frankfurter had taught him of portraying the benevolent, virtuous government agent grappling with a morally inferior corporate representative, in which case the government (on the side of right) *had to* prevail. Lilienthal led Wilke on, while preparing legally to disable C&S—after all, the government needed C&S for a little longer. A five-year contract was signed on January 4, 1934, wherein TVA "agreed" to halt any incursion into C&S markets.

The federal government then began a pincer movement against the power companies of the south, and against utility companies, in general, all over the country. The government began to offer townships 3.5 percent loans for the building of public power stations that would duplicate those that private power companies had already built—and they would be the municipalities' "own," controlled by the federal government. The first communities to sign onto the bargain were Knoxville and Tupelo. And, thereby, the federal government had entered the energy distribution and sales market it had previously agreed not to enter.

At the same time, two other Frankfurter proteges, Benjamin Cohen and Tommy "the Cork" Corcoran, pushed through Congress an addition to the Public Utility Holding Company Act, which outlawed the very structure that energy companies needed and had always organized under, in order to function financially and move capital where it was necessary to invest as a corporate entity. The addition stipulated that all existing utility companies, except those controlling "a single integrated system" of power production and distribution, were given three years to liquidate or restructure themselves. They could not accomplish that mandate. By their nature, private power companies were "multi-integrated systems," they could not function otherwise. In a meeting with Roosevelt, Henry Couch, the President of Alabama Power, pleaded against the act to no avail, finally asking, "Do I understand that any further effort to avoid a break-up of (private) utility holding companies is futile?" Roosevelt answered, "It is futile."

The new SEC was given authority to decide whether holding companies complied with the new act...or were to be liquidated. The rule was coined the utility company "death sentence act," and Tommy "The Cork" Corcoran was the hit man. None other than Joseph Kennedy objected to his *own* authority as SEC chairman, saying he himself did not have the authority to decide the proper operational structure of holding companies! He was soon dismissed from the administration for not showing sufficient prosecutorial zeal. In January 1935, Roosevelt called for "the abolition of the evil of holding companies."

Wilke spoke back publicly against those persons of the present government (and there were many) who assumed "an attitude of superior virtue and patriotism, who paint us who represent private enterprise as...anti-social, unpatriotic despoilers of men!" He stated, further, that his "company had been honestly and efficiently managed...now the government was trying to destroy it!" Then Wilke spoke his hopes. "A true liberal will not tolerate executive or legislative domination!" His hopes were hopeless in the face of the brain trust idealogues.

Arthur Morgan, the head of TVA, later resigned, considering the course that the government had taken as misleading to him and unethical in practice. He later wrote in an *Atlantic Monthly* article that he abhorred the "Napoleonic complex" that the administration was displaying while failing to compromise with the private sector solely because of their ideological animus against private enterprise. In Morgan's view, if a compromise had been reached, the whole venture would have been vastly more economical.

Nineteen power companies launched lawsuits against the TVA, at the point of a last stand against the government's invasion of an entire private enterprise sector of the economy. They held that the TVA had no right to sell power in the marketplace and compete with private companies—and that it was plainly not a level playing field. The case went to the Supreme Court as *Ashwander v. TVA*. After administration bullying, the Supreme Court gave 8-1 in favor of the TVA on the decision. According to the court, the TVA had the right to sell surplus energy and operate in the marketplace. To the brain trust's delight, the Supreme Court, they said, was finally "housebroken."

In the dissent, Justice James McReynolds countered that his fellow justices' view of the case was unrealistically narrow; that the government, "while pretending to act within their powers to improve navigation (on a river) [was] really seeking to accomplish what they have no right to undertake: the business of developing, distributing and selling electrical power." The justice wrote that, in the broader view, what the case was really about was whether the federal government could "destroy every [private] public service corporation within the confines of the United States."

Wilke and his private sector colleagues assessed the new business environment and their adversary—the federal government. Their private companies had only their own earned incomes to spend, while the federal government had everybody's money to spend, including the taxes that the utility companies and their employees paid to it. Government's resources on the ground and in court were literally limitless. The federal government could use tax dollars to effectively bribe any and every township into agreeing to TVA's distribution system. Private companies had to build their distribution systems from reinvestment of rightful earnings, after taxes. While the government paid no taxes, and never had to meet a budget in the same sense.

As leaders of private enterprise, Wilke and his colleagues were answerable to every one of their shareholders; whereas the federal government had become answerable to no one. The government could create more administrative laws at any time, of any kind, to further weaken and destroy private enterprise companies and their shareholders' equity.

Beyond the critical differences between private enterprise and the government, the government had the prosecutorial arms of the IRS and the SEC, which were suddenly all over the utility companies and the people who ran them. The threats of corporate and personal persecutions were real. The government also all but owned the media, so they could turn public opinion throughout the country against any company or any person in a single day. The government did not engage in competition: it engaged in condemnation, regulation, and elimination of competition. It engaged in complete destruction of competitors in favor of itself. There was nowhere for the targeted utility companies to go.

As an act of responsibility to C&S shareholders, Wendell Wilke went directly to FDR (why stop in the middle?). He told Roosevelt, "You and you alone, are the only person who has the power to bring a settlement about." Meaning he wanted FDR to buy out

C&S as it was his last alternative. Wilke was prepared to offer all the holdings of C&S for purchase at the "fair" market price of $95 million. FDR said no.

Wilke wrote a letter to C&S shareholders noting that the damage done to their investments was calculated, industry-wide, to be $3.5 billion, since FDR's inauguration, in real capital terms. And with the new laws erected against their company's ability to function, their future held no better prospect. They were forced by the government into a position of "take it or leave it," on Roosevelt's terms, concerning any buyout of their interests. Wendell Wilke was forced to accept a check from the US Treasury for $78 million—3/4 the price that C&S was worth in a free market even after the government's attacks against it. Three-fourths of the price its shareholders deserved. What a lucky number!

Wilke spoke to the newspapers, saying, "We sell these properties with regret." But that his fears concerning the government were "justified by the hostile attitude of Government itself."

A woman who had invested her pension in utilities, thinking it the best investment, wrote a letter to Mrs. Roosevelt hoping the First Lady would understand and show it to the president: "Personally, I had my savings so invested that I would have had a satisfactory provision for old age. Now thanks to his desire to 'get' the utilities I cannot be sure of anything, being a stockholder, as after business has survived his merciless attacks (if it does) insurance will probably be no good either.... I am not an 'economic royalist' just an ordinary white-collar worker at $1,600.00 per year. Please show this to the president and ask him to remember the wishes of the forgotten [wo]man, that is, the one who dared to vote against him. We expect to be tramped on but we do wish the stepping would be a little less hard."

For every business the government targeted, there were investors who suffered for it, and they did not have the resources of the government's "royalists."

David Lilienthal happily sent two of his New Deal cohorts, Swidler and Krug, to Wilke's office to discuss how to dismantle every private power company in the Tennessee Valley. The scope of the federal government's power had greatly expanded, and the officials had to inventory offices, generating plants, transmission lines, and distribution systems for the purposes of dividing them up for government use. The TVA also had to go into the appliance selling business too, so they were interested in C&S inventories. And, oh yes, there would be some restructuring to do—the government was now a "multi-integrated" power producer, seller, and supplier, just like the monstrous old C&S had been. But the government's angelic subsidiary, the TVA, could structure itself however they pleased; the government would pass no law against *itself*.

David Lilienthal pronounced that TVA (after billions of dollars of taxpayer expense) would produce power for $1.50 a month for regular users—the same monthly price C&S would have provided at no government expense, while it would have filled the US Treasury with tax revenue. Wilke would soon refer to the TVA and the Tennessee as the river that "waters five states and drains the nation." Between 1939 and 1959, the TVA was subsidized with a further $20 billion in taxpayer dollars.

Wilke wanted it noted for posterity that, "Power is just as destructive on Pennsylvania Avenue as it is on Wall Street, and subsidized government competition established in one industry, threatens all industry." Ever since the TVA example, business in America has always been good for the businesses that the Democratic Party favors: those businesses are subsidized, they are protected, and their competitors are disadvantaged or destroyed in the marketplace. It is just the same in economies that are controlled by dictators and monarchs, and it makes business for those who are not Democrats nearly impossible.

And it is the worst scenario for every consumer and every taxpayer searching for a fair tax or a fair price while living and working beneath such a government: one dedicated to the destruction of free enterprise when it suits the party of government's self-interest.

Levying

Prosecution

Roosevelt and the brain trust had seized greater control than had ever been held by the federal government—through control of the financial sector and through massive taxation and expanding dominance over the utilities sector of the economy. The brain trust believed that the three together afforded the best opportunity for concentrating and burgeoning the power of the federal government and its revenues to the greatest degree possible. In addition to the unprecedented rise in tax rates, Roosevelt saw another means of raising more revenue and a way to demonstrate the federal government's new power—through investigations and prosecutions. The brain trust held up the usual suspects for vilification... and collecting more revenue.

Roosevelt did not consider that his tax policies or government domination of the most vibrant sectors of the economy might not be best for the economy. As Roosevelt put it, at fault were the "citizens...they found a trick way of using loopholes." Roosevelt demanded the practice be stopped, that the "loopholes be closed and that the new laws, closing the loopholes, be retroactive." Henry Morgenthau—who had recently added another five thousand to the eleven thousand agents already in his IRS department for investigations—insisted, after performing a number of audits, that most auditors found the use of tax breaks in accordance with the tax code...and legal! How could that be?

Roosevelt offered a different view: that persons exercising tax breaks should be viewed as having malign motives. Where there was any doubt, the citizens—the taxpayers—should be presumed guilty. So, another bill was passed. The Revenue Bill of 1934 would increase revenue by reducing tax evasion; and it was made retroactive...

Attorney Harold Ickes, along with Harry Hopkins and other brain trusters, took a broader view than just income tax returns: ongoing economic weakness could be used to further attack and seize whatever remained of the revenues of big business. The governing philosophy of Felix Frankfurter was brought to the forefront again: the government should portray itself as the virtuous protagonist, while businesses and their representatives were the antagonists who operate with immoral motives to make ill-gotten gains—wealth for which they were unworthy. Roosevelt was listening. Roosevelt wanted more revenue, whether the means was via investigations of individuals or businesses, whether through prosecutions and fines, or whether through new tax laws that were retroactive.

The Administrative State decided to expand the operations of the IRS and the SEC. They put together lists of likely targets. And the media operations ramped up, raising the usual pinatas as the malevolent scapegoats: business leaders and their enterprises. The SEC would proceed against big business with accusations of violations of anti-trust laws, and the IRS would go after individuals who could be hung out to dry in the public square for vilification. When the lists were produced of targets of investigation and prosecution, Roosevelt found some friends on it—and let it be known that he preferred they be treated "softly."

Elmer Irey, who had helped put away Al Capone, was tapped by prosecutor Robert Jackson to investigate the number one target on the list—Andrew Mellon. Roosevelt did not like Andrew Mellon, having referred to him once as "the mastermind among the malefactors of great wealth." But Mellon's success in business was legendary. His service as treasury secretary was so esteemed, it was famously said that "three presidents served under him." Needless to say, Irey was reluctant to go after so respected a man and public servant. Then, Henry Morgenthau phoned, "Irey, you can't be 99 percent on the job—investigate Mellon! I order it!"

Robert Jackson and Homer Cummings brought a case of tax fraud against Mellon before a grand jury in Pittsburgh, requesting an indictment. Mellon's attorneys were legally compelled to provide exhaustive evidence of Andrew Mellon's holdings, which, of course, spilled out into the media. And summarily, the headline was that Mellon actually earned $9.1 million in 1931, not the $6.8 million claimed in his tax return, and therefore he had malignly underpaid his taxes. In addition, that he had used five tax loopholes to *evade* paying the proper amount of taxes.

Mellon's defense was simple: his lawyers proved he had, in fact, earned what he claimed and overpaid the taxes he owed based on his legal earnings in 1931; and, in fact, he would be requesting a refund. His attorneys also noted that he gave away more money to philanthropic causes that year than he paid in taxes. And the loopholes he used were perfectly legal at the time—and he would know, he helped write the tax code. Mellon called the case a "campaign of terror," and fumed that the government ought not be able to prosecute citizens for doing something that is legal.

Mellon and his attorneys might have cited this passage from Alexander Hamilton and the *Federalist Papers* on the subject: "The creation of crimes after the commission of the fact, or, in other words, the subjecting of men to punishment for things which, when they were done, were breaches of no law, and the practice of arbitrary imprisonments, have been, in all ages, the favorite and most formidable instruments of tyranny."

Even Alexander Forbes, a cousin of Roosevelt, deplored the persecutions of persons for having legally taken advantage of tax breaks. He had written in an op-ed in the *Boston Herald*: "The true patriot [would] claim every exemption the law allows and...he may have more to spend on enduring contributions to the betterment of Mankind." Roosevelt's response to his cousin, Forbes: "I do not hesitate to brand you one of the worst anarchists in the United States!"

An indictment requested by the prosecution was not returned by the jury against Mellon. The administration celebrated anyway: they were able to advertise, in a malignant way, the holdings of Andrew Mellon. Soon after, Robert Jackson charged Mellon again with IRS violations in a case that would be brought before the "Board of Tax Appeals," outside the common law system. The "Board" ultimately found for the government, and fined Mellon $600,000.

Then the government opened another avenue of attack. The SEC brought a case through the Justice Department against Mellon's Aluminum Company of America and attached Mellon's family as co-defendants—his nephew Richard K. Mellon, his niece Sarah Mellon Scaife, and his son Paul. Robert Jackson's objective was simple: he wanted the Aluminum Company of America "dissolved." Andrew Mellon died while the case was ongoing.

The government's case against Sam Insull, the immigrant who had earned his way up the ladder of free enterprise—the bringer of light, elevated trains, and opera to Chicago—was not so simple. On hearing that the government was coming after him, but not knowing the extent of what he was going to be charged with and having already re-invested all of his personal wealth to save his business, he needed time to assemble a defense. He fled to Paris, then to Greece, with which the US government had no extradition treaty.

He learned that Harold Ickes, a longtime personal foe from Chicago, had assembled an army of federal prosecutors in their hometown amassing a paper file of evidence against him that was rumored to weigh two tons. Then he learned the charges: mail fraud, based on false promises of profit opportunities in his business; errors made in filing for bankruptcy; and embezzlement (of his own money). In short, he was wanted for making accounting claims that were legal when they were filed, but illegal now by way of the new retroactive laws of 1934.

While the IRS and the SEC were taking a microscope, a copier, and a sledgehammer to Insull's business and personal affairs, the State Department demanded that the Greek government immediately seize and hand over the 76-year-old invalid despite having no legal basis to do so. The Greek government initially promised to deliver the business genius-turned-fugitive. However, the Greek public, animated by their ancient example of individualism and freedom, stood with Insull. The Greek government nonetheless sent the Greek police force to surround Insull and his wife and confined the new prisoner to his apartment with a surrounding police posse twenty-four hours a day.

The US State Department responded that Greece should throw Insull out of the country within forty-eight hours, so he could be captured at sea. Meanwhile, the American consulate assigned more agents to watch Insull, with twenty-four-hour surveillance. Then, on the night of March 15, 1934, the invalid, Sam Insull, vanished without a trace....

The Greek population laughed at their government's blunder. In America, the embarrassed State Department asked Senate Majority Leader Joseph Robinson for emergency legislation granting the extra-territorial powers necessary for US officers to arrest Sam Insull—wherever he might land between the North and South Poles. By exerting overwhelming State Department pressure on the shipping companies in the Port of Piraeus, Athens, Insull was found to have escaped aboard the *SS Maiotis* bound for Alexandria, Egypt. Crowds of people and government officials gathered along the shores of that ancient city looking out for the fugitive ship. On March 23, Roosevelt dropped everything he was doing to sign the new law dedicated to Insull's capture. Then, the vessel *Maiotis,* disappeared at sea...

Most of the waking world became transfixed by one man's escape from a world-circling government vendetta.

Finally, in need of provision, the *Maiotis* went into port at Istanbul, Turkey. Sam Insull, the most celebrated outlaw of his time, was taken into custody by the Turkish government at the request of the Internal Revenue Service, the Securities and Exchange Commission, the US State Department, the US Senate, Harold Ickes, and Franklin Delano Roosevelt—he was surrounded.

Transferred by the Turkish police to his new confine—the ship *Exilona*—was the international terror, Sam Insull...arrested for misfiling taxes. Sam was more than that—he was a great example to every American of the lengths to which the new Administrative State would go to persecute one of its own citizens. The new US "administrative" government had the resources to persecute anyone of its own... to the ends of the earth.

A crowd of three thousand showed up when Sam Insull was brought into Illinois' Cook County Jail. He was just as soon put into the hospital ward, as he was over seventy and in ill health throughout the entire time of his ordeal. Harold Ickes was exultant to have his old adversary, Sam Insull, securely behind bars.

Insull's defense was a simple one. Just as Mellon's team had insisted, the charges against Insull were based on laws passed after the bankruptcy and tax filings in question were filed, and not even the government could change the rules of the game to prosecute whomever they pleased for following those rules when they were in place. "What I did, when I did it, was honest; now through changed conditions [and laws] what I did may not be called honest," Insull said to his State Department escort.

As to the charge of mail fraud in positively marketing his own business shares as a good investment that would realize a profit, Insull noted that he'd reinvested all of his *own* available wealth during "the crash" to save that business—that he *thought* to be the best investment. But Insull was also rendered penniless. Had the utility industry stood up for itself during the withering government media campaign made against it, there might have been something left to save. Insull was tried and found not guilty by a jury of his peers. He was tried a second time and found not guilty by a jury of his peers. Then he was tried a third time—and found not guilty by a jury of his peers.

Some years later, Harold Ickes, the personal foe of Insull since their days in Chicago, who'd helped strategize the big-name prosecutions of the New Deal era, sat on his porch and surveyed his brand new 230-acre "Headwaters Farm" in Maryland. As he looked over the vast, beautiful pastures and woods, he contemplated with pride his career in government—part of which had centered on targeting the wealthy, the "unworthy." He had prosecuted them with the limitless power and resources of the

United States federal government; and even if they were found not guilty or eventually set free, they were personally destroyed. Ickes did have one regret: the government, at one point, had confiscated the remains of Insull's moveable wealth—his furniture. It was thought that the government could make a nifty profit of $100,000 at the special auction that was arranged for the sale. But the whole bundle had sold for only $26,000. Even so, that was all profit to the government.

Sam Insull, once the foremost immigrant success story of the American "free enterprise" system, died in poverty in the street near a metro station in Paris.

At the Democratic National Convention at Madison Square Garden in 1936, Roosevelt spoke exultantly to the gathered crowd about his record. "I should like to have it said of my first administration, that in it the forces of selfishness and lust for power met their match." Then Roosevelt defined government's new role: "I should like to have it said of my second administration that in it these forces have met their master."

It should be noted that Roosevelt's administration succeeded in its own lust and selfishness by levying as much wealth and power as possible into the "Administrative State of America." And by destroying a lot of people along the way.

Fdr's Second Inaugural

Roosevelt's second inaugural speech, given on January 20, 1937, contained the same callings for unity over individualism, and for concentrated federal power as opposed to state and local autonomy. And again, there came the same invectives against the ever-villainous forces of individualism and free enterprise.

FDR vowed…

"To drive from the temple of our ancient faith those who have profaned it." *Another paean sung to the Administrative State's moral superiority.*

"To do that we must find practical controls over blind economic forces and blindly selfish men." *A pretense for stipulating the necessity of federal control over every aspect of the economy.*

"Our forefathers...created a strong government with powers of united action sufficient then and now to solve problems utterly beyond individual or local solution." *Individualism and local self-government, on which our country is based, are obsolete, useless power centers.*

"Nearly all of us recognize that as intricacies of human relationships increase, so power to govern them also must increase." *The central government has a pretense to govern all human relationships.*

"We have begun to bring private autocratic powers into their proper subordination to the public's government." *Subordination to the Administrative State's government.*

"They have been challenged and beaten!" *By their own omnipotent government.*

"We have always known that heedless self-interest was bad morals." *Individual enterprise and self-interest are morally evil.*

"We are fashioning an instrument of unimagined power for the establishment of a morally better world." *The Administrative State, paid for by every taxpayer, is the instrument that is morally superior to every citizen and which will attack any citizen with irresistible power if one disagrees with the Administrative State's univocal moral vision.*

"Dulled conscience, irresponsibility, and ruthless self-interest already reappear. Such symptoms of prosperity may become portents of disaster! Prosperity already tests the persistence of our progressive purpose." *Prosperity itself is morally at odds with the Administrative State.*

The prosperity of individuals and enterprises is the last natural and legal defense of a free and independent people against the limitless redistributive and punishing power of a central government.

Levying

A Senior Partnership

Roosevelt and the brain trust moved on yet another flank to control the economic life of the country. Based on the rationale that inequalities at the bargaining table between employers and employees "aggravate recurrent business depressions," it was therefore the government's necessary role to step into that relationship on a national scale. Senator Robert Wagner of New York sponsored the Wagner Act, which inter-positioned the national government as the senior partner in any labor disputes between ownership, capital, and labor.

A three-person, extra-judicial National Labor Relations Board was empowered to hear cases. Other provisions of the act allowed workers a one-time vote to join a union—thereafter, no vote was necessary, the union leadership was thus empowered in perpetuity over their workers, their companies, and their industries. The act imposed a "closed shop" designation on every company effected: anyone seeking work could be barred from work if they did not join the union. Unions thenceforth had the right to strike against their companies if their demands were not met. And every new approved union worker had to pay part of their salaries out of every check to the union.

Within one year, membership in the Auto Workers Union rose from thirty thousand to 375,000. In the coal industry, membership rose to nine out of every ten workers. Over at the TVA, David Lilienthal, rejoiced that seventeen thousand public employees could now collectively bargain—against the taxpayer, and against their own consumers of energy. At the government-run PWA, the writers and artists went on strike, at which time even Roosevelt objected: "A strike of public employees manifests nothing less than an intent on their part to obstruct the operations of government until their demands are satisfied.... Such action looking toward the paralysis of government by those who have sworn to support it is unthinkable and intolerable." How is that any different than what the Wagner Act mandated to happen to private enterprises in order to expand the coercive power of government? It is no different.

Ford Motor Company held out for a time, citing that after paying higher taxes, after paying to meet new industry regulations, and after paying higher wages to every employee and their union dues—the company had no capital to afford to make new innovations and provide a return to shareholders. Henry Ford held out. Then the government looked the other way when strikers invaded the company's property to stop operations. Strikes began occurring in industries everywhere. Companies all over the country, and eventually Henry Ford, capitulated to the entry of a new force into every boardroom in America, the Administrative State and their protected unions.

At General Motors, after a series of serious strikes and the United Auto Workers takeover, it was found that, while sales of cars and employee incomes were up, as well as union dues paid to the Unions. GM's net income collapsed. Therefore, the equity held by shareholders was suddenly—and from that day to this—down.

Previously, in the free market, in all sorts of industries, a person who worked at a company such as Ford enjoyed their wages, which were sufficient to actually buy the products they built and still have a financial surplus. With the surplus, they were also able to buy stock in their own company (or other companies), and that investment could grow with their contributions to their own company—they were part owners. In the New Deal, government became the part owner of every company's future, and the unions syphoned the money from every union member that otherwise might have been a great investment.

And, lo and behold, every union ever since has paid one party of government continuous dividends deriving from every private enterprise company and associated employee salary.

Since the Democratic Party's passage of what has been called "the most coercive legislation" of the New Deal, it has been receiving donations through every union from every company, shareholder, employee, taxpayer, and, ultimately, every consumer in the country. What a lucky deal.

Levying

The Supreme Court

The primary agencies of the New Deal, the NRA and substantial elements of the AAA, were struck down by the Supreme Court as being too invasive a form of federal governance. Between 1935 and 1936, the court struck down more legislation than it had in its history. Roosevelt had his agencies and his majority in Congress, but he did not have the courts to sanction alterations in the constitutional arrangements between federal and state authorities, and between the Administrative State and the free enterprise system.

Roosevelt became so exasperated by the court's obstinacy on the New Deal that he again launched an invective campaign. Administration mouthpiece columnists started reviling the court as the "nine old men" who work in "the mausoleum of justice." Justice Roberts was assailed as the "meat-axer" of the president's will. Justice McReynolds was either lazy or stupid for not going along with the program. The court was targeted in Roosevelt's second inaugural address when he pointedly demanded that the people "insist that every agency of government use effective instruments to carry out their will."

Roosevelt began to threaten to pack the court to get his agenda confirmed, despite the *Federalist Papers*' remonstrance that, "The complete independence of the courts of justice is peculiarly essential in a limited Constitution." FDR claimed that the court was backlogged with work and needed the help. Chief Justice Hughes replied: "The present number of justices is thought to be large enough so far as the prompt, adequate, and efficient work of the Court is concerned."

Nonetheless, Roosevelt planned to go around state ratification and simply legislate, using his large majority in the legislature, a plan to increase the number of judges from nine to fifteen, with a new judge added for every present judge aged seventy or older. The plan took the form of the Judicial Procedures Bill of 1937, threatening to dilute the impact of the present nine justices. The president railed, "The nation must save the Constitution from the court and the court from itself!" To him, the country required protection from the dangers of 1929 occurring again, that the country needed legislation that was protected, or else the government might need to be ...restructured.

In the face of such intimidation, a miracle occurred. The Supreme Court voted 5-4 to uphold the National Labor Relations Act in the case of *National Labor Relations Board v. Jones and Laughlin Steel*. The decision was termed "the switch in time that saved nine." After that decision, Roosevelt relaxed his intimidation and retracted his packing plan, and the court began to take a view towards broader approval of administration policies—which projected the growth of the Administrative State, just as Woodrow Wilson had prescribed.

Roosevelt was helped by the age of the justices and the longevity of his presidency, eventually naming nine justices to the court who were each like-minded to his ambitions. Of particular note is Felix Frankfurter, Roosevelt's longtime aid, the professor from Harvard—the foremost believer in the expansion of power in Washington, DC—who became Justice Frankfurter through Roosevelt's appointment. Of the American economy, Frankfurter's viewpoint was best expressed by Robert Moley: "The problems of economic life [are] litigious...the government [is] the protagonist. Its agents [are] its lawyers and commissioners, the antagonists [are] corporation lawyers." The new Supreme Court made the invasion of the free enterprise system a judicial cause.

The Supreme Court took a profound turn at this point in time, from a court that was a zealous "originalist" bulwark in defense of the Constitution and its own judicial independence to one that became the flanker for executive branch ambition and fellow masons who laid the foundations for ever-expanding wealth and ever more concentrated power in the Administrative State of Washington, DC.

Felix Frankfurter's influence exceeded his own office and stay on the court. He was the Ivy League's turnstile for persons wishing to clerk at the Supreme Court, a critical stepping stone to high-level judicial or government appointments. Without Frankfurter's approval, it was said, one's chances for a clerkship were nil. Everyone he approved came from the same schools and shared the same views as the brain trust members of the executive, and they started filling the judiciary. Notable among the number of activists from Frankfurter's big government apprenticeship were Dean Acheson, David Reisman, and Alger Hiss.

With that generation and subsequent generations of the court, a dire vision of Alexander Hamilton's was fulfilled, that the court, *"if they should be disposed to exercise WILL instead of JUDGEMENT, the consequence would equally be the substitution of their pleasure to that of the legislative body," and will "have a tendency...to occasion dangerous innovations in the government, and serious oppressions of the minor party in the community."* Such "minor parties" as persons hoping to be involved in free enterprise.

And from that point in time, the court was decidedly given to "party" considerations, which reminds of another warning from Hamilton, Madison, and Jay in the *Federalist Papers*: "On account of the natural propensity of such parties to party divisions, there will be no less reason to fear the pestilential breath of faction may poison the fountains of justice. The habit of being continually marshalled on opposite sides will be too apt to stifle the voice of both law and equity." These Founders of our country, after years of study and deliberation, knew precisely what they were writing about.

The Levy Brakes

The new judiciary began to delight the New Dealers, especially when they rendered a verdict whereby the Supreme Court refused power companies the right to use injunctions against the federal government to stop it from bribing (loaning money to) cities to build power plants. This verdict broke the dam that was keeping the federal government from taking over every power company in America. Harold Ickes, Sam Insull's old "friend," already had sixty-one projects in twenty-three states that were pending and held up by injunctions in the lower courts. It was the last defense of privately operating power companies. When this last barrier fell, Ickes and Roosevelt were exultant about the verdict.

Roosevelt immediately put forward legislation called the "Seven TVAs," bills that would copy the TVA program from the Atlantic to the Pacific—wherever there was a dam on a river, the government would grow and consolidate power through its newly conceived "regional authority." A National Resources Committee carved the country into twelve regions, which would be ruled by federal offices from Baltimore to San Francisco, from Salt Lake City to Dallas, and from Atlanta to Los Angeles. Harold Ickes was delighted, it would mean a Washington, DC, that was infinitely expanding with new federal offices to house the growing federal authority for New Deal projects as far as the eye could see.

Fresh on the heels of this immense ideological success over an entire industrial sector, federal authorities were already looking elsewhere, everywhere, at other market sectors. Only one thing was certain: once Roosevelt got moving against an industry, he would not stop unless someone or something stopped him. General Hugh Johnson, who knew Roosevelt well, famously stated that "Roosevelt...would give up power as willingly as a hungry tiger would give up red meat."

A convention was under way for the American Medical Association in Atlantic City, New Jersey. It would be a mundane affair but for one speaker who was there, a confidant of President Roosevelt from the New York State Medical Society. When Joseph Kopetsky stood up to speak to the 9,200 attendees, he announced a plan in the works which would nationalize the entire health care industry and turn the country's 150,000 physicians into employees of a federal Public Health Service. The doctors were to become federal employees, working under a new secretary of social welfare—they were to become bureaucrats, or at least the arm of bureaucrats. The room stirred with alarm. Two common questions arose: *If we are all to become bureaucrats and government functionaries, where will people go to find a doctor?* And *how can a doctor fulfill the basic Hippocratic oath if they first have to answer to a central government's authority?* The whole healthcare sector of the country froze in its tracks because of the implications.

Adolf Berle and other members of the brain trust also wanted to work in more general terms: *why not just guarantee that every private company employee get certain rate of income across an assortment of industries?* Berle thought the government, on this pretense, might need to take over the railroad, housing, and construction industries... at least.

The ambitions of the brain trust were boundless, like those of the captains of industry—like the railroad builders or like Mellon, Ford, Edison, and Unsell—but they did not invent appliances which provided consumers greater freedom, nor build sources of transportation or sources of light and heat, nor create their own novel power from their individual resources of hard labor and capital through industries of their own making. They centered power in one place: government. And that power had only one source: taking wealth and power from others...who created it.

Just then, when all the brain trust's ambitions were unfolding to further take control over the economy, to nationalize more and more sectors of it, something did stop Roosevelt and the brain trust: the first was the negative market reaction of what remained of the American economy to the New Deal. The second was the election of 1938. And the third were the actions of the socialist and fascist central planners of Europe, who were way ahead of the brain trust in terms of assuming absolute control of their economies and, thereby, of their nations.

The Economy Of 1937

Nineteen thirty-seven should have been a banner year. The New Deal had begun five years before. Then, beginning in March, the stock market began falling, and fell more and fell further, until it had lost 50 percent of its value—again. Industrial production fell 30 percent—again. The nation's gross domestic product shrank 11 percent—again. From September through December, unemployment rose to levels not seen since 1931. There were many causes for the fall, but they all had one source—just like in 1929 it was, yet again, government intervention.

Before that second crash, the Federal Reserve had demanded that banks raise their cash reserves, which took money out of the economy. The Federal Reserve raised the lending rate, so banks did not originate as many loans, which took more money out of the economy. The new Social Security tax started to be collected, after all the other new taxes were collected, taking even more money out of the economy and giving it to the government. The undistributed profits tax, which demanded that every company spend their profits until there was no more capital to re-invest, was taking yet more money out of the economy. The government had taxed, fined, and prosecuted everyone and every big business it could for five years, until it ran out of everyone else's money and had no more money to throw around.

Two other very real factors helped create the second crash. The first was a national sense that government might and could do anything at any time in any sector of the economy, which created a massive sense of risk. There was the living precedent of what had happened to investors in utilities. The risk in the no-longer-free marketplace was exponentially greater than in 1929. Investors generally enjoy as much predictability as they can find; they invest in it.

It was said of Roosevelt that the only thing predictable about him was that he was very unpredictable, and that he univocally "commanded" the economy. *What market sector was Roosevelt thinking about today? What number was he thinking about—do we feel lucky?* Those sentiments reflected how much power suddenly resided in the Executive Office of the federal government. Even the ultra-conservative bond market collapsed, investors did not even trust money anymore. The economy was too bewildered by government's control to grow any further.

Lastly, there were companies that could not afford the Wagner Act. The Democratic Party's new cadre of partisans, the labor unions, could make any demands in any industry of any company they wished and they were defended by a self-interested government tribunal. Or the union could go on strike at literally any moment and shut down and destroy a company if they did not get what they demanded. What became of the investors in the company? Who would want to invest in such an unpredictable quasi-socialist economic environment? This was America in 1937.

In the free and fair elections of 1938, in keeping with the Constitution, Republicans won eighty more House seats, eight more Senate seats, and eleven more Governorships, which meant that any new ambitions to take over the economy by the Democrats would, at least, have to be negotiated.

The Related States Of Hegel

Nineteenth-century German poet Heinrich Hein once wrote, "Thought precedes action as lightening precedes thunder." From 1850 through the 1940s, the lightning that came out of the mind of Friedrich Hegel produced variant thunders and unquantifiable destruction as it influenced the actions of four states who became related based on Hegel's Ideal State—which the reader will remember from our section on Woodrow Wilson. To summarize: Hegel believed that the state was the supreme expression of humanity, not the individual or the family. An individual could only have meaning through the "union" of the individual will with the higher will of the state. The will of the state is known only to the "one" and the "few" who can interpret the people's collective will and then educate the people in that will through an education determined by the state. The will of the state is "one," and is best administrated through "one" historical figure. The goal of the "one will" is the establishment of humanity's next historical phase—the state's achievement of "one utopia."

In Russia, Hegel's ideal state philosophy was adopted as interpreted by Karl Marx and administrated by Vladmir Lenin through socialism. Lenin's Bolshevik Party, a minority party, destroyed the royal family and every competing political party. The party assumed control of the economy, built a special police force, and took over communications. The party then concentrated power and wealth in one party and one person who best knew the people's will. If a citizen did not conform to Lenin's will, they were imprisoned or shot. The Bolshevik Party, after Lenin's death, was assumed by the "one will" of Joseph Stalin and the Communist (socialist) Party.

In Italy, Hegel's ideal state philosophy was interpreted by Benedetto Croce and influenced by Georges Sorel's *Reflections on Violence,* which begat Benito Mussolini's Fascist Party. The Fascist Party subverted the Italian constitution, eliminating every competing political party and intermediary regional power. The party took control of the economy, the courts, the media, the education system, the police force, and the military. And so, it concentrated the power and wealth of Italy into the "one will" of Benito Mussolini and the Fascist Party.

In Germany, Hegel's ideal state philosophy and the fascism of Mussolini were adopted by the Nazi Party, which subverted Germany's constitution and eliminated every competing political party and intermediary regional power. The party took control of the economy, the courts, the media, the education system, the police force, and the military. And so, it concentrated the power and wealth of Germany into the "one will" of Adolf Hitler and the Nazi Party.

In America, Hegel's ideal state philosophy was adopted as interpreted by Woodrow Wilson as being a part of humanity's "progress" to evolving beyond human nature. It was Wilson who proposed that the Constitution had to be corrected and an Administrative

State built to suit the new age, setting in motion the inversion of the relationship between the states and the federal government, which began the further concentration of power in Washington, DC. FDR inherited and actuated Wilson's goals by transferring the wealth of individuals, localities, and states (debilitating local autonomy) to build the Administrative State in Washington, DC, via the expanded income tax and monumental undertakings toward federal control over the economy.

The programs of the Democratic Party were stalled by reverses in the economy in 1937 and by the elections of 1938. Further growth of the Administrative State also hit the brakes because the United States was founded on the natural individual rights philosophy of John Locke—a philosophy based on the individual that is diametrically opposite to the philosophy of the collective "union" of every individual's will with the state, as demonstrated in the socialism that was spreading through Europe. The US Constitution is based on the premise of each person having their own will, and each individual having their own idea of happiness, attained by their own means—not of one "utopia" arrived at by collective means through governmental control. The Constitution also includes a Bill of Rights, which deliberately and specifically protects the individual person, their faith, and their property from the encroachment of the state's "will." America was and is further defended by what remains of state and local autonomy in both the judiciary and the state and local police forces.

The Administrative State stalled in America for another reason—people were learning what the *reality*, not the philosophy, of the ideal state meant. The intelligentsia of the United States were great enthusiasts of Hegel's ideal state philosophy of collectivism, via Marx's socialism, Lenin's communism and Mussolini's fascism, until they began witnessing with alarm what happened when an individual's will was, in any way, at odds with the ideal state's "one will." Persons like themselves—intellectuals, scientists, teachers, priests, philosophers, writers, and musicians—who disagreed with the "one will," whether they were in Russia, Germany, or Italy, began to disappear...never to be seen or heard from again.

Spiritual institutions and opposition political parties suffered the same fate as individuals—whether they were in Russia, Italy, or Germany—because they differed with the "one party." In Russia, seventy thousand churches were closed and torn to the ground. In Italy, political opposition parties were outlawed; some of their leaders were prisoned, tortured, or secretly murdered. In Germany, a whole population lost their enterprises, their properties, and then their lives... for simply practicing Judaism, a faith based on "one" God, who is not a party member.

The intelligentsia class in America became more alarmed when these European states of Hegel demonstrated their collective will by invading neighboring democratic states. When Germany and Russia signed the "Non-Aggression Pact" in 1939 so they could both invade the democracy of Poland, every enthusiasm of the American intelligentsia for socialism and fascism was eclipsed. The founder of the ACLU, Roger Baldwin, described his awakening to reality: "I think it was the biggest shock of my life. I never was shaken up by anything as I was by that pact—by the fact that those two powers had got together at the expense of the democracies." Even Emma Goldman, a one-time socialist, who personally witnessed the effects of the ideal state of the Bolsheviks, wrote of the seduced intelligentsia: "People as naïve as you are hopeless. [You] see the world and the struggle through romantic rosy eyes, as the young innocent girl sees the first man she loves."

It was the collective delusion of the intelligentsia that the "one" and "few" would act any differently than they have over millennia of history since the days of the pharaohs. It was the old tyranny again the same; "humanity's common keep" in a new age. These exemplars of the reality of human nature and the nature of tyrannical government are the very reason that every individual in the world needs protection *from*, not "union" with—any government.

The political class of America awakened when they found that each "one"—Stalin, Mussolini, Hitler, and Hirohito of Japan—had a collective idea of utopia, which involved their own world dominion. Each tyrant thought that they alone were the historical figure whose "one" will should universally subdue the independent will of the world. Joseph Kennedy, as Ambassador to Great Britain, naively thought that America should just try to get along with these tyrants.

When Hitler and the Axis powers ran over Belgium, swept through France, and turned their forces against Britain, and Hirohito demonstrated his appetite for world dominion in China and the Pacific Islands, the free people and armed forces of America had to turn, once again, into a liberating force. This time for the world, in step with the precedent which Abraham Lincoln set in our own Civil War to guide them.

US forces were engaged from the Aleutian Islands to the Coral Sea to the Sea of Japan; from the deserts of Africa and the beaches of Normandy to the frozen fields of Norway and upon and beneath the world-circling seas. Everywhere that US forces died, or were wounded, or were imprisoned or lost, hundreds of millions of people were freed from the deathly stranglehold of tyranny.

In the European theater, the US suffered 135,576 deaths, 365,086 wounded, and 14,238 who were lost never to return home. In the Pacific theater, US forces suffered 161,000 deaths, 248,316 wounded, and 6,242 lost. Total US casualties in World War II amounted to 930,748 who gave their lives for the very individual freedoms based on John Locke's philosophy of the natural rights of the individual, which gave birth to the fundamental rights enumerated in the Constitution. They fought and died against those states that had adopted the ideal state philosophy of Friedrich Hegel and had put that philosophy into practice through socialism, communism and fascism.

World War II produced a series of remarkable ironies. Firstly, it was absolute proof that Wilson's belief in the progress of human nature toward goodness was utterly false and dangerous; therefore, his entire faith in creating an ideal progressive Administrative State was equally false. The period from 1920-1945 proved nothing could be more dangerous to humanity than human nature exercised through Hegel's ideal state. The need to protect every individual from government proved to be *more* necessary than it had ever been in history.

Secondly, the march of the United States toward an "ideal state" of socialism was halted because the United States ended up having to go to war to stop more developed forms of it. The Democrats were compelled to end their war on the free-market system because it was necessary for the government to partner with American industry to build, as Roosevelt termed it, the "arsenal of Democracy" to fight the other Hegel States.

Thirdly, the Administrative State's previous experience of, effectively, a war with the US economy had helped prepare it for the Second World War. The half-built Administrative State was actually strengthened by the war.

The fourth irony was the fact that half of the ideal states of Hegel—Russia and the United States—ended up as allies in the war against the Hegel states of Germany and Italy. And that the US and the USSR, being systems that were by their natures opposed, have been enemies ever since.

The last, most important irony of the war was that while tyranny was defeated on land, on the sea, and through the skies the world over by America and her allies— the DNA of tyranny, which still exists in the destructive lightning of Hegel's ideal state philosophy, was spliced into the DNA of the American system of government.

Our system of government was changed fundamentally by Woodrow Wilson and Franklin Roosevelt. It has become a hybrid system. Part of our government is based on the US constitutional principle of representation and is answerable to the people through elections and through the common law. The Administrative State of our government is based on Hegel's ideal state and is neither representative nor answerable to the people in any way—and is increasingly not answerable to common law. Representatives come and go with elections. The administrative state remains; it has been growing more powerful by the day for one hundred years.

And after the Second World War, the levy brakes on the Administrative State's ever-growing concentration of power were off.

Bill Of Rights

— Light —

Patrick Henry

Patrick Henry, as one of our nation's founders, was born and raised in the 1,700's, a proud Virginian, who had served to free his colony from the seemingly omnipresent force of a distant monarch and his crew of tax-hunting hirelings. He served as a colonel in the Continental Army and as the governor of Virginia as often as the limits on the terms of office permitted. But he is best known for having been the greatest orator of a generation teeming with great orators, having famously demanded, in 1775, "*What would we have? Is life so dear, or peace so sweet, as to be purchased at the price of chains and slavery? Forbid it, Almighty God! I know not what course others may take; but as for me, give me liberty or give me death!*" Patrick Henry was forthright about his convictions.

Henry refused to attend the Constitutional Convention of 1787, as he was extremely wary of having cast off the manacles of a monarch across the Atlantic to have a new domestic pair of chains fashioned at home. He sensed there was more planned than just a design to amend the Articles of Confederation that bound the states, and he did not want to sanction a new central authority. To the proponents of a new and powerful central government, with all the advantages of a vast continent and dreams of empire, Henry replied simply: "Liberty, sir, was...the primary object."

When the proposed Constitution had been written, it had to be ratified by nine of the thirteen states in order to be made effective and a federal government established. In 1788, by the time the Virginia House of Burgesses met to take up the question, eight states had ratified already, and the people of those states looked to Virginia—the most populace state of the thirteen—to confirm she was with them. Yet, Patrick Henry stood his ground, and as he moved to speak, a very real and threatening thunderstorm rolled over the assembly house. It was said that lightning filled Henry's eyes, and that only his voice could thunder and be heard above the surrounding thunders.

He began with his dismay at the Constitution's preamble: "We the People." Was the Constitution not to be a compact between the states? Were the states not supposed to be the barrier from a large central government, to guarantee the defense of individual liberties? Were the state's rights and privileges, then, to be smothered by a greater government? Who or what would defend the individual against so great a power as was designed for the new federal government unless the states were to provide the restraints?

Was the central government to have an unbound power to tax whomever and whatever it wanted, and spend whatever it wished? Would not such a government enrich itself at the expense of the people? What wage of the laborer, what property of the individual or family, what enterprise will exist which so powerful a government could not invade, coerce, or lay claim to as its own when it so willed?

"The whole of our property may be taken by this American government, by laying what taxes they please, giving themselves what salaries they please, and suspending our laws at their pleasure," was Henry's forceful objection.

And what of the problem of human nature, which the Constitution was written to address? About which so much of the document of law was specific in regard to every legislative office being based on elections. Once in power, would the powerful give up power, Henry wondered.

"A willing relinquishment of power is one of those things which human nature never was, nor ever will be capable of," Henry thundered before the assembly.

Henry scoffed at the idea of checks and balances, considering them hopeful fictions. The government would become monolithic, be it immediately or over time—time being the medium through which every government seeks to advantage itself.

Patrick Henry demanded before the House of Burgesses, that previous to any ratification, some defense had to be erected against a government that could become established in such a position of strength. If a federal government were created that could overpower the states, what property or enterprise would it not be able to invade? Then, what rights of the individual would such a government not soon invade to assume evermore power to itself? Henry and his anti-Federalist allies demanded the inclusion of a bill of rights, based on Virginia's Declaration of Rights and John Locke's "Natural Rights" of humanity, in order to preserve the power of the individual to defend themselves, their property, their enterprises, their right to speech and to assembly, their religious beliefs, their ability to redress grievances, and preserve the freedom of the press. Further, every individual had to be secure in their right to trial by jury, as well as every other right that was derived from British Common Law to protect against an overpowering central authority. James Madison stated that such a provision might be made a part of the Constitution, ...after ratification. Henry and his allies demanded his oath on it—his promise. Madison gave it.

Lastly, Henry and the anti-Federalists demanded a guarantee, one that became the 10th Amendment: "The powers not delegated to the United States by the Constitution, nor prohibited by it to the states, are reserved to the States respectively, or to the people." After all, any central government will naturally assume all the powers possible for such a government. Patrick Henry did not think any government should assume such a form of godhood, as it did in the ages past of the pharaohs and as it does today in China.

What did Henry finally say of liberty in his speech, that a new nation had survived a revolution to achieve:

"Liberty ought to be the direct end of your government!"

"Liberty is the greatest of all earthly blessings—give us that precious jewel, and you may take everything else!"

"Guard with jealous attention the public liberty, suspect everyone who approaches that jewel!"

As Jefferson is accounted as the founder most responsible for authoring the Declaration of Independence, and James Madison is accounted as the founder most responsible for the architecture of the Constitution, Patrick Henry must be deemed the most responsible for the incorporation of the Bill of Rights, as the protection of every individual's "Natural Rights" as stated within the Constitution. Again, in the minds of those responsible for these works, they were deemed the foundations of an inviolable "New Order for the Ages" for as long as the people defend our nation's foundations.

Given Madison's assent to incorporating the Bill of Rights as part of the Constitution, Patrick Henry stood before an assembly of his fellow Virginians, who objected to so powerful a conception of a central government, to say that he had done his best with regard to the Constitution with the addition of the Bill of Rights—and that the question had been settled. To keep the peace of a newly unified nation, Patrick Henry appealed to a crowd: "As true and faithful republicans (now) you had all better go home!"

– Shadow –

Levying the Bill of Rights

Franklin Roosevelt gave a speech in San Francisco on September 23, 1932, before being elected President. It contained a very telling paragraph: "The Declaration of Independence discusses the problem of government in terms of a contract. Government is a relation of give and take, a contract, perforce, if we would follow the thinking out of which it grew. Under such a contract, rulers are accorded power, and the people consented to that power on the consideration that they be *accorded* certain rights."

However, the Declaration of Independence does not state that government "accords" citizens their rights. Rather, it states, "We hold these truths to be self-evident, that all men are created equal, that they are *endowed by their Creator* with certain *unalienable* Rights." Meaning: God designed human nature to be fulfilled in an atmosphere of freedom, protected by equal rights. No just government "accords" human rights. A just government, based in human freedom, protects humanity's inborn, natural rights. The natural rights of humanity are to be held inviolable. *That* is a just governments first duty to a free people.

The Declaration of Independence further states: "Among these (rights) are Life, Liberty and the pursuit of Happiness. That to secure these rights, Governments are instituted among Men, deriving their just powers from the consent of the governed." Among the rights to be held inviolable were property rights, which are protected in our Constitution as enumerated in Amendments V and XIV. However, Roosevelt, in finishing the very telling paragraph of his speech, declares: “The task of statesmanship has always been the *redefinition of these rights* in terms of a changing and growing social order”

I doubt that any of the nation’s founders, nor any of the states that ratified the Constitution, nor Patrick Henry who sponsored the Bill of Rights, would have agreed with Roosevelt’s declaration. They did not fight a revolution and form a new nation to have the natural rights of humanity, as derived from God and uniquely protected in America, changed by a single president’s idea of what every citizen’s “Natural Rights” are and are not.

Fourteen years later, after fundamentally changing so much of the American design of government, Roosevelt further advanced what he thought to be the “task of statesmanship” in his twelfth State of the Union Address given on January 11, 1944. Here he announced the “redefining (of) our rights.”

Roosevelt declared that the rights of speech, free press, free worship, trial by jury, and freedom from unreasonable searches and seizures—though they were “our rights to life and liberty… these political rights proved inadequate to assure us equality in the pursuit of happiness.” Roosevelt continued that “true freedom cannot exist without economic security and independence.” He therefore proposed that the central government must take upon itself the power of guaranteeing everyone’s happiness.

And, he insisted, in order to accomplish this, there must be new “rights” which government, not God, accords. They are as follows:

> The right to a useful and remunerative job.
>
> The right to earn enough to provide adequate food and clothing and recreation.
>
> The right of every farmer to sell his product at a return which will give his family a decent living.
>
> The right of every businessman to have freedom from unfair competition at home and abroad.
>
> The right of every family to a decent home.
>
> The right to adequate medical care.

The right to a good education.

Roosevelt claimed, "These economic truths have become accepted as self-evident.... We have accepted, so to speak, a *second* Bill of Rights."

In addition to this speech becoming another pretext for a further, massive governmental invasion into other sectors of the economy, such as housing, agriculture, and healthcare, it also promised wage and price fixing and government control over "undue competition"—which is shorthand for the government being able to do *anything* within or to the economy. And yet, the problem lies even deeper than this. Every right described is something that anyone would want, but up until then, in America, it had been up to an individual or family's dedication and decision making as to how their happiness would be provided for. By this second, so to speak, "bill of rights," the government interposed itself between every individual, every family and their hopes. Government then becomes every citizen's senior partner, governing their happiness. By this standard, the government can then claim its own rights to do anything...

And here, again, we see the government's ultimate fulcrum of power. To guarantee any citizen certain goods such as housing, even that which they do not earn themselves, the money or assets must come from another citizen. For government to give "property" to one citizen, they must take "property" from another. The government does not produce anything—whatever they give, they first must take. Neither is government a generous or a charitable institution. Governments are creatures of power, interested in one thing: more and more permanent power. And it is in the nature of all governments, that more wealth equates to more power. For governments, power equals wealth, and wealth equals power—it pays the government directly to take property and wealth from its citizens. The wealth and power of a government comes at the direct expense of the wealth and liberty of every tax-paying citizen.

The reader will remember that the philosopher John Locke had an analogy for demonstrating earned ownership of property: The *"labor of his or her body and the work of his hands in drawing a pitcher of water from a fountain may be said to be properly his own. [For] though the water running in the fountain be everyone's, yet who can doubt, but that in the pitcher is his who drew it out."*

Following the analogy, this *second* bill of rights places the water in every citizen's pitcher, and the pitcher itself in the hands of the government. The amount of water that may be kept becomes a government decision, and the water taken and then given to another becomes a government provision. Therefore, this second bill of rights is the original Bill of Rights' diametric opposite. The property rights, which our government was established to defend, Roosevelt now proposed to invade based on the indefinable term of everyone's "happiness," which to him gave government the unlimited, indefinable, and thus infinite power and right to provide it.

We become aware of the dangers of turning over our property rights to the government when we revisit democracy's greatest prophet, Alexis de Tocqueville, and his stern warning that, "Those who repudiate the notion of 'natural rights' abandon thereby the principles dictating that government be limited in the ends it may pursue and in the means it may employ." Such a government must also demand "confiscation," and not mere property will be demanded. "To a greater or lesser degree the confiscation of human liberty" itself will be suffered as well. Such an establishment of socialist redistribution of property was, to Tocqueville, "a new formula for servitude."

The Roosevelt administration never put forward this *second* bill of rights before the country, nor through the rigors of a constitutional amendment process, nor has any action been taken through any legislative process to establish it formally because it would be challenged. For, as one contemporary of Roosevelt's, Walter Lippmann, feared—and the country would discover—this method of ever-expanding government is meant "to magnify the power of public officials and extend and multiply their intervention in human affairs." Many Americans at the time would have agreed with Lippmann, and this second bill of rights would never have passed legislative or constitutional scrutiny if citizens knew how it would expand the scope of government growth and control and contract every citizen's liberty and independence.

So, instead of going through a legislative process whereby Roosevelt's proposals might be defeated, the Democratic Party made this second bill of rights, like their idea of the "implicit will" of the people and their idea of "utopia," something to be forever desired, yet never put to a practical vote. It is and has been the guiding lodestar of the Democratic Party—the extra-legal standard of measure for all of its policy since 1944—which has rewritten our rights ever since.

This policy lodestar launched a series of invasions into our rights by Roosevelt's successors, beginning with our property rights, then the rights reserved to our "Original Powers," and finally our rights to the fruits of our own self-reliance! Let us now venture into instances of further light and shadow which have brought our country to where we find ourselves today.

Property Rights

– Light –

Property Rights

As readers of Volume One will remember, Western civilization's concept of property rights began in Rome with the Twelve Tables of Law. Property rights were established as the foundation of British Common Law in the Magna Carta eight hundred years ago. Property rights are utterly fundamental to any democracy because they create a circular defense of individual liberty and law and thereby protect the rights of the individual. Having a base of property gives the individual the capacity, in credit, to defend oneself through the law. And through respect for the law, one defends their own property. By protecting the rights of others in their property, one defends all property rights as a matter of law, including their own. This is a why property rights, and strict laws to defend them, are anathema to tyrannical governments. They are a defense against tyranny's will of universal ownership, with government as the only lessor of property based on a subject or a slave's support of tyranny. It is axiomatic that the less rights of property are enforced, the more government can assume a citizen's property and the more the citizen becomes a subject of government...and the less free that society is. In tyrannical societies, the population is universally weak, and subservient to government for everything because they are without property. In free societies, property rights are the basic rights that provide for a citizen's independent strength.

Which is precisely why our original Bill of Rights, and the Fifth Amendment particularly, are so fundamental to our freedoms.

— Shadow —

Levelling Property Rights

It began simply enough in 1934. As part of the New Deal's takeover of the banking sector, the National Housing Act was passed, creating the Federal Housing Administration. Initially, the administration was created to deal with home mortgage insurance for those banks that the government had not shut down in the Depression—those the government had allowed to survive. The SEC created a web of regulations for the banks to adhere to, and in return for a fee, the banks could carry government-guaranteed insurance against a possible run of home mortgage defaults.

Harry Truman

Like every U.S. government program, it became permanent and grew beyond its original mandate. Its original mission was amplified by Harry Truman's Fair Deal through the National Housing Act of 1949. The act granted the establishment of housing authority in every major urban area. These became federally controlled offices through which to redistribute taxpayer funds. The objective was to deal with the loosely defined circumstances of city "blight." In effect, the Democratic Party partnered with labor and party supporters to redevelop large swaths of urban areas while taking into the group, as junior partners, city mayors and their Democratic Party apparatuses. The federal government offered each city so much money that their mayors could not refuse. It is a regular federal government line, one which exerts tremendous leverage: If you don't take the money now, another city will - tomorrow! Most cities to whom the offer was made acquiesced to this federal coercion and invasion of their political territory…for the money.

What followed were federal master planners, working with the unions and hand-picked redevelopers, to make decisions in Washington DC about cities from the Eastern seaboard through the Midwest all the way to California. It was actually the dream of one of the original New Dealers, Rex Tugwell: "My idea is to just go outside the centers of population, pick up the cheap land, build a whole community and entice people to it. Then go back into the cities and tear down whole slums" There was one problem—there were already people who owned the land that the Democratic Party, the unions, and the redevelopers wanted; they had been there for years and they did not think their home was a slum.

As luck would have it, the feds already had a set of statistics to draw on taken from the SEC regulation of the banks. Based on New Deal regulations, there were areas in every city deemed unfit for mortgage or business loans that were "redlined." As those areas had been federally cut off from banking capital for years because government decided the banks should not allow access to capital in such areas, they must of course be "blighted." The SEC banking statistics were used as a roadmap all over the country for where to move the bulldozers to conduct large-scale demolitions—on the order of whole neighborhoods and hundreds of city blocks.

The partners and planners began the system of demolition in the mid 1950's, in their own backyard of Washington, DC. The Administrative State of our government was growing so big, so fast, that its administrators needed an enormous amount of housing for the exploding numbers of employees, who were coming in to take pay-guaranteed jobs in Washington, DC. The District of Columbia Redevelopment Land Agency set their sights on a neighborhood called Southwest, one of the oldest in the city, for a complete demolition—or, shall we say, *urban renewal.* There were 1,500 businesses there, owned mostly by African Americans, and 23,000 residents, again mostly African American. The government, more specifically the Democratic Party, wanted the property so that government could grow itself by way of land ownership, by way of their law, and by way of centralized master planning according to their New Deal dream.

The method whereby the government could take such property is called "Eminent Domain," an old law which determines that when a private piece of property is necessary for public use (most often for a public roadway), the land can be taken. The owner has to be reimbursed at fair value, and there usually has to be a very real and pressing public need for the property in order for eminent domain to be claimed. Up until then, it had occurred to a property here and there but most people had not heard of it. Residents began objecting to this seizure of their property in Southwest and took the government's claim for eminent domain to the courts.

By 1954, it became the Supreme Court case *Berman v. Parker*. The action was brought by a department store owner, whose property was not designated as blighted but stood in the middle of the demolition zone. He argued that the government's use of eminent domain, in this case, amounted to taking land from one businessperson to give it to another *preferred* businessperson for their private benefit and, therefore, did not constitute a public use in violation of the Fifth Amendment of the Constitution. The justices of the Supreme Court, by now each a New Deal-era appointee, proved to be a capable left flank, using the Court's judicial powers to advance the New Deal-Fair Deal offensive against property rights, voting 8-0 for the Planning Commission and the District of Columbia Redevelopment Land Agency against the shop owner Max Morris. Justice Douglas wrote, in his consenting opinion: "If owner after owner were permitted to resist these redevelopment programs on the ground that his particular property was not being used against the public interest...integrated plans for redevelopment would suffer greatly," and "the...authorized [Administrative State] agencies have made determinations that take into account a wide variety of values. It is not for us to reappraise them."

That is not the end of the story. When it comes to eminent domain, compensation is made solely for the land and not for the value of the business that prospers upon it. Therefore, the businessperson unhappy enough to be in the middle of the redevelopment zone lost everything. And because the surrounding area was designated blighted, the land itself was valued as worth next to nothing. The *Berman v. Parker* case opened the floodgates for redevelopment across the country. The neighborhood of Southwest was levelled. What a lucky deal for the Administrative State, for the Democratic Party, for the unions and redevelopers!

In East Harlem, New York, there was a thriving Italian neighborhood chosen by the planners for demolition... When the New York Housing Authority's own site managers went there to look it over, they could not believe the map was correct—the area was booming! Everywhere the managers looked, they saw that the buildings were, in fact, full of recent improvements, and the neighborhood was aging gracefully and renewing itself naturally. The Housing Authority disagreed. They had already made their plans: the bulldozers and redevelopers were waiting. More than thirteen hundred businesses were levelled; 1,040 of the owners were financially ruined. A further five hundred commercially vibrant store front businesses were razed to the ground. Thousands of residents were forced to move. What a lucky deal, this "Fair Deal." What a defender of property rights was our Supreme Court. The Robert F. Wagner homes were built atop the level ruins of East Harlem and named in honor of the Democratic Senator of New York, Robert F. Wagner, who, upon assuming his office many years before, had sworn to faithfully defend the Constitution, which contains the Bill of Rights and its Fifth Amendment—which had been effectively levelled by the Housing Act of 1949 and the courts.

As heartbreaking as the demolition of the Italian section of East Harlem was for its property and business owners, our African American population would be disproportionately affected by the Housing Act of 1949, with the confiscation of their property in cities all over the country, and as we will find, there was a reason why. As the bulldozers levelled their neighborhoods, they also levelled their Original Powers, once a sacrosanct and protected part of life in America, a center of every citizen's power, the government was never supposed to invade let alone destroy...

— Along the American Road —

General Dwight Eisenhower, who hailed from a simple, modest upbringing in Abilene, Kansas, and led the transcontinental convoy of 1919 to assess the capacity of the country's road systems, went on later to see the world. He travelled from the Philippines to North Africa to France and back home again. Through his expert handling of personnel, his organizational and leadership skills, his meticulous work ethic, and his military and strategic expertise, he rose to become the Supreme Allied Commander of the forces that liberated Europe to the boundaries of Berlin, from the scourge of Hegel's totalitarian ideal where another totalitarian army held the line of the Soviet Union.

In 1952, he was rewarded by the American people with the highest office in the land. His life's experience led him to two great achievements as president. One was his administration's landmark Civil Rights Act of 1957, which federalized the integration of the nation's schools and guaranteed uniform voting rights across the country. The other was the transcontinental interstate highway system. Passed as the Federal-Aid Highway Act of 1956, it was a project that took a decade to construct and cost $25 billion to achieve.

This project was worthy work for a federal authority and was designed in the right way: with national direction while leaving to the states exactly how and where the highways were to journey through their territories. It was a partnership between the federal authority and the states; it was not a dictate of federal dominion. There was a curious coincidence that many cities within the states that fought for the funds the housing authorities brought in also fought for highway construction dollars—which, again, imperiled city neighborhoods where the population was least able to afford it.

The I-10 now flows east to west, connecting Florida to California by way of Alabama, Mississippi, New Mexico, and Arizona. The I-80 connects New Jersey to California by way of Pennsylvania, Ohio, Indiana, Illinois, Missouri, Kansas, Nebraska, Utah, and Nevada. The I-70 connects Maryland to Utah via West Virginia, Ohio, Indiana, Illinois, Iowa, Nebraska, and Colorado. And the I-90 joins Massachusetts to Washington state through New York, Pennsylvania, Ohio, Indiana, Illinois, Wisconsin, Minnesota, South Dakota, Montana, and Idaho.

Going north to south, the I-15 journeys out of southern California to Idaho and Montana via Arizona, Nevada, and Utah. The I-35 joins Texas to Minnesota by traversing Oklahoma, Kansas, Iowa, and Missouri. The I-55 combines Louisiana to Illinois by way of Mississippi, Arkansas, Tennessee, and Missouri. The I-75 flows from Florida to Michigan through Georgia, Tennessee, Kentucky, and Ohio. And the I-95 connects the tip of Florida to the top of Maine by channeling through Georgia, South Carolina, North Carolina, Virginia, Maryland, Delaware, Pennsylvania, New Jersey, New York, Connecticut, Rhode Island, Massachusetts, and New Hampshire! Never was a national road system so meticulously designed since the Roman Empire and the days when they bricked the Appian Way. Just gaze at the number and variety of the traversed geographical regions and states!

With the proliferating use of the automobile and the prosperity of the 1950s, this new road system combined to create a mobile society of families venturing to see their America. Most stayed in campsites, but many enjoyed a burgeoning new service economy along the highways. Howard Johnson motels and Holiday Inns sprang up along every few miles. McDonalds fast food restaurants and Chevron gas stations added convenience to every stop, along with drive-up burger joints and drive-in theaters to accommodate travelers. And in the Golden State was built a gilded kingdom created by one entrepreneur's imagination: Walt Disney built Disneyland, and masses of exhilarated attendees came.

The new highway system facilitated a national communications system, as well, as wire was extended along the sides of every highway. Technology followed with the radio shows produced in New York, which were broadcast to people in such remote reaches as the deserts of Arizona. And whereas the films of Hollywood had traveled to movie houses throughout America since the 1920s, a newly invented media followed with television. The number of households with a television exploded exponentially over the 1950s. Television programming was dominated by New York and Los Angeles studios. Importantly, television news programming was dominated by New York, where it was produced, and Washington, DC, where seemingly all the news from then on was made.

The geography held that if one wanted a career in finance, the news business, or the stage—for money or fame—one went to New York. If one wanted to be surrounded by stardom, one sought the lights of the cinema and the preening ground of celebrity events in LA. And if one wanted control, wealth, and power—one went to Washington, DC. If one wanted a normal, modest working life, one lived and worked somewhere, anywhere, in between.

The new interstate system changed American culture in a thousand unexpected, wonderful ways; and in one particular way that was, again, very predictable. The new highway system ended up stretching 48,000 miles over the contiguous forty-eight states, across a nation that covered 3.12 million square miles in 1955, which came to be governed more and more by one Administrative State in a city the comparative size of a pinpoint, ten miles wide by ten miles long. A central government located on a finite 100 square miles of territory which, through its indefinite promise of "happiness," gave itself a power that is infinite.

President Dwight Eisenhower, in his Farewell Address, warned of one aspect of this gathering power that pertained to the military: to the necessity of continuously defending "the United States...we have been compelled to create a permanent armaments industry of vast proportions. Added to this, three and half million men and women are directly engaged in the defense establishment.... (We) recognize the imperative need for this development, yet we must not fail to comprehend its grave implications. Our toil, resources and livelihood are all involved; so is the very structure of our society.... In the councils of government, we must guard against the acquisition of unwarranted influence, whether sought or unsought by the military-industrial complex. The potential for the disastrous rise of misplaced power exists and will persist.... We must never let the weight of this combination endanger our liberties or democratic processes."

Over the years since, a new ever-growing complex has been added to the permanent circle of power gathering in Washington, DC, through the invasion of America's Original Powers and because of the societal ruins that invasion created...and still creates.

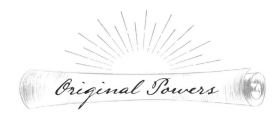

Original Powers

– Light –

THE ORIGINAL POWERS OF AMERICA

As readers of Volume One will remember, the growth of America was utterly unique in one all-important respect: there was no standing European government here. When the settlers arrived, they discovered that the native tribes did not govern in the European manner. They found the Native American manner of self-government was based on individual freedom and self-reliance, from which the settlers learned. There was no overlord and no monarch to whom one was answerable. The individual was neither the chattel nor the pawn of any omniscient, omnipotent pharaoh, aristocrat or king. Among the early settlers, this absence of government allowed the natural powers of the individual, the family, the faiths, the associations, and the economy to emerge and grow unhindered by any dictatorial, overlording power. These are the powers specifically protected by the Tenth Amendment, which states: "The powers not delegated to the United States by the Constitution, nor prohibited by it to the States, are reserved to the States respectively, or to the people."

Family

The power of the family emerged because its parents were not dependents working for an aristocrat—what we today would call a bureaucrat or commissar—the family was *the* authority unto themselves. Neither were a family's children dependent on the goodwill, acceptance, or approval of anyone beyond themselves and the family. Decisions were made based on the free will of every family member. To each their own. The family was the power source that provided the children with the wherewithal to be independent - to be self-reliant.

Education

In America, associations formed naturally around the education of children. The children's parents determined the daily curriculum and they decided who were their educators. The associations of parents were *the* authority, not an aristocrat who determined a certain child of a peasant had to be a blacksmith, or a seamstress like her mother. The families of a locality were *the* authorities in the naturally occurring educational associations of their surroundings. By the mid-1700s, America's schools were some of the best and most practical in the world, because they prepared their students in the best manner possible to be independent - to be self-reliant.

Faith

Perhaps the most important association were those surrounding faith. The authority of the churches in America has always proved a bulwark in the defense of our freedoms, the vanguard of our national conscience, and a power that ever moves outward and forward the establishment of justice. As referred to in Volume One, many faiths were established in America, each free to build their own churches and each becoming an authority that stood distinct from all other authority - relying for their independence on the reply of Christ to the Pharisees in Mk. 12:17: that they were to render unto Caesar what was Caesar's (matters pertaining to civil government) and unto God what belonged to God (a person's spiritual faith, charity, service, and devotion). Throughout America's history, it has been this original power of our spiritual authorities that has been the driving force of a continuous check upon civil authority and has thus brought about better government and greater justice.

Further, it was the various church authorities from which collectively streamed communal charity, whereby the destitute or those suffering would find a hand to help them up and were shown—not given—a path to rise above want or suffering and to so earn a better life. In a wonderful symbiosis, just as Adam Smith's free enterprise system is based on one acting with self-interest, the American churches and each individual's spiritual or humanitarian interests are based on acting in the interests of others... in a perfectly complimentary, free, and voluntary co-respective existence. In this way, religious schools and hospitals were built for everyone. They were spiritual institutions, not civil ones, though each taught civics and religion side by side—the spiritual laws of God alongside the civil laws of humanity. And again, whether the education received was spiritual or civic, or taught in the church or in the classroom, education centered on the practical preparation of students to be free and independent - to be self-reliant.

Occupation And Enterprise

Given the original powers of America, citizens succeed in their lives based on the merit shown in their occupation, which is neither given to them nor demanded of them but is freely chosen. This chosen labor, which one does throughout one's life, is humanity's greatest blessing. It is the fulfillment of one's talents; it is the first source of one's sense of self and pride; it is the means whereby one supports oneself and one's family independently, doing what they *decide* to do. The works and arts of America are not produced as a monarch would sponsor them, or as a despot would demand them, but as the producer would produce them and the community would reward them.

Towns And Neighborhoods

The first form of government among the settlers was the town. Towns occurred naturally and grew harmoniously over time through the creations of free enterprises, which first fulfilled the needs and then the desires of a population. The first civic form to convene was the assembly, wherein every town member had a voice and a vote—it is our American form of the ancient Athenian demos, and it remains the purist form of democratic government we have; all other forms of our government are based on representation. Therefore, as "originally" established, most of the power in America was exercised at this level—the most direct, the most interactive and responsive level.

As towns developed organically, more offices sprang up that tailored to the interests of the people, like the doctor's office and the local bank. And more associations formed around people's interests. And in the middle, at the disposal of the assembly, was the community chest. The local treasury, which distributed funds based on the town's decisions as to what was necessary, whether it was new roads or bridges or civic buildings.

As time transpired, some towns became cities, and within each city the neighborhoods became towns. Over time, the neighborhood became a home. Everyone knew the baker, the butcher, and the banker. Everyone knew the local plumber, the doctor, and the lawyer. Everyone went to the common hospital—likely a church-sponsored institution. Associations for business based on professions, or for the churches based on benevolence, or for the sponsorship of the arts - grew. Neighborhood relationships were reciprocal webs of mutual benefit. Your neighborhood, in part, defined you and you defined your neighborhood. The neighborhood always rooted for its own— you were a member of the home team. And within that unit, there was a democracy of associations and committees which represented the neighborhoods within the city.

The Individual

When the original powers are distinct and rightly aligned, each power helps build the individual into being independent, into being self-reliant. Each original power helps prepare the individual for life. Each power is like a guitar string: when each string is rightly tuned for and by the player, the player is capable of writing and playing any song. The song each citizen creates becomes the orchestrated song of their individual soul.

— Shadow —

Segregation from the Original Powers

As original as this American upbringing was, tragically, a large population of Americans did not experience participation in these original powers. In Volume One of this series, the history of the universal slavery that took root in the southern United States, affecting the African American population, was elaborated upon. The African American in the South resembled the slave and serf populations in every other part of the world, where all decisions in their lives were made by overlords—the *massahs* of the common keeps of humanity. One of the greatest uses of the forces of the original powers of America was the creation of the abolition movement as it spread out from the spiritual centers of the land to move against the government's institutional slavery. It was an unprecedented movement in world history, as was the tragedy of the Civil War, which was an unprecedented sacrifice necessary to slavery's ending. Only in America did such a movement and cataclysm occur; only in America is it possible.

However, following the Civil War, the Democratic Party sought to cling to vestiges of slavery by instituting Jim Crow laws to bar African Americans from exercising their rights, and made African Americans subject to segregation throughout the South. In answer to this continuing oppression, a large migration of southern African Americans bravely moved north, leaving their homes to venture to the industrial cities of the East, Midwest, and the West to find a normal life for their families, a normal education for their children, and the old religion in a new church... They moved in search of work, in search of normalcy, in search of the original powers of America to create the liberty of each individual, for themselves and their children.

While back in the South, the original powers—which faith and family can bring to bear against wrongful law—became, once again, beautifully apparent.

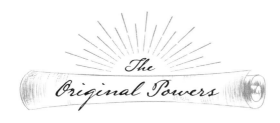

The Original Powers

– The Light of Faith –

THE SOUTHERN CHRISTIAN LEADERSHIP CONFERENCE

In the South, still under Jim Crow law, one of the original powers, those of the churches and their ministers, rose again. This time to fight for equality and against a civil government's laws, which were based on some persons being "other" and "lesser." America's churches stood first as the spiritual vanguard, just as they had for abolition, this time in hopes of finishing the job of equality.

The Supreme Court decided against segregation in 1954 in *Brown v. Board of Education*. But the decision had come and gone, and the ways of Birmingham, Alabama, had not changed. The Civil Rights Act of 1957 came and went, and the segregation of Birmingham never changed. In 1963, things finally did change for the better, and the initial force, as it has been throughout American history, was spiritual and moral. James Luther Bevel, Frederick Shuttlesworth, Wyatt Lee Walker, Martin Luther King Jr., his mentor Bayard Rustin, and Ralph Abernathy—spiritual ministers all—got together to form the Southern Christian Leadership Conference, which was dedicated to protesting for the civil rights that the civil government authorities ignored.

In Birmingham, 40 percent of the population was African American, of whom only 10 percent were registered to vote, but everyone went to church, and everyone bought goods. So, in all the African American churches of Birmingham, the word started going out to boycott Birmingham businesses to bring an end to segregation and to secure actual voting rights. The Birmingham government was unimpressed.

Wyatt Lee Walker and Fred Shuttlesworth decided on a more aggressive, but peaceful, strategy of protest, which they termed "Project C." The C stood for *Confrontation*: an ongoing series of marches and sit-ins that would provoke the civil authorities into arresting persons exercising their rights of assembly and speech—as enumerated in the Bill of Rights and as pertained to all citizens of the United States. Walker knew that the local authorities would react in a way that would alert the media and "induce national sympathy and attention to the everyday segregated circumstance of a person living in the deep south."

Shuttlesworth first demanded that all volunteers to march learn the rules of peaceful protest. Some of the volunteers were adults, others were very young but came with their parent's permission to do what was best for the rights of the "family." Shuttlesworth formed the volunteers into groups of fifty. He sent them from his Bethel Baptist church on 16th Street and told them they were bound for the mayor's office because they wanted to discuss segregation.

In the way of the marchers was the aptly named "Bull" Connor, who met the protestors with water cannons and let loose a group of attack hounds as the response of an uncivil government. This occurred while news cameras rolled, recording the confrontation for the whole country, and the whole world, to see. Walker got it right: one thousand marchers were arrested and taken to the Birmingham jail, occupancy nine hundred. This episode faith-based revolt shocked the moral conscience of the nation.

On seeing the success of the arrests, Shuttlesworth sent an invitation to Martin Luther King, Jr. to join the protest, writing: "If you come to Birmingham, you will not only gain prestige, but really shake the country... If you win in Birmingham, as Birmingham goes, so goes the nation." The Reverend Martin Luther King, Jr. packed his bags.

MLK, Jr. arrived in time to march, purposefully on Good Friday, April 12, 1963. He was arrested for daring to peacefully assemble, this for the thirteenth time since his dedication to civil rights began. He was taken to the Birmingham jail and there held without access to an attorney unless a guard was allowed to be present—another instance of "lesser" and "other" treatment than actual civil rights provide. The Birmingham jail became the latter-day common keep in humanity's struggle for liberty, and the focus of the whole country.

From his cell, King devoted his now-ample time to composing a letter to eight fellow ministers, who had written a letter to a newspaper editor counseling King to stop the demonstrations as they were "untimely, unwise," and bound to provoke violence.

King responded in a letter of his own, as a devout man of God. "I am in Birmingham because injustice is here.... Just as the Apostle Paul left his village of Tarsus and carried the gospel of Jesus Christ to the far corners of the Greco-Roman world, so am I compelled to carry the gospel of freedom." He continued, "Injustice anywhere is a threat to justice everywhere.... It is unfortunate that demonstrations are taking place in Birmingham, but it is even more unfortunate that the city's white power structure left the Negro community with no alternative."

In a spiritual and deeply democratic plea, King made a pointed reference: "Just as Socrates felt that it was necessary to create a tension in the mind so that individuals could rise from the bondage of myths and half-truths to the unfettered realm...we must see the need for nonviolent gadflies to create the kind of tension in society that will help men rise from the dark depths of prejudice and racism to the majestic heights of understanding and brotherhood."

He then cited famous spiritual leaders, such as St. Augustine, who wrote, "An unjust law is no law at all." Paraphrasing St. Thomas Aquinas, King wrote, "An unjust law is a human law that is not rooted in eternal law and natural law." And, in King's own words, he concluded, "Any law that uplifts human personality is just. Any law that degrades human personality is unjust. All segregation statutes are unjust because segregation distorts the soul and damages the personality." And finally, "A law is unjust if it is inflicted on a minority that, as a result of being denied the right to vote, had no part in enacting or devising the law."

King went on to express his happiness at being able to break an unjust law. "One who breaks an unjust law must do so openly, lovingly, and with a willingness to accept the penalty." He cited as an example of breaking an unjust law for a higher law the biblical account of the refusal of Shadrach, Meshnach, and Abednego to bow before a king's image. The rebel act was committed in defiance of the tyranny of Nebuchadnezzar. Then, referencing one of the first philosophers of freedom who defied tyranny, King wrote: "To a degree, academic freedom is a reality today because Socrates practiced civil disobedience." And, in another plea for spiritual authority defying the injustice of tyrannous government, "If today I lived in a Communist country where certain principles dear to the Christian faith are suppressed, I would openly advocate disobeying that country's antireligious laws."

The Reverend then stated, with perfect clarity, the first purpose of spiritual authorities in a free society: "We merely bring to the surface the hidden tension that is already alive. We bring it out into the open.... Like a boil that can never be cured so long as it is covered up but must be opened with its ugliness to the natural medicines of air and light, injustice must be exposed...to the light of human conscience and the air of national opinion before it can be cured."

Later, he warned against placing too great a faith on the inevitability of the good triumphing in the world through the medium of time: "Human progress never rolls in on wheels of inevitability; it comes through the tireless efforts of men willing to be co-workers with God.... Now is the time to make real the promise of democracy and transform our pending national elegy into a creative psalm of brotherhood."

King went on to admonish those spiritual authorities who abjured their proper role as spiritual authorities in a free society and did not stand up beside the SCLC in their efforts to fight the injustice of segregation. "In the midst of blatant injustices inflicted upon the Negro, I have watched white churchmen stand on the sidelines and mouth pious irrelevancies and sanctimonious trivialities." And then he lauded others for their right use of moral authority. "I am thankful to God that some noble souls from the ranks of organized religion have broken loose from the paralyzing chains of conformity and joined us as active partners in the struggle for freedom."

Near the end of the letter, King wrote of his hopes: "One day the South will know that when these disinherited children of God sat down at lunch counters, they were in reality standing up for what is best in the American dream and for the most sacred values in our Judeo-Christian heritage, thereby bringing our nation back to those great wells of democracy which were dug by the founding fathers in their formulation of the Constitution and the Declaration of Independence."

Back on the streets of Birmingham, James Bevel devised a plan to begin a "Children's Crusade." Parents of families, though knowing their children would be put in certain danger, brought them to Minister Bevel, who told the gathering youth, "It's up to you to free our teachers, our parents, yourself, and our country." Then he gave each child a toothbrush...to be used during their foreseeable time in jail. New groups of fifty youths per group set out again from the Bethel Church on 16th street and headed for city hall with a spiritual plea to the civil authority, while singing "We Shall Overcome." Again, Bull Connor let loose the hoses and dogs of segregation for the world to witness. In the span of the day, twelve hundred children were arrested and incarcerated in the Birmingham jail.

That evening, the recently released King assured the families of the imprisoned minors, "Do not worry about your children who are in jail. The eyes of the world are on Birmingham. We are going on in spite of dogs and fire hoses. We've gone too far to turn back." Indeed, the seeds of a civil rights revolution had been cast and there was no turning back.

Finally, on May 13, the U.S. Attorney General, Robert Kennedy dispatched three thousand federal troops to restore order in Birmingham, and the Kennedy administration began drafting new legislation. Along the way, it was stopped again by the Democratic Party's southern bloc of segregationists, until—as the Governor of Georgia, Richard Russell, said, the segregationists were overwhelmed by the churches who had joined the civil rights lobby.

The National Council of Churches, comprised of Catholic, Protestant, and Jewish clergy working with hundreds of thousands of church and temple members throughout the country, began to identify members of Congress and told their congregants to swarm their representative's offices with regular weekly petitions in support of the new bill. In the spring of 1964, it was said that you could not walk through the halls of government without being surrounded by clerics and rabbis. Martin Luther King, Jr., the minsters of the SCLC, and the children and families of Birmingham had inspired their spiritual brethren and a nation to overcome their government's immoral laws and extend the frontiers of justice. They had moved the earth under Washington, DC, from their family homes, from their churches and from their jail cells in Birmingham.

On July 2, the Civil Rights Act of 1964 was passed in one of the greatest episodes of our spiritual and political history, and one of the greatest expressions of the rightful force of America's original powers through the individuals, families, and ministers of faith who made it happen. The act, by law, prohibits discrimination on the basis of race, color, religion, sex, or national origin. It also bans discrimination on the basis of sex and race in the business areas of hiring, promoting, or firing. The act opened public accommodations to all on an equal basis and promised equality in consideration of federally funded programs. It strengthened voting rights until the greater remedy of the Voting Rights Act of 1965 was passed. And the act laid the legal groundwork for the desegregation of schools.

Would the promise finally be real? Would those treated as "other and lesser" finally be equal? Would our brethren, our fellow Americans, finally be free?

An African American scholar, Thomas Sowell, after the great victory, sounded a note of caution that this victory was not all that was necessary and that "to expect civil rights (legislation) to solve our economic and social problems was barking up the wrong tree." He noted that the black community had to also look inward and "toward our own self-development as a people." Self-development in America had always relied on those original powers which the government was supposed to leave alone.

With a little time, in every northern city that the African Americans ventured to, there came another cultural, economic, and artistic blossoming like that in Harlem N.Y, during the jazz age. Detroit had its Black Bottom and Paradise Valley neighborhoods, St. Louis had its Mill Creek, Washington, DC, had its Southwest, Los Angeles had its West Adams; these were thriving neighborhoods African Americans developed themselves. Like every other ethnic neighborhood—those of the Italians, the Poles, the Irish, and the Jews—African American neighborhoods were a hometown with a home team, which had all the elements to create progress within the neighborhood through the original powers of America. If only they were left to exercise them...

But a predictable thing happened. The federal government decided that it had the right to invade the provinces of the original powers of America and assume such powers unto itself, to the great affliction of the very people the government sought to "benefit"—the African American population that had not so long before moved north to escape oppression. Based on the Housing Act of 1949, bulldozers levelled their neighborhoods, and as they did so, they levelled a once sacrosanct, vital, and constitutionally protected part of America life, an area which neither the local, the state, nor the federal government were ever supposed to invade let alone destroy...

JOHN F. KENNEDY

In his domestic program titled "The New Frontier," President John Kennedy proposed to allocate some federal funding to education, to medical care for seniors, and to get some resources to poor pockets of the country, such as Appalachia. He wanted to balance the budget and revamp the tax code to stimulate the country's economy. To do so, he would lower taxes to produce more government revenue—based on the concept of America's private economy having more liberty, and therefore a greater capacity to create more wealth and resources for private investment, and thereby more revenues for the government. He also wanted to land a man on the moon. All but the last objective was a measured, practical policy. Kennedy and his coterie viewed any expansion of New Deal policy or programs with great skepticism. The reader will remember that JFK's father left the Roosevelt administration because he refused to "get with the program" regarding the federal government changing the economy fundamentally, and even dictating the way in which utility companies were to operate in the "free enterprise" system.

In foreign policy, JFK had stared down Nikita Khrushchev over Cuba. He also found himself, like the rest of the country, skeptical about our efforts in Vietnam. Because of this, he had sent a large number of advisors on different missions to secure one thing: an accurate assessment of the likelihood of success for a viable democracy in South Vietnam. Kennedy had sent 16,000 troops there in a support capacity, not in a combat role. Each of the advisors JFK sent came back with differing answers so much so that Kennedy openly wondered if they had visited the same country. All of the reports about Vietnam, though told in different ways, were bad news. By October of 1963, Kennedy ordered completion of the McNamara-Taylor mission statement, in which he demanded a schedule that 1,000 troops be withdrawn by the end of 1963, with a complete withdrawal from Vietnam accomplished by 1965. On October 1, he enforced the schedule by signing National Security

Action Memorandum 263, which likewise ordered the withdrawal of 1,000 military personnel by year's end with the remainder of all troops withdrawn in 1965.

Then, shots rang out in Dealey Plaza, Dallas, Texas and the trajectory of America's future, at home and abroad, changed on November 22nd, 1963, forever...

— Shadow —

The Great Society

Lyndon Baines Johnson had been a creature of government his entire life. He had been a congressional staffer before being the youngest person ever elected to Congress at the age of twenty-eight. Unlike Kennedy, Johnson was a stalwart disciple of Roosevelt's, a true believer in the New Deal regardless of its many failings. He believed, like Roosevelt, that if a program failed, change the name and do it again...and again. Johnson also believed in Roosevelt's mode of securing power by creating constituencies, which became dependent on government services funded by wealth redistribution, then making those programs permanent, thus making the Democratic Party's power base - permanent. Like Roosevelt, Johnson believed in using every lever of power possible. And no one knew how to do so better. LBJ could be ruthless.

Lyndon Baines Johnson

Johnson's inner circle was a mix of persons from his own history and the Kennedy administration, whom Johnson called the "Harvards." There were some, like Robert McNamara, who believed in active management from the top, meaning directly from the Administrative State. Others, like Patrick Moynihan, believed in transforming society based on statistics, agreeing with Wesley Mitchel, the social scientist, that the quantitative analysis of society is the sole road to societal improvement. Another part of Johnson's inner circle were members who believed, with a religious zealotry, in expanding the power of government to improve society, such as Sargent Shriver, a devout Catholic, and Bill Moyer, a Baptist preacher. A third arc of the circle were people from Johnson's long background in government called the "Texas Mafia," who knew from long experience how to railroad legislation through Congress.

The other members of Johnson's inner circle were union chieftains, led by Walter Reuther—a believer in European Socialism, who once said he could shut down any company in America with a snap of his fingers. And there was George Meaney of the the American Federation of Labor and Congress of Industrial Organizations. These labor leaders were some of the first people Johnson called to discuss policy when he assumed the presidency. And there was a vast new group of unions forming, which were greatly interested in the growth of government. Executive Order 10988, masterminded by Patrick Moynihan, made public sector workers new union members, at a surplus cost to every taxpayer. The new federally created and protected unions, by the necessity of their existence, negotiated against taxpayers for their own higher wages, benefits and guaranteed positions.

The team suited Johnson's purpose, which was to use statistical rationale to assume ever more power to the state. The guidebook of inspiration for this next transformation of America, beyond the New Deal and the Fair Deal, was written by a proud, self-avowed Marxist socialist, Michael Harrington, who authored *The Other*

America and *The Twilight of Capitalism*. He famously remarked to Johnson that the Democratic Party had another ready constituency, which would be as reliable as the labor vote for the Democratic Party if it were, in effect, unionized - the poor. Harrington also said, "Of course, there is no real solution to the problem of poverty until we abolish the capitalist system."

There was a roadblock. During the Eisenhower years, there had been a massive increase in the average citizen's purchasing power—of roughly 300 percent—and the Gross National Product had increased 30 percent during that time. Since the Kennedy tax cuts had gone into effect, the news got even better: the country was growing at a rate of 5.5 percent per year, with 3.5 percent unemployment (the statistical equivalent of full employment) and an inflation rate of only 1 percent. The capitalist economy was succeeding brilliantly. People were making their own way out of poverty, where it existed.

Life Magazine wrote that America was experiencing "cornucopias full of abundance that no other country in the world has ever known." *U.S. News and World Report* noted, "Tax relief in massive doses, appears to have achieved something like magic!" The success of capitalism also meant money was pouring into the Treasury - revenue was up 60 percent. For the adherents to the Administrative State and for the Democratic Party, only one question arose: how do "we" spend all this money?

Where was poverty to be found? Patrick Moynihan, in digging into his statistics, found that African American families that stayed together and were outside of the south were earning as much as white families. So, where, outside of the isolated mountain areas of Appalachia, could they find poverty?

A Johnson advisor, Robert Lampman, had an idea: why not widen the definition of poverty outward? He said, "Some people would say poverty means lack of money income, [but maybe it should be viewed like] a spiritual concept; or it's a participation in government concept; or it's a lack of self-esteem...or it has to do with lack of public facilities like schools and so on. That's what makes people really poor." By this lack of definition, everyone could be called poor. The Johnson administration redefined poverty, inventing the term *cultural poverty*, until one in five people within America were defined as poor - in the richest, most modern country that ever was.

Unlike FDR, who had the crisis of the Depression to claim emergency powers, LBJ had to create a climate of crisis… for one to exist. He began with the "Economic Report of the President." Kennedy's last report in 1963 did not use the word *poverty* once. Johnson's first report, in 1964, referenced poverty 196 times. Suddenly, the poverty found in remote corners of Appalachia became a plague about to spread west from Maine to the shores of the Pacific and had to be dealt with as if it were a war. Thus, a new marketing term was born: "The War on Poverty." Suddenly, thirty-five *million* people in America were considered poor. Just as suddenly, all the powers in Washington, DC, had to be marshalled to expand the Administrative State - again. The federal government had to assume to itself all the wealth that the success of capitalism was generating—just as it was raising everyone's prosperity. And the Democrats had an advantage: they had ridden a tidal wave of sorrow over the loss of John Kennedy to landslide victories for Congress and the presidency.

The new war had to be branded well to succeed. It had to sound moderate. Advisor Robert Lampman cautioned to "avoid completely any use of the term *inequality* or the term *redistribution* of income or wealth." Tom Hayden, one of the Students for a Democratic Society, the SDS, pointed out: "We (the Democratic Party) will be 'out' of power if we are explicitly socialist, but we can be further 'in' power if we are willing to call socialism - liberalism." Robert McNamara advised that if the country thought the administration was going soft on socialism at home, they could show how hard they could be on socialism—in Vietnam.

Suffice it to say, the incident in the Gulf of Tonkin, which expanded America's commitment to the Vietnam War, and the incident of the poverty law's passage, were coincidental. The impasse in the Gulf of Tonkin occurred on August 4, the passage of the Economic Opportunity Act was debated during that very time and passed the House on August 20, 1964. The Johnson administration decided thereafter to bomb socialism abroad, while levelling neighborhoods and the original powers, in order to build socialism at home.

— Shadow —

Levelling the Neighborhood and the Original Powers

Where justice is denied, where poverty is enforced, where ignorance prevails, and where any one class is made to feel that society is in an organized conspiracy to oppress, rob, and degrade them, neither persons nor property will be safe.

Frederick Douglass

And yet, there was no reason for the Johnson administration to worry about amplifying poverty statistics is some areas - Democratic Party policy was creating poverty all over the country in the major cities, mostly in African American neighborhoods because their homes, their businesses, their neighborhoods, and their lives were being levelled by the Housing Program—and the inner circle of the Democratic Party, the unions, and their chosen redevelopers.

As previously discussed, since the migration from the South began, African American neighborhoods outside of the South were maturing to prosperity, just as the Irish, Italian, Polish, and Jewish neighborhoods had in the major cities. A good example of typical African American urban neighborhoods were the Black Bottom and Paradise Valley areas of Detroit, noted for their arts scene and the fact that so many African American-owned businesses were thriving in the area—including 71 beauty shops, 57 restaurants, 30 drugstores, 25 dress makers, and 15 fish and poultry markets. There were a multitude of night clubs such as the Flame Show Bar, the Horseshoe, and Club Harlem. The area was a national jazz mecca, with acts from Ethel Waters and Ella Fitzgerald to Duke Ellington and Louis Armstrong making regular stops there to perform. There were all sorts of theaters filled with actors, actresses, and audiences. There were 151 physicians, 85 lawyers, 36 dentists, 25 barbershops and 20 hotels—some of them as nice as any in the country, such as the Gotham Hotel, where you might meet a jazz virtuoso on any given evening.

The neighborhoods were thriving, most everybody knew everybody else; they cared about the "neighborhood." They cared that the schools were teaching their children. They took pride in their forty churches. They took pride in their occupations and enterprises. They looked out for one another's property and protected it against thieves and vandals. They cared whether a neighbor's son or daughter was in school or had gotten the job they wanted. The dentist was their neighbor, the grocer was on the corner, the doctor was down the street, and everyone knew them by their first names. It was all local. It was all home. The residents of Black Bottom and Paradise Valley, and residents of a multitude of other neighborhoods in urban America, had a home.

Until planners in Washington, DC, decided that such neighborhoods should not be anybody's home. The government levelled Paradise Valley and Black Bottom and replaced them with union leader Walter Reuter's vision of what a neighborhood should be: the Lafayette projects, just one of the results of the government's invasion of private property rights. Such projects were creating prosperity for the chosen redevelopers and the unions, while creating inner city poverty throughout the country—a poverty that Lyndon Johnson now said the country had to wage a war against. You see, when politicians and "redevelopers" level a developed neighborhood, other things are levelled beyond what some professor at Harvard can see on a statistics sheet. You raze critical relationships necessary to every citizen's independence and well-being. You level an individual's wider societal family, which raises the young in an environment of trust and love. You level the original powers of American society to the dust...

The new society planners of LBJ were busy, working all hours. The lights were burning in Administrative State offices deep into the night as this new coterie of "Harvards" decided on how to restructure the fundamentals of human society, which they determined to do with an urgency suited, as Johnson put it, to "the moral equivalent of war."

Levelling

The Family

One of the first effects of levelling a neighborhood is that all the jobs are ground into the dust left by the bulldozers. The redeveloper's jobs, building the new projects, were going to the unions. The unions were not hiring people from the old neighborhood. The doctors went away, so there was no need for nurses. The lawyers went away, so there was no need for legal assistants. The restaurants went away, so there was no need for chefs or waiters. The movie houses went away, so there was no need for managers or staff. The nightclubs went away, so there was no need for the bands. The theaters went away, so there were no more jobs for stagehands. What replaced the multitudes of independent businesses and professionals were "government approved" convenience stores, fast food chains, large institutional hospitals, and law firms.

When what was needed were the jobs the government had bulldozed... Government's solution was to increase the minimum wage, so anyone out of work stayed that way, particularly the heads of families trying to keep their families together. The government held out hope - welfare benefits were increased to be above the average wage paid for inner city workers. But to collect such benefits, to maximize your benefits, and to have a place to live in the projects because your home was gone - you had to be a single parent.

At Pruitt-Igoe in St. Louis, social workers inspected the residences based on the "Man in The House Rule," to make sure there was no father of the household present. If he was, the family was evicted. To be allowed to stay in the Pruitt-Igoe projects, the family had to prove to a social worker that the father had left the state. If a father returned "to visit" the family, the children were told to lie to the social workers about their own father. If someone in the projects was lucky enough to find a job or get a raise—the rent in the projects was based on one's level of income, lo and behold, the rent just went up and the government got the raise.

Neighborhoods are impossible to recreate once they are levelled. So is the father of a family, once a government drives his home, his neighborhood, and his job into the ground and creates circumstances whereby his family is better off without him. Whereby his family is better off as dependents of government. But the government was there, again, to provide by expanding the Aid to Families with Dependent Children—government benefits attainable only if the family was broken. The new "father" of all such families became the federal government, upon which the war on poverty was making the urban poor completely dependent. This became something you could depend on for generations: urban dependency, and therefore, urban poverty.

Levying

Education

A major part of the war on poverty involved the federal takeover of another sacrosanct local responsibility, since before the nation's founding. A local responsibility that guaranteed the independence of the American school system from grade school through to the universities. The takeover began in the many areas where the private or neighborhood schools in urban areas had been levelled. Also levelled were the connections every student had with their teachers and their school fellows. The takeover took root when the new teachers of the students arrived. They were members of the American Federation of State, County, and Municipal Employees—a union directly controlled from offices in Washington, DC.

The connection parents had with the schools that educated their children fundamentally changed. Parents no longer controlled their children's education—control passed to the union and the federal government. If a parent did not like the curriculum, that was tough. If a group of parents did not like a teacher, so what. A teacher's position was not up to the parents—the teacher's position was given and guaranteed by the union. Did the parent wish to take it up with the principal? He was a member of the same union. The only way to get ahead at the school was through the union.

The second path of invasion was the usual route: through federal funding. It began with Head Start, a combined food and education program for preschoolers. Taxpayer money poured into Head Start offices in the urban centers of the country; like their Housing Authority cousins, they were federal offices. This outpouring ensured two things: first, the family was no longer together for their meals, a central component of family life; and second, the federal government was serving more than food for intake, it was taking over what every child was learning. Even the Democratic stalwart John Connally was alarmed by this new federal power, saying the government was not going into education to form a system of cooperation with local education authorities and parents, Connolly knew that the Administrative State wanted control. Many voices arose equally alarmed that this sacrosanct province of parental and local control was being invaded. They were shouted down by those who answered that it was a question of getting inner city children fed. Ultimately, 44,000 people were hired to administrate the Head Start Program – to take the place of two parents.

The program worked so well in bringing pre-education children into the federal realm that two bills quickly followed, one establishing federal funding for kindergarten through twelfth grade, and another that would finish the job of the invasion with federal funding for colleges and federal financial aid to students for higher education. This all looks like generosity; it is not. It is the federal government taking tax money from individuals, localities, and states—all of which had funded an independent school system—and levying control of the education system to the federal government. Or, I should say, the Democratic Party.

Our friend de Tocqueville had an observation on this assumption of power over education by a central authority: "The State receives and often takes the child from the arms of its mother in order to entrust it to its agents; it takes charge of inspiring sentiments in each new generation and furnishing it with ideas. Uniformity (then) reigns in studies as in all the rest; (while) diversity, like liberty disappears from it day by day."

Inner city education has been failing parents ever since this change in the once independent American educational system took place. And in a remarkable instance of coincidence, elementary, secondary, and higher education has ever since become more and more uniform in their antagonism to a civic education founded on the principles of freedom.

Levelling

The Faith

As in any neighborhood in America, so it was in urban areas that when you went to a certain school, you likely went to a related church. The persons you saw at school during the week were usually whom you saw on Sunday at preaching. There was a wonderful symmetry involved in learning the ways of the world and in learning the ways of one's God. The vast majority of African

American neighborhoods in the 1950s were comprised of Christian denominations, mostly Baptist. For most of these denominations, the whole message of Christianity is given to making oneself better morally, of being a better person in society, of caring for those around us as much as we care about ourselves. When the housing program levelled the large swaths of urban areas, perhaps no greater loss was felt than the loss of the houses of faith.

What is more valuable to a neighborhood than the place where everyone gathers in hope, surrounded by a message of love? What is more important than that caring congregation to which Martin Luther King, Jr. devoted his life? Where families discussed each other's aspirations, where the passages of life were honored on the sacred ground which was the neighborhood's common house. Where, if someone had a problem, an answer was found through neighbors of a shared faith bond. Houses of faith have been one of the primary societal builders and sustainers of neighborhood life.

In St. Louis, where Mill Creek was levelled for the Pruitt-Igoe projects, forty three churches were levelled while only one was spared. The government made no plans to rebuild those that they destroyed. One of the only priests left, John Shocklee of St. Bridget's, worked tirelessly, devoting years of his life, becoming a conduit for families to get outside of the projects and into a family home – a property they could own.

Faith is something that no just civil government can replace. But it is where tyranny always begins—with the overthrow of faithful institutions. Communists burned down seventy thousand churches, butchered the priests and carried off the chalices and crosses for smelting. Modern socialists prefer to work quietly, unnoticeably taking upon themselves all the offices of the church, in order to become the first, the last and then the sole resort of the poor; seeking to be the sole repository of all belief—a belief in government and government alone.

Here again, we can afford ourselves the wisdom of de Tocqueville: "The rulers may not care very much about doctrine," but they are intent on "laying hold of the will of the man who explains" this doctrine. First, "they take from the clergy their property. [Then,] they assign to each a salary, [and finally,] they divert and use for their advantage alone the influence the priest possesses.... They make of him one of their functionaries and often one of their servants, and with his assistance they penetrate the ultimate depths of each man's soul."

Levying

The Faith

LBJ had his man—actually an exceptionally good man. Sargent Shriver was a veteran of World War II, he had fought in the swarming hell of Guadalcanal. He was a Kennedy family member through his marriage to Jack and Robert's sister Eunice. Under Kennedy, Shriver had founded a great civil service institution, the Peace Corp. He was a strict lifelong Catholic, a daily communicant who believed in the services the church provided, the charity it dispensed, the education it gave, the help up it offered to all who were in need no matter their background or belief. He loved the church so much and believed in its services to such a degree that he thought he could duplicate it through government, in those areas where the government decided to tear the churches down... He was not the first to be wrong about civil government being able to take over the authority of faith; that lineage goes back to the Emperor Constantine.

LBJ made Sargent Shriver, who sincerely believed government could take over the offices of faith, his point man in the war on poverty. Johnson's advisors told him he needed a better name than the Office of Poverty, so he made Shriver the head of the "Office of Economic Opportunity" (OEO) and made that office a cabinet level position. The office was to "stimulate urban and rural communities to mobilize their resources to combat poverty." The act authorized public and private organizations to operate "community action programs," or CAPs. The bill demanded "maximum feasible participation" by local residents.

Sargent Shriver began by asking for submissions of applications for grants of money. His offices were flooded with requests. In return, a flood of money poured out of Washington to urban centers around the country. Mayors around the nation were delighted and quickly set up offices for the receiving and dispensing of the funds to community action agencies. In Chicago, Mayor Daley created his own agency and made himself the head of it so he could control the money. He did what was natural to him. He hired one thousand loyal Democrats as community representatives, expecting them to perform the Democratic Party's three - step tango: take taxpayer money from the government, take the patronage job (which pays union dues, and makes cash contributions to the Democratic Party), and go hold a shovel where the mayor tells you to.

The OEO wanted more direct federal control rather than to give slush funds to city halls, so it demanded that the agencies be independent of city halls around the country. The OEO required mayors to find some "poor" people and get them to engage in "maximum feasible participation." The OEO produced a 262-page handbook on how cities could apply to the federal government to begin their own poverty program. One of the ways to get to the head of the line for funding was to prove your organization would "facilitate opportunities for the poor to participate in protest actions." If an organization proved successful in teaching protestors how to protest, it would get more grant money. Saul Alinsky, who achieved wealth and fame as an activist, got his start by organizing the Woodlawn Organization on the south side of Chicago through funding from taxpayers. Junius Williams, an activist himself, said the war on poverty set up a new government—one for the opposition to government. Walter Reuther, the socialist union leader, encouraged LBJ to support this federally funded culture of protest.

In the flurry of funds the OEO was throwing at urban areas, Sargent Shriver, with good intentions, gave a grant of $957,000 to the Woodlawn Organization for job training and motivation programs. It became the entire treasury of a criminal south side street gang: the Blackstone Rangers of Chicago.

Mayors around the country started to wake up—vocally. Richard Daley was furious; he used an inside line to contact the White House. "What the hell are you people doing? Does the president know he's putting money in the hands of subversives?" Didn't the Johnson administration know these protestors might bring down the American government? A fellow mayor noted, "We are experiencing a class struggle in the tradition of Karl Marx... and we don't like it!" Even Jim Rowe, a fellow New Dealer and supporter of Johnson's, warned: "The political implications of using public funds to instruct people how to protest are...obvious."

This critical period in U.S. history marked the time when the Democratic Party cornered the market as being the party that demands the federal government grow until it has absolute power. And, it also became the cool, rebellious, hippy party that protests against government power. The Democratic Party also cornered the market on urban unrest: it has controlled the protestors and the police department unions of inner cities ever since, for sixty years.

What replaced the churches of faith in the inner cities of America was a government-funded belief in socialism, which is antagonistic toward all religions and democratic governments because it is a "religion" whose faith is in tyrannical government.

City governments around the country found that once you let the federal government in, you could not get them out. Neither the mayors nor the governors of the states could close the OEO offices. Nor could they repurpose the funding; the Democratic Party was determined to keep that power. Congress passed a bill, which Johnson signed, allowing OEO dictates to override the vetoes of state governors. The accepting of federal money looked good, until the cities and states discovered the cost: allowing still more power to be levied to Washington, DC. And the cities, like large populations of their citizens who became dependent, became dependent themselves on federal largesse through the building programs, the poverty agencies and the activist agencies—with each creating the necessity of the other and each depending on the Democratic Party taxing everyone in the country.

The Great Society was created with a single motive: to eradicate poverty. The Great Society programs did the opposite: its social restructuring destroyed the wealth naturally generated by America's original powers and the free enterprise system and traded that wealth for dependence on government at every point. The Great Society took property rights and replaced property with government rental housing; it took the natural neighborhood and replaced it with centrally planned projects; it took away enterprises and occupations and replaced them with "benefits"; it took away the family and replaced it with bureaucrats and social workers; it took away parental control of education and replaced it with federally controlled curriculums and unions. It took away houses of faith and replaced them with socialist activism. Sargent Shriver's sincere attempt to do "God's Work" through government, drove God out of the communities that needed faith-based institutions the most. The sincere attempt became a tragedy, that is ongoing.

Civil governments and faith-based institutions can only coexist in an enlightened partnership of opposition, recognizing the necessity, the rights and the benefits of each other's existence as our Constitution does. Or else a dominant, tyrannical civil government destroys faith institutions and their authority within society and persecutes all practitioners of faith. For reference, one may study China's treatment of Hindus, Buddhists, Christians, and Muslims, to name a few. Or the contrary may occur, a theocracy may assume power and do away with civil codes of law and civil institutions of power that are a threat to the theocracy; therefore, creating another system of tyranny. America's founding was unique: it was based on an enlightened separation of civil and spiritual power, which was deliberately done in order to form a barrier to such civil or spiritual forms of tyranny, by making these centers of power competitive and complimentary. The American design goes back, again, to Christ's answer to the Pharisees in Mk. 12:17: "Render to Caesar the things that are Caesar's, and to God the things that are God's."

Another power, the one most fundamental to a life of freedom and the freedom of a nation, was being levied to Washington, DC, by the Great Society. It is a power whereupon our freedom rests and has rested for centuries. A necessary power in any free society, a necessary power for the individual's independence: the power of self-reliance. Without one's property, without one's neighborhood, without one's family, without one's education, without one's faith, the original foundations of strength are taken from the individual rendering the citizen dependent on government. Individual independence can only survive if it is dependent on one thing alone, self-reliance: the key to the jewel of American liberty.

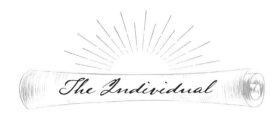

The Individual

– Light –

THE ULTIMATE ORIGINAL POWER

Ideally, when one is born on the American continent north of the Rio Grande River, one is born to freedom. One's life is not dictated by one's birth beneath an overlord or a monarch, a dictator or a bureaucrat. One may become anything, riding along the limitless horizon of an individual's imaginings.

The miracle of creation abounds with undisputed evidence that, in nature, no two things are the same. Indeed, if one peers upon the faces of every grain of sand over the vast reaches of our southwestern deserts, one will find without exception that no two grains of sand are the same. Neither are any two flakes of snow that fall on the Niagara, nor the drops of rain that flood New Orleans or Seattle. Nor are any two individuals the same in the massive number of our population.

When born into this world, there are billions of variables that come into play and harmonize based on every individual's DNA. Some persons are born with a physiognomy to become an offensive lineman in football; some to play center in the WNBA; some are best suited to be jockeys. One's physiognomy, one's physical strengths and weaknesses, are their own and no other's.

Everyone's intellect is equally various: some are born with minds built for numbers and math; some are given to the gifts of the sciences; some are given to a facility with words; some are given to the arts; and some are sensible in how best to cultivate the earth.

Everyone's nature, their mental strengths and weaknesses, are their own and no other's.

Further individualizing characteristics come into play based on one's force of personality—how they manage and nurture their talents. What power of will does one bring to the field of their endeavor? What virtues of self-discipline does one adhere to that make for success? Ask any professional athlete and they will confirm that their success does not depend solely on the circumstances of their physiognomy or their mental strengths—the streets are full of would-of-been, could-of-been athletes. What one does with their unique gifts determines one's optimum self-development as the individual they become. That is the power of their personality and no other's.

It is not an irony to find that the vast majority of those who develop most fully make their way upward through circumstances of the most adversity. Some, in fact, by making strengths of their weaknesses. One becomes the best mountain climber by rigorously training and dieting to achieve peak performance. One must learn to mountain climb by book and experience to chart the best courses a chosen mountain offers. One must overcome the ascent over every cliff and through the travail of every crevasse that may seem in the way at first glance but might, in fact, help in the climb. To master the craft, one must take the time and repetition to build endurance, to deal with less oxygen in the atmosphere, to sustain pace in adverse weather. This corollary of mountain climbing applies to every human endeavor. What mountain you design to climb is your journey and no other's.

From acuity of mental faculties to physical prowess building, to learning and decision making, to dealing with adversity—power depends on mental, physical, and moral exercise against opposition. The power of one's character to overcome obstacles of opposition becomes a cumulative force. Any great achievement is based on the adversity that is overcome as the mountain summit is won. The achievement of overcoming obstacles is yours and no other's.

How one achieves their individual summit through the mental and physical gifts they are born with, through the moral discipline of their personality, and through the disciplined overcoming of adversity, chisels the character of their soul. The path taken and the summit surmounted is each individual's own self-development, their own personal grail. The summit that each individual achieves is as unique as every grain of sand in creation but comes by way of a common key: individual self-reliance. And that key of self-reliance unlocks life's foremost treasure—the jewel of individual liberty.

Who has more liberty than the self-reliant? Who has more liberty than one who can fulfill every necessity within their own responsibility and achieve their dream independently? Who can say—atop their achievements while hoisting up the grail of their own filling, "This is I and no other!"? This was the ethos of the Native American, this was their great gift to America's ethos and the designing principle of our original government. This was the vision of the pioneers, who each settled a unique frontier.

There is yet another life one develops, beyond the self yet based on individual achievements as unique as the person. As Machiavelli noted in his *Il Principi*, our progress is dependent on a very human characteristic. "Human appetites are insatiable," nature has created persons in such a fashion that they are "able to desire everything," but not "to secure everything." Their "desire is always greater than their power of acquisition." Therefore, as one cannot have everything, what one chooses to be their property, what one labors to acquire, and how one uses it, is equally a fundamental liberty—a "natural right" and the "property" of one's individuality. And, by extension, a natural right and property of individual families.

The choice of an inventor might be to invest in the most refined technological tools. An artist might want a city loft full of light, the better for working. A lawyer may want to invest in the best computer system on the market. The choice of a military family might be different from that of a farming family, which will be different from that of an entrepreneur's family. The military family might spend on education what the farmer will invest in a barn, or the entrepreneur might spend on expanding manufacturing. What we have and what we earn, we invest in our hope based on a life plan that is our own. It depends on what one person, or one family, considers the key to success and happiness.

Does one choose to invest the most in their home or in the education of their children? Does a family live in a smaller house, so they might invest in a business? Does a family accumulate earnings through savings or investments? Or does one spend their earnings and sell their property to see more of the world? In a free country, how one develops their self, how one pursues self-fulfillment and their family's fulfillment, is a decision that is their own and no other's. And it is predictable—every individual and every family will have a unique answer of what exactly happiness is, as broad as the spectrum of possibility.

The benefit of self-reliance for each individual and family is that they achieve their own fulfillment. The benefit, which derives to society of every individual and family doing what renders them happy, creates an utterly unique country—one of abundancy in the beautiful and useful fruits and flowers that springs and teems from every branch of human capacity to invent, to create, to build, to harvest, to share.

The rights that produce our liberty are again termed "natural rights," as enumerated by John Locke: rights in one's own "life, health, liberty, and possessions." The choices each individual and family make for their fulfillment are those fundamentally protected by our Constitution and the Bill of Rights through personal property rights. The right to the fruits (property) deriving from one's own labor—that is the right to one's own income. As James Madison, the architect of our Constitution, said: it is from "the diversity in the faculties of persons [that] the rights of property originate [and] the protection of these faculties is the first object of government."

— Shadow —

Levying Reliance

At every turn, the Housing Program and the Great Society took an original power which contributes to self-reliance and replaced it with dependence, rendering millions of Americans dependent solely on government. And there is odd math about that: for every dependent, everyone loses a measure of freedom and a measure of self-reliance.

The amount of money the government takes from its citizens to support a system of dependency can be measured as the personal liberty of its citizens. Let us say that a family earns $100,000, of which the federal government takes $35,000—a roughly accurate measure in 2021. Just $15,000 of the money government takes every year could be the difference in choosing between an average university or a better one for a family member. It could be the choice between living in a more run-down house and neighborhood or a better one. It could be the working capital to invest in a business. Every dollar a citizen earns is a measure of liberty achieved through their own hard work. The very definition of freedom is being free to make choices—that is liberty's jewel. For every dollar the government takes from any citizen, it takes away choices, and that is a measure of a citizen's liberty to choose. It is also a measurable resource of self-reliance, which the government takes away and the citizen has lost.

A government that equalizes citizens economically, for the sake of happiness, must confiscate the property which the virtues of self-reliance create: the virtues that make for success. Virtues such as discipline, diligence, and husbandry must be penalized by government taking more money (property) from the citizen, thus diminishing one's liberty. While habits which make for dependence, such as laziness, negligence, and wastrel spending are the means to government benefits and a motive to remain dependent. And while the key of self-reliance opens the way to ever more liberty simply by its regular habit, when one is reliant on the government and receives more benefits based on derelictions—one becomes locked in a prison of one's own weaknesses. In this grotesque relationship, everyone loses a measure of their life's jewel—their liberty, their independence *from* government.

Let us turn again to Machiavelli's revelation regarding human nature: that we are a species whose wants are insatiable, by our nature we desire everything. If one depends solely on their own initiative to attain what they desire, it leads one to self-development and self-fulfillment—to the growth of the individual and the family. However, if one places reliance on government to provide "happiness" as each individual would variously define it, humanity's infinite source and variety of desire becomes government's infinite source and variety of growth.

For proponents of the Great Society, government must also be omnipresent, the opposite condition of America's founding when, as far as the individual could see, there was no government. Only America's original powers existed. If government is responsible for every citizen's happiness, it must become as de Tocqueville foretold in *Democracy in America*: "The State should situate itself unceasingly beside him (the citizen), above him, around him, to guide him, protect him, restrain him (and) sustain him." That is the opposite of individual freedom; it is government omniscience; it is governmental omnipotence.

Further, there can never be equality in the "pursuit of happiness" between the self-reliant and the government-reliant. Those who are self-reliant create in themselves the engine of self-development and its rewards. While those who are reliant on a government never start, let alone drive, the same engine of development. The idea of a happiness that can be created by government and given away to the masses is, in fact, a delusion. In reality, dependence on government is a prison whose bars are comprised of the debilitating weaknesses that such a government sponsors, when government levy's reliance for everyone's happiness unto itself, for its own empowerment.

The reader may remember a passage from *The DNA of Democracy* on the Grail of the Round Table and Arthur. The Grail could never be achieved by the king, nor could a king give it away: it was not his to give. Only those knights whose strengths, virtues, and daring led them to explore alone the never-trod forests of their original vision could achieve it. The Grail was only found through diligence and sacrifice: it had to be earned. What the fruits of the Grail are depends on the Grail's pursuer—the individual. The myth, like all myths, holds a thousand truths and among them is this key: that the Grail contains every unique *individual's* self-fulfillment—not the kings. That individual fulfillment is the jewel of liberty, and it is what renders the individual happy. No king or government can fill that cup, not even Arthur. No one who is dependent on government can find fulfillment; they can only awaken from the delusion, while in the heartbreaking prison of their own confinement.

— Shadows —

of Flame

In July1967, Black Bottom was gone. Its sorrow remained. Fifty thousand families were displaced. The businesses were gone. The churches were gone. The schools were gone. The "homes" were gone. The families were gone. Individuals moved on.

The jobs were gone. The senior partners—our government, the unions, and the auto manufacturers—were pricing themselves out of the competition for our own domestic markets and decided to move any new auto-building operations and facilities out of the city of Detroit to the suburbs. The blue-collar jobs and the people who worked them went along. The costs of city taxes were too high for the bottom line if the auto companies were to survive, when added to the union dues and the corporate taxes they had to pay.

The former residents of Black Bottom had a choice: They could move into the new projects and be studied there by social workers from Washington, who were keeping statistics on African Americans as though they were in a science lab to highlight the progress of the "Great Society." Or they could take up residence in Virginia Park, a one-time perfectly integrated and mature neighborhood which was now overrun by what amounted to a migration of refugees from a war zone. Virginia Park, like neighboring Black Bottom, was transformed.

Where there was a banker, there came a pawn broker. Where there was a doctor, there came a drug dealer. Where there was an employer, there came a gambler. Where there was a preacher, there came a Marxist militant. Where there was a home, there came a flop house. Where there was a wife, there came a prostitute. Where there were children, there came orphans. Where there was caring, there came chaos. The Fair Deal Housing Program and the Great Society's redistribution of wealth funded the entire transformation: the destruction of Black Bottom and the corruption of Virginia Park. They flooded an area with money that no one had to earn; money no one knew where to spend. For every individual, where there had been a neighborhood's strength, there came hordes of opportunities for self-destruction. Every individual was surrounded not by positive societal influences to achieve self-reliance, but by temptations to fall into dependence. The new society created and paved an open avenue to the degradation of the Human Personality, as Martin Luther King Jr. had termed it.

Wonderful things, jobs, families, and neighborhoods. You know where and how you have to earn every dollar, and you know how you have to spend every dime for yourself and your family to be alright; to be happy and to thrive.

It's fine...the new social workers are here to help. Of course, you cannot get a job, so here is a government check. Of course, you cannot be responsible for the education of your children; we will take care of that! Of course, you cannot feed yourselves; so the government is here with food stamps. Of course, you cannot house yourselves; the government is here with an apartment in the projects you can rent from us. Of course, you cannot care for your own children; the government school is a nursery too. Of course, you are other and lesser and cannot do anything for yourself. The government will take care of you. We will be your new overlord.

One of the architects of the Great Society, Daniel Patrick Moynihan, aptly stated his political party's arrogant attitude toward the good people of Detroit in an NBC documentary when he stated: "They are not particularly able people." That is synonymous with "other and lesser," the language of *Massahs*. This classification as being incapable is the definition of racism. This classification was the foundation of the Great Society.

The Great Society created the opposite of what the new civil rights laws promised: Equality. That contrast became the dry kindling for a national wildfire, waiting for the mismatch to strike.

The Blind Pig

On July 23, 1967, Willie Scott was operating a "blind pig" establishment, a social club that operates outside the normal statutes governing bars. Scott was operating his out of the United Community League for Civil Action office on 12th Street in Detroit. There was a crowd of eighty-five people involved in a celebration, welcoming home two soldiers who had survived their tours in Vietnam. It was a great time. The spirit of the old neighborhood, Black Bottom, was in the air...until patrol cars rolled up to make a nuisance raid at the unlicensed social establishment at 3:45 a.m. on that Sunday morning and decided to pick a fight with the wrong Marines. The proprietor and the patrons protested that they were free people, in a free country, who were celebrating the homecoming of soldiers who had fought for their freedom. The officers countered that the place was not sanctioned by the city for social gatherings with liquor service at that hour of the morning and began arresting everyone in the bar. While officers were arresting and forcibly securing the bar patrons, a larger crowd of two hundred onlookers were surrounding the police cars.

At 5:00 a.m., a bottle was thrown through a police car window as the exchanges between the police and the onlookers grew angrier and the atmosphere more ominous. A large wastebasket was hurled through a storefront window—and the battle began. The officers called for more back up, while the neighborhood began to awaken to what was going on at 12th Street. Hundreds more people joined the hundreds that were already there. Around 6:30 a.m., a chain reaction began, born out of anguish, anger, and frustration. People on the street began breaking into the shops, looting the contents and setting the stores ablaze. When fire trucks arrived to battle the fires, which were burning out of control, they were embattled by the crowds until they retreated.

Hastily organized meetings of fifty to seventy people were assembled in some area basements. Marxist militants were ready, they were trained, and they took the reins to give a goal to the anger, saying of the gathering riot, "Let's make the best of it." Many of the leaders were white. The unrest spread from 12th Street to Linwood Avenue, then on to Dexter, then on to Grandview, with stores burst into, looted, broken, and abandoned while a growing fire followed with a twenty-five mile-per-hour wind at its back. The fire department was battling over 1,200 fires, and everywhere they went they had to battle the crowds, who did not care if the city burned down to the ground—it wasn't theirs.

A hurried meeting was arranged at the White House. Among the Great Society's original planners, Daniel Patrick Moynihan noticed something about the group: there were no African Americans. None. What could be done?

Back on 12th Street, John Conyers, the district's congressman, stood up on a car and demanded calm. He was taken down by incoming bottles, bricks, and rocks. Nothing could stop the mayhem of a populace that had suffered such unequal treatment. At 5:30 p.m., Detroit's mayor Jerome Cavanaugh began the process of calling in the National Guard, followed by Governor George Romney's request of the same.

Pitched battles between the police, the fire department, the people of Virginia Park, and the militants occurred spontaneously and sporadically as fire, ash, and crowds of rage interflowed through a hundred city blocks. Until night fell....

Hubert Locke, an African American assistant to the police commissioner, climbed up onto the rooftop of the thirteen-story police building. He looked over the vast darkness, interspersed and defined by columns of smoke and moving masses of withering flame. "Detroit looked like what I imagined Dresden looked like after its fire-bombing in World War II. You could just see flames... all across the city, east and west. That was enough to be one of the saddest moments of my life, for a city that I grew up in, loved dearly, and still have a passion for." Hubert Locke grew up in one of Detroit's neighborhoods that had not been bulldozed to the ground. He cared.

The firefighters were made to abandon the hundred-block area where the fires raged. Sniper fire coming from multiple rooftops was being aimed at them. One white Marxist militant was witnessed shooting two national guardsmen. By 11:00 p.m., five looters had been shot by shop owners protecting their stores. Random gangs roamed the streets passing homes that were now ablaze, calling to those who were emotionally stricken on their own front yards "Uncle Toms" because they owned the homes. By midnight, 1,000 people were arrested. After twenty hours, the riot was still gaining energy.

At 2:00 a.m. Monday morning, Governor George Romney ordered 800 state police officers and eight thousand national guardsmen into the city. President Lyndon Johnson followed by ordering forty-seven hundred paratroopers of the 82nd Airborne's elite division to move on the city to restore federal control. The sniper fire continued randomly against any government representative within range until July 27. By then, much of Detroit laid in ashes, as levelled as Black Bottom had been by the bulldozers.

During the riots, forty-three people were killed and 1,189 injured. Twenty-five thousand stores were looted and seven thousand people were arrested in the worst riots in American history. In the wake of the riots, the federal government called for a special commission and named it after its head—Otto Kerner. The Kerner Report identified more than 150 riots that had occurred between 1965 and 1968. The commission declared: "Our nation was moving toward two societies, one white and one black, separate and unequal." The New Deal and the Great Society central planners had made it so. It is what occurs when government invades and literally levels one of America's greatest societal strengths: her original powers.

African Americans did not want a new project, they wanted the societal strengths of their old neighborhood. They did not want a house given to them, they wanted to build them. They did not want to make a rent payment in a project, they wanted to own the houses they built. They did not want a benefit check, they wanted to earn their wealth. They did not want social workers studying them and telling them what a family is, they wanted to raise their own families as they will. They wanted to educate their own children to be self-reliant. They wanted to do the work they chose and start the enterprises they desired, without government interference. They did not want special treatment—they wanted equal treatment.

A survivor of the riot was asked why it had all happened, and what was the answer to the tragedy. His answer said it all in one line: "A man must be a man, or he is nothing."

In a democracy, the individual is everything. In a tyranny, the individual is nothing. Our Constitution was conceived and our federal system of government was organized based on that idea alone.

However, a party of our government, in direct contravention of the Constitution's Fifth and Tenth Amendments, disregarded property rights in areas that it targeted to destroy, and then sought to bandage the wound by further setting itself up as a socialist alternative to those natural rights of every individual, which are supposed to be sacrosanct in our federal system. This is what can be expected when our Bill of Rights is overturned, and government assumes its own rights to intervene in the lives of individuals, to "help" them. It is government arrogance and hubris at its highest. Like trying to solve the problem of Vietnam with napalm, a party of our government thought it best to burn down the natural societal structure of the African American and created thereby a whole population dependent on one political party, left with nowhere to go for hope other than to those who destroyed it...

Additionally, that same party of our government went even further by invading the powers and prerogatives of the states, cities, even the neighborhoods, which our federal system expressly forbids. These are acts of a tyranny. And it is an extremely dangerous tyranny, which can claim that it acts for the people's own good - whether they want help or not.

The good people of America did not mind the Great Society government taking so much of their wealth, if it could help the poor among them...it appeared to be charity. Neither did the faith-based organizations mind this invasion of their normal authority if it would help the poor among them. But this massive confiscation of wealth and authority did not do that. As previously writ, governments are not churches—they do not function as charitable organizations, which give without demanding anything in return.

What the taxpayer funds, and where then government money goes, there flows a political assumption of control. Where government extends its control, it creates dependents; a dependency which is anathema to city and state autonomy and to individual liberty. As Hamilton noted in the *Federalist Papers*:

"In the course of human nature, a power over a man's subsistence amounts to a power over his will."

The same holds true for individuals and for cities dependent on federal funding. This creation of dependency has given a monopoly of government control to the Democratic Party over America's cities for sixty years with horrific results.

How misspent were our tax dollars then? How misspent are our tax dollars now? Therein lies the irony: the mismatch between equality and dependency is still igniting fires nationwide. What occurred in Detroit and around the country in 1967 occurred again in 2020. The riots and the ensuant battles between Marxist militants, who want to burn every city down to the ground, and the police and fire departments who try to save them, are both controlled to this day by the same political party. The Democratic Party controls the police and fire departments of every city because they control their unions; they also control the city administrations through federal dollars; and they control the militants through government grants and slush funds which become the treasuries of militant protest groups. And every Democratic city mayor, after every different riot, does the same thing: blame Republicans.

There are three groups who suffer from every city neighborhood that is burned down: The dependent residents, who are stuck in a state of dependency in those cities and suffer the loss of lives, businesses, and properties. The families of every police or fire department officer injured or killed. Then there are the taxpayers from Bangor to Honolulu, who pay for every government funded urban militant organization and every building they burn, through the confiscation of their wealth as it is… redistributed.

In the end, with his policies in ruins, LBJ took a familiar page from FDR and claimed his programs were working, that they were a great success, and he merely chose to retire from another run for the presidency. He had had enough, he had to stop. LBJ did succeed in securing another constituency that could be relied on as

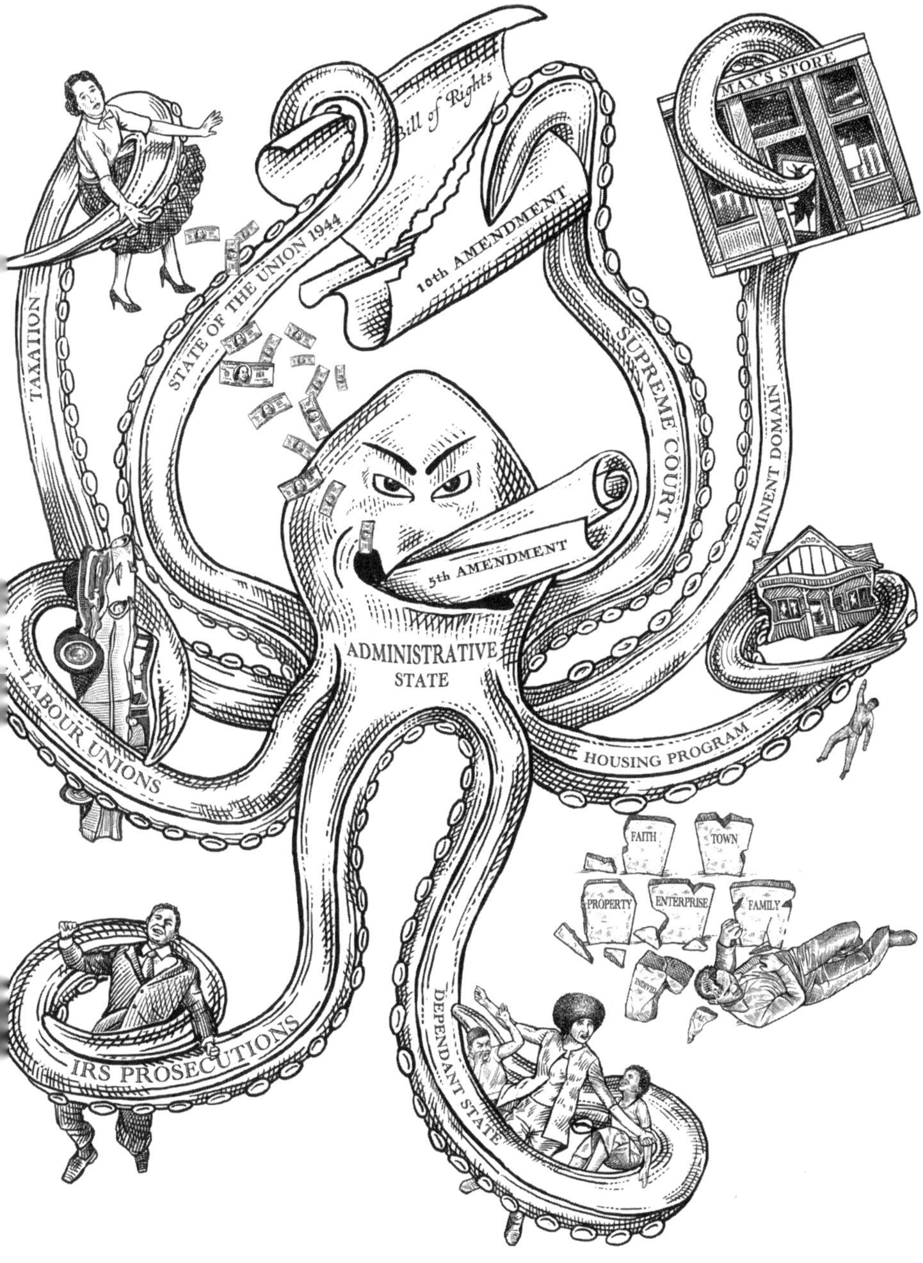
Bill of Rights
10th AMENDMENT
5th AMENDMENT
MAX'S STORE
TAXATION
STATE OF THE UNION 1944
SUPREME COURT
EMINENT DOMAIN
ADMINISTRATIVE STATE
LABOUR UNIONS
HOUSING PROGRAM
FAITH
TOWN
PROPERTY
ENTERPRISE
FAMILY
IRS PROSECUTIONS
DEPENDANT STATE

much as union labor—the persons he reduced to dependency, the African Americans, just as Michael Harrington had predicted. The realignment shocked one of the original Black Power movement leaders, Stokely Carmichael, who said: "To ask Negroes to get in the Democratic Party is like asking Jews to join the Nazi Party." But it happened. Left with nowhere to go for hope—other than to those who destroyed it—the African American community has been the most faithful monolith in support of the party of government which succeeded in reducing the African American's hopes to one: hope in more government.

The electorate in 1968 acted to stop the growth of the "Dependent States of America," with a landslide victory for a Republican presidency, but it could not stop the Dependent State's advance, because an aggressive collaborator pressed for national solutions to every American problem. And because a person who was elected as a conservative, to defend the original constitutional framework of the country, went along with the media and the opposition party, for the sake of individual power.

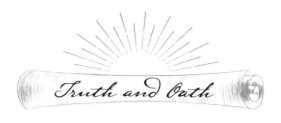

Truth and Oath

– Light –

TRUTH

There is no power more important in a democracy than the knowledge of the truth. According to *Webster's Dictionary*, the truth is defined as *the state of being the case* and *the body of real things, events and facts*. The truth is that simple: it is definition. And there is nothing more important for every single citizen than the accuracy of knowing the *what, where, why,* and *how* of events and circumstances upon the path of self-determination, on which our democracy exists. What events brought our nation to where it finds itself? What are the present circumstances of its existence, based on the body of real things, events, and facts? There is nothing more important to the course of a democracy than knowing the truth regarding challenges the nation confronts based on real and truthful alternative courses which may be taken in its future, because it is everybody's future. In any democracy, the truth is the most important basis on which to collectively make decisions. On this foundation, every single good outcome of a democracy absolutely depends. In America, we enjoy a unique freedom of the press, a free media, on whom everyone relies - to be the faithful bearers of the truth.

— Light —

An Oath

An oath which one gives is a species of the truth, indeed, the first definition of truth is fidelity, constancy. The oath which every federal representative of our democracy takes is unique, it derives from an obligation written into our Constitution in Article VI, clause 3: "*The Senators and Representatives before mentioned, and the Members of the several State Legislatures, and all executive and judicial Officers, both of the United States and of the several States, shall be bound by Oath or Affirmation, to support this Constitution.*" There is no ambiguity. The oath to be taken by representatives was written as the first act of the first Congress, as follows:

"*I, John Hancock, do solemnly swear or affirm (as the case may be) that I will support the Constitution of the United States.*"

The Oath of the President is an obligation demanded in Article II, Section One, Clause 8, of the Constitution and follows:

"*I do solemnly swear (or affirm) that I will faithfully execute the Office of President of the United States, and will to the best of my ability, preserve, protect and defend the Constitution of the United States.*"

There is no second Constitution, there is only one. It is as it was written in 1787, with its amendments applied over time. These oaths taken by the servants of the American people, every one of them, demands a fidelity to the Constitution. Webster's further defines an Oath as *a formal calling upon God to witness to the truth of what one says or to witness that one sincerely intends to do what one says*. Any servant of the people who has not faithfully supported the Constitution, has been derelict in their office regarding the first obligation of that office.

Every servant of the people makes an implied oath before the explicit one they take on entering office; they take one before their constituents in a pledge that they will do what they say they will do in office, they will faithfully espouse the policies they have defined their support for—as they have promised to their constituents. There is nothing more important in a representative government than the people's representatives truthfully representing the will of their voters. Persons are not sent to a representative government to represent themselves—they are given the honor of representing others, the folks back home.

— Shadow —

A Turncoat

He was the poster boy of the conservative party. He was the vice president to Dwight Eisenhower. He was the paragon of the Republicans. He was the definition of conservative, who promised to govern based on conservative principles. But he had a fatal flaw, one that plagues most members of humanity: he wanted to possess power, and once possessed by it, he would do anything to keep it, including not representing those who elected him and not following his oath of office. He was also a politician who craved to be liked by the media and respected by the Harvard grads among the Democrats. He wanted to be a member of their inner club. Richard Nixon was a tiger whose flaws changed his stripes.

When Richard Nixon assumed office in 1969, he very deliberately chose persons of both parties as his advisors. Rather than serve those who elected him, he sought a wider popularity which would guarantee, in his mind, continuation in office. Nixon began proclaiming his admiration for the architect of the Administrative State, Woodrow Wilson. The favorite of his new administration was Daniel Patrick Moynihan, one of the keystone builders of the Great Society. These signals and appointments alarmed his party and bewildered his constituents, who thought they knew whom they entrusted to barricade and turnabout a wildly growing government.

Moynihan came to spend more time with Nixon than any other advisor. Moynihan had Nixon's ear, telling him tales of the glorious history of Benjamin Disraeli, the conservative Tory who, by adopting liberal policies, became the beloved leader of his country. Moynihan's sincerity convinced Nixon that this could be his destiny. Rather than do what he was elected to do by his conservative constituency, which wanted to do away with the Great Society, Nixon determined to solidify the Great Society's foundations and attempt to expand its "benefits" to the middle class.

The media and democratic politicians cheered Nixon as he extended New Deal and Great Society programs, which the people of his party had elected him to eliminate. Nixon even kept the Office of Economic Opportunity and put one of the most liberal democrats in Washington at its head, Leonard Garment. The Republican Party wanted the OEO abolished. Nixon was delighting the media and the opposition party, who could not believe their luck that someone who was elected in a landslide to roll back the Great Society was reinforcing and extending it. It was as though Nixon sat at a poker table with key Democrats of his day, George McGovern and Hubert Humphrey, and when they proposed $10 billion in more spending on the Great Society as a bluff, Nixon did not call the bluff, but raised... to $20 billion.

Nixon and Moynihan did not merely wish to keep the dependent state, they crafted a Family Assistance Plan which would nationalize welfare and make it accessible to middle class working men and women throughout every part of the nation. The new reform would not cost a billion more, it would cost billions upon billions more and add thirteen million more people to the rolls of those eligible for federal government "benefits", aka government dependence. The frontier of government services was not receding as conservatives voted it should; it was expanding.

The foundations of the Great Society programs, which had failed even according to their creator Moynihan, were being solidified by a very useful ally: a Republican, at a crucial time in history, who turned into a liberal owing to his love of power. Moynihan told Nixon he thought the Great Society might finally succeed, if only welfare programs were expanded, pleading that this was "the moment to spend money for education, health, poverty, or whatever…and to hell with the details." Nixon said, "the present welfare system has to be judged a colossal failure." Therefore, it had to be enlarged.

Nixon's own party was of the opposite view. They considered the Great Society for what it was, an ever-expanding mechanism of wealth redistribution that was leading millions upon millions of people into a condition of absolute and permanent dependency on the federal government—the opposite of the American ideal of individual self-reliance and independence *from* government.

After much political wrangling, the Family Assistance Plan did not succeed in passing, because even the conservative Democrats in the Senate thought it went too far to a level commensurate with socialist European governments, and created too much dependency. It proposed redistribution of too much wealth. But this failure succeeded in another way—by keeping the failed programs of the Great Society in place. Nixon even lauded himself, exulting that government entitlements—meaning dependency payments—exceeded the entire cost of the military, in the middle of a war.

The costs of Great Society programs were taking an unprecedented toll on the economy. And it was not just the welfare programs draining the treasury; the Johnson administration had taken over a large swath of the health sector, with extensions of the Social Security Act to include Medicare and Medicaid, under titles XVIII and XIX, for funding medical services solely for the poor and the elderly who could not afford it. This partial takeover of another sector of the free enterprise system added a massive new bureaucracy and administration costs to the already bloated Administrative State. The world noticed.

Foreign nations were beginning to doubt America's fiscal strength as political policies were making the once-capitalist economy more socialist in nature by the day. The dollar was weakening as spending budgets were exploding. There was an unbalancing of the international monetary system. European and Asian nations began purchasing gold out of American vaults in response. Arthur Burns, the chairman of the Federal Reserve, warned that the normal "rules of economics are not working in quite the way they used to." He warned that the growth of government spending comparative to the nation's GDP had risen more in the past nine years than it had in the previous two hundred years combined, and the economy was in uncharted waters... The unemployment rate reached 6.1 percent, meaning there was excess labor in the marketplace. Yet prices were continuing to rise as the inflation rate reached 5.85 percent. An election was coming in a year—if Nixon was going to have a good economy by Election Day and ensure re-election, he had to act.

Nixon performed his next feat with the same objectives in mind as when he attempted to expand on LBJ's policies: he wanted to please the media, to gain the great regard of Democrats, and to stay in power through the approaching 1972 elections. To do so, Nixon used the same *modus operandi* he had before: he chose another leader of the Democratic Party, John Connally of Texas, a close colleague of LBJ, to be his treasury secretary, to the great alarm of everyone in his own party. He decided, as a Republican, to lead a further government intervention, like the Democrat Roosevelt had, into the United States economy with a force that startled the world.

Nixon convened a secret meeting with Connally and some of the nation's top economists at Camp David from August 13 to August15, 1971. The meeting dealt with a wish list that Connally had prepared for Nixon—a list which would deal with the exploding costs of the new economy. It was a liberal wish list that included delinking the dollar from the gold standard, by which every nation in the world had determined currency values since 1944, so the value of the dollar could "float" or devalue relative to competitor currencies. It included wage and price controls to stabilize the "new" value of the dollar. It included ceasing the sale of gold to foreign persons or governments. It included raising tariffs, through an entry tax on all imports of 10 percent, to bolster American trade.

The unilateral act of the Nixon administration was announced on a Sunday night, August 15, 1971, to the shock of his own party and the world. It was the first rise in tariffs in America since Herbert Hoover, and it was the first delinking of the dollar from gold since Roosevelt. It was the kind of government intrusion on the free market that Nixon had spent his whole career speaking against. It was an act of socialist economic planning which took the virtuous pricing found in a free-market system and replaced it with a federal review board dedicated to wage-price fixing.

Nixon's own party was struck by the arrogance of the act and the reasons why. It was all considered a political maneuver to bolster the economy before the election, to keep Nixon in power. It was considered the first act of a re-election campaign, in a move that did not serve the Republican party but was an answer to the growing costs of socialism - by actions that only socialist governments made, in direct contravention of capitalist principles. It was an attempt to dull the growing effects of socialism on the economy with acts of even more central socialist planning, more than any president had attempted before.

The venerable and respected British weekly, *The Spectator*, declared, "President Nixon, like (our own) Mr. Wilson, is turning socialist." The immediate impact of the policy did help get Nixon re-elected. But it helped that his opponent in 1972 was a person even more outwardly given to socialism than himself—George McGovern. Nixon could still speak in conservative terms.

The effects of the policy, which were not immediately apparent, were that this delinking from the gold standard has come to be considered by many to have created the monetary policy responsible for every economic bubble the US economy has suffered since 1971. The effects of Connally's wish list were also responsible for the runaway inflation of the 1970s and early 1980s.

Nixon set another precedent: he became the paradigm of the useful Republican. The Republican politician who gains office by voicing opposition to Democratic Party policy, only to go along with that policy when in office—it is the best opposition one can have; it only pretends to be a force of opposition. It is in reality a politics of betrayal which breaks one's oath to those who, in good faith and with their votes, oppose Democratic Party policy.

Since the 1930s, the Democratic Party has written the song of an ever-growing, ever more concentrated government: they determine the tonal key, the melody, the lyrics, and the chord progression. The Republican Party, if allowed to play at all, plays the minor chords and the contrapuntal notes, that provide just enough tension to fill out the song as they follow the Democratic lead. Many Republicans thrive in this role. If the Democratic party has done wrong in promoting ever more socialism, which is tyranny, the Republican party has been wrong in what it has failed to do: it has failed to stop the progression of socialism. It has failed to defend the Constitution; it has failed to serve its own constituency. These Republicans substantiate tyranny, by minimally opposing it, as tyranny gains strength incrementally and continuously.

Nixon got what he wanted. He won re-election, he even stooped to criminality to do so, setting up a break-in of Democratic Party headquarters at the Watergate Hotel. He should have spared himself the trouble, he should have just told the Democrats again what they knew already —that Nixon would betray his own constituency, that he would do whatever the Democrats wanted him to do. In the end, the media, whose love he courted, hated him. In the end, the Democratic Party, whose great regard he sought, reviled him. And the Republican Party which he pretended to serve and actually betrayed, cornered him into doing the right thing: retiring from office. Even in leaving, he proved, once again, to be the worst kind of Republican: the odium of his crime stuck to his party, becoming part of the brand. Richard Milhouse Nixon is to this day, by any measure, the best and most productive Democrat the Republican Party ever produced. He is the Democrat's idea of the gold standard for a Republican.

— Shadow —

The Changelings

Since before the Revolutionary War, the free press on this continent was always the first to respond to political wrongs acted out by government. At the time of our founding, it highlighted the wrongs committed by the British Empire against the lives, properties, or rights of the citizens that the press sought best to serve by publishing the truth. The *Boston Evening Post* and the *Massachusetts Gazette* marshalled the city of Boston to an awareness of British wrongs, which inspired the Boston Tea Party. The press chronicled the wrongful acts of King and Parliament, that the colonists would know how rightfully to respond. The press in America, at its best, was dedicated to espousing the truth, the concept of individual liberty and the rights of man. The press in the colonial period was a great defender of the rights of Englishmen, and later, the rights of Americans. The press supported every step of the advance of Constitutionalism.

The press can be a double-edged sword—a two-sided shield at times. The northern press was a great supporter of the abolitionist movement. But some of the press, even in the northern states, also harried and attempted to demoralize Abraham Lincoln on nearly every day that he was in office, never accounting his genius until the day he died.

As noted in Volume One of this series, newspapers in America served as political physicians, illuminating the causes and effects of political wrongs, and served as prescient to possible societal cures. In the main, journalism was alert to any wrong done by the government to a vulnerable citizen, whether it was a matter of life, or rights, or property. The press alerted the community to remind that, when it comes to having a common government, whether it is local, state, or federal, what occurs to one citizen can occur to every citizen. The press served, as did the institutions of faith, as a vital check on civil governance overreaching its rightful powers. When a government wrong was newsworthy, the press generally prescribed the recruitment of every intermediary power of society, whether the local government or the churches or community families or the business community, to take up the general cause against the agency or politician by whom the wrong was committed. The press protected the locals, rather like a shepherd would the flock from the powerful wolf: it chronicled the daily wrongs of government in order to hold politicians responsible and accountable to the people.

As time passed, technology changed the manner of delivery of the news. In the 1930s, one did not go to town anymore to get the newspaper, it was delivered. The radio started to broadcast news on an hourly basis. News became less a matter of local events and more a matter of national concerns. The major producers of radio programming were in New York, and the news, as the central government grew more and more by the day, was made in Washington, DC.

In the 1950s and 1960s, houses filled up with television sets. One could do more than just hear the news; one was guided through the news by a trusted news "Anchor." A familiar voice and face came into everyone's living room every evening after work. Never was the power of television more elaborately or meaningfully shown than on July 21, 1969, when every person in America watched images of Neil Armstrong making his first small step onto the surface of the moon. A whole world leaped.

Levying

The Truth

By the end of 1960s, the media acquired the power to bring the truth into every American living room, or to decide to bring falsehood. At the end of the tumultuous 1960s, just after the technological evolutions that enabled news to become available within every family's living room, attended by the truth's anchor, a strange thing began to occur: the truth began to blur.

Joseph Goebbels, the head of the Nazi Ministry of Public Enlightenment and Propaganda, famously wrote in his diary: "It would not be impossible to prove with sufficient repetition and a psychological understanding of the people concerned that a square is in fact a circle." In the late 1960s and early 70s, an example of the capabilities of the American media to shift the truth occurred. Though the Democratic Party had first involved the United States in the war in Vietnam, though Lyndon Johnson vastly expanded the war and therefore its casualties, and though the Democratic Party determined that the United States would lose the war—the Republican Party began to be blamed for the entire conflict. Responsibility was firmly placed, on a daily basis, on the Republican's shoulders by the media. After constant repetition on the evening news, of Republicans being to blame for the entire conflict, the blame stuck... and has to this day.

Another power began to be exercised by the media beginning at that time. It paralleled an ancient military axiom: the most important ability a general can possess is to make the many seem like few or to make the few appear to be many. One can thereby manipulate and maneuver a much larger enemy force to do one's own will. It is equally so in the case of the media directly effecting government policy. The small number of the media may use a small proportion of the population, through the manner whereby they describe and portray reality, to move the will of the nation. A camera lens and a reporter can make a hundred-person protest appear to be 100,000. Or make 250,000 appear to be 250. The truth can be manipulated by the editing.

Beginning at the pivotal point of the 1970s, continuing through today, by way of daytime programming and news reporting the media has continuously trumpeted our societies normal ills, which are to be found around any nation of our size, and magnified such problems until they become national portents of disaster. The problem reported may be of a meager kind, affecting very few people, or of an infinitesimal character, but according to national media outlets every single problem our nation has had for over fifty years has had only one prescribed solution—a new federal program, a new federal agency, and a vast new bureaucracy to extricate a painful thorn discovered on the pinky finger of a schoolboy in the back hills of Paducah, Kentucky.

By this blurring magnification of reality, the media magnifies its own importance into being the lords of the national oracle. This corrupt methodology has served to magnify, in real terms, the size and scope of the dependent and Administrative States, as the media determines the shape and scope of the truth and prescribes the invariably single cure of federal government intervention and growth for the sake of healing every single personal problem. The daily sensationalism of the media has become the federal government's perfect growth medium.

According to the media, the solution of getting a thorn out of a child's finger, no longer lies with an individual's self-reliance, nor with a family's support, nor with the inspiration of an institution of faith, nor with a private business addressing a need in the marketplace, nor with the swift response of a local governance. Only one solution will do: more money and more power funneled into Washington, DC, where an agency will fund hiring a hundred thousand new federal employees and spend billions of dollars for some union plant to produce hedge clippers for the removal of a 12-penny nail from the foot of an eighty-year-old farmer in Winnett, Montana.

Such is our media, since 1970, upon whom every citizen must rely for the single most important foundation on which a democracy relies for its best decision making—the unmanipulated truth.

Since the same point in time, the media began using another power, one known from ancient times as well: the strategy of the hounds to the hunters for flushing out a quarry of foxes. Richard Nixon was a sly fox indeed. He attempted to be the best liberal democrat, the best proponent for government growth, any American era ever produced and be a Republican too, in order that he might secure to himself the most power. The media began to sense its own power as it scented an opportunity to do something without precedent in American history: to drive an elected president from office.

It began with two reporters and one leak within Nixon's administration. The story grew every evening as it led off the TV news programs, and every morning filled the front pages of every city newspaper. A crime was committed. A cover-up existed. And for two years, the hounds drove their quarry, Richard M. Nixon, to the hunters of a certain end. Nothing untoward—the sly fox Nixon deserved his end.

What the media discovered by the resignation of Nixon was the power it possessed when it acted together simultaneously and sought to hunt someone down, even a president. That is a very dangerous power to possess in a democracy, it tempts the media to act as a herd, based on taking down a target rather than on upholding the truth.

The phrase could not say it better: *there is only one truth - there is no substitute*. The health of ours or any democracy relies on it. Those who do not relate the simple truth do our nation and everyone in it a grave harm. Just as the definition and dissemination of truth in a democracy is its greatest power for good, there is an equal, opposite evil power a democracy will suffer by the creation of falsehoods.

And certain questions arise within the penumbra of these shadows of falsehood, with regard to the truth. If the media, whose sole devotion ostensibly should be the transmission of the truth in the service of the American people, instead purvey falsehoods, whom do they serve? Is it their own power? If politicians are elected and given office based on the promise of serving the people as their representatives and to protect the Constitution, but instead do not represent their constituents nor protect the Constitution, whom do they serve? Is it their own power? The odds are fairly sure that the answer has to do with serving themselves. This disservice to the American people and the Constitution, comes not only at the people's expense, but it comes at the graver cost of national misgovernance.

— Along the American Road...with the Band —

From 1965 to 1975, the artistry within American society exploded with variety. Bright colors, flowers, and paisley decorations adorned everything from jewelry to clothing, to housing, to the cars people were driving. The artistic soul of the country was reaching out through various colorful forms of beauty. It was a rebellion against the formal black, white, and grey backgrounds of the 1950s.

No artistic field spawned more novel creations than that of music during the era. Though country music was still coming out of Nashville, folk music was pouring out of Greenwich Village, NY. Blues was rising out of smokey bar rooms of Chicago and through Chess Records. Soul music and R&B was rolling out of Detroit and Motown. Southern Rock was being born in Macon, Georgia. And a new, self-revelatory style of acoustic music was ascending the clouds above Laurel Canyon in LA. There were many more forms of music than just these pulsating over the nation's radios, lest we forget Brian Wilson, Burt Bacharach, or Jimmy Webb.

People gathered by the thousands at music festivals all around the country, such as the Newport Jazz Festival, which was dominated by folk music or the Gathering of the Tribes in San Francisco, largely given to psychedelic music or the festival in Monterey which featured a heavy dose of rock and roll. And, of course, Woodstock which had artists who came with it all, from Santana to Country Joe. Most of the music that was played, all of the hundreds of songs sounded with a common lyrical feature: they were songs of rebellion.

Rebellion was the dominant mood of the nation, visible on university campuses nationwide in administration take-overs and sit-ins. Every uprising, like the songs, had a common theme: No more government, no more bureaucrats, above all, NO MORE establishment! The establishment was the campus administration, the establishment was made up of the leaders of industry, the establishment was the federal government. The counter-culture was led by an ever-expanding circle of fire comprised of artists who demanded that the government establishment get off their backs and out of every aspect of their lives. It was a profoundly American movement.

Then a strange thing happened, again. An entire generation was convinced that the political party that created, ruled, and metastasized the federal establishment throughout our society, was actually the same party that represented its opposite, the freedom aspired to by the counter-culture. The owners of the establishment, the Democratic Party, credited themselves as rebels who were fighting *against* their own establishment. The Party marketed itself as if on the front lines fighting against an establishment which they were in fact furiously building off camera.

This one generation, in reality, witnessed the greatest expansion of a governmental establishment in the history of the world. The generation which wanted absolutely nothing to do with government, has since voted perennially for the the federal establishment's expansion into every crevice of our societal existence. It tells you something about the marketing power of the establishment—it was able to turn a fiery circle of rebel artists, and their whole generation, into a square...

This generation can still prove itself revolutionary, in keeping with the country's founding, if it would vote like a perennial rebel, to have the now omnipresent establishment - dismantled.

A Little Levy

Conclusion

Thus, we have recounted how were laid the foundations of the administrative and dependent States:

It began with Theodore Roosevelt, in a landless capital, seizing lands in thirty-eight states, marking the first imperial presidency, and greatly expanding the arbitrary power of the Executive office over the states and industry. Theodore Roosevelt expanded the territory of the federal tiger and roared sufficient to be heard east to west, along the rails from the Atlantic to the Pacific and south to Panama. It continued with Woodrow Wilson, elaborating the philosophy of the Administrative State based on Hegel's German State Theory. This furthering of federal empowerment effected the bursting of constitutional barricades erected by the Founders, subordinating the states out of their "proper, practical relations to the Union" as Lincoln so eloquently put it. One of the last acts of Lincoln's life—what he gave his life for—was to restore the proper role of the states within the Union at the end of the Civil War. Wilson broke those constitutional barricades and left the federal authority fewer barricades to overrun. Wilson set the foundations of the Administrative State by building its first administrative agencies, whereby the federal tiger developed progeny in the form of federal offices to carry out national policy in every state; setting the footholds for a central government's exponential growth.

Wilson's precedents of national agency building were taken up by Franklin Delano Roosevelt, who expanded upon it until his administration had created so many agencies that they used every letter in the alphabet as acronyms to signify the state's new powers, each of which were calculated as an invasion of the country's economic life—including the takeover of a whole industry of the economy via the Tennessee Valley Authority.

FDR took another unprecedented step whereby at the end of his administration, he proposed a second bill of rights, which turned our original Bill of Rights upside down, affording a Bill of Entry for the federal authority into every aspect of our lives to provide for every citizen's happiness by whatever means government deems necessary, including the regular invasion of property rights. Thus, the territoriality of the government state became one without bounds. Roosevelt, thereby, set the foundations for the Great Society and the Dependent States.

Lyndon Johnson took Roosevelt's foundations and extended the federal reach into areas of each citizen's personal sphere of power, which no American government authority was ever supposed to breach, levelling the original powers of whole populations for their stated benefit. This is the rationale of the greatest expression of the nature of our federal tiger: for our benefit it may assume, when it wills, absolute power over every aspect of a citizen's life, taking property from whomever it wishes and giving it to whomever it wills, while taking *our* powers and wealth unto itself. To pay for the ever growing benefits that provide for one population's dependency, a measure of another population's freedom and self-reliance were taken via ever-expanding confiscatory and progressive tax policies of the federal government, thereby assuring our federal tiger a boundless food supply and a limitless scope of power.

It was forewarned centuries ago, before the Revolutionary War, in a publication of *Cato's Letters* that: "It is natural for power to be striving to enlarge itself, and to be encroaching upon those who have none." The nature of power has proved true. The powers levied have been in one direction: to the central government and to one branch therein, the executive. The fundamental changes in how we are governed have been so profound as to levy what the term *federal* means in our system.

How much has our central government's power grown? How far has the tiger assumed new territory? How many children has the tiger produced? How much wealth does the government and its progeny consume? How large and how strong is this tiger?

The Dependent States

The Great Society began as a war to eradicate poverty from small, distinct neighborhoods of inner cities and from small, rural pockets here and there in the countryside, such as remote, rural areas of Appalachia. The system was nationalized by the expansion of the Aid to Dependent Children Act, and the creation of the Food Stamp Act of 1964 and the Child Nutrition Act of 1966, which have come to be known as TANF and SNAP. The Social Security Administration was expanded into Supplemental Security Income (SSI), which has become the nation's largest welfare system. The number of persons who now receive welfare every month is estimated to be fifty-nine million. The number of persons on assistance through the above programs is sixty-eight million—which equals 21.3 percent of the population. Outside of these programs, 184 other welfare programs have been created, on which citizens are said to be dependent, which brings the overall dependent population, or those taking some form of benefits from the government, nearer to 50 percent. As of today, the number of persons receiving food stamps exceeds the population of twenty-five of the individual United States... combined.

When the war on poverty began, using the broadly expanded definitions that LBJ, Robert Lampman, and Michael Harrington invented to categorize what poor was, thirty-five million Americans were described as poor. That was the number that the war on poverty was supposed to convert to zero. After sixty years, and the redistribution of $22 trillion of wealth, and the creation of an ever-growing cascade of programs, the number of people on direct welfare programs has doubled and the number of persons receiving some form of government-assisted benefit has multiplied to many times that number. What a successful war, this war on poverty...

There are some curious anomalies in the welfare system, which has become one of *institutionalized* dependency, and it is the inverse of what one finds in an efficient economic system such as capitalism. If success is deemed to be getting people *out* of poverty, people in administrative offices who dispense money to the poor are rewarded for failure. The more people come into federal poverty programs, the more administrators and their employees are rewarded. When such an agency makes up a budget, they are not rewarded for reducing costs, they are rewarded only if their costs increase. A federal program is only deemed important if it expands, not if it succeeds in contracting the numbers of dependents. The more dependents an agency assumes, the greater the power of the administrator, the more employees an agency employs, the more wealth the agency gains. That is a federal agencies' profit motive—that is the measure of their success.

The success of dependency agencies, therefore, is the taxpayer's failure, for it is based on an ever-growing number of people being regarded as and made dependent, while those who are not dependent pay ever greater sums for the more than sixty-eight million persons who are directly dependent.

Yet, there are more dependents than appear in the above numbers. There is the dependency of the population who take stipends, of whatever form, from the taxpayer through the government; then there are the persons who administrate and work in the offices that redistribute the funds; then there are lobbyists and law firms that determine what money goes where. And finally, there is the political party, which depends on those who are dependent on or employed by the agencies. The political party is dependent on the dependent—to maintain their own power. It is in the interest of that particular political party, and those agencies, that this war on poverty is never won, that it goes on forever. Their wealth and power depend on it. It is in the vital interest of dependent state employees that the number of dependents in America and "in the system" always goes up. For this perpetual war is also a particular political party's means of exercising an iron grip on perpetual power.

In Mk 14:7, Christ reminds us: *For ye have the poor with you always...* In America, where dependency has been institutionalized, we have a political party that literally counts on it—on the poor being poor, always. This is what one can expect when government takes over the charitable offices of the institutions of faith, which had helped the poor *out* of poverty for 175 years of our history. It is what we can expect to happen when government takes over the offices once performed by families. It is what happens when government levels neighborhoods, schools, and churches and assumes control to itself. It is what we can expect to happen when government cripples the self-reliance of individuals, because as poor dependents, they are a political asset. It is what happens when government seeks to maintain poverty at the poor's expense, and everybody else's.

Let us look at the other side of the equation. In America today, there are just 125.3 million individuals who pay income taxes which fund the federal agencies. When we add the fact that taxpayers directly support sixty-eight million dependents in the country, in addition to the entirety of the country's government employees—a total of another 22.8 million persons, we reach a population of nearly ninety-one million people in the country being supported by only 125.3 million taxpayers. It, therefore, appears to the author that the citizens who pay taxes support themselves, and their spouses, and their children, and their schools, and their churches, and their businesses, and their employees, and their community charities, in addition to paying for every person who is dependent on government and for every government employee—that is a massive and grotesquely unjust tax burden on every taxpayer.

In 1902, the total cost of local, state, and federal government equated to 7 percent of the nation's Gross Domestic Product. Today when we add the local, state, and federal governments together, which only tax-paying citizens of this country presently pay for, the amount of expense is 45.8 percent of the total Gross Domestic Product of this country or roughly $10.2 trillion. When translated, this means that out of the entire wealth that every working person in this nation produces annually, fully half of it is spent on or through government. It also means that every taxpayer works half the year, from January to June, just to pay for government's grotesque burden. While those who pay no taxes at all have an inverse view of government: if all that government does is benefit you, you'll want nothing more than more government...which is exactly how one political party in America wants it.

Even so, with all this wealth being seized from taxpayers, our federal government cannot contain itself at this astronomical cost. As of today, our federal debt alone is over $30 trillion, which is a debt owed by every *taxpayer* of $226,000.

When we total all the debts of localities, states, and the federal government, along with its unfunded liabilities, every *individual* today out of a population of 330 million owes a debt of $444,729. While, if we add all the assets of the population and divide them among every individual, each person would have assets equaling just $487,541. If we do as some in Washington, DC, wish we would and redistribute every dime of wealth in America, every citizen and the country as a whole, would be as flat broke as Venezuela. But we do have some luck, for we now have a means of guessing the size of our federal tiger—its size can be estimated by the infinite enormity of its intake of wealth and by the sheer weight of each citizen's astronomical debt. It can also be measured by the extent of its economic reach into our society...

The Adminstrative State

Let us now turn from the Dependent States to the Administrative State. How far into our common economy has our tiger ventured? How far has the Administrative State grown? It will be remembered that Theodore Roosevelt brought under government control the largest industry of his day when he broke up the railroad companies.

It will also be remembered that Franklin Roosevelt literally invaded the next big financial star on the free enterprise horizon when he broke the Commonwealth & Southern Company and its shareholders, as well as every other utility company that once served the people in the southeastern United States as investments, as employers, and as utility providers. So, where thrives the tiger in our economy today? How far has federal control spread into our once-free enterprise system? Who, again, pays the price of this government ownership and control?

The Administrative State has been extremely active in its proliferation since its founding one hundred years ago. There are now over four hundred federal agencies, each of them busy in expanding its own power base. Each of the over four hundred agencies work to expand its number of employees, to expand its expense budget, and expand its territory. Since the beginning of the Administrative State, its favorite territory has been the economy: that is where the money is. That is where the power is. Not coincidentally, our once-free enterprise system has been the Administrative State's, and the media's, scapegoat for every economic calamity in our society since the Great Depression. A depression created, deepened, widened, lengthened, and made "Great" not by a failure of free enterprise, but by government's invasions of the free enterprise system. Every calamity in our economy since has been from similar government perversions of the marketplace. To add injury to injury, when foreseeable financial bubbles burst, the very government which creates economic calamity, engages in further invasions it deems "necessary."

Such invasions follow a pattern. A small proportion of the population are said to be underserved by the free marketplace, just as was claimed about the people of the Tennessee River Valley where the private economy was actively and regularly expanding until it was attacked and overtaken by the Roosevelt administration. Then there is a government study and biased statistics are produced to favor government's argument. A sensational media barrage follows, demanding the need for an immediate government intervention, which *may* only be temporary, and *will not* cost the taxpayer much—in fact, the effort may pay for itself. What is said to be certain is that there is no time to solve the problem through the private marketplace. A massive government agency is necessary, so it is built and placed within an economic sector. In America, some sectors for these invasions are the health sector, the housing and home mortgage sector, the student loan sector, and the energy sector, to name few.

The moment government enters a sector, the economic dynamic changes. There ceases to be a competitive relationship between relatively equal competitors on that economic field. From that point, the invaded marketplace turns into an ecosystem of one predator—the federal tiger—and a field of prey. Some of the prey will stand opposed and fight the predator; and like Commonwealth & Southern during the Roosevelt years, they will be consumed. Others will join the tiger in a predatory pack allying themselves with government—endorsing and applauding Administrative State policies enthusiastically… to survive. And they will subsist —while they are useful.

In addition to regulations, a targeted sectors private enterprise companies come under the proverbial microscope, firstly by the Internal Revenue Service through audits and investigations to weaken so called "bad actors"—or "the prey"—in the private economy. Remember, the Adminstrative State has infinite resources and staying power; it has resources supplied by every taxpayer and company, including the taxes paid by the companies it attacks. The state has the collaborative power among its agencies to win any litigation. Or if they lose, the Administrative State will simply bring another investigation and another charge. Each taxpayer and every private enterprise pays for these attacks on our free-enterprise system—for the regulations, for the investigations, and for the litigations made by the Administrative State; as well as the expenses necessarily paid by private enterprises for the adaptations and defenses necessary to confront the ambitions of a self-interested government.

Let us look at a few examples of the sectors which have been invaded. Take the housing industry and Fannie and Freddie Mac—the massive home mortgage agencies. A political party policy was espoused, to make home ownership more affordable, which launched a regulatory strategy which forced financial competitors in the home mortgage sector, through administrative law, to create home mortgages on unstable terms with financially unstable clients. This arbitrary policy was contrary to industry standards of historical standing, which were necessary for market stability. Meanwhile, the kindred Securities and Exchange Commission kept interbank rates at unrealistically low levels, which drove housing speculation, housing demand, and housing prices up meteorically from 2000 to 2007. The bad mortgages were packaged in bundles and spread throughout the financial marketplace, which created the conditions surrounding the economic crash of 2008, and drove much of Fannie and Freddie Mac's home mortgage competition the "bad actors" out of business. The only survivors were the institutions that the Administrative State allowed to survive.

That crash affected not only the home mortgage industry, it threatened the financial structure of the country and did financial injury to every single American in the fallout zone of the arbitrary, politically driven policies. Meanwhile the government entities Fannie and Freddie Mac's portfolios were expanded and the SEC, which helped cause the crash in the first place, was given greater power. Fannie and Freddie Mac now underwrite 90 percent of the home mortgage industry, that is nine out of every ten mortgages written in America today. The Administrative State controls those mortgages; it also determines mortgage rates. A great number of home buyers in America are, thereby, *dependent* on government for the roof over their head. Another way to view the Administrative State's control of the home mortgage industry is that we are all just renters of property ultimately owned by the State: which is becoming America's universal landlord.

The government always enters a sector, with the assurance, of being 'helpful in a necessary situation.' Financing is always an easy means for the entry of government into an economic sector through an agency. They have more access to money than anybody because the government's money *was* ours. Let us take the example of financing student loans for higher education, one political party launched a policy drive to 'make education more affordable.' Getting a loan for one's son or daughter used to be a transaction between a family, a neighborhood bank, and an educational institution. It was one of the proudest moments in a family's life: earning the credit, receiving a loan, and making the financial commitment to send a family member to a university in hopes of expanding that person's opportunities. Then the government *had* to intervene in the student loan market, promising to make the costs 'more affordable.' This intervention, this invasion, of the student loan industry, has actually brought about meteoric increases in the costs of education, as government has assumed more of the student loan marketplace. With government as a financial partner, universities have raised tuition and residency prices and every related expense of education across the country, doubling, tripling, quadrupling the costs of an education until few can afford a higher education *without* the government. There is no need to worry about the universities, they can count on the money—their partner, the government, guarantees it. The problem is with those American families who have nowhere else to go for the loan: it is now a massive family or personal expense… it has become one of the largest expenses in the average American's lifetime. The Administrative State, on its mission to make higher education more affordable, has made it unaffordable. And again, the citizen becomes *dependent* on government; if a family wants to put a family member through college, there are fewer choices of institutions which fund college and the costs are far, far, higher than they would be in a normal marketplace.

Financing higher education has a particular side benefit for a government. There is an adage from ancient Greece, as true today as it was two thousand years ago: "To wealth all things together are obedient." Such a paymaster as our government has become over the universities will, sooner or later, influence university curriculums. In so far as money that funds our university system comes mainly from a central government, the university system runs the risk of being centrally influenced. The independence of our educational institutions and the university system was the glory of American society, since the 1630's.

Today, the Administrative State underwrites 100% of the student loan industry, totalling $1.6 trillion.

In the health care sector, Medicare and Medicaid were specifically created to help the relatively small populations of the poor and elderly: to 'make healthcare more affordable.' From that beach head, government has invaded the health and pharmaceutical sectors of the economy. Due to the massive bureaucracy and regulation of the industry; due to government's guaranteed payments to providers it approves; due to litigation against providers the federal government does not approve—the costs of healthcare have spiraled to the point of being, yet again, unaffordable. Meanwhile, the Department of Health and Human Services makes the rules as to what treatments are approved, who gets what treatments, who gets reimbursed and in what amounts. The central influence on the industry of HHS policy has so perverted the marketplace that nobody knows what the real costs of healthcare are anymore.

In America today, a citizen turning sixty-five years of age, who is not independently wealthy, *must* abandon their private insurance plan and *must* join the federally controlled Medicare Health system. The government *allows* a citizen to choose between five supplementary plans which expands a little, the bureaucratically dictated choices of physicians and hospitals. A government agency created to benefit only the few poor and elderly who could not afford health insurance is becoming the only insurance allowed by the government, at a time of life when the citizen needs healthcare the most.

The Administrative State is not a disinterested competitor in economic sectors, it has a self -interested ambition to succeed against its competitors. Healthcare represents 17 percent of our Gross National Product. The ambition of Administrative State is to own and control as much as it can of the sector. Then the State—

as the universal paymaster to which all things together must be obedient—will control who gets care, who gets *what* care, and who gets *no* care. The Administrative State's ambition is to make citizens *dependent* on government for the most personal service in their lives: the care of their life. Then one's healthcare *will not* be decided by doctors who abide the Hippocratic Oath; the service you need and the care you receive will be decided and rationed by bureaucrats whom no one knows, whom no one votes for, whom no one can argue with, and whom no one can fire.

In 2022, we have another real-time example of the Administrative State's predatory pattern in action. It is occurring in the energy sector, on which everyone depends for light, heat, transport... and everything else. The energy sector comprises 8 percent of the nation's Gross Domestic Product, upon which the other 92 percent of the economy directly depends to function. To control the energy sector is to control the economy, as it can be a conduit to placing indirect taxes on every product and service ordinary people use every day. Career Administrative State regulators know exactly what this wealth and power represents; they know how much it means. This single, vital economic sector influences the costs and prices of everything, through control of this sector, the government can tax and, therefore, control human behavior. Elements of our government are determined to universally control the sector.

The premise for which the government *must* take control is that the average temperature of Earth's atmosphere has risen 1.1 degree since the 1,800's. It is contended, but is *unproven*, that this can only have occurred by the burning of fossil fuels... It cannot be because our sole source of heat is the Sun, which is 92,955,828 miles away. It cannot be because the Earth spins at a velocity of 1,000 miles per hour or because Earth rotates around the Sun at 67,000 miles per hour or because our galaxy is careering through the universe at 490,000 miles per hour. With all this motion, the Earth, of course, has not moved one inch nearer the Sun... No, the temperature must have increased a single degree over the past century because the Administrative State does not entirely control the most vital sector of the U.S. economy.

A marketing campaign began some time ago to suggest that an oncoming apocalypse can only be averted if the Administrative State seizes another 8 percent of our economy. It began in earnest with Al Gore's production of *An Inconvenient Truth* in 2006. In the documentary, Gore claimed that based on scientific research it was evident that global temperatures were rising, that as a consequence, the North Pole and Antarctica would melt. And that the melting of ice off Greenland would shift the North Atlantic Gulf Stream current.

Gore predicted that within a decade, there would be no more snow in Kilimanjaro and parts of a consistently sinking Florida would be underwater. Lastly, the occurrences of hurricanes, typhoons, tornadoes, floods and droughts would be increasing in frequency and severity. The threat is immediate and it is planetary. And...there is no exit. Do you feel cornered yet?

The only solution? A government invasion and seizure of another economic sector.

There are several inconvenient truths...Satellite measured temperature data, outside of the recent El Nino current, has shown no significant warming has occurred for the last twenty years. The Kilimanjaro's northern ice field is still 131 feet deep. A Kilimanjaro National Park ecologist, Imani Kikoti stated, that though studies are being carried out "preliminary findings show that the ice is nowhere near melting." The North Pole and Antarctica are still icebound too; so is Greenland.

Australian scientists studying the North Atlantic Gulf Stream have affirmed that the current is not weakening, that "claims of strengthening or weakening of the AMOC are...pure speculation. And since 2006, hurricane, typhoon and tornado frequency has decreased... As to Florida, a National Snow and Ice Data Center scientist, Ted Scambos, has stated that if Florida is ever to sink, "this will take centuries [Gore's] model was the most pessimistic." No kidding.

This is pessimistic: on January 21, 2019, Anastasia Ocasio Cortez, a leader of the Socialist wing of the Democratic Party stated unequivocally: "The world is going to end in 12 years if we don't address climate change, and your biggest issue is how are we gonna pay for it?" For government's interference in the energy market, on the way to seizure of the energy sector, every one of us is going to pay for it in wealth and liberty.

The Administrative State already determines where energy companies can and can't mine for resources; it already heavily regulates fossil fuel companies, the IRS already audits them, and the Justice Department investigates them and we, the consumers, pay for the innumerable regulations, indiscriminate audits and investigations, because the costs to energy companies to defend themselves are passed on to the consumer.

On the other hand, if you are an alternative energy company, in favor with the Administrative State, your firm will be given research grants, subsidies, government financing and tax breaks, which are paid for by the taxes, again, paid by every taxpayer.

This invasion of the energy sector will cost everyone more than just higher prices for every product and service effected by energy costs going up. It will cost more than just in the tax levies necessary to destroy one member of an economic sector in favor of another. It will cost everyone with regard to the liberty they lose to make choices. With the takeover of the energy sector, the Administrative State will determine what kind of car you *must* drive, what batteries you *must* buy, what electrical system you *must* have in your home, how warm or cool your house *must* be, and what light bulbs you *must* use, after all, it will be administrative law. Administrative law that no one ever votes on, administrative law that is administered by bureaucrats that no one can argue with and that no one can fire.

It goes further: the State will determine how much every private business in America that uses energy (and that is every company in America) *must* spend on retrofitting plants and equipment to meet new regulations, which, of course, will benefit the chosen, licensed unionized vendors of the State. Of course, these licensed friends of the state will be given the government contracts to retrofit government buildings – at the taxpayer's expense.

Just as the pattern of the invasion, destruction, and assumption of the market in industrial sectors by the Administrative State are the same, so are the effects. Taxes are raised nationwide to support a new policy and new agencies. Costs to every consumer for every product and service rise within the invaded sector. The number of free enterprises within the sector go from many operating in an efficient, low-cost marketplace, to a few operating in a perverted marketplace, in which prices are highly inflated by governmental meddling. The marketplace then becomes quasi government-owned and controlled in which nothing is affordable (without more government control.) Then the kinds of goods and the quantity of services, who receives them, and what they cost become determined by government bureaucrats. And finally, the number of choices a consumer has is reduced to one: A very expensive government service or product... or one that is prohibitively expensive. Then the once-free, normal consumer becomes the *subject* of government provision. Then you and I, citizens, assume a new position, because,

"The lowest form of living,
Is having no choice"

America (The Band)

When I approached having to research this section of the book, I was bewildered. How does one quantify what the Administrative State controls in our economy today? I started at ground level and below, with mining. It turns out the Administrative State now "owns" 28 percent of the United States' land mass (not to mention how much the State owns as the underwriter of 90 percent of all the housing loans in the nation). Pretty nice sum, having grown from the ten-by-ten square miles of land agreed to by Jefferson, Hamilton, and Madison as the limit of the national government's landless existence, designed by the founders. Today's Administrative State determines who gets the leases and who gets the mining rights to the resources on every square inch of that land. Thereby, the Administrative State alone determines who mines what and where. That is just what the federal government owns that effects the mining sector. They control the rest of the mining industry through the EPA, the Army Corps of Engineers and the Department of the Interior.

I was struck by the reality that I might need a hundred years to detail how much ownership and control the government exercises in our economy. So, I turned to a friend of mine, a neighbor, an accomplished investment analyst. I thought to ask what research institutes I might go to, to quantify how many sectors and businesses the Administrative State owns or controls. How does one quantify to what degree private enterprises are controlled when government is active in a sector or just one that is affected by the sector? I had thought of how in-depth this study had to be: the idea is daunting. My neighbor responded, saying it was not really complicated, the answer was short and simple: In our economy today, the government controls everything. Government does not need to own every sector of the economy to control the whole economy. It has only to own the more vital sectors, like finance, health, and energy, and regulate the rest. Government does not need to own something to control it - that they can do through administrative regulation. What is sure as the sunrise, with every sunrise, the Administrative State keeps assuming more control of the remains of our free enterprise system.

With regard to our expanding Administrative State involving itself in a democracy's economy, there was a phrasing by Thomas Paine, one of our founders at the time of the Revolutionary War, which bespoke the colonial frustration over England's growing control of the economy in the 1770s:

"We still find the greedy hand of government thrusting itself into every corner and crevice of industry and grasping the spoil of the multitude. Invention is continually exercised, to furnish new pretenses for revenue and taxation. It watches prosperity as its prey and permits none to escape without a tribute."

While, in the *Wall Street Journal's* June 21, 2021, edition this passage appeared in an article by Kim Strassel:

"In his first 100 days in office, Mr. (President) Biden signed more than 60 executive actions, many sweeping in character. His regulatory agencies, under the guise of preventing climate change,

are ramping up to run nearly every sector of the economy by executive fiat."

In an ever-changing world, one can count on one constant: the foreseeable pattern of a tyranny.

Going back to our ever-expanding dependent state, creating ever more dependency, a near contemporary of Paine's, Alexander Fraser Tytler, took pen to paper to describe how, over time, democracies change and end up looting the wealth of their citizenry, transforming their form of governance into tyranny. And why democracies, if not defended in terms of respect for the law and the rights of property, are bound for a very certain demise:

"A democracy cannot exist as a permanent form of government. It can only exist until the voters discover that they can vote themselves largesse from the public treasury. From that moment on, the majority always votes for the candidates promising the most benefits from the public treasury with the result that a democracy always collapses over loose fiscal policy followed by a dictatorship. The average age of the world's greatest (democratic) civilizations has been 200 years."

Today, the United States is more than 230 years old. Tytler further wrote that the lifespan of history's infrequent but glorious democracies follow a certain cycle, proceeding from tyranny's *"bondage to Spiritual Faith to Great Courage to Liberty to Abundance to Selfishness to Complacency to Apathy to Dependency and back into (the) Bondage..."* of tyranny.

This begs the question, fellow citizens: what part of the cycle do you believe we are in?

Of we citizens, who are said to rule ourselves, this one has a question: how much wealth will the dependent state redistribute and take for itself and its clients? How much will this Dependent State grow at everyone's expense, rich and poor? Will the Dependent State ever be content with the wealth and power it has gorged? When will the Dependent State stop? When will the Dependent State stop consuming our nation's wealth and liberty and stop converting it into the continuous expansion of its own centralized power?

Of we citizens, who are said to rule ourselves, this one has one other question: how many private enterprises will be destroyed? How many industrial sectors will be taken over before the Administrative State is content with the hoard of wealth and power it has confiscated from our economy? When will the Administrative State stop? When will the state stop consuming our nation's wealth and liberty and stop converting it into the continuous expansion of its own centralized power?

The State

The answer to both questions is a common one, the State, this composition of the administrative and dependent states, will never stop of its own will. For it shares the nature of the tiger. The State is a creature of power, and such creatures never divest themselves freely of power—ever.

This State will not stop until it is forced to stop with what remains of the nation's democratic processes. They are the sacred legacy of our Constitution—the democratic process. This tiger must be voted back behind the sensible barricades by which our nation was framed. It will require a century of brave generations who believe in our nation's original purpose—liberty for all. It will require generations who believe in the uncompromised structure and processes of a real democracy that promotes and defends every citizen's property and liberty—equally. Or our government will proceed on its arbitrary way into being a tyranny.

There may be readers who wonder what harm there can be in allowing our benevolent federal government to grow further? To that question, our own history provides the answer: What is wrong with a vigorous central power, which operates in a distant capital, that is unanswerable to the people, which taxes ever more wealth, which demands ever more of everyone's liberty, and which has no respect for the Constitution of our laws? I state to you, fellow citizens, that these are the very reasons for which our Revolutionary War was fought.

– Darkness –

The New Circle Of Power

Over the past century, there has been one subtle and one dramatic shift of power away from our Constitutional moorings. Power in America, upon a time, emanated from each individual and flowed outward into and through a vast number of intermediary powers, by way of what I termed the "American Arch" in Volume One. When this Arch is conceived horizontally, it forms the cornerstones of each individual's original ring of power. In this recounting of the levies of power, which mark the growth of the State, there is a common pattern. As the State has grown, federal levies have subtly removed from power the intermediary entities that created the glory of our democracy, built upon and around the individual and every individual's natural rights.

The diffused light of these intermediary powers of families and faiths, enterprises and industries, associations and trades, localities and states, once the glory of our democracy, once a defensive ring around each individual—have been driven steadily, inexorably out of power, while the single State casts an ever-expanding shadow of a monopolistic dominion over every aspect of our society making each individual subject to a new, centralized circle of power emanating out of the distant capital of Washington, DC. Our government has assumed a dark tendency over the past hundred years in keeping with tyrannies around the world: tyrannical governments do not suffer the barricades of intermediary powers; a tyrannical government assumes those intermediary powers for its own use, to penetrate the natural rights of every individual.

The more dramatic shift of power regards the extent to which we citizens are represented in the decision-making processes of our governance. America was originally designed as a direct democracy locally and a representative republic at the state and federal levels. It was constitutionally designed that each citizen was to be represented at every level of government wherein laws were made; that each citizen's voice or the voice of their representative would be heard before the passage of any law, at any level. This book has chronicled how and why power has been levied up and away from every local and state authority to the federal level of government where every citizen is represented *least*.

At the federal level, this book has further chronicled how the executive branch alone now produces more administrative law, via agencies it controls, than the legislative branch does as the Representative House of the people. Alexander Hamilton termed the Legislature of the United States the "Original Fountain of all just authority." For one hundred years, the executive branch of the federal government has levied power from the representative legislature of our government into a bureaucratic State which is unanswerable to the people and increasingly unanswerable to the people's representatives. Our representative legislature has become little more than a rubber stamp for the State's ever-expanding budget. Our legislature has become little more than the State's ineffectual complaint department.

The Constitution defined the Executive's role as that of Commander in Chief, out of which rightly grew the Departments of Defense, State, and Veteran's Affairs. The Executive office is also consigned the responsibility of taking care that the laws (passed by the legislature) be faithfully executed, out of which grew the Departments of Justice and latterly, of Homeland Security. That is the extent of the executive branches' authority as detailed in the Constitution, along with the naming of federal officers, ambassadors, and judges in conjunction with the approval of the Senate.

The executive branch of our government was never constitutionally assigned the roles of chief economist, or chief housing officer or chief of labor or the chief of human development or chief health giver or chief provider of happiness, or chief hand holder… these and a hundred other new roles of the Presidency now inhabit within the executive branch; all of them invented since 1920. This shift has concentrated power within that branch, and among the over four hundred departments and agencies writhing for power under the Executive Branch's umbrella.

I wish to take the reader back to Eisenhower's warning in his Farewell Address, about the Military-Industrial Complex, that, "we have been compelled to create a permanent armaments industry of vast proportions." Indeed, to fulfill the first role of the Executive as Commander-in-Chief, and as part of the Department of Defense, an armaments industry is vitally necessary. However, in the case of these other departments and agencies, there is and was no necessity. These invented departments have nothing to do with the Constitution's role of the Executive. This arrangement is utterly contrary to the Constitution's definition of the limited role of the Executive and of government. Nevertheless, to again paraphrase Eisenhower: these invented departments have, exactly like the Defense Department, "brought in millions of men and women directly engaged in the…establishment." Thus, Eisenhower's further warning applies: "We must not fail to comprehend its grave implications. Our toil, resources, and livelihood are all involved; so is the very structure of our society." Eisenhower was referring concisely to the Defense Department's power, but it is equally true today of these invented departments and agencies of the "State" that what he says applies:

"In the councils of government, we must guard against the acquisition of unwarranted influence…The potential for the disastrous rise of misplaced power exists and will persist…we must never let the weight of this combination endanger our liberties or democratic processes."

This combination of misplaced power already does endanger our liberties and our democratic processes…

Most of our laws today come out of agencies controlled by the Executive branch of government alone. This "progress" of the national government's growth has been in one continuous, invariable direction, toward a centralization of power—over our Constitution's deliberately formed barricades and moorings—and proceeds at a retrogression of the rights of every intermediary power between the central government and each individual. We have moved from being a nation whose citizens were a power unto themselves, who were represented under local and state rule and left alone by the federal authority, other than in the case of war, to today, when the "State" within our federal government is everywhere. Our states, towns, industrial sectors and enterprises, faith associations, educational systems, families, and individuals are intermediary entities that have seen their rightful powers usurped as this central national power has grown. The very cornerstones of our unique, democratic diffusion of powers have been seized from us and have been assumed by an ever growing, ever more burdensome, ever more intrusive "State."

The creation of most of our laws occurs in a different circle of power now. Laws are made among Washington, DC,'s hundreds of domestic and foreign lobbyists, her over four hundred administrative agency executives, her over 184 welfare heads, and her self-interested twenty-eight thousand consulting lawyers. In this cauldron of influence peddling, they decide whose money is taken and to whom money is given. They decide what enterprises are targeted for ruin and which are financed and protected. These State positions of influence provide their holders the ultimate power and wealth in this nation. They hold the determining scales of who succeeds and who fails. It is not direct democracy or representative democracy; it is the exercise of influence on the part of lobbyists and the use of permanent positions within the State to determine policy and law. It is not free enterprise, it is not justice, it is judgement in self-interest…

This lobbying has become the Washingtonian's family business. It is so lucrative a business that Washington, DC, and its surroundings have become one of the wealthiest places to live on earth. This political family business wealth is accumulated at the expense of every one of us. We the citizens have utterly *nothing* to do with this process of administrative law making - we merely pay the bill for every decision they make and every dollar of ours they spend.

Who would defend such an anti-constitutional arrangement? What members of a free society would condone it? The first defenders of this new circle of power are members of the media and the intelligentsia of our universities. In the early days of our democracy the free press and the universities were on the front lines fighting for liberty and the new philosophy of the natural rights of humanity. Today, you may tune into any major news program or visit a university campus, and if any citizen objects to the government's takeover of the healthcare or energy industries, or against the consolidation of power in Washington DC., the shock troops of the media will make that citizen a target of national defamation; that rebellious citizen will be publicly held up to a relentless ridicule.

It is a tremendous irony that part of the traditional media's social oath and boast, regarding their profession, is that they have the unique courage to speak truth to power. The members of the media should have the courage to look in the mirror and speak the truth to themselves: they are the spear point of the new centralized circle of power in Washington DC. A circle of power that the citizens of this country need to defend themselves against.

It is another irony, that America's university professors, who are deemed wise, are the intellectual apologists for the socialist policies which are emanating these days from the same circle of power. Apparently, few of these professors have the wit to view the societal ruins socialism has created throughout the world for the last hundred and fifty years and are unable to judge that socialism is not a unique road to an undiscovered utopia. It is, as the chronicle of history amply testifies, the often travelled, shortest path to tyranny... and living hell on earth.

So, here we are. We as citizens no longer have a say in who makes the vast majority of the laws by which we are governed and we have no power to object, unless we wish to be ruined...That kind of tyrannical, oppressive condition was *the* direct cause of our American Revolution.

Are we already beyond the tipping point into tyranny? The State is already of far greater size and power than the comparatively meager representative federal government we elect. This State exists beyond our electoral processes. This State acts in its own interest. The vast majority of those who work within this State hold membership in and dedication to one particular political party which invented this State. And this State presently controls the interior lines of a new circle of power dedicated to its own preservation, its own growth, and its own profit.

And by this State's new circle of power, every individual in America is now surrounded...

So what harm is there, really, in this new arrangement? It is *our* government, isn't it? These are our fellow citizens, right? They do obey the law, don't they? They believe in our Constitution... don't they? These are nice people... right?

The real harm begins when a State, operating under the control of a few, accumulates so much power in a society that it is no longer answerable to the people or to any intermediary societal power... or to the law. Such a power becomes dismissive, it becomes intolerant, it becomes arrogant, it becomes insulting, it becomes vengeful, it becomes unwilling to give up *any* measure of its power, to the point that it becomes... immeasurably harmful. Such a State becomes a creature of the worst human nature.

As the reader will soon discover, as we are now amidst, the gathering Shadows of the Acropolis.

PART TWO

Leviathan Rising

INTRODUCTION

"These lawyers and men of learning, and moneyed men that talk so finely, and gloss over matters so smoothly, to make us poor illiterate people swallow down the pill, expect to get into Congress themselves. They expect to be the managers of this Constitution and get all the power and all the money into their own hands. And then they will swallow up us little fellows, like the great Leviathan."

Amos Singletary

The foremost threat today to the United States form of governance does not consist of an invader, storming over oceans to overwhelm our borders. If any invader so appeared, like a modern-day Genghis Khan, there is no doubt the whole of the American population would rise up in arms and do battle, as we did to erase tyranny's semblance of Fascism from the Earth.

But the threat of such an invasion is only an attack of one kind. What of a subtler assault, one by a quiet systematic ambush? What of the threat, not of an army overcoming defensive works, but one that tunnels unnoted and unobserved, seeking the fracture of our nation's foundations? What of a belligerent's will, not to overcome an American army, but to wrench the carefully crafted design of our democracy? What of a foe who doesn't measure miles of territory to be occupied, but works in a measured fashion to weaken the American mind and accustom it to dependency and, therefore, slavery?

What if the enemy does not need to drop a biological bomb, but only to work slowly and methodically to splice the DNA of tyranny into the American DNA of democracy? What of the foe, who does not need to put us in chains, but has only to weaken us by a thousand assaults, seeking to destroy our faith in ourselves?

Lincoln was right when he attested: “If this nation…is ever to fall, it will be from within,” as it was for the America of the Civil War. It is the hardest thing to admit that the foe is not an “other;” what if it is ourselves? What if the invader is within and engages in a thousand assaults, while the many allow the crime to occur to weaken our democratic structure, our democratic nature? What if the foe is composed of those who seek to destroy the American design of democracy—and of those who do not recognize the destruction is going on?

Our civilization’s laws and freedoms represent more than two hundred generations and thousands of years of hard earnings: the real sufferings of those who were born to adversity, to tyranny, to slavery and who, by their ultimate sacrifices, supplied us with our present liberty and our ease—it should not be for us to lay by, while a power contrary to democracy is gathering. Should we lay by in gathered silences, while witnessing our government intrude by imperceptible degrees upon every entity of America’s original powers? Should we lay by while we are witnessing the overthrow of our Constitution’s balance of powers? Should we lay by while the protection of our rights and the equal application of common law is disappearing? Should we lay by while an Administrative State intrudes with its colossal shadow into every aspect of our economy, our society, and our individual existence, owing to the invariable nature and allure of unanswerable power?

This is where the next true story begins, with the forbidding constructions of America’s federal castle.

Jimmy Carter

By the time the Georgian, Jimmy Carter, was elected president in 1976, the Democratic Party had just about everything it dreamed of. Big industry in America was run by big labor, the party's economic and political partner. The population of the poor in America was expanding exponentially with the multiplication of government agencies and programs proliferating daily in the nation's capital, growing a dependency industry the Democratic Party controlled. The taxes on corporations, individuals, and investments were at all-time highs. The State was dictating what prices could be charged to consumers. Big Labor was dictating what wages would be demanded from corporations and from consumers. The State's regulatory power was expanding throughout the economy with the amount of regulatory law doubling annually. And, in the *coup de grace*, a Republican president took a Democrat's advice and dismissed the Gold Standard, which untethered the federal government from any spending restraints.

In precisely 50 years, the Democratic Party had enacted, through a continuous stream of little levies, almost the entire Socialist Party policy platform enunciated by its candidate for the presidency in 1927, Norman Thomas, because they never called it socialism during any election. They called it liberalism and levied power and wealth, not all at once, but by degrees, by countless little levies of wealth and levies of power. The dream achieved one of its greatest manifestations, under Jimmy Carter, in 1977 when the National Energy Plan was launched. Like LBJ had said about the Great Society, it was a "necessity," which had to be imposed with the "moral equivalence to war." It was an Administrative State regulatory plan to control every British Thermal Unit of power in the energy sector. The plan would throttle American energy production during an inflationary spiral and cripple what remained of the free enterprise system: the Democratic Party was on the verge of their dream scenario.

But the heaven dreamt of turned out to be a practical hell for the economy and for every producer, for every consumer, for every taxpayer. It was the perfect economic storm for businesses and investors: higher taxes, higher union labor costs, an avalanche of often unpredictable regulations, and government spending operating like a vacuum, inhaling every dollar out of the economy for the government's own growth. The government grew in wealth, in size, and in power by another 20% between 1970 and 1980 alone.

To provide one example: the creation of the entitlements Medicare and Medicaid were projected to cost at most $400 Million, in its first year, they actually cost $1 Billion, a massive sum at the time. After the programs launched, health care costs skyrocketed 30% between 1968 and 1969 alone, as the cost of the partial nationalization of the industry came to bear; costs continued rising meteorically throughout the 1970's (and ever since).

In another example: the State controlled the price of oil while a plethora of regulations were heaped on energy industry production during a period when the world's energy consumption rose 85% between 1965 and 1973, ensuring that the US share of world oil production would fall dramatically, and the price of oil, like healthcare, would skyrocket too: from 1972 through 1981, prices rose by 900%.

When the costs of energy, health care and government climb that fast, the increases flow to every taxpayer and consumer, through the cost of every product and service in the economy. This was reflected by an inflation rate in 1974 of 11%, which climbed to 14.8% by 1980. Such is the stuff Democratic Party dreams are made of.

Detroit, Michigan, once a thriving jewel of the unique American free enterprise system, was a city proudly built on the strength of American capitalism. So how was it fairing during the Democratic Party's dream decade? Detroit's unemployment rate in the 1970s was 25%. The number of Detroit's population who were on welfare was 35%. Between 1979 and 1980, 6,800 of Detroit's private, locally owned businesses went out of business forever. One political party's dream became Detroit's and every citizen's nightmare.

Even Jimmy Carter woke up, for a moment of mental clarity - based on common sense. He proclaimed in his second State of the Union address, "Government cannot solve our problems; it cannot eliminate poverty or provide a bountiful economy or reduce inflation or save our cities or cure illiteracy or provide energy." No kidding.

Rather than listen to the momentary common sense of its leader, the Democratic Party allowed a battle to develop instead for the next Democratic candidacy for president in 1980. and the Party confronted Carter with the most liberal senator in America, Theodore Kennedy. This party division ensured that the Democratic party leader would be defeated in the election, but that Democratic Party policy and its "dream" would be defended and advanced as a still unachieved, achievable, unspoken socialist Utopia.

Only one man arose in America in fifty years, who would meaningfully stand up against the avalanche of government growth and socialism's inexorable tide. He was the twice elected Governor of California.

Original Principles

– Light –

"I shall here, perhaps, be reminded of a current observation, that where annual elections end, tyranny begins..."

Alexander Hamilton, **The Federalist Papers**

Ronald Reagan proclaimed himself unashamedly for the virtues of liberty, expressing truths concerning government's size and ambition which sounded like echoes of the original principles of our nation's founders:

"Either you will control your government or government will control you" he noted. "Unless bureaucracy is constantly resisted, it breaks down representative government and overwhelms democracy." Also, "When a government can tax a people with no limit or restraint on what the government can take, then the government has become the master." Finally, "Man is not free unless government is limited...that is as neat and predictable as a law of physics: as government expands, liberty contracts."

With regard to the Great Society's programs and its premise of "helping" the poor, Reagan said citizens must "...remember that every government service, every offer of government financed security, is paid for in the loss of human freedom" and that "... government is never more dangerous than when our desire to have it help us...blinds us to its great power to harm us."

With regard to taxation, Reagan held that "the problem is not that people are taxed too little, but that government spends too much...Revenues should be increased not by increasing tax rates on the individual but by building a bigger economy for everybody." And on government spending other people's money, Reagan used the form of a joke to state another fundamental truth: "Government is just like a baby. An alimentary canal with a big appetite at one end and no sense of responsibility at the other..."

Of the conditions in America at the time, he justly stated during the 1980 campaign that: "Extreme taxation, excessive controls, oppressive government competition with business, frustrated minorities and forgotten Americans are NOT the product of free enterprise. They are the residue of centralized bureaucracy, of government by a self-anointed elite." This same truth holds as true today: it is eternal. As the State exerted more and more control over the economy from the 1930s thru the 1970s, the effects were showing more and more in the economic and political ailments of America.

One may sum up Reagan's philosophical view in one simple line: "Government is not the solution to our problem; government is the problem." The American electorate listened and voted to right the direction of the country in November 1980, with Reagan's landslide victory for the presidency.

Ronald Reagan

The new President embraced the supply side economics of Jack Kemp and Arthur Laffer and he appointed David Stockman as the head of the Office of Management and Budget. The team's goals were fundamental: stop printing money and stabilize the value of the dollar. Lower taxes to allow capitalism to work on its own—to create more wealth. Shrink the size of the Dependent and Administrative States to lessen the unprecedented burden of government on the economy and the taxpayer, enough to allow the economy to renew itself for the benefit of everyone.

In Washington, they had a problem. For fifty years no one had ever asked how to reduce the cost of a program. For fifty years the only thing the people in government and at the Office of Budget and Management had done was add: add more programs or add further to already existing programs. No one knew how to shrink the size of government by an inch or by a dime, the very idea of *reducing* the size of government was unprecedented.

David Stockman came up with what he termed the "Grand Design." He would phase in budget cuts across the whole Administrative and Dependent States, in measures that would be acceptable in Phase One and grow more difficult in Phase Two; during Phase Two the benefits would become apparent. For instance, there would be cuts to public jobs programs like *Comprehensive Employment and Training Act (CETA),* while there would be reforms to exploding programs. Some programs had grown so fast, the spending was out of control: as with the Food Stamps program. In Stockman's plan, there would be caps on bigger budget outlays as in Medicaid payouts to the states, which had never been capped or controlled before. Then in Phase Two, the big entitlements like Social Security, Medicare, and the federal pension system would be targeted for reform, while the economy was growing.

Parallel to this trimming of the dependency system, Stockman proposed to end corporate welfare. A system of subsidies had been created and managed by Washington's lobbyists, who are specialists at securing taxpayer money from the treasury for their clients. Subsidies (or corporate welfare) in the 1970s were even being paid out to large Fortune 500 companies, like Boeing and General Electric. Lobbyists represented a plethora of various interests from rural electrical co-ops to the major airlines, to automotive companies, to mass transit companies, to large and small oil companies, to dairy consortiums and home builders, among a thousand others. Subsidies were also going out to whole industries, like agriculture, in order to fix the rate of production and therefore "fix" commodity pricing. This subsidy system has been, and is, the cash cow of D.C.'s class of lobbyists: every such lobbyist client gets a government subsidy at the taxpayer's expense, every client pays the lobbyist with a portion of that subsidy, again, at the taxpayer's expense. This is how the inner circle of power functions; how it profits. The lobbyists who live in the Washington D.C. area have made it one of the wealthiest areas on earth.

Stockman also wanted to eliminate unjust tax write offs, such as the loopholes millionaires enjoyed for their second and third homes and their yachts. The Grand Design approach was to work with an even hand across the entire economy to end the injustices created by the government's ever-expanding, self-interested interference with entitlements, subsidies and loopholes. These payouts benefitted the edifice of the State, the lobbyists, the politicians and their "favored" clients. And did so at the expense of every taxpayer.

The most critical part of the plan was discipline, the budget cuts, the ending of subsidies, the closing of tax loopholes had to all come off together. If one constituency was spared, the plan would sink: it had to be all in. Reagan's watchwords were simple: no favoritism and "No compromise!"

The new president was very excited to make this unprecedented effort to control by subtraction and reduction the system of cronyism he had watched grow for fifty years, and which were crippling the economy. Many Republicans he spoke to agreed enthusiastically with the new plan, saying: "We are with you Mr. President." "We're all for your program, (we're) ninety-nine percent for those budget cuts!" It looked as if the Republican Party might finally end its fearful, puerile role as the minor partner in the Administrative State. The voters were with Reagan. He found that he and his proposed polices had become ever more popular with the citizenry of the whole country.

Even the Democratic Speaker, Tip O'Neill said: "I can read Congress, they go with the will of the people, and the will of the people is to go along with the President." Then O'Neill said a very telling thing to his fellow Democrats: that there was no need to worry, "time cures all ills," meaning the Democrats should disregard the public will by withstanding the popular wave of policy sentiment, until it would be safe to operate "the system" again.

In the spring of 1981, Ronald Reagan, a real American rebel, led his team as they rode a wave of popularity, right into the outer wall of the inner circle of power's impenetrable castle. And if you listen, you can still hear the laughter...

— Shadow —

Leviathan's Castle Keep

In Volume One of this book series, I touched on the history of William the Conqueror's system of castles, a castle system of tyranny the Norman's constructed, with each stronghold built not more than one day's horseback ride from another in order to "nail down" the countryside. The castles served as armories for garrisons which harvested all the wealth of England for the Aristocrats and the King. The castles themselves were impregnable with concentric defenses beginning with an outer moat in front of a draw bridge, which became an impassable portal which sealed shut the fortress. If one did not drown in the moat, boiling oil was poured from the castle towers upon would-be incomers. If one made it past the moat, the boiling oil and the portal, another inner defensive wall, bristling with archers and swordsmen, would prove yet another hurdle to the entrant. One never saw nor knew where from the next force of defense would emerge, as circle after circle of defenses had to be surmounted before one came to the castle's inner towers. Each tower was unscalable, a defensive fortress unto itself, and worked to fire on any interloper who had made their way within the castle. The last defense of the Baron—the King's enforcer and tax collector—was the central citadel where the treasure raked from the surrounding population was kept.

Often times, the aristocrat and king set up skirmish lines just the other side of the outer walls of their castles, with soldiers who were the least loyal, where they had to prove their loyalty by facing any on comer first, one or the other or both would die, to the king and baron's delight. As one penetrated the castle and moved further toward the center, one came upon the loyalists, the aristocrat and king's inner circle of power, the family's party, and its immediate dependents.

The irony was this: it was the wealth ripped out of the countryside which paid for the building of the Norman castles; thereafter, the strength of the castles was used to reduce the people of the countryside to perpetual servitude and to keep them subdued.

Unlike the many Norman castles, which were each separated by a day's horseback ride from one another, to support a common defense system, there is only one American castle and one may drive from end to end of it, as our politicians do, by a limousine ride across the bisecting roads of Washington D.C. within a single day. The skirmishers outside the castle walls, whose loyalty is suspected, is the sometime opposition party to the Administrative State. While on the walls are politicians of either party. Inside the castle proper are the loyalists, the inner circle: Democratic Party operatives, the lobbyists, the administrative and dependent state's life-long employees, the consulting attorneys, and the business and union leaders benefitted by the State. And, of course, the ever-present media, ready to drown in the moat or scald with oil or scold with insults, anyone who disagrees with their Inner Circle.

With this analogy in view, we may see what occurred, when a modern American knight, a rebel, dared to tilt an effective spear in the castle's direction, as Ronald Reagan and his team did in 1981, with David Stockman's Grand Design.

There was a prophetic meeting that February, when a gathering of the governors of the states was held in Washington. At the meeting, the governors disputed over some policies but all agreed on one thing, when the subject of the budget cutting program came up. None of the fifty governors wanted any cuts in the money which their states expected to receive.

Nonetheless, the economic program of Stockman got off to a roaring start on May 12, 1981, when the Senate voted 72 – 20 in favor of Reagan's budget resolution. In the House, 50 conservative, southern representatives, called the Boll Weevils, were siding with Republicans in favor of the program. Even in the liberal north-eastern districts of the country, a group called the Gypsy Moths were also bucking the liberal system, in favor of exhilarating the economy by putting reins on government's overspending and over-controlling nature. The program called for budget cuts of $118 billion dollars in savings by 1984, based on an overall 1981 annual budget of $740 billion. The targeted savings for 1982 amounted to $38 billion or an overall budget reduction of 5.14%.

The progress slowed when Ed Meese, a member of Reagan's cabinet, demanded to know what would not be cut. The media were banging down his door, demanding to know. Stockman answered that in the first phase of cuts, Social Security, Head Start children's program, Veterans benefits and Summer Jobs for youth would not be cut. Meese went out immediately and megaphoned to the media that these programs would *never* be cut, even though there were to be cuts in Phase Two; these programs became "walled off," from the start by the media and one of Reagan's closest advisors.

When General Alexander Haig, the new Secretary of State, was told his department was targeted for $7.5 billion in cuts/savings over the next four years, he turned into a ballistic missile and shot into Reagan's office. Haig demanded, "Mr. President, if you accept the OMB proposal, your entire foreign policy will go right down the drain!" Reagan asked Stockman what the hang-up was, Stockman answered that part of the cut was trimming personnel back by 591 persons, out of an employee payroll of 22,000 persons.

Haig fumed. Reagan asked Haig if he could trim back half the number, just 295 out of the 22,000? Haig declared he could not. The other part of the budget cuts was to come from foreign aid outlays. Haig's department did a curious thing by alerting foreign embassies around the world that cuts were being made to U.S. foreign aid. Couldn't the embassies generate some blow back from their governments, against the policy? The media were right there to exclaim that there were foreign concerns germinating about a policy crisis if foreign aid were cut by the State Department. Under the Grand Design, the State Department was only asked to trim their entire budget by 2.6%. In the end, hardly a dime was cut from the State Department.

This cycle was repeated throughout the agencies which the Reagan Administration had just begun to run. At the massive Health and Human Services department, which devoured so much budget capital, only $2 billion per year in budget savings was expected. What was returned by Dick Schweiker and HHS to the OMB was a list, 185 pages long, of complaints as to why the budget could not be cut at all.

The Housing and Urban Development department responded to the call for savings by alerting every major metropolitan mayor, and concerned urban developer in the land, and suggesting they flood the White House with phone calls railing against any cuts which were contemplated for HUD.

At the Justice Department, newly installed AG, William French Smith, demanded that his department could never cut 2,000 employees from his 54,000-payroll base. For that matter, his department should not be the first, but the last department which should be looked to for savings! The Justice Department payroll did not change.

Then Stockman had an unexpected confrontation from an unsuspected source. Howard Baker, Reagan's own Chief of Staff, had seen a list of the budget cuts proposed at the Department of Energy. On it was a nuclear reactor project that Stockman thought a rip-off and Baker thought a necessity in his own political district.

The problem was, if Stockman could not cut a project that was jeered throughout Washington as one of the worst examples of "set-aside pork", how could there be any other meaningful cuts to the energy department?

The skirmishers outside the walls of the castles were fighting against themselves, fighting against their own agenda. How does a new cabinet official, in a spanking new office, with a fat budget and tens of thousands of cheering new employees, cut their newly gained department? Instead, they proved their loyalty to the castle by fighting against themselves. They fought against the larger goal, which was to reduce the size of the castle.

Atop the castle's outer walls, stood other defenders. Elected officials that could sometimes be toppled from the wall by outsiders, by the electorate, imagine that! When Stockman proposed to cut the Job Corps, which had an allocated budget of $12,000.00 for every job, which was a sum at the time which Harvard did not charge for a full year of undergrad education, someone unexpected strode through the door to defend the Corps, the Republican Senator from Utah, Oren Hatch. Hatch was one of the loudest cheerleaders for the Reagan Program, yet here he was, asking Stockman to set aside the Job Corps—after all, it did not amount to much in the grand scheme of things. The Grand scheme of things could not be done without all the little things.

Leviathan's Castle Keep

Everywhere Stockman turned to find savings, a defender of one program or another was there to defend a program every time. He ran into the Republican Senator from South Carolina, Strom Thurmond, who looked Stockman right in the eye to say "Now, we're all behind the President's program, yuh heah? But you take good care of those REA's, them's some real fine peoples." REA was the Rural Electric Administration whose lineage went back to the destruction of the Commonwealth and Southern utility company during the Roosevelt Administration. The REA's were still being subsidized by the government, for doing what C & S would have done for free for the last 50 years. The subsidies had gone up every year like clockwork, they were on auto pilot; people depended on them—they could not be cut.

Back in the House, it was more of the same. The 50 Boll Weevils, who were otherwise gung-ho for Reagan's program, wanted to keep agricultural subsidies in place; they wanted the federal government to continue to control production, control crop prices and thereby farm income. That meant subsidies for a multitude of farmers, paying them to produce nothing. Again, the subsidies were part of FDR's industrial invasion that was still in operation; it was akin to Soviet central-planning and had been going on for 50 years: people expected the money. This central planning involved production controls, price supports, subsidy payments and even the financing of exports to foreign nations with U.S. taxpayer money. All of this effort and the work of tens of thousands of employees at the Agriculture Department for over 50 years was done to arrive at a price, which could have been established and maintained for free, if only Adam Smith's invisible hand were allowed to move. The Boll Weevils turned on the Grand Design, threatening the whole agenda, if the agricultural status quo was not maintained.

Across the aisle in the House between 30 and 50 Republican members were in minority leader Bob Michel's ear morning, noon, and night assuring him that they were for the Reagan agenda, while asking him not to make any cuts whatsoever that effected their congressional districts. They demanded that the status quo be maintained. Fifty Republicans plus 50 Boll Weevils equaled nearly half of the votes necessary in the house to do anything. They were also 100 political districts, each of which expected the "allotment of pork" (so to speak) they had always received from the central monetary exchange of the Administrative State.

Finally, Bob Michel exploded. In front of the group, he slammed his fist onto his desk and said, "When are you guys going to recognize that this is just a budget resolution? It doesn't cut anything! If you've got problems, we'll take care of them later."

Later came when the budget arrived to the interior of the castle, the chambers of 15 House committees, headed by Democrats at the time. This group decided what a final bill would look like that reconciled the House and Senate versions of OMB's budget proposal. The committee chairmen held their positions based on seniority. They created the status quo; they were therefore as determined as adamant to keep it. They began to do so by using different accounting methods than those established by OMB. Then they found savings by inventing new spending items which they would cut, if only to show they were reaching savings targets. The meat of programs, like those supported by the dairy lobby, were never actually cut. In the end, each of the 15 committees cheered their own cleverness at how successful they all were in maneuvering around an intended budget cut.

A Republican, Ralph Regula, went before the media to say: "We've been very pleased with the results so far. The indications are that most of the committees are coming up with real cuts..." In fact, of the $118 Billion in budget cuts OMB called for, $55 Billion in "paper" cuts came out of the committees, when they completed their work on the bill. Regula, like other Republicans, did not fully realize that the foundations of the Grand Design were sinking with every step of the process.

Then another phase of the bill's passage was entered, when the addition of the votes had to equal 218 yays. The count was short. There had to be an auction held for votes based on adding back programs which had been cut. So, Amtrak had to get back $112 million in financing to attain necessary votes. The CETA youth and job training had to be refunded with $200 million to attain more votes. The Department of Energy had to be funded a further $200 million for public facility weatherization, for votes. By the end of the Auction, billions were added back for everything, down to a single railroad crossing in Schenectady, New York. In the end, the politicians of both parties protected the castle walls.

The bill was passed with only $25 billion in real savings, mostly in discretionary spending, over four years, which equaled 1.28% of the fiscal budget. It represented the most elaborate exercise imaginable on the part of an entire government to cast a deck chair off of the Titanic. Reagan once said that the closest thing on earth there will ever be to an eternal life form is a government program. Reagan's immense efforts of good faith on behalf of the taxpayer, and their failure, proved that to be as true as possible.

But the bill did do something not done for 50 years. The Gramm–Latta II Omnibus Budget Reconciliation Act of 1981 constrained the growth of government for the first time since 1930, restraining welfare spending to an additional 1.4% per year from 1981-1989. It also helped allow the passage of the Kemp-Roth Tax Bill of 1981, and the Tax Reform Act of 1986, the first significant, if slight, victories for free enterprise and capitalism since 1930. The Reagan Administration reduced the highest individual tax rate from 70 to 28%, the corporate tax rate from 46 to 34% and reduced the rate at which investments were taxed from 28 to 20%. The effects of the tax reductions were to replenish the economy with investible capital which had previously been dead and buried in the bureaucracy.

Another cornerstone of Reagan's agenda was to reduce government's control of the economy through deregulation of industry. In just the transportation sector, this brought about a meteoric rise of innovation which created a revolution in transportation logistics, dramatically increasing efficiencies, reducing costs, and launching new carrier airlines like Southwest to compete in the marketplace. The Reagan Administration oversaw the breakup of AT&T, which brought dynamism and innovation to a communications industry that had been constrained by the monopoly. Deregulation in the energy sector made oil exploration and production possible again, which drove down the price of oil, and the reduction of those costs in the marketplace brought down inflation throughout the economy. These are just a few of the success stories which the Reagan agenda could claim.

Ronald Reagan's economic initiatives allowed just a little free enterprise and some of capitalism's great virtues back into an economy still dominated by the Democratic Party and the State, operating in the castle. The results were magnificent. The average wages of Americans increased across the country, while inflation and unemployment both dropped below 5%. Whether an individual invested in a company, or a company invested in itself, with the increase of new capital and the costs of regulations decreasing, the number of entrepreneurial start-up firms exploded in kind and number. You might have heard of some of them: Adobe Inc., Compaq Computer, Intuit, Dell Computer, Cisco Systems, America Online, and Stairmaster, to name few.

During the Reagan years the Gross Domestic Product of the country rose 30% and the equities markets, as a measure of entrepreneurial, technological, and industrial strength rose 135%.

So, how were things inside the castle? The Inner Circle of Power was aghast at the success it did not create and could not control. Free enterprise was succeeding wildly, and the people of America were responding. Reagan won reelection in 1984 by a landslide of 49 states to one. A broad spectrum of the media, which serves as the Inner Circle's sensory nervous system, was in agony. The media let the country know from its castle tower, that they were disgusted with Ronald Reagan: they set out to systematically ridicule him.

Tom Brokaw, an NBC anchorman, said of Reagan, "I don't think he really understands the enormous difficulty a lot of people have in just getting through life, because he's lived in a fantasy land for so long."

Jonathon Alter of Newsweek said Reagan's presidency "tended to lead the country backward."

Bryant Gumbel said because of Reagan's policies, "more people are becoming poor and staying poor in this country than at any time since World War II."

Brokaw, Alter, and Gumbel were making these reports while the economic statistics of the time, such as reduced unemployment and rises in real wages told the opposite story. As *USA Today*'s Sarah McClendon wrote that it would take a hundred years for government to recover, saying Reagan "hurt people, the disabled, women, nursing mothers, the homeless." in fact, the average American worker and family were far better off. African American unemployment had dropped from 15 to 10% during Reagan's presidency. And truth be known, Reagan did not cut social spending, he merely constrained its growth. The media had to report an opposite tack, because Reagan and the idea of just a little free enterprise were succeeding.

The barrage was not finished. Clark Clifford a senior Democratic Party member and media maven called Reagan "an amiable dunce."

David Broder said Reagan's staff's principal job was to "water the desert between Ronald Reagan's ears."

Columnist, Jimmy Breslin, called Reagan "shockingly stupid." The media's insults of Reagan's character and intelligence were characteristic. Reagan's great sin was his success, and that success threatened the State's arrangement of power, which disliked any success that it did not arrange through the inside channels of its own Inner Circle. In fact, Reagan dealt with only fringes of the State's power. By holding federal government's growth rate to 1.4% per year from 1981-1989 and by reducing a small amount of the regulatory burden of the State upon the economy - Reagan could not diminish the real power of the State further. There was a reason. Our federal castle is as carefully constructed as those Norman castles which still stand today, after a thousand years.

It was Woodrow Wilson's genius for the accumulation of power that led to the harvest of the whole nation's wealth into a single treasury. It was Franklin Roosevelt's genius for the expansion and retention of power that turned the treasury into a dispensary benefitting his own political party through financing interest groups who were loyal to the party, above all other considerations. It was Lyndon Johnson's genius for the further expansion of the Democratic power base, and making it permanent, that he created a dependency industry based on the poor and branding it a necessary charity with all the sacrosanct aura of holy writ. It was the Democratic Party's genius to make even its opposition defend the castle's walls, by allowing some Republican pet projects to be funded from the castle. If any stone of the castle comes under threat, every stone holder, every pet project defender, becomes a defender of the whole castle, including those opposed to much of the castle in general. It is our representative system of government turned from outside in to inside out. One of our founder's wrote about just such a system:

> *"When once such a vicious system is established, it becomes the guard and protection of all inferior abuses. The man who is in the receipt of a million a year is the last person to promote a spirit of reform, lest, in the event, it should reach to himself. It is always his interest to defend inferior abuses, as so many outworks to protect the citadel; and in this species of political fortification, all the parts have such a common dependence that it is never to be expected they will attack each other."*
>
> *Thomas Paine*

Another of Paine's comments obtains:

> *"What at first was plunder, assumed the foster name of revenue; and the power originally usurped, they affected to inherit."*

In our federal castle system, the walls are not made of stones but of government programs. Instead of many aristocrats spread throughout many castles, we have one castle filled with many bureaucrats who occupy the castle's walls and towers, whose powers extend to the lengths of the nation. Instead of courtiers surrounding an aristocrat or king, we have lobbyists who encircle a single citadel of power, living off government's plundering of taxpayers.

The implications of this castle system within our democracy are very real. For hundreds of years, our thousands of unique public squares, were locales where the concerns of local populations were heard and addressed in every township. The power once exercised in these thousands of public squares has been turned over, into a single private courtyard inhabited by a very select few who now wield a national rule over and above every township. Instead of *We the people* having representatives who represent our will, we have politicians who defend their own interests first, in this castle system, even if they hold just one stone of it. The protection of the castle keep has become more important to the political class than the rightful representation of we, the people. It is a representation usurped by politicians, courtiers and lawyers in the new circle of power, more devoted to keeping the wealth they plunder, than representing any defense of the property and liberties of we, their constituents.

And, as with the Norman system of castles, it is the wealth of our country, which has been plundered, that provides every adamantine stone in the American castle's walls; it is the wealth of the nation, which provides the sealing mortis between the castle stones. It is the bounty of our country which has built and sustains this castle which becomes ever more devoted to our common oppression, even to the point of government making decisions which used to be determined by ourselves as individuals, or by our families, or by our faiths, or by our associations, or by our towns, or by our states.

Lastly, this castle system has changed our nation from one nation comprised of *We the people* to a nation divided between those who are within the castle and those who are outside the castle. *We, the people* have been divided into *us* and *them*, the *us* who defend the castle and are benefited by the inner circle and them, the unimportant outsiders who are fired upon if *they* intrude in the castle's works. If you are one of us and inhabit one of the castle's towers, you are unlike them; "Us" are the extended family party, who gather herd-like in nature for the benefit of us alone. While "they" who are outside the walls pay for it all, even their own oppression.

As Americans, we should not feel unique—this manner of bureaucracy can be viewed fully operating in Europe, that continent of castles. The castle of the federal European bureaucracy is in Brussels now. They too have created a permanent administrative state, they too have created their own dependency industry, in the place of its charitable institutions of faith. Their bureaucracy, too, controls finance, healthcare and energy industries from the central capital. Europe is as Europe always was, with a castle dividing *us,* the bureaucrats, and *them,* the new peasants. In America's original, unique design of a federal system, *we* were never supposed to be a part of such an old-world castle system.

During his presidency, Reagan had one other great initiative: to win the Cold War against the tyrannical socialist empire of the Soviet Union. He was asked once how he might succeed where every other president had failed; he said it was easy: "We win, they lose." He was right again. The Soviet Union dissolved into ruins because of Ronald Reagan's efforts. The pity is, he had more success dissolving the Soviet Union than he did taking one stone out of the castle walls of our own Administrative and Dependent States.

George H.W. Bush

Reagan's twin initiatives of bringing back free enterprise through deregulation and tax cuts and of defeating the Soviet Union cost the country the precise amount of money not saved by the Grand Design's attempted reduction in the Administrative State. That failure took the form of a large national deficit.

That deficit became a Y in the road for Reagan's successor to the presidency, a man who was unlike Reagan, for George H.W. Bush was a life-long insider. Bush's father was Senator Prescott Bush. George H.W. Bush served with valor in World War II in the Pacific theater. He was by every measure, an honorable man but he was also one to the castle accustomed.

The alternatives of his presidency were: would he use the deficit to apply pressure on Congress to find some further means of reducing government's growth, so the wealth generated by the re-emergence of the economy could pay down the debt? Or would he do as previous presidents, such as Nixon had done, and go along with the staggering momentum and costs of government's growth? The country thought it knew which road Bush would take after the convention of 1988 in New Orleans, where, as an honorable man, he pledged:

> *"I'm the one who will not raise taxes. My opponent [Michael Dukakis] now says he'll raise them as a last resort, or a third resort. But when a politician talks like that, you know that's one resort he'll be checking into. My opponent won't rule out raising taxes. But I will. And the Congress will push me to raise taxes and I'll say no. And they'll push, and I'll say no, and they'll push again, and I'll say, to them,* 'Read my lips: no new taxes.'"

In 1990, instead of applying pressure against the State, Bush was feeling under pressure from his friends *inside* the State. Bush decided to do what was customary for 60 years—he about-faced. He betrayed the conservative constituents of the Republican Party, he was supposed to represent. He decided that rather than rocking the boat, he would expand the ship of State, again. He came to a grand bargain with the Democratic leadership in Congress. Bush agreed to raise taxes definitively, based on the Democratic leadership's undefined promise to look into cutting the budget. They all lied. Bush lied about his pledge and the Democrats lied about the budget.

The tax hikes hamstrung the economy, turning a boom period into a recession. The Republican Party split its formerly solid majority between Bush and a conservative third-party candidate, Ross Perot. The Democratic Party then deftly used Bush's broken pledge, his tax increases and his recession, which the tax increases caused, as the premise to win the 1992 presidential election with 43% of the vote. Bill Clinton won the presidency with the same percentage of the vote that Michael Dukakis badly lost by four years before.

George H.W. Bush proved himself another very useful Republican, this time to the opposition party. The Republican Party and its constituencies were betrayed, divided, and then played like a fiddle, again. Thus, the invulnerability of the castle stood intact, again. The System was still growing—under Democrats the government grew by leaps, while under the Republicans, like the honorable George Bush, it grew by bounds, need I say it, again.

The increases in taxes during the Bush presidency, as tax increases always are, were used to further remove power from the people and their representatives: to build more unanswerable power within the Administrative State, aka the castle. Since 1992, the insiders have never felt more secure or safer from the pesky vagaries of elections. No matter which party is elected to office, the State has grown in wealth, in power, and in invulnerability.

Equal Justice

– Light –

"Why should there not be a patient confidence in the ultimate justice of the people? Is there any better or equal hope in the world?"

Abraham Lincoln

As pertains to domestic governance, there are two kinds of justice, economic justice and criminal justice. Our government was formed based on the ideal of equal justice for all concerning both realms of justice. Regarding the economy, it concerns having a level environment and common law for businesses, so that the family farmer in Wisconsin has an equal chance to succeed when competing against a large Agri business corporation. Or a single fishing boat running out of Gloucester, Massachusetts has an equal chance for success as has a fishing fleet going after the same catch. That is the American ideal.

With governments interposition in our economy, the effect of government on the economic playing field has increased in proportion to its growth. Since the New Deal, government has become a major factor in which companies succeed or fail. Rules written in agencies can make or break the fortunes of two competitors, who are supposed to be equal before the law. Hence, the more the economy is affected by agency "rules," the more the number of lobbyists multiplies, for they are specifically paid based on their ability to curry favor and gain "privileges" for their clients. The existence of lobbyists and lobbyist profits are based on their ability to unlevel the playing field in their client's favor.

The administrative state has become the central exchange of such favor and privilege. Some politicians build their careers based on dispensing such favors through influence in the State's agencies. It is a consequence of the omni-presence of government in our economic system, that unequal justice has become omni-present. A government designed at the founding to keep opportunities equal based on common law, has grown to be a State which sells privilege through the rules it invents for lobbyists and their clients. It is a system today, which creates unequal justice. The only means of securing something like equal justice in the economy would entail getting the government out.

In the criminal justice system, our founder's ideal was best spoken by John Jay when he proclaimed: "Justice is indiscriminately due to all, without regard to numbers, wealth, or rank."

Equal justice is owed to the person who shop lifts from a store, as well as to one who robs a bank, as well as one who robs people through a computer program. Offenses of a kind are treated in kind and every transgressor is equally answerable to the law.

There is another equality, that persons before the law should not be exempted from being answerable because of who they are or what particular position they hold. Persons who commit criminal acts, even if they are in political positions of government, need to be as prone to judgement as anyone walking the street. However, we are witnessing in plain view, in our present day, that the agencies which are supposed to effect just outcomes, are, like their kindred economy based agencies, unleveling the justice system to favor persons "of" the State, creating a justice system of privilege for special members, thereby creating injustice in the criminal justice system. It is particularly dangerous when one political party is immune from justice - for this breeds unanswerable persecutions on that party's political rivals – granting to the wrong doers the privilege of immunity, no matter how criminal their acts.

— Shadow —

Leviathan's Privilege

Then a couple came into the executive office, who were of a unique kind, who found new, personal ways to enlarge the already gorged powers of the presidency. We now turn from the castle becoming invulnerable and the State becoming unanswerable to the castle's insiders, who inhabit the castle's towers, becoming wise and adept in the practices of tyrants.

BILL CLINTON

Bill Clinton had been planning on assuming the presidency for most of his life. He even married a woman as centered as he was on his assuming the nation's highest office. Even before Bill Clinton was elected governor of Arkansas, he set out to serve three two-year terms and then run for the highest office in the land. When the election of 1992 approached, the Clinton's found they had a problem: they had gathered a lot of politically radioactive baggage during Bill's years as Attorney General and Governor of the State of Arkansas. In Bill's own words to David Ifshin: "I can't open my closet. I'll get crushed by the skeletons." Bill was not alone, Hillary had some things in the closet too.

For years, the Clintons had engaged in a type of political family business in Arkansas. Bill Clinton became Attorney General of Arkansas in 1976. At the same time, the firm of Witt Stephens,

Stephens and Co., and the Worthen Bank in Arkansas became the Clinton family's financial advisors. Also in 1976, Hillary entered the Rose Law Firm.

When Bill Clinton became Governor (with the help of donations from the Stephens family) the state awarded millions of dollars of bond underwriting contracts to Stephens and Co., while the legal work for the bond issuances were awarded to the Rose Law Firm, where Hillary became a critical link in the area of public-private business initiatives. The same arrangement was made with another bond brokerage house affiliated with Bill Clinton, that of Collins, Locke and Lassiter. A three-step dance was formed: The first was campaign donations, the second was state awarded work, the third step was awards of work to a firm where a relative of the governor was a partner.

Tyson Foods and Tyson executives were also great benefactors to the Clintons' political ambitions. Clinton's election was step one, helped by Tyson donations. Step two took the form of Tyson supporters being appointed by Clinton to state regulatory agencies which oversaw Tyson operations. And the third step: Tyson was represented by the Rose Law Firm before the same agencies.

The Clintons were brash about this political "family business" relationship. When confronted by the fact that he regularly flew on a Tyson private jet, Clinton quipped that it spared the state the expense of having to buy a private jet for him. He also noted that Hillary flew commercial; what he did not say was that her travel expenses were often paid for by Tyson, and she flew first class. So, the three-steps in this case were political donations, state protection from regulations, and again, a family relative, privately benefitting financially.

A fellow democrat, Jerry Brown, summed up the ethical problem during a debate with Bill Clinton. "I think there is an electability problem," said Brown. "He is funneling money to his wife's law firm for state business. Number two, his wife's law firm is representing clients before the State of Arkansas agencies—his appointees. And one—a key poultry industry—which his wife represents."

Brown concluded: "So, it's not only corruption; it's an environmental disaster and it's the kind of conflict of interest that is incompatible with the kind of public servant we expect from a president of the United States."

And then there are other benefits of this political dance.

One of Tyson Food's outside counsels, Robert Blair, decided to advise Hillary Clinton on commodities trading, about which she knew nothing. Blair advised Hillary to work with a former Tyson employee, Robert L. "Red" Bone, who worked with Refco, one of the largest commodities trading companies at Chicago's Mercantile Exchange. To begin, Hillary purchased cattle futures contracts worth $12,000 for $1,000. Though Hillary invested only $1,000, she was able to hold onto the contracts through daily losses, even though any deficits in contract valuations are usually settled on the Merc Exchange at the end of every trading day, through margin calls. On July 17, 1979, Hillary lost as much as $26,460 in a single day, yet there was no margin call. Miraculously, at the end of 10 months the same 10 cattle contracts purchased for $1,000, sold for roughly $94,000. The Merc exchange later charged ol' Red Bone with violations of records keeping and margin requirement rules and revoked his license to trade. He violated rules that Hillary Clinton never had to observe. Nothing personal, it's just another division of the Clinton's family business.

These Clintons were different, they were more blatant in their arrangements, more manifest in their transgressions; they believed themselves above everyone else, and above the common law. They thought nothing else mattered if in key arenas, they were making a proper showing for their political audience. As an example, Bill Clinton attended services on Sundays in Little Rock's Emmanuel Baptist Church, where he knew they were recording for television. He made sure to sit directly in front of the cameras, in the best light, so he could be seen singing hymns and praying. Bill and Hillary know how to arrange a stage for political gain.

None of the above skeletons worried the Clintons at the beginning of the 1992 presidential campaign as much as the skeletons of

Bill's paramours or sexual harassment victims, depending on your point of view. Bill had an unoriginal point of view about power. It is a point of view that has been shared by persons in power for millenia; it is a problem of power which our Constitution sought to end. Bill Clinton thought his power entitled him. At the mansion he had maids, servants and several chefs; on the mansion grounds he had gardeners and groundskeepers; on the road he had drivers, bodyguards and state troopers, all at the tax-payers expense and all at Clinton's beck and call. To many, Bill Clinton appeared to treat some women the same way.

While he was governor and living in the mansion, during the 1980s, Bill stepped out on most Saturday nights; he and his brother, Roger, could be found in downtown Little Rock at Buster's bar, until the early hours. Bill was often surrounded by a circle of women. His wife was never among them. When the 1992 presidential campaign started heating up, so did rumors alleging over a half a dozen women received "unwanted advances" made by the governor. And there were rumors of affairs and some of the rumors were coming from the women involved, such as Myra Belle Miller, Miss Arkansas 1958 and Gennifer Flowers, a cabaret singer. These skeletons had to be dealt with – by the woman who was never there on Saturday night; but who desperately wanted her husband to be president.

– Shadow –

Spinning Leviathan's Web

"Oh, what a tangled web we weave,
When first we practice to deceive."

Shakespeare

The Democratic campaign of 1992 was waged on two tracks. One was through the "War Room" operated by James Carville and George Stephanopoulos. Carville was famous for saying to his campaign staff: "Don't complicate the simple." The way this track of the campaign was run wasn't complicated. Campaign spokespersons used phraseology that was simple: "It's the economy stupid," "You've had twelve years trying it your way, it's time for a change," and "don't read his lips, look at his actions!" It is as old as politics itself that to convince people of something, confine yourself to a few points and repeat them over and over and over again. And Bill's appearance was simple too, as run from the War Room, he was always made to appear a devoted family man... and was shown to be so over and over again.

On the other track of the campaign, the rumors of affairs and unwanted approaches by the Governor of Arkansas needed an organized response. Betsey Wright, Clinton's one time Chief of Staff, was specifically assigned to deal with what Wright termed, the "bimbo eruptions." And aides to the campaign, a defense team of mostly women, were assigned to act as detectives to identify problematic persons who might have any information about all of those skeletons. This group was called the Bunker, the left flank of the War Room, and began compiling a doomsday list, which categorized each woman who had been involved with Clinton according to how vulnerable they were, what trouble they might cause and how they might be stopped.

Hillary Clinton herself called Ivan Duda, a Little Rock detective, to direct him: "I want you to give me the names, addresses and phone numbers (of Bill's women) and we can get them under control." The number of women Duda and his fleet of detectives found out Bill Clinton was seeing regularly or sporadically were many. Hillary separated them into two columns: the women who were safe and the women who were trouble. Detective Duda was ordered to find out all he could about the women on the list and what their vulnerabilities were. Then Hillary hired another detective, Jack Palladino, to confront the women on the list with the information that had been gathered, telling them they had to sign affidavits denying they had any involvement with Bill Clinton, or else. A democratic operative was even unleashed to threaten Miss Arkansas, who decided not to go public about that rumor.

There was one woman who initially agreed to keep her long-term affair with Bill Clinton quiet, and did so for two years, until she, Gennifer Flowers, was confronted with a tangential lawsuit in the case of Mike Nichols, wherein she might be called and deposed, under oath. She did not mind keeping quiet; she did mind lying, and being convicted of perjury. When *Star Magazine* phoned to let Ms. Flowers know they were printing a story about her affair with Clinton with or without her consent, she questioned whether she should come forward. When she heard Bill Clinton lie about the affair, she knew she had to come forward or the truth might never be known. Ms. Flowers was the only woman who could not be threatened into being quiet; the only woman Bill Clinton admitted having a relationship with and then lied about it.

One of the War Room's specialties was a lightning response to the news, while adapting a new story, for their candidates benefit. When they learned the Flowers affair was coming out and had to be dealt with, they turned to *60 Minutes* producer Don Hewitt, who immediately provided 15 minutes of exclusive airtime, following the most watched program of the year, the Super Bowl, which provided a lead in audience of 84 million people. This sort of programming, benefitting one candidate of one political party was unprecedented. The interview took place on January 26, 1992. Steve Croft conducted the interview. Croft was handed an exact script, as he was to word it, by War Room operatives. The whole appearance was to show the Clintons in the best possible light, while deflecting all of the rumors in the short span of one show.

Croft played his part, saying: "*TIME Magazine* just anointed Bill Clinton the front runner of the 1992 campaign. The tabloid magazine *The Star* put out a story that was picked up by the mainstream media, unsubstantiated…Keep in mind all of the allegations are unsubstantiated; all have been denied by everyone involved." Croft characterized the opponent and the article as, "The Flowers interview appeared in a tabloid article for which she was paid."

Then the Clintons followed a script as well: "Admit nothing, deny everything, make counter allegations, discredit the opposition."

Croft: "Describe your relationship [with Gennifer Flowers]."

Clinton: "Very limited."

Croft: "She accuses you of carrying on a 12-year affair."

Clinton: "That allegation is false."

Listen to the script, the question is very defined as a 12-year affair, therefore Clinton could say the allegation was false, knowing that the affair was 11 years and 363 days long or 12 years and one day long. Very lawyerly.

Then, Clinton made counter allegations and discredited Flowers, the opposition: "It was only when money came out that she changed her story…."

Then he discredited all future witnesses, when Clinton said, "You can expect more and more of these stories as long as they are handing out money."

Lastly, Clinton gave a non-answer which served as a denial, Croft asked: "You categorically deny ever having an affair?" Clinton: "I've said that before."

The script worked perfectly. The Clinton's seemed like the victims of the tabloid press, and they had suffered enough! And it appears that they never told the truth.

Back in the War Room, campaign volunteers were upset by the news of the Flowers affair. James Carville soothed their worries, reassuring the concerned that "Roger Ailes is behind the Flowers accusation."

After the interview, all rumors of Clinton's affairs were dismissed as "old news." When Flowers offered her taped conversations with Clinton to the press, they were discounted as edited, taken out of context, and fake.

In the wake of the interview, the Clinton's unleashed their media fixer, Syd Blumenthal, who began a personal destruction campaign against Gennifer Flowers by describing her as "the woman in red, trimmed in black to match the roots of her frosted hair..." When other women saw how Syd Blumenthal orchestrated the media's attack against Ms. Flowers, no one else dared to come forward.

Back at the Arkansas governor's mansion, the troopers who were Clinton's custodians, his drivers, his bodyguards knew better. They started talking among themselves about the affair and all the time, over the years, that Clinton had spent with Gennifer Flowers. When their supervisor, Raymond "Buddy" Young heard the scuttlebutt going around, he contacted each of the troopers individually to threaten them: "'Don't talk to the press, if you know what is good for you."

On March 8, 1992, an article about a scandal called Whitewater appeared in the New York *Times,* written by Jeff Gerth, who had researched the tangled finances of the Clinton three-step in depth. The article proved too successful. Gerth's editor at the New York *Times* told him he had to stop writing about the Clintons because the Clinton's were criticizing the article. Therefore, Gerth had a conflict of interest with any story he might write about the

Clintons. Gerth was effectively shut down on reporting a story he knew better than anyone else in the media, because he knew the story and it put the Clintons in a negative light.

That summer, another stage was carefully set when Bill won the Democratic nomination at the convention. The Clintons came out on stage with Chelsea, their daughter, beaming into the cameras, with Bill looking down at Hillary, calling her: "My Valentine Girl."

Just before the general election, George Stephanopoulos took a phone call from a reporter with a question about yet another scandalous Clinton behavior. Stephanopoulos listened for a second, then let the reporter know what was and was not a reporter's job in the Clinton era: "If you push that article, you will never work again in politics," he threatened. At the same time, within days of the election, the Clinton campaign was demanding press coverage of a leak from within the Justice Department, that a close associate of George H.W. Bush, Casper Weinberger, was being indicted; the indictment implicated Bush as having lied during the Iran Contra affair.

This would be the Clinton's *modus operandi:* to engage in scandalous financial, political, and personal behavior, because they are entitled and do not believe normal rules apply to them. Then the Clinton political organization engages in a systematic campaign threatening individuals who know the truth. Then a perfectly studied and expertly presented architecture of a non-truth is constructed and displayed, as in the *60 Minutes* interview. This is not the surreptitious lie of a child caught in some trivial misdoing. It is a cold, meticulously constructed, deliberate and organized web of deceit that bears false witness.

Joseph Goebbels's once wrote in his *Diary,* that if you repeat what is false often enough, you can convince anyone that a square is actually a circle, and a circle is a square. The Clinton machine is still working with the major media's full cooperation to this day, to make themselves seem as they want you to think.

Remember 1992? It was the "Year of the Woman." During which the media portrayed, and the public believed, that Bill Clinton was a trustworthy, devoted family man, who cared deeply about women.

In the 1992 election, Bill Clinton won with 43% of the vote, the same total the Democratic Party lost with four years earlier, and the Clinton administration proceeded to spin webs of deceit throughout his presidency. In the swirl of scandals, another three-step occurred that went largely unnoticed in the folds of the web but was more important in its implications and more grave in its effects, which have had dire ramifications to this day.

– Shadow –

Leviathans Bargain

We the People of the United States, in Order to form a more perfect Union, establish Justice, insure domestic tranquility[and] provide for the common defence...

The Constitution of the United States

Many readers will remember the fall of the Berlin Wall on November 9, 1989. It was the culmination of efforts by the U.S. and North Atlantic Treaty Organization since the end of World War II to defeat the tyranny of socialist communism in Russia. A great measure of the success of that strategy is owed to the discipline of the western democracies in having had a steadfast policy of controlling the exportation of technology, which could be converted to military uses.

The strict export policy began during World War II. After the war, it was administered by the Coordinating Committee for Multilateral Export Controls or COCOM. COCOM served as the economic arm of NATO, dedicated to keeping the Soviet Union and other Communist states, which included China, from achieving technological parity with NATO. The Reagan and Bush administrations went further, establishing a nine-point template, in assessing critical areas of technology which could not be sold to any state which posed a security threat to United States or to any U.S. ally or friend. All applications for export licensing were finally passed through a rigorous vetting system at the State Department, the only department which could ultimately approve the exportation of sensitive advanced technologies.

The U.S. and NATO therefore, developed a technological edge over the Soviet Union best exemplified by Ronald Reagan's "Star Wars" defense system initiative. It was a frontier of technology the Soviet Union could not keep up with financially, given their centrally planned economy. And it was technology they could not steal given COCOM controls. The Soviet effort to match U.S. and NATO's technological advances bankrupted their economic system, brought down the Berlin wall, and freed millions upon millions of peoples who had been trapped in Eastern Europe. The tyranny of communist Russia, which plundered its own people and the peoples of neighboring states, sustained by a totalitarian military, gave way because of the pressures emplaced against the Soviet Union by the world's democracies.

After the Soviet Union's fall, the only major communist state in the world to survive was China. In the late 1980s, China was far behind the U.S. and the world in its technology capabilities. Like the Soviet Union, China was barricaded by a strict regime of COCOM technological controls; after all, theirs is a totalitarian system.

In that same year of 1989, China had shown their determination against making any democratic reforms by invading its own capital of Beijing with a tank division to drive out of existence groups of thousands of their own citizens who were demonstrating peacefully for the same legal and political reforms which were sweeping through Eastern Europe that year. Thousands died beneath banners dedicated to the Chinese people's will for freedom. The international tide of democratic reform died right there in blood-soaked Tiananmen Square.

China's only real military threat at the end of the 1980s was its multimillion-man army. China had no satellite defense system. China had no super computers. Nor did China have accurate guidance systems for their "Long March" rockets, which are akin to our ICBMs. They had thousands of medium and long-range rockets in silos, but the Chinese were notorious for not being able to hit the side of a barn at 10 miles distance with any of them. And Chinese technology was not likely to improve, because the murderous acts in Tiananmen were not likely to inspire a relaxation in trading restrictions.

China was also notorious for selling whatever limited military technology it did possess, such as their rockets, to third world states who would pay their price. In the early 1990s, they were found to be selling their M-11 short range missiles to such states as Pakistan and North Korea. During the Bush administration, that transfer of dangerous weaponry was met with even stricter controls on COCOM compliance of technological exports. Then, all of a sudden, the conditions were changed, and the world became free to arm a blood-soaked tyranny to the teeth.

China's goal was not to democratize or to become a free enterprise market. The ambition of China's Communist Party was to become a better militarized tyranny, for which they needed a few things. On the technology front, China wanted the capacity to get military purposed satellites into orbit. They wanted guidance systems for their short range and intercontinental ballistic missiles. China wanted to acquire super computers necessary for command-control capability and communications in a military theater. On the intelligence front, China wanted U.S. based political and economic information. Finally, on the economic front, China wanted to convert its outdated industrial base from military production to civilian manufacturing of common products; then to use the profits of their exports to reinvest in the creation of a modern military capability.

To attain many of their goals, China needed three very specific sorts of people they were adept at identifying. First, an ethnic Chinese businessperson with operations inside and outside of China, who would work with Chinese military intelligence in return for large scale Chinese state business.

Enter number one, Mochtay Riady.

Mochtay Riady was an ethnic Chinese, Indonesian businessman, whose ancestors hailed from Fujian Province, China. Mochtay was enormously successful, having founded the Lippo Group, which began in real estate, insurance and banking in Indonesia, and later branched out into textiles, mining and land development that included a multitude of projects inside China. During the 1990s, in his ancestral province of Fujian alone, Riady interests were valued at $2 billion. The Riadys have worked with the central Chinese government in Beijing, as well as regional and local governments on all manner of public projects. In some of its holdings, the Lippo Group in China partnered with China Resources, a company controlled by Chinese military intelligence.

There are many convolutions in the Riady global network of business entities and financial institutions within China and Indonesia and around the world. *Newsweek* once reported that "moving cash around the globe and tangled webs of transactions has always been the Riady way." The Riady empire was valued at $12 billion in 1996.

Some of Mochtay's sons joined the family business. Steven Riady was educated in the U.S., whereafter he was put in charge of Lippo's China and Hong Kong business interests. James Riady was educated in the U.S as well, becoming a permanent resident. Whereafter, James undertook Lippo's Indonesian operations as well as the operations of a little venture in Little Rock, Arkansas.

James Riady partnered with a firm the reader will remember, (Witt) Stephens Inc., one of the largest private American investment banks outside of Wall Street. James Riady also partnered with Witt's son, Jackson Stephens, to become the co-owners of Arkansas' largest bank, the Worthen Bank, underwriters of State bond issues for Arkansas, while Bill Clinton was governor. It is a small world after all.

Chinese intelligence analysis in the late 80s and early 90s categorized America's politicians and U.S. political processes as highly prone to bribery and influence.

Enter number two, Bill and Hillary Clinton

Bill and Hillary Clinton, two persons described by those who know them best, as persons interested in money and power; as persons interested to gaining and keeping both.

Enter number three, a go-between, John Huang.

Huang was born in the same area of China the Riady family hailed from: Fujian Province. Huang went to the University of Connecticut and became an American citizen in 1977. He speaks five different dialects of Chinese perfectly. His manners and social graces are impeccable. He was hired by the Riady family, who stationed him for two years in their Hong Kong offices, from which he travelled throughout China and Asia extensively and met a great many officials. Huang spent another two years in Los Angeles and a further two years in New York, before he joined James Riady and the big time in Little Rock.

Like the Stephens and Riady families, John Huang supported Bill Clinton for governor. And when Clinton ran for president, they all knew what it meant: they had their man.

The donations began in earnest when Clinton was in trouble during the lead up to the New York primary. The campaign chest was empty and one of the biggest states in the primary season was very uncertain. Clinton had a private talk with James Riady. The Worthen Bank, which Riady controlled, issued $3.5 million in lines of credit to the campaign to get Clinton through the critical state of New York.

Following victory in the primaries, James Riady pledged $1 million for the general campaign. Then John Huang got busy: he donated a check in August for $50,000 from Hip Hing Holdings, one of Riady's American companies. A matching amount was wired to that account from Lippo in Jakarta Indonesia, the next week. Huang controlled funds from two other American Riady companies, San Jose Holdings and Toy Center Holdings which were funneling donations to the Democratic Party, totaling $800,000. In September, with the general election closing in, and Clinton in need of yet more money. And the money came again, from the Riady family, from Riady associates, and from Riady company executives totaling another $600,000 which was systematically funneled to various Democratic party operations in toss up states to help with operations.

By the time Bill Clinton was elected, the largest single donor to his campaign was not an American labor union, it was not an American industrialist, it was not an oil magnate or a Hollywood starlet, it was the Riady family. To celebrate, James Riady and John Huang donated another $100,000 each to inaugural festivities; they had a lot to celebrate.

On taking office, Bill Clinton made a pledge that included himself and his staff:

1. No lobbying for five years after they left government.
2. No activity on behalf of a foreign government.
3. No representation of a foreign government or foreign corporation for five years after being engaged in a trade negotiation.

Clinton promised to serve the American people first. And so, he signed an order that no American satellite with sophisticated technology could be launched on board a Chinese rocket to preserve the security of the American people. Clinton further warned the Chinese that they had one year to make "overall significant progress" in human rights violations or their most favored nation trade status would be removed. At the time, the United States was the world's sole superpower and could put pressure any nation, through trade policy, into observing the rights of humanity, based on America's unique founding doctrines.

Then a letter arrived on Clinton's desk, marked "Personal and Confidential" from Mochtay Riady, urging that rather than threatening withdrawal of China's trading status, "the best way of achieving political reform in China is through capitalist interaction." The interaction with Mochtay Riady helped change the policy of the world's lone superpower. America, the leader of the victorious free world and of a surging wave of international democracy, changed its policy from one of pressure towards a socialist tyranny to one of economic and strategic "engagement" with China. The change in policy came from the top.

The first step in Clinton's new policy began with a new appointee, Deputy Secretary of Defense William Perry, who over road NSA recommendations, Joint Chiefs of Staff objections, and long standing COCOM international law. In doing so, the Clinton administration approved the sale of advanced fiber optic communications technology to the Chinese company Hua Mei, which had ties to the Chinese military, the principal enforcers of China's tyranny.

The change of American policy continued. In the Pacific theater, the sole possessors of super computers were Japan and the United States. Such technology could be dual purposed for either civilian or military uses. On September 29, 1993, Clinton reversed long-standing U.S. and allied policies against export of sensitive technology to China and announced the U.S. was lifting the controls on the sale of supercomputers to China, without consulting America's longtime ally, Japan.

The transfer of such technology was governed by standing law in the United States under the Export Administrations Act of 1979, which had duly passed both houses of Congress and been signed into law by President Carter, as a national security control measure. The Clinton administration first attempted to rewrite the EAA laws. When Congress objected, the administration dismantled the law by going around it through new executive branch regulations, without consulting Congress, the houses of the people's representatives. The Clinton administration decided unilaterally to kill the COCOM accords which had contained advanced weapons proliferation since World War II on technology exports to dangerous states; and did so without consulting Congress or the democratic states of Asia or other U.S allies.

On September 30, 1993, Commerce Secretary Ron Brown issued a report stating that there would be a new export strategy that would create 20,000 American jobs for every $1 billion of U.S. exports, regardless of who the buyer was; and regardless of former restrictions on technology.

C. Michael Armstrong, head of the Satellite division of Hughes Electronics was the next to recommend policy changes to the new administration, this time regarding satellite technology. Armstrong wrote Clinton two letters, stating that U.S competitors were profiting from sales of satellite launchers to China, while American firms were excluded from Chinese markets. Armstrong reminded Clinton in a threatening manner, and in detail, regarding his financial support of the Democratic Party with $2.5 million of donations since 1991.

A Hughes Electronics partner, the Loral Corporation's CEO, and longtime Democratic fundraiser, Bernard Schwartz sent a further donation of $100,000 to the Democratic National Committee on the proviso that he could join a trade mission being organized by Ron Brown based on Brown's new export strategy. It was understood that the going price for the trip and high-level introductions to Chinese counterparts, was $100,000. When Schwartz returned from the trade junket, he rejoiced that the trip "helped open doors that were not open before." Schwartz came home with a very profitable accord with the Chinese government to sell it a state-of-the-art mobile telephone network. A network which would require the very latest satellite technology. The Loral satellites would be launched on Chinese rockets – precisely what the Communist Party of China wanted – at any price.

The satellites, which were part of the $650 million sale by Hughes and Loral to General Shen Rongjun, were of a kind previously used solely for spying upon enemies of the United States and its allies. The same caliber of satellites would now be used by China to spy on the U.S. and its allies. The satellites are also excellent for communications and command-and-control uses in conjunction with supercomputers when a military force is making a coordinated invasion, over the sea, through the air and with amphibious forces when one wants to conquer a sea-surrounded land mass, like that of a friend of the U.S.: Taiwan. In fact, the sale of the collective security of America and its democratic allies in Asia was going cheap.

But there was another hurdle to undergo for corporations like Hughes and Loral. The licenses for the sale of the satellites had to be approved by the State Department. Bernard Schwartz assured the Democratic Party that further donations could be expected....

And what of American security back home, in Washington DC., where China wanted intelligence gathering? Re-enter number three, John Huang, the go-between. John Huang was to leave the Lippo Group and join the Department of Commerce, he was given a severance payment of $788,750 from Lippo.

In December 1993, Bill Clinton appointed John Huang to the post of Deputy Assistant Secretary for International Affairs. It is the highest posting in the Commerce Department which *does not* require Senate approval of the appointment. At the end of January 1994, Huang received a top-secret clearance. A top-secret clearance had never been associated with the position Huang assumed, in fact, it was exceptionally rare for any person ever employed at Commerce. This clearance allowed Huang to see *any* intelligence reports on China. During the week of his appointment, Huang met with the President several times at the White House, in the company of James Riady.

Though Huang was supposed to deal with international trade involving every region of the globe, he told his CIA briefer he wanted intelligence on Southeast Asia, with more specific reference to China, Taiwan, and Viet Nam—countries of interest to both the Communist Party of China and the Riady family. While at Commerce, John Huang received 37 one-on-one CIA briefings. While at Commerce, Huang read between 370 and 500 products of United States CIA intelligence. A sample period of Huang's phone traffic from Commerce included 400 phone calls to various entities of the Riady empire and 140 phone calls to China, Indonesia, and Hong Kong. His Commerce office was not John Huang's sole communication center.

Across Pennsylvania Ave. from Commerce is the Willard Hotel, renowned for its history and its beautiful lobby, from which America uniquely derives the descriptive title of "lobbyist." Among the offices in the old building is one which was leased by Stephens Inc. of Little Rock, Arkansas; an office Huang used for free. Huang was known to come into the Stephens Inc. offices several times a week. He always carried a briefcase. He would send and receive faxes; he would send and receive mail and packages. Huang used the copier machine to copy documents. He regularly used the private phone in a side office. The secretary at Stephens Inc. distinctly remembered, that on the day of Huang's first CIA briefing, he stopped by the Stephens Inc. office in the afternoon and sent a fax to Lippo Ltd. in Hong Kong: the central office of Lippo operations in China. Huang often logged his daily events in his office calendar; his visits to the White House were recorded. His visits to the Stephens Inc. offices were never recorded.

Just a few of the CIA intelligence products which Huang received were: "Economic Issues Confronting Taiwan and China," "Investment Opportunities in China," "Succession of Power in China," "China Technology Transfers," "Investment Climate in Hong Kong." Each of these top-secret CIA intelligence products, paid for by American taxpayers, would be of extreme interest to any investment group or to any government. But they would be of particular interest to the Lippo Group, Stephens Inc. and the Chinese Communist Party: it is the American Government's state-of-the-art view on those subjects. No information on earth is more valuable to governments or to large scale investors. The information formed a new international component to the Clinton's old three step.

John Huang had a very busy year working for the American people in 1994, as did the President. On June 2, Bill Clinton again followed Mochtay Riady's advice and extended China's most-favored nation trade status. On July 13, Clinton issued presidential waivers #PL 101-246 to allow US satellites to be launched from Chinese rockets. Yet, there was still the licensing necessary from the State Department to export the technology to contend with.

But something else happened in 1994. The Republicans won a landslide victory in the House of Representatives, gaining the majority in that chamber for the first time in 40 years. Bill Clinton and his policies were that unpopular. Worse news emerged in 1995, Bill Clinton himself was underwater in the polls for the next presidential election, so much so that an old friend from his Arkansas days, Dick Morris, raised the alarm that without a substantial media effort, Clinton might soon be out of power. Morris advised that millions of dollars needed to be raised and an ad campaign begun immediately to stave off disaster at the polls in '96. From that moment, Clinton became even more obsessed with how to raise more and more and more money, with the single purpose of staying in power.

Terry McAullife had acted on a method of raising funds earlier in the year. He had suggested Clinton meet personally with major supporters and charge $50,000 or $100,000 for the privilege. The strategy had worked, some events were even held in the White House, in contravention of White House Counsel, Bernard Nussbaum's admonition that "no fundraising calls or (campaign) mail may emanate from the White House or any other federal building, and no contributions may be accepted at the White House or any other federal building." Despite Nussbaum's recitation of campaign law, McAullife's strategy was adopted and then adapted.

A meeting was held on September 10, 1995. In attendance were Bill and Hillary Clinton, Harold Ickes, Leon Panetta, and DNC Chairman, Don Fowler. The question: should Dick Morris' all-in strategy on fundraising be undertaken? The goal: raising $44 million in excess of campaign spending limits by raising "soft money" contributions, the kind that did not count under Federal Election Commission rules.

The strategy became one of raising contributions through a myriad of menu offerings to major donors including: Democratic Party committee memberships, overseas trade mission memberships, seats at the President's Box for Kennedy Center performances, seats for trips on Air Force One or Air Force Two. Donations would also be accepted for the private use of the White House tennis courts or the pool.

Or one could have coffee inside the White House. Attendees of the coffees were of two kinds: first, political appointees who held jobs within the Administrative State, who determined federal regulatory policy and, second, wealthy businesspersons with issues before the same appointee's agencies, whose businesses were benefitted or beleaguered by regulations the appointees oversaw. Everyone knew the price of the ticket was higher based on how much influence one wanted to buy. One could also "buy in" to attending high-level policy meetings in the White House. A strange thing about these coffees and meetings: *none* were ever noted on Bill Clinton's official presidential schedule and no reporters were ever invited.

One didn't necessarily have to buy into such events. When either Bill Clinton or Albert Gore Jr. had a minute to spare, they were on the phone, pushing for more money. A donor who contributed $100,000 after one Gore phone call, later admitted: "there were elements of a shakedown about the call. It was very awkward. For a vice president, particularly this vice president, who has real power and is the heir apparent to ask for money, gave me no choice. I have so much business that touches the federal government – the telecommunications act, tax policy (and) regulations galore." On another call, a conference call with a few donors, Gore was questioned about the legality of asking for contributions from his office as vice president, he gave the same answer repeatedly: "my counsel advises me...there is no controlling legal authority that says any of these activities violated any law."

In fact, Clinton and Gore were legal and fiscal micromanagers of this massive fundraising effort. Along with going over the law, they went over the budget with Harold Ickes and noticed their accounting needed adjusting. In case of a federal audit, they added a line-item of $1.5 million. And there might be an expense for fines from the Federal Election Commission, they added a line-for fines of $1 million. How to fill the budget hole? Harold Ickes thought he might start a program for large contributors which would result in better coordination and appointments to boards and commissions. You know, the kinds of Boards and Commissions that control the economy.

Another money-raising idea surfaced during a meeting in September 1995 in the Oval Office, with James Riady, John Huang and the former Chairman of the Rose Law Firm, and now Lippo counsel, Joe Giroir. Why not move John Huang out of Commerce and over to the DNC to handle Asian contributors and Asian money? John Huang would have to keep his top-secret clearance, of course.

The efforts of the fundraising plan raised $27 million from 103 White House coffees that served 358 paying guests, which equals $75,419 per coffee. That is a lot to pay for a coffee, something else must have been served. The Lincoln Bedroom itself was used to raise donations to the Democratic Party. Four hundred four guests slept in the room Lincoln himself could never sleep in, as he paced the room every night during the time he spent in sacrifice, trying to save America's experimental democracy. The Clintons sold the room and the democratic process, for $13,366 per night.

Among the donors was Loral CEO Bernard Schwartz, who gave an additional $1.5 million to the Democratic Party during the 1996 election campaign. On March 12, 1996, President Clinton signed a decision memorandum, overriding the policy of his own Secretary of State, Warren Christopher, and transferred authority for satellite exportation licensing from the State Department to the Commerce Department of Ron Brown. Thereby, Hughes and Loral were awarded the licenses to export their satellites and the technology to China. On May 23, 1996, Bill Clinton again renewed China's most-favored nation trade status.

This is the problem with an Administrative State that controls so much of an economy, one it regularly invades and always regulates. Decisions are made for a whole nation within the confines of one room where coffee and public policy are served to the highest donors. A room wherein there are no voting citizens or their representatives, wherein there is one law in the form of the one person who controls the Executive Branch and can sell it. It's not just an Administrative State run by the executive branch that controls an economy – it's a business, a very lucrative political family business.

It's a family business that might have escaped the public's notice, if some of the donors who attended the White House coffees hadn't been noticed, while they were funneling foreign money into an American political party.

Johnny Chung had been a visitor 49 times to the White House, usually on the authority of Hillary Clinton's office. He had donated $366,000 to the Democratic National Committee. Chung remarked that he saw the "White House is like a subway: you have to put in coins to open gates." Some of those coins, $300,000 worth, were given to Chung by Chinese General Ji Shengde, who said to Chung, "We like your president very much. We would like to see him reelected...You can give it to the president and to the Democratic Party."

Another regular visitor was Yah Lin Trie, who had contributed $177,000 to the Democratic National Committee while earning an annual salary of $30,000. Trie personally escorted Wang Jun to a White House breakfast with President Clinton. Jun was a Chinese weapons manufacturer and exporter to rogue states, who was interested in acquiring dual use technologies from American companies. Trie later became a tip-off to persons curious as to where all of this foreign money was coming from, when he showed up unexpectedly at the office of Michael Cardoza, Executive Director of Clinton's Presidential Legal Defense Fund, with hundreds of checks and money orders stuffed in a manila envelope, in amounts of $500 and $1,000 exactly, totaling $460,000.

Other foreign contributors were more systematic, and worked through the official channel of John Huang, the go-between who was made Vice Chairman of Finance for the Democratic National Committee. One such couple were Soraya and Arief Wiriandinata, who contributed $450,000 to the Committee, after having received $1 million from Soraya's father, Hashim Ning, an Indonesian business partner of the Riady family.

Another method, oft used, was to funnel contributions from American Riady companies through Huang to the DNC, followed by a reimbursement of those accounts from foreign Riady holdings. Huang would also donate funds personally, and later be reimbursed directly from Lippo with cash. Huang funneled a total of another $3.5 million dollars to the committee.

John Huang also organized fundraisers; one of which was co-produced with Maria Hsia, a long-time Gore fundraiser at the Hsi Lai Temple of California. The speakers at the event were Albert Gore Jr., Robert Matsui, a House representative from California, and Don Fowler, the National Chairman of the DNC. The event raised $140,000 from Bhuddist Nuns and Monks who had taken sacred vows, committing their lives to poverty. One can see how some of these events would raise attention.

None the less, while John Huang was working for the DNC, he visited the White House 78 times; he was also a sometimes visitor to the Chinese Embassy on Connecticut Avenue NW. During that time, James Riady visited the White House 20 times, and in September 1996, just before the election, Riady spoke to Clinton again to lobby personally for better trade relations between the United States and China, with the sole person who had single handedly done so much to change those relations already.

Then in that same September of 1996, a story began to break about all that money. And pictures began to appear on every

American TV screen of Al Gore posing at the Hsi Lai Temple of California. The images said a thousand words.

— Shadow —

Leviathan's Defenses

Justice is the end of government. It is the end of civil society.
—Alexander Hamilton

When the fundraising scandal broke, the Administration faced a barrage of questions, in answer, Don Fowler held a news conference, representing the DNC, he stated: "Never has there been any desire, plan, or intent to evade requirements of applicable laws and regulations."

White House Press Secretary, Michael McCurry addressed the media himself to affirm, that: "To the best of my knowledge, no one here had any knowledge of" misdoings with the Chinese.

When asked by a reporter about receiving money from Johnny Chung in the White House, Margaret Williams, Hillary Clinton's Chief of Staff, said it did not violate the law, "if you receive a contribution and all you do is pass it on, and you've been involved in no way in any solicitation on public property and you just pass it through; that is what the regulation provides for!"

It is accurate to say that, over time, Bill Clinton's answers evolved. Right after winning the election, Clinton gave his first press conference on November 8th and stated he had "absolutely not" been influenced in foreign policy by foreign donations. He was so outraged at the idea, Clinton called for campaign finance reform. Later he said, "I do not know whether it is true or not. Therefore, since I don't know, it can't and shouldn't affect the larger long-term strategic interests of the American people in our foreign policy." To further defend himself and the Chinese, he stated: "Chinese President Jiang Zemin emphatically denied to me personally that their government had tried to do anything to influence the outcome of this election."

As clamoring for an independent counsel grew loud, Clinton's response became more legalese: "I don't believe you can find any evidence of the fact that I have changed policy solely because of the contribution." Clinton defied anyone to absolutely prove that there was not one other reason for which he changed policy, other than a contribution. Clinton did take a preemptive legal action though, in February 1997, when he signed an executive order making transfers of technology, such as Loral's to China, legal. Thus, taking the teeth out of any future legal inquiry into Loral and Bernard Schwartz and all of that easing of trade barriers for the sale of sensitive technology to a tyrannical state.

Representative Gerald B.H. Solomon, representative for New York, asked FBI Director Louis Freeh to investigate John Huang and the Lippo Group for legal cause over "economic espionage against the United States by a foreign corporation having direct ties to the Peoples Republic of China."

When we speak of the Administrative State's castle keep, it is about a fortification with circular lines of defense—mechanisms which defend against the imposition of common law so that the power of the State stays in the hands of those the State favors. As the curious in the country became many, a defense had to be mounted to defend Clinton, who had just won an election, and Al Gore, the presumptive heir, who *had* to win the next.

Rumors began to circulate through the corridors of power that Janet Reno, the Attorney General since 1992, might not be renewed by Clinton for a second term. The Administrative State's defenses began to stir. In the early stages of the political crisis, the Justice Department moved swiftly to have Inspector Generals from the Commerce Department do the investigating, rather than the FBI, so that Commerce could investigate itself. That did not happen; it was too obvious a conflict of interest.

Suddenly, dozens of the would-be witnesses to a new investigation began leaving the country. Many other witnesses, like Pauline Kanchanalak, a friend of John Huang, who donated $679,000 to the DNC, started removing her computer hard drives and collecting her other business records, presumably to destroy them. At the Commerce Department, they began hiding and destroying files related to the trade mission junkets.

Then the Justice Department's original Los Angeles investigators assigned to look into the dealings at the Hsi Lai Temple were abruptly taken off the case by a career man, Lee Radek. Radek sent them a "cease and desist immediately" order and then assured them that they needn't worry, an independent counsel was being assigned to take over the investigation. On the same day, Lee Radek assigned an inexperienced Justice Department neophyte named Laura Ingersoll, to lead the investigation and to report and work directly for him.

Meanwhile the cries grew louder for an independent counsel, led by a demand from Senator John McCain. Janet Reno said no. Then, President Clinton and Atty. Gen. Reno held a personal and private meeting, with just the two of them in the room, about the size of a plane fuselage on a tarmac, on December 12, 1996. On December 13, 1996, Clinton confirmed that Janet Reno would continue as Attorney General.

Laura Ingersoll directed her investigators "not to pursue any matter related to solicitation of funds for access to the President." When asked why the core of the investigation could not be investigated, Ingersoll replied, "That is the way the American political process works." In fact, Ingersoll oversaw the agents with a microscope and frustrated them when they asked to execute customary search warrants to stop the destruction of evidence. Ingersoll would not allow it.

An FBI agent, Ivian Smith, wrote a letter to FBI Director Louis Freeh, saying he had a "lack of confidence" in the attorneys the Justice Dept. assigned to the case: "I am convinced that the team leading this investigation is, at best, simply not up to the task. The impression left is the emphasis on how *not* to prosecute matters, not how to aggressively conduct investigations leading to prosecutions."

Freeh responded by sending a memo to Reno requesting that Lee Radek and his team be removed from the investigation because they were "not capable of conducting the thorough, aggressive kind of investigation which was required." Reno denied the request. Freeh also objected that he was not consulted on whether the case warranted an Independent Counsel, such a consultation would have been customary. Objection ignored. Freeh wrote the FBI's general counsel that he was worried that the FBI was being cut out of the fund-raising probe and that the investigation was being singularly managed by Reno's Justice Department.

Finally, as part of the investigation, there had to be interviews of Bill Clinton and Albert Gore Jr. The terms of the interviews had to be negotiated. According to White House Counsel, the interviews could only go ahead if Clinton and Gore were not asked any questions related to or about the Riady family, the Lippo Group, John Huang, or the fundraiser at the Hsi Lai Temple. The Justice Department agreed to the terms. They became interviews about nothing.

And what about the go-between John Huang? Huang refused to testify without immunity, so his testimony was missing. As were his DNC telephone logs, his outgoing correspondence, his travel records, the details of his visits to the White House, details of his visits to Clinton campaign headquarters; and there was no remaining evidence of business he conducted outside of his DNC office, such as at Stephens Inc.

The U.S Senate voted unanimously on March 11, 1997, to hold hearings on the growing scandal. The committee of inquiry was to be chaired by Senator Ted Thompson. The hearings would be hampered by the fact that of more than 100 necessary witnesses, many fled the country, such as Yah Lin Trie and Pauline Kanchalanak. Other would-be witnesses, such as James Riady and John Huang, refused to testify. And dozens of others pled the Fifth Amendment against self-incrimination. Finally, Janet Reno directed the FBI not to share information with the Senate Committee.

The scandal divided the Senate right down the middle. The Democrats formed a procedural ring for the administrations defense, just as the Justice Department had formed a defensive ring around the evidence. The Democratic Party denounced the hearings as partisan and one-sided; they refused to sign onto necessary subpoenas to demand evidence. The Democratic Party defended those who did not testify and those who pled the Fifth Amendment. And they used every procedural opportunity to stall the hearings and run out the clock by a preset date, to cripple the inquiry.

The media formed another ring of defense as Ted Thompson and the Republicans were regularly vilified for wanting to bring down a presidency. The inquiry was framed as one that was a waste of the people's time and money and a distraction keeping government from doing the people's business.

The most ironic media defense was voiced by Katie Couric in an interview with reporter Bob Woodward, on her newscast, Couric asked, "Are members of the media too scandal obsessed, looking for something at every corner?" The Clinton administration had created so many scandals with Watergate, Travelgate, etc., that the multitude of scandals defended against the people of the country taking any single scandal seriously and left the country exhausted.

Bill Clinton took the time to express a sad regret to the media, telling reporters that he was "sick at heart" that the Democratic National Committee may have accepted foreign donations.

Even with all the defenses erected by the castle guards: the Justice Department, the Democratic Party and the media, the Senate Committee still found that:

> "The President and his aides demeaned the offices of the president and the vice president; that the administration and the DNC pulled down all the barriers that would normally be in place to keep out illegal contributions. What was left was the strong suspicion that they were not only selling access to high-ranking officials but selling policy as well."

After the Senate hearings, both Louis Freeh and Charles LaBella, the head of the Justice Department's campaign-finance task force, sent separate memos to Janet Reno strongly recommending that the evidence so far obtained overwhelmingly suggested the necessity of an Independent Counsel who would have the legal power and independence to discover the truth. Janet Reno ignored both memos.

That is when another scandal emerged to eclipse the stories of influence peddling. In January 1998, the story of Monica Lewinsky broke in the press. Janet Reno decided to hand Kenneth Starr the power of an Independent Counsel to investigate the affair. Starr had already been demeaned by the press as a hopelessly biased partisan, and the stigma stuck. Thereafter, it seemed that the media's focus became that all of the investigations were just about sex and the accusations did not rise to the level of an impeachable offense. The media and the country were riveted by every word out of the mouths of Linda Trip, Monica Lewinsky, Betty Curry, Vernon Jordan, and Syd Blumenthal. Meanwhile they never heard a word out of the mouths of James Riady, John Huang, Johnnie Chung, Yah Lin Trie, Maria Hsi or Pauline Kanchalanak about influence peddling and possible treasonable acts.

The Administrative State's castle defense system against a possible impeachment for treason was complete.

After the Senate hearings, other hearings took place in the House, which the country largely ignored. The hearings were specifically about Hughes and Loral. The committee was of the view that the Hughes Corporation and Loral Space and Electronics illegally assisted China with satellite and rocket technology, which was used to modernize China's military missile program. It also believed that the Clinton administration deliberately lowered the sensitive technology standards, which allowed the companies to do it. The sensational media parade of stories about Bill and Monica and what is or isn't sex eclipsed the committee's findings.

The Price of Leviathan's Privilege

Here we have, in capsule form, what is wrong with how our government has concentrated in one place over the past century.

Our Administrative State has become an insular circle of power. The notorious Clinton White House coffees merely moved the power dealing that is the day-to-day commerce of the State from the corridors of agencies and lobbyists to the environs of the White House, where it was more noticeable. In the corridors of power, it is determined who is favored and who is not based on tribute money which keeps the party handing out favors in power. The problem is that this system of influence peddling has been growing and concentrating in Washington D.C., since FDR invaded the economy and assumed to one branch of government so much centralized power, that it could be sold over coffee. Choosing between two U.S. companies in a sector and deciding who wins and who loses is now the day-to-day business of our State. The more that choice is concentrated in a single authority, the more tyrannical that system is. The reader will note that there were no teachers or carpenters or plumbers or librarians or policemen or firemen or family doctors or other regular citizens at the coffees held in the White House, the nominal "people's home."

Once caught, the inner circle's castle defense system went to work as line after line of defensive circles moved to protect the wrongdoing and the wrong doers, rather than the Constitution. From the Justice Department, which formed a protective moat around the investigation; to the Democratic Party, which barricaded the truth from being viewed by the American people; to the media which spun its arrows at Republicans while shielding the DNC and the Clinton administration. This inner circle of the State built a concentrated defensive system that established injustice, coverted evidence, and made those who would inquire after the truth, the villains.

What made this episode unique is that the inner circle of an enemy state was purchasing influence in the inner circle of our State through donations which helped, to a measure, in Clinton/ Gore assuming and preserving power in our government. What made this episode intolerable is that the actions were defended by the full apparatus of a political party and by agencies of the State, when our common national security was at stake. What makes the episode relatable to the present day, is that it set the precedent that those in the inner circle are for all intents and purposes untouchable, if they are of one particular political party and work in synergy with politically interested agencies, something never conceived in the innocence of Woodrow Wilsons's ideals

And what of the effects of this policy shift towards China by our State's inner circle? When the Clinton administration began, China had no satellite defense system, China had no super computers, and China did not have missiles with reliable guidance systems. At the end of the Clinton administration, China had a growing satellite defense system. China had hundreds of supercomputers operating in the service of the Chinese military. And China had intercontinental ballistic missiles with the guidance technology necessary to make precision-strikes on American cities. China fulfilled most of its ambitions.

On-going favoritism towards China fulfilled the last ambition. While the Administrative State attended to its regular business of creating ever more taxes on American businesses, as it continued to create volumes of costly new business regulations for American manufacturers to follow, it opened our domestic consumer markets to Chinese products made by slave laborers in the Chinese manufactories, that used to make their antiquated military weapons. With the profits our consumers provided, the Communist Party of China financed its modern military, one that today is a threat to our own.

Such have become the effects of the prerogatives exercised by a central power, operating in a manner that is unanswerable to the American people and is increasingly unanswerable to the law.

No one from either Loral or Hughes ever paid a penalty for modernizing China's military. No one other that Johnny Chung, who received probation for unlawful contributions, paid a substantial price for making foreign contributions to influence American government policy.

Bill Clinton, in one of his last acts of office, revoked his and his administration's pledge not to work on behalf of or lobby for foreign governments and not to lobby in matters of trade his administration had negotiated… Everyone was free to make more money.

Lastly, America, the leader of the world's democracies, allowed communist China to flourish upon our wealth, while China acquired the military and policing technology necessary to further strangle their own people in a totalitarian prison. That has been America's answer to China's freedom fighters, who gave their lives on Tiananmen Square in hopes of becoming a democracy.

George W. Bush

Nine months into George W. Bush's presidency, a horror occurred in New York, which reduced blocks of the city center to cinders. Over 2,600 persons were murdered in an act of terror after the hijackings of American Airlines Flight 11 and

United Airlines Flight 175. In Washington, another 125 persons lost their lives as American Flight 77 caved-in the Pentagon. And over Pennsylvania, four hijackers were overtaken by 40 American heroes aboard United Flight 93—who determined that no other Americans would die, and did so at the cost of their lives.

The events of 9/11 were seismic. President Bush spoke that afternoon through a teleconference to his security team, and stated that his first term of office was, in effect, at an end. From that moment, the activities of his administration would have one designing principle: "We are at war against terror. From this day forward, this is the new priority of our administration." The events of 9/11 had shown how porous our country could be when faced by a merciless, implacable foe.

The United States has a 5,525-mile border with Canada and a 1,989-mile border with Mexico. The combined lengths of our multitudes of shorelines are 95,000 miles. In 2001, along our borders and via our seaports and airports, there were 350 official ports of entry. Within the interior of the nation is an area of 3.4 million square miles in which to hide. How does one even begin to secure all of that?

At the time of 9/11, homeland security was a responsibility diffused among 100 different bureaucratic organizations. The Bush Presidency's designing principle became that of consolidating responsibility for America's security into a single, new federal organization: The Department of Homeland Security. Under the new department's umbrella shifted the Coast Guard, the guardians of our shores; the Border Patrol, who stand as sentinels protecting our frontiers with Mexico and Canada; the Immigration and Naturalization Service, who vet all of those entering the country; and the Transportation and Security Administration, the gatekeepers who monitor the over half-a-billion people traveling in and out of the United States every year.

In addition, Homeland Security would be in charge of preparation for federal emergency response. The department would evaluate the vulnerability of critical infrastructure such as energy, communications, and public safety and health systems. These are all critical functions of a commander-in-chief that are necessary for the security of a people in the modern era. It is not a matter of federal *ownership* of industrial sectors, but the authority of mobilization of assets *within* those sectors in times of emergency that was the aim of Homeland Security's consolidation of authority.

There was another critical area of the nation's defenses on 9/11 in which the nation felt failure the most: its lack of sufficient intelligence about the foreign terrorist network that launched the attacks, and of the activities of the hijackers who had planned and carried them out from safe-havens *within* the United States. Because of this, President Bush wanted to merge the capabilities of a number of previously separate intelligence organizations. Some, like the CIA, were created for foreign intelligence collection, and others, like the FBI, were focused on domestic law enforcement and intelligence. Ultimately, Homeland Security would contain an office whose directive was to assemble, analyze, and fuse intelligence from a myriad of government sources—among them the CIA, NSA, INS, DEA, DOE, DOT, and Customs departments. The DOJ and the FBI would maintain their roles as the country's main law enforcement entities, with new priority given to enhancing counter-terrorism capabilities.

On May 29, 2002, Attorney General Brent Ashcroft and FBI Director Robert Mueller announced that the FBI was being reorganized to affect better coordination with the CIA. Likewise, the Department of Homeland Security was created in 2002—combining twenty-two different federal departments and agencies to work in synergy under one cabinet-level agency charged with the security of the American people. A new office was also created by the Intelligence Reform and Terrorism Prevention Act. The director of national intelligence would oversee America's newly unified intelligence community.

The Homeland Security Department's mission was, and is, to protect the homeland of the United States. By extension, and as has been said many times, it was created essentially to protect "the American way of life"—the citizens of the nation in their natural rights, as codified in the Constitution as well as in the laws, liberties, and democratic processes uniquely framed in America. The creation of the Homeland Security Department was one of the great achievements of the Bush Presidency.

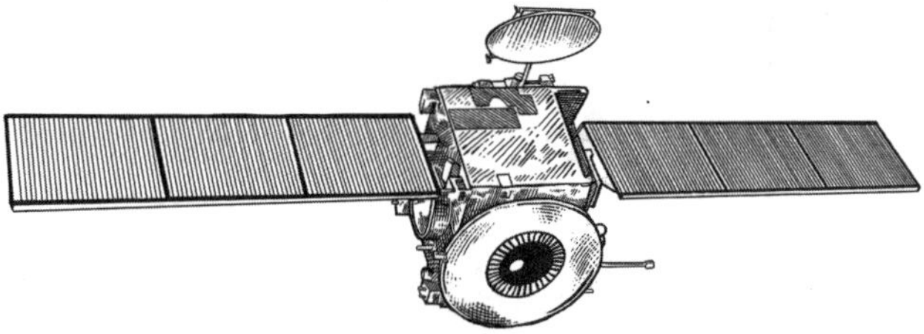

— Along the American Road —

One of the most wonderous characteristics of free enterprise and capitalism is the endless horizon the system opens to life altering innovations. In an open system functioning under common economic law, the possibilities for invention are literally infinite.

In the 1960's – 1970's, IBM created a massive mainframe computer with the capacity of holding all the known information in the world. In the next decade, Steven Job's Apple Corporation brought that capacity into a computer that was a personal model, available to every individual and home; which could be attached to one's home phone for access to the accumulated knowledge in U.S libraries. At the same time, phones were becoming "mobile" and took on the new name of cellular.

In the 1990's, the incorporated computer phones, began having global reach, literally connecting individuals from the distant ends of the earth to a common communication system.

In 2004, the new phenomenon of Social-Media opened with Facebook. Participants joined in a new common "digital" square to share information and ideas... The square soon became one of the world's largest marketplaces.

In 2006, Apple led the way again, with the innovation of the smart phone or I Phone, a computer, which in the 1960's might have filled a gymnasium, was contained in a 3 x 6 x ¼" oblong box, with a phone application. If you are reading this "book" on your I Phone, you are holding more technology in your hand right now than was aboard ship on the Apollo 11 mission that landed on the moon in 1969.

If you were sitting in your home in 1969, watching the moon landing, you had to be watching one of only three available network channels. Sitting in your home today, you have access to thousands of channels and every entertainment property ever made, through your home entertainment center's satellite feed connection to every streaming distribution company in the world, from Hulu, to Amazon, to Netflix to Disney...

We are now entering the verge of virtual reality: video games, and the creation of a digital reality that appears to *be* the reality of yet another new frontier, digital universes available in a microchip.

As I put it earlier in this work, when television was invented, it brought the world into everyone's living room. Today, everyone's living room is viewable to the world...Our new phone's, our new computers, our new televisions are all two-way systems: they can be used for viewing or be used as a viewing port camera. They can be used to listen to or they can be used as a microphone for listening...Everyone's telephone is, of course a two-way system, but can also be invaded by a third party seeking intelligence, about any user.

New technology is always the ultimate temptation to those in power. Through all the advances along technologies frontiers, governments find the nearest way to intrude into the individual's private, personal sphere. For example, China uses every technological step forward to further surveil the activities of their own people to ensure that they are doing what they are supposed to do, or their people face pain and punishment. In the United States, we have a government as technologically capable as China's, the question is whether our government is using that capability to secure our rights of privacy or to invade them?

It raises a critical question: who monitors that? Does the government alone decide how invasive into a citizen's privacy it can be?

This may prove to be the present and future's ultimate dividing line in determining a government's democratic principles - whether one applies technology to invade individual rights and privacy, or applies technology to protect an individual's rights and privacy, which means a government must barricade itself from becoming an intruder into the lives of its citizens.

Again and again, it has been said...the hardest thing for any government to do throughout human history is to control itself, to acknowledge that there is a power it should never possess or exercise.

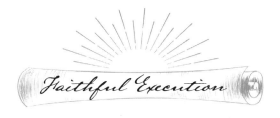

Faithful Execution

– Light –

The foremost of our founders, George Washington, provides the deepest well of the American experience. It is a sacred well, which never runs dry. The reader may remember that Washington used his power, during the Revolutionary War, always under the authority of the people's assembly, earning the praise of Thomas Mifflin, president of the Continental Congress, who said of Washington: "You have conducted the great military contest with wisdom and fortitude invariably regarding the rights of the civil power through all (the war's) disasters and changes." Washington had proven to be an unswerving servant to the people's representatives. When the war was over, after he'd endured those years of insufferable trials for America's freedom, he just as dutifully returned the power used to secure victory back to the Congress and the people—rather than using it against them to empower himself.

The reader may also remember that Washington was called upon to preside over the Constitutional Convention, where he sat every day, always listening, as fifty-five of the people's representatives from thirteen new states wrote what they believed to be a document of law that would secure the citizenry of their new country in their natural rights and liberties. It was a document of barricades against the assumption by any central government of an omnipotent power over the states and the people. Washington dutifully sat and listened as the Constitution took shape, and established a diffused system of power through legal processes which would keep in harness the ambitions of an American federal government. The Constitution would also contain a catalogue of rights, deemed to be derived from nature and nature's God, which would secure the people under a system of constitutional common law rather than under Washington or any other person. It was created to be the highest law in the land to which all other future legislation would be subject—as all future law would have to prove in-keeping with the original laws of the nation.

The Constitution of the United States is composed of the words that define our highest law. More than any other single thing, it defines what America is. It is, as well, a definition of law created to guard America from becoming what she is not and should never be—another tyrannical prison-keep of humanity. The wisest man on the world's living rim when the Constitution was writ, Benjamin Franklin, wept when he read it. He possessed that great a faith in the Constitution as a unique social compact that created our Republic. James Wilson, another of our founders, said of it: "We should consider that we are providing a constitution for future generations and not merely for the circumstances of the moment." Our Constitution was considered by those who wrote it as the "new order for the ages"—not the new order of the hour. Human liberty was a new being in that era of revolutions. And of all the revolutions of that time, it took root only in America. The founders desired that after all the sacrifice, fighting, and war, American liberty would continue by way of our highest law, which they uniquely forged for eternity like those physical laws which create the patterns of the stars.

After the Constitutional Convention, Washington had yet another duty to perform for his country. As written in the Constitution, only the House and Senate could create legislation. Only the judiciary, in the form of a supreme court, could validate new law as being in keeping with our constitutional law. And only the executive could "faithfully execute" the laws so created. Laws that are written and not enforced are not effective, they may as well not exist. Worse—if not executed, the opposite of the written law becomes, in effect, the law. If one does not enforce a law against littering, the ability to litter freely is essentially the law. As the Constitution is our highest law, the faithful execution of law is the president's highest duty within our form of governance. Otherwise, the Constitution does not work, and the people's rights are unsecured

Washington was not only the first wartime officer to arrive at constitutional government; he was also one of the first citizens to approve the Constitution through the execution of his signature. And, on becoming the first citizen to assume the office of president, he became the first to enforce Article II, Section 3 of the Constitution, which requires that the president "take Care that the Laws be faithfully executed."

In all the prison keeps of human history, enforcing the law has been easy. Those who *oppose* the pharaoh or monarch or emperor are punished to varying degrees until they come into conformity with the one will of the tyrant. In America—the reason we are different—is that the president has to *protect* those who oppose him. It is the president's first duty to be the faithful executor of the Bill of Rights, which enumerates the legal protections of every U.S. president's *opponents*. If a president only protects those who adore him or her—that is the stuff of tyrants.

So, it was rendered that a president of the United States, who faithfully defends the Constitution's provisions, cannot arbitrarily seize the lands of those one does not like...or break up associations one does not believe in...or muzzle a reporter one might disagree with. Neither can a president who is faithful to the Constitution create laws that one thinks are superior to considerations of constitutional law, as there is nothing in this land superior to constitutional law. The executive office is not a master overlording the people, but the servant of a constitution constructed to protect the people from anyone that would be their master. It is through this instrument that we arrive at our just common laws—the equal execution of which is the president's first duty.

Finally, when faithfully executed, every member of our government, high and low, and most importantly the president, is subject to the same law as the farmers in Virginia or the ranchers in Wyoming or the schoolteachers in Louisiana—that is the law as given to us by our founders, and to which George Washington himself was as subject as any other citizen. George Washington gave his entire life to America's opportunity to be a constitutional democracy, to the Constitution's creation, and to the example of its proper execution. It was a life well spent and an example well given to every president since.

Another fierce proponent of our constitutional government was one who fought through the crucible of the Civil War to preserve it. In 1838, Abraham Lincoln said this about our constitutional Law:

> *"Let every American, every lover of liberty, every well-wisher to his posterity, swear by the blood of the Revolution, never to violate in the least particular, the laws of the country; and never to tolerate their violation by others. As the patriots of seventy-six did to the support of the Declaration of Independence, so to the support of the Constitution and Laws, let every American pledge his life, his property, and his sacred honor; let every man remember that to violate the law, is to trample on the blood of his father, and to tear the character of his own, and his children's liberty. Let reverence for the laws, be breathed by every American mother, to the lisping babe, that prattles on her lap—let it be taught in schools, in seminaries, and in colleges; let it be written in Primers, spelling books, and in Almanacs; let it be preached from the pulpit, proclaimed in legislative halls, and enforced in courts of justice."*

It was Lincoln who gave his life that the promise made in the Declaration of Independence that "all men are created equal" could be emblazoned into our constitutional law through a four-year war that cost over a million American casualties. However, take note that even Lincoln did not just proclaim this statement to be a law—that would have been unconstitutional and against everything for which the war was fought. One cannot right the Constitution by wronging it.

Instead, Lincoln envisioned the design of amending the Constitution as the best, most just outcome of the war. After

Lincoln's death, his political heirs shepherded his legal design through the constitutionally appointed means of the amendment process, whereby the 13th, 14th, and 15th Amendments were passed and became part of the highest law of the land, giving all citizens equal rights and protections under common law—no matter their race or color—because all persons are created equal. No longer were citizen's rights compromised constitutionally as being "other and lesser" because of race. The nation went through one of the most painful crucibles in human history to mend the Constitution's greatest flaw, making the equal execution of the law meaningful to all. Such was both the founders' and the reformers' love of and devotion to our Constitution.

— Shadow —

Leviathan's Lash

Then came a president of another kind—the founder of our "administrative state." The reader may remember that Woodrow Wilson did not believe that human rights are either "natural" or "unalienable," but that human rights are contingent on the times—therefore, rights and laws are changeable! As Wilson said: "We are not bound to adhere to the doctrines held by the signers of the Declaration of Independence; we are as free as they to make and unmake governments!" Wilson was the inverse of Washington and the founders. He believed the state—not the citizen—has rights. Therefore, Wilson professed, it made no sense to put limits on the power of a centralized Administration as our

Constitution does—the state has a right to determine what the administrative state's rights are, and therefore what the citizen's rights are *not* relative to the state.

Conversely, our highest law, the Constitution, is a document which defines the "natural rights" of every citizen at the expense of government's ambitions. The whole document is a definition of governments limits. Ideally, government has no rights or functions other than what the highest law says they are.

But Wilson believed in the creation of a new form of democracy, one not "ruled by the many" constitutionally through elections, but "ruled by the whole" through executive appointments. The best rulers of the "whole" were the one and the few who knew better the people's will than the people do themselves. Government, in Wilson's view, should be left to the one and few such as the Ivy League's intellectuals.

Sovereignty, according to our "administrative state's" founder, is *not* in the individual who possesses God given natural rights. Sovereignty is neither to be found in a document of highest law, which protects and defines individual rights and defines the limits of government.

Sovereignty, in the view of Woodrow Wilson, is found in the unified will of the state. This higher being of the state will be realized in a unified will brought forth by "one" leader and the "few" well-educated elite—who dictate that unified will, through administrative law, to the people. This, the progressive movement's sovereign belief, is the diametric opposite of our constitutional system as it was founded. In our original constitutional system, the individual is the sovereign—the government is the servant.

This creature, the "state" that Wilson's presidency gave birth to at the beginnings of the 20th century, has grown by leaps and bounds into the 21st. Thousands of powers have been delegated (unconstitutionally) from the people's original fountain of authority, the Congress, to the "State's" agencies. From these agencies, thousands of rules, which have the force of laws, are (unconstitutionally) created annually through the executive branch. These administrative laws enjoy a special designation: they are (unconstitutionally) given "judicial deference," meaning they are assumed to be constitutional by the judicial branch—the vast majority go judicially unreviewed. The enforcement of these laws is uniform because the same branch of government that univocally creates them univocally enforces them—through the "State's" enforcement agencies of the DOJ, FBI, and dozens of others.

Wilson and his successor progressives have been very successful in creating a condition of governance which one of our bearers of light, Charles Louis de Montesquieu, the philosophical father of our federal separation of powers, most feared. He wrote, "When the legislative and executive powers are united in the same person or body (as they are in our "state"), there can be no liberty, because apprehensions may arise lest *the same* monarch (president) should *enact* tyrannical laws to *execute* them in a tyrannical manner." Herewith, the conditions of tyranny exist.

By 2008, our executive branch of government exercised unilateral power over the administrative state (and thereby the economy), the dependent state (and thereby every dependent), the retaliatory state (and thereby intelligence and law enforcement) and the military state (and thereby the military-industrial complex) of our government. It is now an unimaginable, unprecedented amount of power stowed in one office, which sits behind the walls of our federal castle, the impenetrable fortress. One would think it would be enough power for anyone.... Yet, someone came along with very human longings who, given all that power, wanted one more thing—power to do anything.

Barack Obama

The Democratic Party found the perfect candidate. He was urbane, cultured, well spoken, graceful in motion, perfectly modulated in voice, often dressed immaculately, and when paired with his wife Michelle, Barack Obama cut a beautiful figure. Better yet, he practiced politics in a Democrat stronghold—the streets of Chicago, where Obama had been a professor and community organizer. He had been educated at America's finest schools and was therefore steeped in the progressive, socialist philosophy. He was and is militantly progressive—down to his perfectly woven Armani socks and his perfectly polished Gucci shoes.

Like Woodrow Wilson himself, and like countless contemporary progressives, Barack Obama does not seem to believe in the United States constitution. Obama has derided our highest law as a charter of "negative rights," which is exactly what it is. Our highest law is a container—a container which holds government power in by dictating how far government can go, and no farther. The Constitution keeps government from intrusion into the "positive natural rights" of every individual. The rights of every property owner, of every faith, of every family, of every association, of every state. Progressives do not like to be told where government cannot go, which is what our Constitution was designed to do.

There is another critical similitude between Obama and his fellow progressives. They believe that a "higher justice" can often only be created outside the Constitution. They believe themselves so wise as to be unconstrained by our highest law. Indeed, they believe they are chosen to go outside of our highest law to achieve a higher justice. Which is a critical difference from our nation's founders, who believed justice can only be created through the Constitution. It was created as the highest charter our nation has—as the foundation for the highest form of common justice.

So, there Obama stood on April 28, 2008 in Invesco Field in Denver, Colorado. Where a temple had been erected that looked like it was dedicated to Apollo...not Athena. Dedicated to an enlightened god, not to a goddess of a people of freedom. Throughout the field, chants and their echoes resounded: We are the one's (the few) we have been waiting for! Obama is the 'one' we have been waiting for!!!

There is a problem in our democracy, one which Lincoln constitutionally solved by giving his life to rid the nation of the idea that there are persons who are "other and lesser" in our body politic. The same problem comes to exist when any "one" is considered "other and greater." It makes every citizen other than the one and few "other and lesser."

So, there Obama stood on January 20, 2009, on the Capitol steps, taking an oath to protect and defend our highest law, our Constitution. And there he stood, making a vow to perform the highest duty of the office of the presidency—to faithfully execute the law, even the laws he disagrees with. He also made the vow to enforce the laws that protect his political opponents....

Lashing

Arizona

Barack Obama entered office with majorities in both chambers, sufficient to pass any law he chose to devote his administration to. There had been a southern border problem for two decades, as one political party sought amnesty for illegal aliens while the other wanted stricter border enforcement. A compromise stood plainly before them: amnesty for a given number of illegals, combined with strict enforcement of the border. And there would be no more illegal alien problem, just a standardized legal immigration system. Such a compromise, established through congressional law, would have provided a valuable lesson on how the Constitution can work to perfection for the establishment of common justice.

The states bordering Mexico were desperate to see the federal government achieve such a compromise. Texas, Arizona, New Mexico, and California were overrun, and not just by hordes of persons seeking seasonal work. The whole length of the border was becoming a war zone, with zealous Mexican gangs trading in drugs, guns, and human traffic. With borders many hundreds of miles long, the states needed federal support to manage it. This is a primary duty of the federal government. Immigration and naturalization are assigned constitutionally to the Congress. The duly-passed federal law that was on the books "mandates the initiation of immigration removal proceedings whenever an immigration officer encounters an illegal alien who is not clearly and beyond doubt entitled to be admitted." It is the constitutional duty of the executive branch, as executor of law, to work with the various states' law enforcement to faithfully execute immigration law.

The Obama Administration chose not to take the constitutional path, which stood directly before them. It would have been an easy, landmark victory with large Democratic Party majorities in both chambers. Instead, as head of the executive branch charged with enforcing the standing law, Obama chose not to...and he let everyone know it. It was not a matter of insufficient funding, or of manpower, or equipment necessary to faithfully execute the law. It was a president proclaiming he did not like the law and, therefore, would not enforce it despite the oath he took to do so. The administration claimed it had "prosecutorial discretion" in matters such as immigration enforcement regarding any laws it did not like.

The gangs involved in running guns, drugs, and humans got the message. The hordes invading the border states increased, knowing there were no penalties. The chaos at the border area and the personal danger to American citizens for having no border security increased dramatically. The reverse of standing law became law: it was effectively legal for anyone, for any reason, to cross the southern border.

The state of Arizona got the message too. Russell Pearce, a state senator, sponsored and helped shepherd the passage of Arizona Statute SB1070. This new Arizona law simply codified the standing federal law into state law, which requires aliens to register and carry their documents with them per federal statutes 8 USC 1304 (e) and 8 USC 1306. The law's passage would allow the state to deal with the chaos that the federal nonenforcement of the same law had unleashed. The state had the right to do so under Section 287(g) of the Immigration and Nationality Act, which allows state and local law enforcement to enforce federal law.

Not content with not faithfully executing the law, the administration was outraged that Arizona acted to protect the lives and property of its own citizens, the safety of whom the federal government had effectively abandoned to murderous gangs. The Obama Administration sued the State of Arizona for "preempting" the Federal government's duty—the duty that it was not performing. The case of the United States of America v. the State of Arizona was filed as 10-CV-01413 on July 6, 2010. The administration argued that it was "unconstitutional" for state or local police to investigate anyone suspected of being an illegal alien.

The administration went further. Attorney General Eric Holder launched a campaign from his office persuading the attorneys general in the border states to do as the federal government was doing and ignore standing federal immigration law. The administration then let Arizona know that it would not process or accept any illegal aliens that the Arizona police sought to transfer to federal custody—which again, is the law. In fact, the administration told Arizona it would not cooperate with the state on anything pertaining to the border problem. The governor, Jan Brewer, was left with nowhere to go saying, "Arizona is under attack by violent Mexican drug and immigrant smuggling cartels...and under attack in court from President Obama and his department of justice." Obama's actions were a pronouncement that he, and he alone, could determine what the law is. And his actions were vindictive towards those who disagreed with him.

Obama expanded his administration's disregard of immigration law by endorsing cities to designate themselves as "sanctuaries"—where too, no standing laws would be enforced. His administration even directed funding to cities that adopted such a status, while financially punishing states that tried to enforce those laws that were constitutionally passed.

Finally, for some time, the congress had considered a bill which would legalize, by way of an amnesty, illegal aliens who were brought into the country before they were sixteen years old. The bill failed to pass both houses of congress, and so it rightfully did not become law. President Obama decided on his own that it should be the law. He issued an executive order proclaiming, as a king might by decree, that an amnesty was granted for a category of illegal aliens and that the failed bill—known as the Dream Act—was the new "law."

Thus, in the person of President Obama, we have one who decides which laws are *not* laws, by not enforcing them, and which bills that have failed to pass by constitutional process should have the force of law! This brings about the following condition: By not enforcing law and instead enforcing unconstitutional, unilateral decrees, the Obama Administration denied every citizen in America their birth right—to live under constitutional law. That is the definition of tyranny. It is a condition which some, who helped create our system of constitutional government, warned about:

> *"Exceeding the bounds of authority is no more a right in a great than in a petty officer, no more justifiable in a king than a constable."*
>
> *"The legislative or supreme power of any commonwealth is bound to govern by established standing laws, promulgated and known to the people, and not by extemporary decrees...."*
>
> *"For without this the law could not have that, which is absolutely necessary to its being a law, the consent of the society, over whom nobody can have a power to make laws but by their own consent, and by authority received from them."*
>
> *John Locke*

> *"This state will perish...when the executive power, assumes corruptly, the power of the legislature by execution of non-laws or the non-execution of standing law."*
>
> *Charles Louis de Montesquieu*

Beyond Obama's actions being unconstitutional and a betrayal of his oath of office, the practical effects of his unilateral decisions were disastrous. By not enforcing the existing law to secure the border, by allowing drug dealers and human sex traffickers to move at will within our country, Obama failed in his first duty as the foremost law enforcement officer of the nation. Everywhere that immigration law was not enforced, the Obama Administration acted as an accomplice, an enabler allowing a massive network involving the smuggling of humans and drugs to be created from the lawless southern border to each of the sanctuary cities. Within these cities there was a correlated rise in an array of crimes related to the illegal drug industry, from assault, to robbery, to rape, to murder, to the tragedies of drug overdoses, which happen mostly to children who don't know what they're taking. And then there is the human sex trade, which also spawns the same array of crimes along with prostitution—whose victims, whose *casualties*, are always women. And who profits? The smugglers, the drug dealers, and the inner-city gangs.

Many of the victims of these crimes are American citizens that the government is bound to protect. There are other instances where the victims are the very people this lethal negligence in law is said to help, but because they are illegally allowed to enter and remain in this country, they have no rights and recourse to protection by the law. This anti-constitutional policy has created a vast population of persons who are functionally "other and lesser," and outside our constitutional protections precisely because constitutional law was not followed. Where can the victims of the smugglers go for justice? They are, in effect, the smuggler's slaves. Any crime can be committed by smugglers against the people they traffic into the country and the smuggler will face as much law enforcement as Obama dedicated to the border—none. Such is the injustice that comes of lawlessness.

Our constitution's prescribed process for the making of law creates just law, because it derives from a long process where, through a multitude of views, all the implications of causes and effects of proposed laws are detailed, considered, and debated by all involved, including opposing parties. This acts as a political filter system to prevent bad law. It is like water emerging from deep within the earth through many various substrates, which then rises through a narrow spring, creating purity. Univocal dictates are the stuff of dictators.

Lashing

Property And Enterprise

The Clean Water Act of 1972 was legislation passed by both houses of Congress, signed by President Nixon and deemed constitutional by the Supreme Court. The act was landmark environmental law, which interdicted the discharge of pollutants into the major "navigable waters" of the United States such as the St. Lawrence Seaway, the Hudson River, and the Great Lakes. The CWA did not specify how far upstream into tributary waters the act applied. The act's provisions were overseen by both the Environmental Protection Agency and the Army Corps of Engineers.

The Obama Administration took the Clean Water Act and unilaterally added, without congressional approval, the "Clean Water Rule." Obama stated that the "rule will provide the clarity and certainty businesses and industry need about which waters are protected by the Clean Water Act.... With today's rule, we take another step towards protecting the waters that belong to all of us." The only "us" referred to in the lexicon of government - is the government.

The new rule expanded the definition of what waters fell under federal jurisdiction. In the Clean Water Act it referred to "navigable waters." The new "Waters Of The United States" rule covered waters as defined by the Corps of Engineers: "mudflats, sandflats, sloughs, prairie potholes and wet meadows;" down to "water filled depressions," which means puddles. The new rule widened the scope of federal jurisdiction over the waters of the United States to include almost all the fresh water within U.S. boundaries and the privately owned lands attached thereto. Making all the waters and lands effectively *subject* to federal agency purview, oversight, and regulation—which means control. The Army Corps of Engineers made it clear that water need not be standing necessarily on the land they now control, it could be a dried-up old ditch that once had rain in it.

The EPA lamented that the administration was forced to take such action because every bit of water in the country was likely poisoned by weak state and local regulation. In the United States, up until then, the states were the primary regulator of land and water resources both within their borders and owned by their citizens. This new rule not only invaded another power of every state in the union, but also the property rights of every citizen and private enterprise. Senator Joni Ernst of Iowa had a study performed, based on the new administrative "rule," and found that 97% of the land in her state was subject to the rule. A rule which threatened every property owner, such as Iowa's small businesses, farmers, and every manufacturer. By the new definition of what constituted "wet meadows" alone, the EPA and the Army Corps of Engineers asserted federal jurisdiction on land use on over half of the state of Alaska without the need for any other designation.

In Minnesota, the Hawkes Co. are miners of peat moss. Peat moss only grows in musty sorts of areas where water and earth combine. Once mined, peat moss is perfect for improving the soil, such as soil under the greens of golf courses. That is Hawkes Co.'s business. The company wanted to expand their existing mining operation but were stopped by the Army Corps of Engineers. The land they wanted to expand their operation into—the land they owned and wanted to mine—was a threat to the Red River. The river was 120 miles away. But they were told they needed a permit, which on average takes 788 days to receive and costs on average $271,596. The Corps also said that the company would need to submit numerous property assessments, likely costing another $100,000. Hawkes was simultaneously warned by the EPA that they might spend all that time and money and not receive the permit. And, if they went ahead without a permit, the penalties would be immediate and severe enough to put them out of business.

I ask the reader: who owns the land that Hawkes Co. purchased for their business?

In Wyoming, Andy Johnson, a rancher—with a wife and four kids to support from the proceeds of his daily labors—was putting in a stock pond to water his animals. It was nothing big, just the water necessary on a ranch if you want your stock to be healthy. It was only a bit of land, to be made into a pond to water stock that was nowhere near a "navigable water." Johnson was served with a compliance order from the EPA, which threatened him with fines of $37,500 per day if he finished his pond and watered his stock—and another $37,500 per day for acting in defiance of the order. The EPA bureaucrat told the Johnson family that the pond fed a ditch used for irrigation, which was a "navigable waterway." Johnson replied that he agreed, it was a waterway...for his chickens.

Such are some of the actions taken these days by our federal regulatory colossus, whose stride and shadow now covers this country from the Atlantic to the Pacific in their perpetual war against businesses and private citizens—who they can step on wherever a raindrop falls.

The average American should feel assured, however, because Melissa Harrison of the EPA has decreed: "The clean water rule was developed by the agencies to respond to an urgent need... for identifying waters that are and are not protected by the Clean Water Act, it is based on science and the law!" It is neither. It is a massive federal agency assumption of power over the states and every property owner by way of an agency rule—not a law. The rule does demonstrate one of the laws our "administrative state" lives by: Never to be content with how much it has grown or how much it controls. It must "rule" over every pond, every puddle, and every bit of the land that surrounds it...wherever rain falls.

The Clean Air Act of 1963 was a great piece of legislation, like the Clean Water Act, when it was voted and signed into law. It assigned the Environmental Protection Agency to create national ambient air quality standards which would help rid the atmosphere of harmful toxins, such as ground level ozone or O3, carbon monoxide or CO, particulate matters PM10 and PM 2.5, sulfur dioxide or SO2, and nitrogen dioxide or NO2. The legislation was amended in 1971 to include photochemical accidents and hydrocarbons. In 1976, lead or Pb was added to the list of toxic agents that can be airborne. By 1990, amendments to the law classified that there were 187 toxins that rightly came under the purview of EPA regulation. Such standards have proved very effective in cleaning the air.

The reader will note that carbon dioxide, CO2, is not on the list above nor among the 187 classified pollutants, for a very good reason. All of the animals on the earth, including reptiles and fish and worms, take in oxygen and respire carbon dioxide. While all of the plant life on Earth, from the sequoias and cedars to the bushes and flowers to the grass in your yard, take in carbon dioxide and respire oxygen, which we humans, every one of us, breathe in and then exhale as carbon dioxide. It is a beautiful, miraculous symbiosis between animal and plant life here on Earth...until the prospect of global warming became a government driven, government sponsored, government funded theory treated as fact—which changed everything.

To echo an earlier passage of the book, a "*strong consensus*"—which means it is not proven among "experts" (who are paid by governments for their results)—"indicates that global warming exists and threatens a precipitate rise in sea levels, severe irreversible changes to natural ecosystems, significant reductions in winter snowpack, all of which will result in the spread of diseases and a greater frequency of ferocious weather events...and there will be grave economic impacts." In other words, according to one party of government we face the apocalypse, and the primary culprit is the mother of all photosynthesis on Earth—carbon dioxide. Literally, the air you breathe out, like every other earthly animal, is pollution!

The experts theorize that if governments can control carbon dioxide, they can control the world and the temperature! It would be like controlling every drop of water and every bit of land that rain falls on! One problem: the EPA never classified carbon dioxide as a pollutant, because the idea was ludicrous...until the prospect of the Apocalypse.

We must do SOMETHING or we're all going to die! We are on Earth and there is no way to get off!

Do you feel cornered yet? We must be taxed to death for being in an earthly prison and polluted by our own breath.

Some liberals are really smart—they know how to operate. They know the legal tricks to expanding the powers of the state. One instance can be found in *Massachusetts v. Environmental Protection Agency,* a case brought in 2006. A liberal state, Massachusetts, sued a liberal federal agency, the EPA, before a liberal court, the DC Circuit court, to get a result they all wanted: an expansion of federal power to take control of carbon dioxide. Literally, the air we breathe. Massachusetts brought the suit based on "respected scientific opinion" (which means *it is unproven*) that environmental changes have resulted from a significant increase of "greenhouse gases" in the atmosphere, therefore, the EPA must begin to regulate such gases, including carbon dioxide. The EPA declared that it had to deny the petition because there is no proven causal link between greenhouse gases and increases in global surface temperatures—which was true at the time the case was brought and is still true today!

Then one of the judges on the court declared that the administrators (EPA) might exercise "judgement" as to whether a pollutant could "reasonably be anticipated to endanger public health or welfare, based on *scientific uncertainty*"—rather than on *scientific facts*. This "judgement" expanded the definition of pollutant to include "any air agent...emitted into the air, embracing all airborne compounds of any stripe," including carbon dioxide, which might, with *scientific uncertainty*, be a pollutant. It was a rendering rather like changing the definition of a "navigable water" to a "water filled depression." But this change wasn't done by a new "rule"—it was done among a liberal state, a liberal agency, and a liberal court to vastly expand the EPA's jurisdiction over the very air we breathe.

Massachusetts v. EPA turned the Clean Air Act and EPA's mission on its head. Rather than the EPA defining what a pollutant is within the air, based on scientific facts, in order to control pollution, the EPA could now assume based on *scientific opinion* that everything in the air might harbor the severe effects of a pollutant and therefore is subject to EPA oversight, purview, and regulation based on the Clean Air Act amendments of 1992. In an instance of irony, with the change in rules the EPA can only avoid regulating carbon dioxide emissions if the EPA proves global warming does not exist.

The case was heard by the Supreme Court on November 29, 2006. The verdict was rendered on April 2, 2007. Four conservative judges dissented against the judgement of the DC Circuit and four liberal justices decided in concurrence, with the ever-ambivalent Justice Kennedy deciding with the liberals for the supreme judicial act to change the law by way of a rule.

With the new apocalypse on the horizon, the devil making it happen turned out to be the coal industry—which at the time supplied 50% of the least expensive power generated in the United States. That is a lot of power to take, even for an ambitious administrative state.

In 2008, then candidate Barack Obama was interviewed by the *San Francisco Chronicle* and made his ambitions plain: "If somebody wants to build a coal powered plant, they can…it's just that it will bankrupt them because they are going to be charged a huge sum for all that greenhouse gas that is being emitted." Candidate for vice president, Joe Biden, chimed in: "We're not supporting clean coal." One man's threat was an American industry's peril. President Obama, on taking office, vowed to bankrupt the coal industry.

Democratic Senators Waxman of California and Markey of Massachusetts wasted no time in putting forward the Waxman-Markey cap and trade bill, which would make the federal government the central exchange for control of the national emissions of carbon dioxide, an emission common to every power plant in the country as well as every person and every animal. The bill would give the "state" the power to "cap" greenhouse emissions, which would affect 85% of energy production. That is the amount of U.S. energy that was carbon based. For "permits," a proposed tax would be assessed on every kilowatt of energy produced in America. The state would "permit" every emitter of greenhouse gases—you may only emit carbon dioxide with government permission. The government would become the central exchange, which decided who would benefit and who would be penalized for their emissions.

It was, in fact, as Senator Bill Posey of Florida claimed, the most expensive tax proposal to be placed on the American people since the Income Tax was imposed in 1913. The Competitive Enterprise Institute argued that the bill was, essentially, "the largest tax hike in world history." The bill was projected to take $9 Trillion of wealth out of the economy and cost 2.5 million jobs—and every American family between $1,500 and $3,500 per year in added energy bills.

The effect of the bill would be infinitesimal. A report published by the Heritage Foundation found that the impact it would have on global temperatures by the year 2100 would amount to a reduction in temperature of 0.2 degrees Celsius. Senator Oren Hatch asked a common sense question about the legislation: "Are we going to make our country uncompetitive with the rest of the world just to get a .07% decrease in emissions over the next 100 years? I mean it does not make sense."

But there would be a benefit...to the wealth and power of the "state." The tax would bring in massive sums of money to be parceled out to companies the federal state favored—at the expense of companies the federal state did not favor. The state, with control over all the energy emissions in the country, could decide what companies would thrive with subsidies, grants, and tax breaks and which would be ruined through regulations, fines, and taxes. That is the business the state is in, and the state does better depending on how much money it taxes and how much of the economy it controls—period.

The Waxman-Markey Bill was brought to a vote in the House on June 26, 2009, where it passed by a vote of 219–212. The Senate, as is its prerogative, chose not to take up the bill knowing the votes were not there to pass the legislation. Obama was not pleased. He calmly stated that there were other ways of "skinning a cat." He was right, the recent changes in the EPA's control over emissions brought to the office of the president another power unimagined by the founders: a power to crush an industry that the Senate had sought to save by not voting for the cap and trade bill. As stated previously, there is a lot of wealth and a lot of power in the energy sector of our economy—too much for the administrative state to leave alone.

Based on the new designation of carbon dioxide, Obama did what he promised—he waged a war on the coal industry through the EPA's "Cross State Air Pollution," "Coal Combustion Waste," and "Cooling Water Intake" rules, combined with application of the "Maximum Achievable Control Technology" rule. In short, the allowable emissions related to these rules were severely reduced, and immediate retrofits of coal-burning electric utilities were demanded by EPA to meet compliance of new emissions per the MACT rule. The retrofitting of coal-fired plants alone would cost $130 billion.

The effects of the new EPA "rules" were immediate. Fifty-seven coal burning plants went out of business because of the MACT rule alone. The largest coal company in the United States, Peabody Energy, went bankrupt. So did other venerable firms such as Alpha Natural Resources, Arch Coal, and Patriot Coal. Their owners and investors lost their investments, and their employees lost their jobs—every one of them. The total energy-producing capacity of the coal power plant fleet in the country dropped 22% over the next ten years. Energy costs rose across the United States. During the same period, billions of taxpayer dollars were annually funding 700 new government programs dedicated to dispersing wealth taken from taxpayers and funneling it through Wall Street to alternative energy start-up firms—like Solyndra.

Obama did from his single office what the congress decided not to do by law. He may not have made the ocean levels fall as though he were Poseidon, but with his new rules he reminds of Darius, the Persian emperor-god, who demanded he would "so extend the empire of the Persians, that its boundaries would be God's own sky and God will not look on any ground that was not ours!" With Obama's assumption of the office of the presidency, the administrative state assumed control of all the waters, all the lands, and the very air over America, everything beneath the sun.

With the new "rules," the EPA became an agency empowered like a Goliath, lording over every property owner, who became like a new David. The EPA is invested with the limitless resources it takes from every taxpayer, including those it rules against. The EPA can litigate with any one person or any enterprise to the end of time. The EPA can fine anyone or any industry until they can no longer afford to live or operate on the land the EPA assumes is under its absolute control. Go ahead, try to sue them—they are funded by tax dollars you give them. It is the payment you send to them for your own oppression.

Lashing

Associations

Readers of Volume I may remember the vital role played in the creation of America by associations. The early days of the revolutionary movement were organized through associations, such as the Sons of Liberty. Later, the abolitionist movement was spearheaded by associations of like-minded persons who conceived that America's promise of freedom for all and equality of all had been compromised at the time of the Constitutional Convention, and could only be corrected through a reformation by organized democratic methods of objection to slavery. The associations dedicated to emancipation held together through the Civil War, and saw their objective achieved through the 13th, 14th, and 15th amendments to the Constitution.

The rights of association have had protections under the Constitution's right of assembly for as long as the country has existed. This right to assemble without government control or interference has been a bulwark of defense from the intrusions of government since the Mayflower Compact was signed. As de Tocqueville described them:

> *"There is no country in which associations are more necessary to prevent the despotism of parties or the arbitrary rule of the prince than those where the social conditions are democratic."*

In 2009 and 2010, political associations began to spring up spontaneously around America that were devoted to the original principles of the country. The most successful of these was the Tea Party movement—a loose collection of like-minded associations formed from Concord, New Hampshire, to Albuquerque, New Mexico. They, like every other political organization since the Sons of Liberty, were formed around common ideas. To share their ideas and promote them through publications, promotions, or political candidacies, associations require patronage—they need money. The giving of patronage to such free assemblies for the promotion of ideas is entirely voluntary and has been protected by the Constitution since the founding.

To raise money in our contemporary era, such associations are only feasible financially if they apply for tax exempt status with the IRS through 501(c)(3) or 501(c)(4) categories of organization. As everyone in America knows, the IRS is one of the most powerful agencies in our country. The IRS has, quite possibly, the most information our government holds on each citizen: what job a person has, how much they make, how much they spend, what house they live in and where, how many children they have, how many family members they have, what churches they support, what school their kids go to—and what associations they donate to.

According to Woodrow Wilson, the whole hypotheses of the administrative state possessing an unthreatening nature was that its agencies would exist beyond political accountability, and doing so, the agency's lifetime-appointed employees would remain politically neutral. Because of their special status, they would be above the temptations of human nature, they would act in the interest of the nation as a whole not in the interest of any particular political party, and certainly not in the interest of themselves. Agency employees would enjoy a certain enlightenment because they would be insulated *from* accountability. But there is one accountability agencies do have: they are forbidden from taking any action which violates the Constitution. The body that is supposed to hold agencies accountable to the Constitution is the Congress.

In 2009 and 2010, hundreds of applications were being dutifully filled out and sent into the IRS to enfranchise Tea Party and other similar organizations nationwide. The majority of the applications were submitted for 501(c)(4) status, which, though it does not make donations tax-deductible for individuals, it does make donations to the organizations tax exempt. Normally, an application would be sent to the IRS to be evaluated on an individual basis, solely on the activities of the "social" organization. If less than half of its activities were dedicated strictly to politics, the application was approved within a few weeks. Or, the submitting organization would be notified that the application was denied, in which case they were allowed to appeal the negative decision immediately.

With regard to the new Tea Party organizations and others like them, something strange occurred: They were not receiving replies. Months went by…no approval, no denials…no replies. Limbo. Meanwhile, the media airwaves were filling with derogatory references to conservative groups. President Obama began "warning" the country, through nine distinct speeches, of the "illicit" activities of conservative groups with patriotic sounding names actually being fronts for "foreign controlled corporations." Obama opined, "The only people who don't want to disclose the truth are people with something to hide!" Things got worse. On October 14, 2010, Obama called conservative groups "a problem for our democracy." On October 25, 2010, Obama called conservative groups a "threat to our democracy." The Democratic National Committee, along with certain Democratic senators such as Chuck Schumer, Max Baucus, and Jeanne Shaheen, began to demand investigations of such associations. And the media filled out the chorus of objections to these shadowy new "conservative groups."

Coincidently, the most frequent official visitor to the Obama White House over his first term in office was Internal Revenue Service Commissioner David Schulman, who visited Obama over 150 times.

Still no determination of status—no approvals, no denials. The only replies from the IRS contained questions that were very abnormal for the application process. The IRS questioned Tea Party organizations about their donor lists and their donors: who were they? The IRS wanted to know what social networks the Tea Party groups operated in? What internet postings they made? What family members they had? What books they read?

The IRS contacted a chapter of the Waco, Texas Tea Party to requisition printouts of its webpage and social networking sites and copies of its newsletters, promotional bulletins, and flyers. The IRS wanted copies of stories written in local newspapers about the organization. The IRS wanted transcripts of any radio interviews the chapter had given. The IRS asked an association that shared members with the Tea Party—the Christian Voices for Life—about their prayer vigils...the IRS wanted to know the content of their prayers.

In Hollywood, the IRS demanded that a conservative group within the entertainment industry, the "Friends of Abe," grant them access to the "Friends" security-protected website—a site which contained its membership lists.

Many of these conservative groups, in normal discussions with one another, were awakening to the very abnormal activities at the IRS. At the same time, *none* of the groups were obtaining any determinations on their application status—there were neither approvals nor denials. The activities of 471 conservative political associations were frozen in place from the spring of 2010 through the presidential election of 2012. They could not legally raise money—it would have been a violation of IRS rules governing tax exempt associations, which encompass every normal political association.

In the spring of 2013, the concerns of the Tea Party were echoing through the halls of Congress with the question, "What is going on?" As if on cue, at an obscure American Banking Association conference on May 10, 2013, Lois Lerner, a senior official of the tax-exempt organizations division of the IRS, took the podium to blithely announce—in answer to a carefully planted question—that some rogue IRS agents, confined to an office in Cincinnati, were targeting conservative associations on their own without the direction or knowledge of anyone in Washington D.C.—that the conduct was "absolutely incorrect, insensitive, and inappropriate." Congress, as part of its oversight duty to the Constitution, decided to schedule hearings to get to the bottom of a very sudden scandal, which took years to uncover.

Barack Obama and Attorney General Erik Holder called Lois Lerner's assertion, if true, "intolerable, outrageous, inexcusable, and unacceptable." Then, Obama demanded that the IRS' screening of conservative organizations warranted additional scrutiny—just the kind the IRS was now being accused of doing.

Among the flurry of responses to the Lerner admissions, Press Secretary Jay Carney stipulated that the "inappropriate conduct was confined to rogue agents at a small office in Cincinnati." On May 13, Erik Holder opened a joint investigation to be handled at the DOJ by Barbara Bosserman, a long-time liberal donor to Obama, and at the FBI by newly-elevated Director James Comey.

When Congress went about its duty to subpoena Lois Lerner and her associate's emails, the IRS informed Congress that Lerner's emails and those of six of her close associates had all been lost. When Congress asked the IRS for Lerner's hard drive, they were told the hard drive had "crashed." When Congress asked for the physical hard drive to be delivered to them, they were told the hard drive had been destroyed because it had crashed. When Congress asked if they could have Lerner's Blackberry, they were told the IRS had destroyed that too. When Congress asked for the hard drives of Lerner's six associates, they were told it was a remarkable coincidence but all seven hard drives had crashed—at the same time. When Congress asked for the subpoenaed parties' backup email files, which were required by law to be kept by the agency, the IRS answered that all 422 backups of the subpoenaed emails had been lost.

Obama told a national television audience, while the investigation was ongoing, that "there was not even a smidgen of corruption in the IRS' actions." He went on to commiserate with the media about all of these "phony scandals."

Congress scheduled hearings for July 18, 2013. The congressional committee subpoenaed Lois Lerner to testify. She asserted she had done nothing wrong and flatly refused to testify, claiming she stood by her Fifth Amendment right not to incriminate herself. The committee asked for any information the DOJ and FBI might have pertaining to the scope of the hearing—the DOJ and FBI declined to comment or contribute to the hearings as theirs was an active, ongoing investigation. The committee did hear from a pair of the principal agents who were accused of going rogue, and from the inspector general of the IRS, Russell George.

Ms. Elizabeth Hofacre testified that, in April 2010, she was an Exempt Organizations Determinations specialist. That April, as part of her assignment as an "Emerging Issue coordinator," she was tasked to supervise all applications identified as "Tea Party" associations seeking determination of 501(c)(3) or 501(c)(4) exemption status. Associations with "Tea Party" or "Patriot" or "9/12" in their names were part of a new "emerging issue." They were segregated as part of a "be on the look-out" or BOLO list. Ms. Hofacre was immediately assigned twenty Tea Party applications, which she dutifully segregated. Other applications from liberal groups, with liberal names, were sent to general inventory as normal because they were not a part of the "emerging issue." As of the end of May 2010, 298 conservative association applications had been segregated.

Ms. Hofacre met with her managers, Steven Bowling and John Waddell, who told Hofacre they were working to consolidate a single document of instruction for this group of applicants which were classified under the BOLO. She was instructed to work under the supervision of Carter Hull, a senior employee with forty-eight years of experience at the IRS. Mr. Hull, too, was working on this "emerging issue," and had taken two test cases from the 298 applications to work on. Hull and Hofacre were to work together on "development letters," to fashion language to respond properly to the applying associations—as far as they knew. Ms. Hofacre would send Mr. Hull trial edits and he would send comments back. This correspondence was active for a while...then the communication stopped.

During this time, Carter Hull took his test cases with the language he and Hofacre had worked on and sent them, per request, to Chief Counsel William Wilken's office for review. Hull took a meeting with his managers, Elizabeth Kastenberger and Judy Kindall, to recommend that, rather than treating the applicants as a group, they should be treated individually—that was normal protocol. Kindall asked Hull to forward the recommendation to the chief counsel's office. Thereafter, Carter Hull waited for direction from management on the test development letters and his recommendations. He could not direct Ms. Hofacre on how to proceed with the growing number of Tea Party applications without direction from higher up. The pair were in limbo. During that time, Ms. Hofacre received more and more applications and phone calls about the status of received applications. She could only respond that they were being worked on.

An entire year passed, during which Elizabeth Hofacre transferred out of "Emerging Issues" because she was uncomfortable with the delayed applications process. In the summer of 2011, while all the applications were still unaddressed—neither approved nor denied—Lois Lerner convened a meeting. Attending were Carter Hull, his supervisor Michael Seto, his managers Holly Paz, Ms. Kindall, and Mrs. Kastenberger, and a representative from Chief Counsel William Wilken's office. Lois Lerner instructed everyone in the room that the files previously segregated and referred to as "Tea Party" applications should be changed and titled "Advocacy" applications.

In August 2011, during a meeting with Don Spellman, David Marshall, and Amy Franklin—each of the chief counsel's office—Carter Hull was informed that more current information was necessary for a "multi-tiered" review of the applicants and that Hull should write another development letter. The applications were soon after transferred out of Carter Hull's office. And they were further delayed...

During the congressional hearings, Elizabeth Hofacre was asked by Congressman Duncan: "I understand that in your fourteen years of experience, these cases were handled differently? How common was it that you would be told by someone in Washington to hold up applications?" Hofacre answered, "It wasn't common at all." Congressman DesJarlais asked: "Have you ever seen anything like it?" Hofacre responded, "I wasn't aware of any situation that was...where applications were treated in this fashion." Chairman Darrell Issa then asked Carter Hull: "You have forty-eight years of service, can you give us a single valid reason for groups to be lumped together and not granted for so long a period of time... nearly three years and counting? You don't have any experience of seeing it before?" Mr. Hull answered, "I have no experience—no."

IRS Inspector General Russell George's report to Congress made three key findings: "The Internal Revenue Service used inappropriate criteria that identified for review organizations applying for tax exempt status based on their names and policy positions, rather than on tax exempt law and Treasury regulations, that the applications experienced unprecedented delays and that the IRS made unnecessary and burdensome requests for information."

After his statement, Congressman DesJarlais asked Inspector General George: "You've been doing this for about a decade. Have you ever been involved in a case quite like this?" George responded, "This is the most unprecedented example I have ever experienced, not only as an Inspector General but as a former member of this very committee staff for almost twenty-five years...I have never experienced anything like this."

One of the conclusions of the committee was that the IRS policies guaranteed that the applications from conservative associations would not be approved before the November 2012 election. The policies succeeded. A massive population of conservative voters were *not* organized into a potent political force of associated voters and ideas because one of the most powerful agencies in the country turned political and acted "systematically" against half the country's voters through prejudicial acts against conservative associations.

Hundreds of conservative associations (471 to be exact) were frozen out of the political process, along with hundreds of thousands of voters who those associations would have organized; and millions of dollars in donations which those associations might have collected and put to use in the political process. The systematic targeting and crippling of conservative political associations likely worked to change the results of the 2012 election.

The delay of applications was not the only malicious act of the IRS during this period. The IRS leaked dozens of the confidential applications they had blocked from the approval process to ProPublica for publication. They also leaked the private information of donors to the National Organization for Marriage, another conservative association. And, in perhaps Lois Lerner's greatest service to her particular political party, she sent 1,250,000 pages of conservative voter's confidential tax returns to the Department of Justice's criminal division in case they needed the information—*before* opening an investigation.

The IRS was also inspired to audit conservatives—for being conservatives. In April 2012, President Obama referred to a Mitt Romney donor during a speech. He said Frank VanderSloot was a typical Romney donor: a person who was wealthy and had a "less than reputable record." Twelve days after the speech, Mr. VanderSloot was informed he was being audited by the IRS. Mr. VanderSloot was audited three times during Obama's presidency.

Catherine Engelbrecht founded a Tea Party association called "True the Vote," and dutifully sent an application to the IRS for tax-exempt status. The IRS did not respond to the application, but it did audit Engelbrecht's small business. Then the Engelbrecht's were investigated by OSHA, and by the FBI, and by the ATF. During Obama's presidency, 100% of the conservative associations that filed tax returns as 501(c)(4) and were founded before Obama took office were audited while he was in office.

It was later found, owing to a successful judicial motion under the Freedom of Information Act made by Tom Fitton and Judicial Watch in October 2013, that the IRS auditing of conservative associations was as systematic as the segregation and delay in applications. A meeting was held on April 30, 2010, attended by Lois Lerner, Steve Miller—chief of staff to IRS Commissioner Nicole Flax—and other IRS officials. The subject of the meeting: what was to be done about the exploding number of Tea Party or Patriot associations. Henry Kerner stood up and suggested, "Maybe the solution is to audit so many...that it is financially ruinous (for them to continue)." Lerner responded that it was her job "to oversee it all."

Just as Lois Lerner oversaw it all, the DOJ and FBI overlooked it all. Barbara Bosserman, who was in charge of the DOJ "investigation," allegedly spent 1,500 hours on the case. No charges were filed. James Comey's FBI did not interview a single Tea Party group or member about the illegal actions of the IRS. Steve Miller, by then IRS Commissioner, put in his resignation on May 15, 2013—fifteen days before he was scheduled to retire. Lois Lerner received $129,300 in bonuses for her work between 2010 and 2013, then retired quietly with full pension. None of the IRS agents involved in the targeting were ever even disciplined.

The "state's" castle defense system worked perfectly. They worked in service to one of their own—the most powerful agency in land, the Internal Revenue Service—rather than the American people who they are sworn to serve and to the Constitution. The

DOJ and the FBI helped to cover up rather than either investigate the truth or establish justice—again.

Lashing

Privacy and the Press

From the time of the Democratic Convention through the inauguration of 2009, Obama had a very special relationship with the press. As alluded to earlier, his figure, his carriage, his grace in public elicited a kind of adoration from almost everyone, but particularly from members of the press. Obama's approval numbers among those of that profession were astronomical, incomparable with any former president even at their height of fame. When questioning the president, press members behaved differently—with a tremendous deference to his person. When Obama spoke, the room, whatever room, hushed to a silence, hanging on his every word and gesture. The press appeared as the ancient figures of petitioners kneeling before the magnipotence of Zeus, admiring of his throne and reverent of his dreaded thunderbolt. He was the absolute head of his political party and the idol of an awed press. Then along came a person who was a strict servant of the truth—who, before all else, served that one devotion.

Sharyl Attkisson, at the time of Obama's inauguration, was a seasoned, multiple award-winning investigative reporter in both print and broadcast journalism. During Obama's first term, Attkisson worked as a lead reporter and sometime anchor for CBS news. Attkisson knew where the news was and how to cover it in the finest American tradition: without favor and without fear.

Two years into the Obama presidency, in February 2011, Attkisson covered a story on the Bureau of Alcohol, Tobacco, and Firearms named "Fast and Furious" about deadly U.S. firearms being, literally, walked by a United States law enforcement agency into the arms of Mexico's drug cartels for use in the drug and human trafficking trade. A follow-up story on March 3, 2011 featured evidence given by ATF Special Agent John Dodson, which showed that the agency's bureaucracy was lying to the press about the operation. It was a blockbuster news story, and a negative one about Obama's DOJ—something the administration was not accustomed to.

The administration's outrage at the story was made known to CBS news and to Attkisson. There were demands from the Department of Justice to know who had leaked details of the story. Being rightfully protective of her confidential sources, Attkisson declined to give them up. Attkisson, in fact, did another dozen follow-up stories throughout the course of 2011. One installment in October of that year proved that Attorney General Eric Holder had blatantly lied in a statement regarding when he first found out about the "Fast and Furious" operation.

In January 2012, Attkisson brought another news story to the public titled "Green Energy Going Red." It was about the $90 billion federal slush fund being parceled out to green energy companies, which resulted in the failed investment of *$535 million* in solar panel producer Solyndra. Again, CBS news and Attkisson were harangued by the administration, which again demanded to know details about the "leakers" related to the story. Attkisson was not intimidated by the pressure. She had uncovered another dozen failed energy "investments" to relate to American taxpayers who paid for these "investments." That is what reporters who do not kneel before a political party, or a person, are actually supposed do: bring taxpayers the truth.

On October 5, 2012, CBS News offered another Attkisson story titled "Libya: Dying for Security," about the Benghazi massacre. The story and its confidential administration sources were critical of the security lapses at the U.S. Embassy Compound that resulted in the deaths of Ambassador Christopher Stevens and three other brave American souls. Again, the administration bristled—wanting to know who had been letting loose the true information about Benghazi, about the terrorist attacks. The press was supposed to be reporting that it began and ended with a video. Sharyl Attkisson proved to be a journalist the administration could not control.

Attkisson was privately approached by several U.S. intelligence community insiders. They warned her that she had better watch her back because the odds were very high that she was under surveillance by an administration that did not like negative news broadcast about it. What even this seasoned veteran of the media did not know was that the Department of Justice was vastly expanding its electronic eavesdropping capabilities in the name of national security. Nor did she, or anyone else, know that on October 3, 2011, the administration had secretly changed long-standing legal practices governing surveillance that protected the privacy of U.S. citizens, by opening up a "loophole" in the law to engage in "backdoor searches" of "within borders" communications of U.S. citizens. The administration was turning practices used to find terrorists abroad on their own citizens at home—it was an unknown extension of and based on the precedents of the Patriot Act, passed under GW Bush.

What Attkisson and her family did know is that, beginning at around the same time the "loophole" was opened, her house took on characteristics one would associate with a poltergeist event. In the middle of the night, the work and family home computers turned themselves on, then without being touched turned themselves off... repeatedly. On other occasions, the home alarm system would signal trouble—the sort that only occurred during storm conditions when the lines went down. But there was no storm. Sometimes, again under clear skies, the television and computers seemed possessed, such was the interference experienced in the signal reception. The Attkisson's land and mobile phone lines would drop connections surreptitiously, or at times become unusable because of massive static.

In December 2012, Attkisson began telling colleagues and friends by phone and email about the chronic problems she was having across her work, personal, and family devices. It was happening to everything outside of the family toaster. A concerned contact who had worked in the intelligence community offered help by referring a computer expert—an associate and another veteran of the intelligence community—to check on Attkisson's

CBS work computer, a Toshiba laptop. The computer tech recognized his client and offered some insight: "Reporters used to be off-limits…it was sacrosanct. Obviously, that's changed." He continued, "Taps aren't usually done on people's homes anymore. It's all done through Verizon—they cooperate (with government surveillance)." Verizon happened to be the Attkissons' sole service provider for phone, internet, and satellite service. Everything in the house was connected to and through Verizon except the toaster. The tech continued, "There is no need to come to your house, we (the intelligence community) can get everything we want through a phone company."

After taking the computer for analysis, the tech's findings concluded that there was clear evidence of an intrusion involving a technology and malware that could only be associated with an intelligence agency of the United States government—no one else uses it or is capable of mirroring it. The technology allowed for keystroke monitoring, acquisition of data, access to email, and monitoring what was done. By connection to Attkisson's network, the "intruder" was even able to enter CBS' internal network and computer systems. Lastly, the intrusion allowed the acquisition of personal passwords—and through a method of activating Skype audio within the computer, gave the ability to listen to everything going on in the Attkisson household twenty-four hours a day.

The tech believed the surveillance had been going on since at least early 2012, while "Fast and Furious" was still a story and "Green Energy Going Red" was becoming one. The tech's last observation to Attkisson was a dire warning: "Three classified documents… were buried deep in your operating system. In a place that, unless you're some kind of computer whiz specialist, you would not even know exists. I'd say whoever got in your computer planted them… to be able to accuse you of having classified documents if they ever needed to." Having such documents is a crime punishable with prison.

The Toshiba laptop computer examined was CBS property, and the internal CBS computer network had been compromised through it. Therefore, Sharyl Attkisson took the matter immediately to CBS Washington Bureau Chief Chris Isham. The two agreed that an independent analysis of the computer was immediately necessary. If two independent examinations concurred on the findings, they would have a case to make to leadership—and a story which would have been unbelievable if they did not know it was true.

An independent private computer forensic analyst was hired by CBS to look at the Toshiba. Jerry Patel confirmed what the previous tech already discovered: an "intruder" had been at work on Attkisson's CBS computer. He also found that the "intruder" tried to remove the evidence that he was ever there. Patel found a gap in the Toshiba's internal event log, between December 10 and December 11, of 22 hours and 55 minutes where the logs had been removed. "Oh boy," he said, "that is suspicious behavior."

Attkisson prompted Patel to check the family iMac computer as well. He went directly to the December 9 to 12, 2012 logs—the dates around which the Toshiba computer log had been altered. "Oh, shit," Patel said, "that's now a pattern—we have (another) gap. That is not normal." The iMac had an internal event log gap from December 8, 10:12 PM to December 9, 3:18 PM—17 hours and 6 minutes. "Someone did that to your computer," Patel said with growing astonishment. "Two separate instances, showing the same MO. That shows knowledge of event logging, and it shows skill. Somebody deleting days of messages (about their activities within the two Attkisson computers). That shows skill." The dates of the deleted logs corresponded exactly with when Attkisson started communicating with friends and colleagues about her devices and the suspicions she had about them being tapped.

Patel told Attkisson flatly that whoever intruded would never be caught. The evidence Patel found proved the intruders were too sophisticated, too skilled—beyond even the best *nongovernmental* hackers. They know how to cover their tracks. It's what they do... as though they were never there. Patel later sent an email to CBS' Isham and Attkisson, writing: "It is my professional opinion that a coordinated action or series of actions have taken place. I don't wish to go into details because (as the analysis proved) the integrity of email is now in question."

Isham and Attkisson now considered the concern that they had previously voiced to be proven real. Attkisson said to Isham, "I can't be the only one they're doing this to." Isham returned, "I know...you can't be."

Five weeks after Patel's email, a senate hearing was held on March 12, 2013 during which James Clapper, the director of national intelligence, was asked a very direct question by Senator Ron Wyden of Oregon: "Does the NSA collect any type of data *at all* on millions or hundreds of millions of Americans?" Clapper answered directly, "No, sir." Senator Wyden asked again, "It (the NSA) does not?" Clapper answered craftily, "Not wittingly."

On May 13, 2013, a story broke about the United States government very wittingly spying on an entire news syndicate—the Associated Press. The AP is not a local newspaper or a local television station, or even a national news organization. Today, much as in 2013, the AP operates an international hub-and-spoke news organization through 250 offices, which connect 700 newsrooms and 65,000 subscribers to services around the world. Literally half the world reads, watches, or listens to an AP-distributed news story every day. The AP is not a minnow, it is a great blue whale that intakes the news like plankton and spouts stories the earth over. The Obama Administration and Eric Holder did not think twice about secretly spying, for two months, on 100 editors and writers through twenty different telephone lines including at AP offices in New York and Washington and AP's dedicated press line within the U.S. House of Representatives. The spying also included records from the cellular and personal phones of reporters and editors. To "spy," the government normally needs probable cause—and given that, a news agency normally receives notice of a subpoena being issued and can address its validity in court. That did not happen.

A group of fifty news organizations put together a letter to address the issue. They sent it directly to Eric Holder: "In the 30 years since the (Justice) Department issued guidelines governing subpoena practice as it relates to phone records from journalists, none of us can remember an instance where such an overreaching dragnet for newsgathering materials was deployed by the department, particularly without notice to the affected reporters or an opportunity to seek judicial review." Eric Holder did not bat an eye.

Gary Pruitt, president and CEO of the Associated Press, wrote Holder a letter stating in part, "These records potentially reveal communications with confidential sources across all of the newsgathering activities undertaken by the AP during a two-month period, providing a roadmap to AP's newsgathering operations." Perhaps that is precisely why Holder's DOJ did the spying.

A week later another story broke, this time regarding a single reporter, James Rosen of Fox News. Eric Holder himself signed a search warrant that dubbed Mr. Rosen a criminal co-conspirator who, with his sources, violated the 1917 Espionage Act. Holder wanted to search Mr. Rosen's emails and his parent's communications too. When questioned about this episode of his department's spying, Holder denied it. He testified: "With regard to the potential prosecution of the press for the disclosure of classified material, that is not something I've ever been involved in, nor heard of, or would think would be wise policy." At a later hearing, when faced with the search warrant he signed, and being reminded that subpoenas are generally issued following a crime, Holder testified: "Just because the Justice Department was investigating a reporter for commission of a crime did not mean the Justice Department was actually considering prosecuting the reporter for committing the crime." So, on that basis, what reporter can't the Justice Department investigate?

An internal memo was circulating among executives at Stratfor, a global intelligence firm which worked regularly with the intelligence community. The executives were stunned to read a memo about the Obama Administration's initiative to target journalists. The email stated: "(John) Brennan (the director of the CIA) is behind the witch hunts of investigative journalists learning information from inside the Beltway sources—they are after anyone printing materials negative to the Obama agenda."

Two weeks later, on June 5, 2013, a story broke that eclipsed those that had come in rapid fire before it. There had been a viewer of Clapper's testimony back on March 12 who knew that Clapper was "directly lying under oath to Congress," and could not let it go. Edward Snowden, a computer intelligence consultant, had worked for the CIA and NSA for years and knew what the truth was. He had been preparing to share it with his fellow citizens for some time. Snowden had worked out of the NSA's Hawaii regional operational center and had learned first-hand the surveillance techniques employed by the Chinese Communist Party. In fact, Snowden taught methods of defending against Chinese hackers to high-ranking officials and military personnel. He could not bear to see the same degree of surveillance the CCP practiced in China being used on United States citizens, without their knowledge. So, he broke the story.

Snowden began funneling documents through reporters Glenn Greenwald and Laura Poitras, which were sent to the *Guardian* and the *Washington Post*. Over the next few months, he spread the documents among publishers around the globe from Der Speigal in Germany to O Globo in Brazil. Snowden had copied as many as 1.7 million NSA documents to prove that what he was revealing about global surveillance programs was true. Among the trove of documents were 160,000 intercepted emails and 7,600 documents taken from 11,000 online accounts. This proved the NSA was working with telecommunications networks to spy—on anyone.

Glenn Greenwald informed the public that Snowden had "to take documents with him that proved that what he was saying was true, he had to take ones that included very sensitive detailed blueprints of how the NSA does what they do." On the release of the first tranche of documents, Snowden said in warrior fashion, "I understand that I will be made to suffer for my actions and that the return of this information to the public marks my end. All I can say right now is that the U.S. government is not going to be able to cover this up by jailing or murdering me. Truth is coming and it cannot be stopped."

The onslaught of documentation that followed from Snowden proved the existence of the following surveillance programs run by the NSA:

- The "PRISM" program allowed the NSA direct access to Americans' Google and Yahoo accounts with a court order.
- The "Boundless Informant" program was run based on a "secret" court order, which required that Verizon hand over to the NSA millions of phone records of U.S. citizens on a daily basis
- The "Bull Run" program was harvesting millions of emails, harvesting contact lists, searching emails, and mapping cell phone locations. The program also utilized cookies through internet advertising to find targets for government surveillance.
- The "MUSCULAR" program tapped undersea communications cables to clandestinely harvest information on millions of Yahoo and Google account holders.

These programs were financed through a top-secret NSA "Black Budget," where from payments were made to U.S. tech companies for access to their networks. Snowden's document drop also revealed the NSA's plans for the future, which bears out the ancient axiom that the powerful, no matter how much power they have, will always seek more power. An NSA mission statement was revealed titled "SIDINT Strategy 2012–2016." In it, the following cause was written: "(The NSA goal is to) dramatically increase mastery of the global network, to acquire adversaries' data from anyone, anytime, anywhere."

That is a loaded word, "adversary," as adversaries come in many kinds. They can come in the guise of an enemy nation whose system of government is contrary to your own. Or an adversary can be closer to home, in the form of an investigative journalist like Sharyl Attkisson or James Rosen who write stories that are "adverse" to another person's will. Or it can be a massive news entity, like the AP, through which some adverse stories are distributed. Or the adversary could be you if you disagree with a political party's policies.

When Edward Snowden was monitoring Communist China's surveillance system, he was watching a tyranny systematically holding its 1.6 billion people down. Our NSA complains that, with the same system, they are protecting our freedom by using powers that are contrary to the privacy protections of our Constitution.

Snowden apologized for his exposition of the NSA's surveillance system, saying, "I do not want to live in a world where everything I do and say is recorded, my sole motive is to inform the public as to that which is done in their name and that which is done *against* them." It is we the citizens, who are said to rule ourselves, that pay the taxes for this surveillance done *against* us.

The usual things occurred in the wake of this scandal. For all of Congress' complaining, that is all it could do—complain. Erik Holder openly scoffed at Congress' oversight role, knowing the only weapon Congress can wield is impeachment. He openly dared them to try it.

James Clapper lied to Congress in front of cameras and a microphone. He kept his job and was assigned to address the concerns of the public and their representatives. Clapper was allowed to proceed with his ambition of a "sweeping system of electronic monitoring that would tap into government, financial and other databases to scan the behavior of many of the 5,000,000 federal employees with secret clearances; current and former officials." It's a system now operating near you. The NSA can afford the finest state of the art surveillance system on earth—it's built with your money.

Lashing

The Faithful

By the end of 2009, the Obama Administration had done all that it could to formulate a manner to pass Obamacare, yet with massive democratic majorities in both houses of Congress, they still needed votes. On their own side of the aisle, Bart Stupak, U.S. Representative of Michigan's first congressional district, was a stand-out along with several other democrats who objected to federal funding of abortions and abortifacients—which was a part of the bill. Obama had already promised that his bill would not invade religious liberties. To gain the necessary votes, he needed to be more concrete, so Obama pledged that no manner of abortions would be federally funded through Patient Protection and Affordable Care Act provisions. He went so far as to sign Executive Order 13535, which paralleled the Hyde Amendment—another government assurance written by Henry Hyde of Illinois—that federal funds would never be used for abortions. Given this promise, this pledge, and this order, Bart Stupak and his group of democrats became the last votes needed for the PPACA's passage without a single Republican vote. The administrative state thereby seized regulatory control of one-sixth of the United States economy.

There was more to the bill than even Nancy Pelosi could foresee when she said Congress had to "pass the bill so that you (the voters) can find out what is in it!" After Obama promised not to use his healthcare law to violate religious liberty, after his pledge to Bart Stupak not to use federal funds for abortions or abortifacients, and after his executive order of compliance with the Hyde Amendment, Obama went ahead and did through regulation what he could not get passed through constitutionally required means of law.

Obama directed Kathleen Sebelius and her Health and Human Services Agency to mandate that insurance companies cover "preventative services," and in that category, abortifacient drugs such as Ella and Plan B as well as contraceptives and surgical sterilizations. Though the government would not supply the funding directly, it demanded by mandate that employers and their health insurers *must* cover for their employees what several Democrats and every Republican said should never be funded through the PPACA.

The HHS decided that it would be "tolerant" of religions by exempting the health insurance plans of churches, synagogues, and mosques—just those persons specifically employed in the holy sites themselves would be exempted. What were not exempted were schools, universities, hospitals, and charitable orders, such as the Little Sisters of the Poor. Such institutions were forced, by a mandate never voted on by representatives of the people, to provide the funding for abortifacients, including the Plan B drug, with an FDA label that warns it "can destroy life." Something the Catholic Church and its faithful have vowed never to do for two thousand years. Since some of the first Christian lives were slaughtered for sport throughout the Roman Empire, the religious orders of the Catholic Church have vowed to behold life as a sacred gift.

The great irony of this passage is that America was literally founded as the first safe haven on the globe for all religions.

Yet we cannot blame America's founders, they could not have foreseen the menace posed to our government by the Little Sisters of the Poor. An order comprised, as Mother Provincial, Sister Loraine Maguire gently noted, of "a group of women who make religious vows to God.... We dedicate ourselves to serving the elderly poor (in the inner cities) regardless of race or religion, offering them a home where they are welcomed as Christ, cared for as family and accompanied with dignity, until God calls them to himself." The order of the Little Sisters of the Poor had been selfishly performing this practice for 175 years, until the order was threatened with being punished out of existence by a mandate of Obamacare.

This order of Catholic nuns follow their conscience, and the doctrinal teachings of the Catholic Church, which demands a devotee's respect for all life, and they therefore must oppose the life-threatening use of contraceptive and abortive drugs as well as sterilizations. Such devotees deem life to be as sacred in its seed as it is in the poor and elderly, whom the sisters spend their lives caring for. The sisters were informed that if the twenty-five homes they devoted to the poor did not conform to the mandate and pay the bill for abortifacients, the order would face federal fines payable to the federal government of $70 million. The fines were to be imposed by a tax-payer funded federal agency, to punish an order of women who are pledged to their own poverty. The order of nuns refused the government's order.

Kathleen Sebelius demanded that the Little Sisters of the Poor had to conform. The HHS was on the frontline in a battle of the "War on Women." Nancy Keenan, the president of the pro-abortion group NARAL, chimed in that "all women should have access to contraceptive coverage, regardless of where they work!"

Sebelius finally relented, she would offer a government *accommodation*: If the Sisters would sign a document known as Form 700, whereby the they agreed that not *they*, but their insurance company, would pay for the "preventative services" directly, then the fines would not be applied. The Sisters again stood firm, for according to their faith and the faiths of many another, there is no moral difference between an individual doing a sinful act or that same person authorizing the same act be done by another than themselves.

The administrative state was beside itself. It's just a piece of paper! Can't you just sign it! The Sisters could not. It was a matter of something higher than a bureaucracy, something to do with one's judgement as to what is sacred. A little something one cannot quantify or qualify or renounce on a piece of paper. It is a matter of God's gift of human life—which the nuns contended is sacred… and therefore not within the province of governments.

This central argument, in the context of the province of government control, represents much more than just an HHS mandate or a form. By creating this mandate, our state threatens the remains of spiritual institutions that serve in America. One hundred years ago, most of the hospitals in this country were faith-based. One hundred years ago, most of the educational institutions were faith-based.

One hundred years ago, most of the social services in this country were faith-based. Today, there are only the remains of these institutions that linger on, as the administrative and dependent states have assumed more and more control of our society; as our society has become more and more *dependent* on a single, central government. This HHS mandate serves as a final wedge to further drive the remains of faithful institutions to have to decide between the services they provide and the dictates of their consciences, which are the driving spiritual force of those services. It is the state's last hurrah in driving every independent, intermediary societal power from our society altogether, that the state might finally be in absolute control of everything we think and every service we need. This answers the question that Sister Loraine asked when her punishment began: "Why is the government doing this to us?"

Lastly, this is the last place where the state must grapple for absolute control—in the sacred province of every citizen's soul. Why must so few remaining independent institutions bother a state which controls over 95% of the universities, the hospitals, the schools, and the social services? And why do a few nuns, who ask and want nothing, but who refuse to conform to the state's rules, bother the state? The state has grown so great, it hates the idea that it does not control everything! Like the land we stand on, the water we drink, or the air we breathe. The administrative state demands even the conformance of our beliefs. Even the conformance of our deepest held thoughts about what is sacred, about what is life and death.

We must accept the state's lash as an instrument to bind us to its unconstitutional, unrepresentative "rules" or we must suffer the state's lash—applied with a whip that is merciless.

LEVIATHAN RISING

Conclusion

We have chronicled Leviathan's rise, which began by describing the irreducible castle walls of the impenetrable fortress the administrative and dependent states now enjoy, fortified by the stone and mortis of thousands of government programs that have all the sanctuary and certainty of eternity normally ascribed to holy writ. We have observed a sincere conservative fail to reduce the walls by even a single stone, though a vast majority of the nation voted for him to do so.

We have witnessed influence-peddling on a massive scale with the placating of an enemy's will at the peril of our own national security. However, the wrong doers were shown to be defended by the very law enforcement agencies that are supposed to investigate crime and prosecute the offenders of our common law. Further, we observed the process of the entire Democratic Party choosing to, rather than defend the Constitution and our laws as they were sworn to do, defend wrongdoing and the wrong doers to maintain Democratic Party power. We witnessed the spectacle of a media spinning a web of deceit, which turned the villains into heroes and turned the committees convened to bring forth the truth into villains...all perfectly orchestrated to make a mockery of the truth and our common law.

We have observed a president fail in the first duty of his office to faithfully execute the law, in violation of Article II of the Constitution. And viewed the same president decree laws to exist, which were definitively rejected by the people's representatives. We have looked on as the same president punished states that abided by standing immigration laws, and reward states that defied the same laws. We have witnessed an attorney general who swore to "faithfully discharge the duties of the office" counsel the various states' attorneys general not to enforce standing immigration laws—or their cities and states might be financially punished.

We have observed an agency of the administrative state, the EPA, change definitions within laws to expand its jurisdiction from the oversight of oceans and seas, Great Lakes and rivers, to having legal authority over who may fill a pond on their family ranch in Wyoming or who may harvest peat moss in Minnesota.

We have viewed a liberal state, a liberal agency, and a liberal court redefine the definition of what constitutes a pollutant, to include the air we breathe out, and redefine science from a determination of facts to a rendering of opinion. This change of definition was done deliberately to create a means for fashioning rules based on *scientific uncertainty* and fulfill a scheme to take control of the entire energy industry. After the people's representatives refused to do so by law. Over a very few years, these combined EPA machinations have expanded the jurisdiction of the administrative state to include all of the waters, the lands, and the air of the United States. Our central government, which the founders originally confined to a capital that could occupy an area no larger than ten square miles, now makes a jurisdictional claim to every square foot of land, every puddle of water, and every breath of air over the breadth of the entire continent. These schemes to bring everyone's private property to being under a federal authority is in direct violation of the Constitution's Fifth Amendment, which states that no citizen will be "deprived of life, liberty or property without due process of law; nor shall private property be taken for public use, without just compensation." Yet, common citizens have now to litigate against a federal authority with infinite financial resources for the use of their own lands, their own waters—even their own air.

We have witnessed one of the most powerful agencies of the administrative state, the Internal Revenue Service, determine who can and cannot organize themselves into a legal political association. We observed applications being side-tracked for years. We saw applicants being investigated for the lists of their members and the contents of their prayers. We have seen IRS authorities ship the confidential information of innocent applicants to law enforcement authorities for possible investigations.

This prejudice against certain associations of which the state does not approve can be viewed as in direct violation of the First Amendment of the Constitution, which states, "Congress shall make no law…prohibiting the free exercise…of the right of the people to assemble." The administrative state took it upon itself to deny that right to hundreds of Tea Party assemblies. It is also against the very design of our Constitution, which uniquely provides protections against the persecution of one's political opponents—if only the constitutional law were faithfully executed.

We have viewed a courageous journalist convey vitally important, truthful stories to the public, which have antagonized an administration in power. We have witnessed her home being digitally invaded, her computers systematically harvested, and her phones tapped because forces within the administrative state did not like what she was writing. Whether it was the DNI or the DOJ or the FBI—a woman who had committed no crime was harassed by her government for what she was thinking; for what she was writing.

This action, by the administrative state, is in direct violation of the First Amendment, which guarantees the freedom of the press. It is also in direct violation of the Fourth Amendment, which secures, "The right of the people to be secure in their persons, houses, papers and effects against unreasonable searches and seizures." The administrative state set up a digital camp in the Attkissons' living room for a year, searching and seizing whatever it wanted. Sharyl Attkisson was not the only journalist who wrote stories the state did not like, and she was not the only one who was spied on. There were a hundred writers and editors of the Associated Press, and there was James Rosen. Again—the state's perceived opponents.

Lastly, we witnessed a president make promises not to invade the provinces of faith. A president who made a pledge to get the votes necessary to pass a law, knowing he would add a rule which contradicted his promise and his pledge once the PPACA became law. President Obama waited until the Health and Human Services Agency assumed control of 1/6 of the United States economy, then created a "rule"—a mandate—as an extension of the law, which could be used as a consequent wedge to attack the relics of our society's faithful institutions. The "rule" was made even though in direct contradiction to the First Amendment, which plainly reads: "Congress shall make no law respecting an establishment of religion or prohibiting the free exercise thereof." Congress, as prescribed in Article I of the Constitution, is the sole authority that is supposed to make *all* of our common laws. However, the central state now unconstitutionally makes all the rules. Rules no one votes on; rules that are not always judicially reviewed for being in keeping with the Constitution.

We have observed a central state power failing to faithfully execute constitutional laws it does not like; a central power fabricating laws the people's representatives reject; a central power treating the states with contempt; a central power laying legal claim to every square foot of a continent; a central power disabling associations it disagrees with; a central power making itself a spy in private citizen's homes. And we have witnessed a central state power trying to manipulate faithful souls into acting against the faith they know. Such is our central state's infinite thirst for control.

We have witnessed this power become so secure in itself that it does not care what constitutional laws it breaks. It does not care who it injures. It does not care about the nation's voters. This state does not protect its opponents, as designed by our Constitution, but threatens them.

So, what are we to do as voters?

Listen! Rising from the castle's towers...you can hear laughter.

What would such a state do if we the people voted to elect someone that the state does not approve? What if it were someone who threatened their inner circle? What if it were someone who threatened the comforts of the castle? What if it were someone who wanted to rewrite or remove some of the state's "rules." What if it were someone who wanted to reduce the amount of taxes raked from the population? What if it were someone like Ronald Reagan, who threatened to reduce just a small measure of the state's long gathering, monolithic power?

That is where the end of the *Shadows of the Acropolis* will begin—for Leviathan is risen....

PART THREE

Leviathan Arisen

Fair Elections

– Light –

FAIR ELECTIONS

In the early pages of Volume I, *The DNA of Democracy*, we visited the most direct democracy in human history as it was constituted in Athens, Greece. From that time to this, democracy has never existed unless its basis was in the right of the citizenry to vote. In Athens, all of the free citizens voted on the major issues of their day together in assembly in the *Ecclesia*. Volume I later recounted the Romans' "Republican" system of voting—for representatives to stand in office and "represent" the will of their voters. In England, the representation of the people is housed in the national Parliament, to which the peoples of the various counties vote in their Members of Parliament to faithfully represent the people's interests. The vote has been taken in England for centuries, and it is the vital key to their democracy's stability. Neither democracy, nor its species of representative government, exist outside of the process of voting, whereby the will of the people is placed in government. If ever one or a few decide who should rule over the multitudes—rather than that decision being in the hands of the voters—then such a government is tyrannical by definition.

In America, voting began within the councils of the Iroquois, the Cherokee, and the Algonquins. For the first Europeans on their way to America, voting began on the decks of the Mayflower as she made her pilgrim voyage. Voting is so important to the foundation of our nation that a large section of our Constitution is dedicated to defining who determines how the vote will be accomplished within the states, how often the vote will occur, and the lengths of terms of office before another vote renders representation of the multitudes ever fluid. Ours is a nation where the government was made to be forever reflective of the people's will.

The phrase that animated the Constitutional Convention—as it defined every American's voting rights—was: "Where annual elections end, there slavery begins." America's founders viewed regular elections as the foundational basis of liberty itself. Without the vote being faithfully taken and faithfully observed for each lawful "citizen" of the nation, all of the other rights we have are worth nothing. A tyrant may emerge, who then denies the determination of the people as to who should rule, and by one more step can dispossess the people of all their other rights. Elbridge Gerry, one of the Constitution's framers, said in regard to annual elections that they were "the only defense of the people against tyranny." As it was then, so it is now.

In ranking which type of vote is most important, at the time of our nation's founding it would have been easy to give this award to the local vote. The second most important would have been the vote to determine who would be the assembly members and senators of the state. Then, who would be voted in as governor. Who would be sent to the distant national capital to deal purely with matters of war, the mint, and commerce was arguably the least important vote of the time.

Since then, so much power has been taken from the localities and states and heaped into the single administrative state that the echelons of importance among the offices we vote in is essentially reversed. So much power has been poured into the single office of the presidency that all our other votes barely matter. It is the tell-tale sign of our times as to how far our nation has strayed from its original federalist design—a design which the founders adopted from the councils of the Iroquois, the Cherokee, and the Algonquin peoples, and felt any government should govern the least so that the people could experience liberty the most. So far have we strayed toward a governmental body thoroughly dependent on a single office—whose power and reach have become central to every citizen's life.

The election of 2016 became a referendum on this ever-gathering, omnipotent central power, when a candidate emerged who was the ultimate example of the outsider. Donald J. Trump had never won an elective office in his life, and he had never even been a Washington lobbyist. Donald Trump's main campaign promise was to "Drain the Swamp." A candidate had emerged whose greatest claim to fame was a reality television show on which he coined a simple phrase that had become a cultural mantra: "You're fired!" So, when the people of America heard that line, many believed its author was going to take the sentiment to Washington DC and, literally, "fire" some measure of the mammoth bureaucracy.

— Shadow —

Leviathan's Web

Donald Trump's opponent in the presidential election of 2016 was the foremost example of a person of the administrative state. In fact, she was the queen of the castle. Hillary Clinton had lived her entire life "inside" government—as the first lady of Arkansas, then as first lady to President Clinton, then as a pampered senator of New York, then as the secretary of state under the Obama Administration. She was a member of the "us" castle club, and she freely let the rest of the nation know what she thought of all of "them." While speaking at a fundraiser in New

York City on September 9, 2016, Hillary bellowed the following: "You could put half of Trump's supporters into what I call the basket of deplorables. Right? The racist, sexist, homophobic, xenophobic, Islamophobic, you name it...unfortunately, there are people like that!" That came straight from the heart of one of the "us" crowd.

The crowd in the castle laughed and jeered at Trump and those people who supported him. And they feared him. By March 2016, it was becoming clear that Trump could win the Republican nomination, and it was clear to the "us" crowd that Trump had to be stopped...he was a threat.

Enter Fusion GPS, a private research firm hired in April of 2016 by Mark Elias of the law firm Perkins-Coie, for his clients Hilary Clinton and the Democratic National Committee, to attack the candidacy of Donald Trump. Fusion GPS would be paid $1.02 million for its efforts.

On staff at Fusion since October of 2015, Nellie Ohr—a one-time CIA contractor—had already been compiling "open source" research on Trump through the internet by scouring Russian sources, news journals, legal notices, business records, and so on for another GPS client, the *Washington Free Beacon.* She was tasked to research Trump, his associates, his aides, and his business ties to Russia. And she was to produce reports of any negative connections Donald Trump possibly had with Russia. It was precisely this same research on Donald Trump that the Hillary Clinton campaign and the DNC were looking for.

Fusion GPS does more than just gather research. It was founded by Glenn Simpson, a former reporter, and Peter Fritsch, a former editor for the *Wall Street Journal.* Together the pair have extensive connections with journalists, editors, and the whole news media hierarchy of Washington DC and New York across both print and broadcast outlets. Fusion management knew how to develop a story—and how to get their stories distributed throughout the media.

Soon after Fusion was hired, stories began to proliferate through news journals such as *Politico*, where reporter Evelyn Farkas wrote an April 3 article postulating that Donald Trump was a greater threat to America than Vladmir Putin. An associate at *Politico*, Michael Crowley, wrote an article that appeared later in the month which called Trump "the Kremlin's Candidate." *New Yorker* magazine's Jonathan Chait wondered, in an article placed in the April 28 edition, "Why is Donald Trump a patsy for Vladmir Putin?" Nellie Ohr's research was being disseminated throughout the media and was finding its way into finished articles within a month of Fusion's hiring. Most every story painted a connection of Trump to Russia based on Nellie Ohr's "open source" research.

To add credibility to the research and the reporting that was in development, Fusion turned to one of Britain's former MI6 spies whom Glenn Simpson had known since 2009—Christopher Steele. Coincidentally, Steele had also known researcher Nellie Ohr and her husband Bruce Ohr since 2007. Through the spring of 2016, Nellie's unverified research was not only finding its way out into the media, but was becoming a part of a document that looked like an intelligence product, courtesy of a spy who knew how to write one.

When Glenn Simpson was later asked about Christopher Steele's trustworthiness to compose an intelligence product, Simpson replied, "Chris Steele deals in a very different kind of information, which is human intelligence information. So, by its very nature, the question of whether something is accurate isn't really asked." Yet, what Nellie Ohr and Chris Steele were writing, and Fusion GPS was feeding to the media, was getting into the daily news stream where it was portrayed as the truth. With many voices repeating it, the stories were multiplying like a virus.

During the same time period, various persons affiliated with the early Trump campaign were running into different people in scattered parts of the world who were stating the same sort of things and asking the same sort questions. George Papadopoulos was attending a conference in Rome when he was approached by a Maltese professor named Joseph Mifsud, who happened to mention, out of the blue, that he knew some Russians who "had dirt" on Hillary Clinton—something in her emails. Two weeks later, in London, Papadopoulos was contacted by a former Australian foreign minister, Alexander Downer, who wanted to talk over a drink, out of the blue, about "thousands of Hillary's emails."

Meanwhile, Robert Goldstone, a British publicist, began emailing Donald Trump Jr. offering documents and information that would "incriminate" Hillary Clinton. And Michael Caputo was approached by a man going by the name Henry Greenberg, who Caputo handed off to Roger Stone, and offered damaging documentary information on Hillary Clinton. Stone turned Greenberg down. It was later learned Greenberg had been an FBI informant for seventeen years. In fact, there were six occasions when various Trump campaign personnel "encountered" people who were connected with the FBI, the Clinton campaign, or Western intelligence agencies and wanted to know—you know—about all of those emails.

The creating of a storyline and the random contacts with Trump campaign operatives was apparently a hound-and-fox operation: certain hounds related to the FBI were chasing the Trump foxes into the hunter's developing storyline—that Donald J. Trump's campaign was connected to the Russians and that both their objectives were to reveal all of those emails and the dirt on Hillary.

In July 2016, the number of stories multiplied but all maintained the same theme. On July 4, Franklin Foer wrote in *Slate* that Trump was "Putin's puppet." On July 18, Jonathan Chait wrote in *New York* magazine that Trump had a "relationship with Russia that is disturbing...and frightening." Also on July 18, Josh Rogan wrote in the *Washington Post* that the "Trump campaign guts GOP's anti-Russia stance." Then, in a July 21 *Washington Post* article, Anne Applebaum claimed Trump was being used as a Manchurian Candidate and that Russia "was clearly participating in the Trump campaign."

Then a perfectly-related story broke. On July 22, 2016, *Wikileaks* released a tranche of emails that were hacked from the Democratic

National Committee's computers. The press jumped on the story to complete their narrative: The Russians must have done it. Trump must have helped. It was part of the same developing story....

Clinton campaign operatives then took what had been a print story to the broadcast media at the perfect time—*during* the Democratic National Convention. On July 24, Robbie Mook told Jake Tapper of CNN that the Russians had hacked the DNC emails to help Trump. He added, "I don't think it's coincidental... on the eve of our convention." Jennifer Palmieri and Jake Sullivan began feeding the broadcast media a variation of the same line: the Trump campaign had suspicious connections to the Kremlin.

On July 31, directly after the Democratic National Convention, agencies of the administrative state decided to join the party. FBI Director James Comey opened a counter-intelligence probe into the Trump campaign, which FBI Special Counsel Lisa Page named "Crossfire Hurricane." The investigation was opened based solely on a conversation at a London bar between Alexander Downer and George Papadopoulos that mentioned Hillary's emails. It was not opened on the basis of any intelligence, or any crime that needed investigating.

Because it was a counter-intelligence investigation, the activities of the FBI were protected from congressional oversight. The investigation, and all of its fruits, could be deemed "classified"—at least while the investigation was ongoing. And though most FBI investigations originate and are maintained at FBI field offices, this investigation was different: it was controlled by a select few FBI agents at FBI headquarters, in what Deputy Director Andrew McCabe called an "HQ Special."

In August, the CIA got involved. Its director, John Brennan, began sharing what would be popularly titled "the Steele Dossier" with democratic congressional members and the media, declaring that he had "information indicating that Russia was working to help elect Donald J. Trump president," as quoted in the *New York Times*. Brennan ended up in Senate Minority Leader Harry Reid's office on August 25, telling him about the dossier and offering it as proof that "the Russians were backing Trump." This meeting formed a pretext for Harry Reid to send an official letter to FBI Director Comey—a letter everyone intended should get directly to the media. The letter stated, in part: "The evidence of a direct connection between the Russian government and Donald Trump's presidential campaign continues to mount and has led (former CIA Director) Michael Morrell to call Trump an 'unwitting agent' of Russia and the Kremlin."

Then, on September 8, another extraordinary thing happened. FBI Director James Comey and Homeland Security Chief Jeh Johnson called an emergency meeting of the "Gang of Twelve"—an expanded grouping of the normal "Gang of Eight" congressional intelligence heads. Comey and Johnson told the representatives that Obama wanted a joint statement reflecting "solidarity and bipartisan unity" on the part of Congress in light of Russia's attempts to shape the upcoming presidential election. No proof was offered of these "attempts." It appears to have been a gambit to get the Republicans to endorse the developing story. The Republicans did not prove useful on this occasion—they saw through the ruse and then wondered what was going on.

The media picked up Reid's letter to Comey and claimed it was further evidence that the Russians were supporting Trump's candidacy. The media picked up on the "urgent" meeting calling for the Gang of Twelve and cited that as further evidence. To further amplify the widening story, Christopher Steele went on a celebratory media tour with Glenn Simpson, touting the dossier that was becoming the heart of a political storm. Steele and Simpson visited Fusion GPS contacts at CNN, the *Washington Post*, the *New York Times*, and *Yahoo News*.

So, what was in the Christopher Steele dossier that made Brennan start brandishing it all over town? It was not an "intelligence" product as any CIA or FBI investigator—or any decent reporter—would know if they merely studied it. It was an elaborate political hit piece made to look like an intelligence product—with some real-life characters who did not do what was alleged in the dossier.

Leviathan's Retaliation

To present two cases-in-point: The dossier alleged Trump was being cultivated by the Kremlin for five years going back to 2011. But the dossier does not supply evidence, nor has there been anything presented since, to show that Trump has had *any* ties to the Kremlin - none. The dossier alleged that Trump was subject to blackmail by the Russians based on episodes it claimed happened while Trump stayed at the Ritz Carlton in Moscow. Yet, the episodes described never happened...

In autumn of 2016, the dossier, as a work of rumor and pseudo-fiction, was already doing tremendous damage because the media continuously portrayed its contents as true. And this non-intelligence document could be used for another purpose: when endorsed by the directors of our CIA and FBI it could be used to further invade the Trump campaign to find what no one had yet found—any real, factual evidence of a Trump connection to Russia. But there was a problem. The Dossier, given strict examination, would be laughed out of a normal U.S. court of law. However, given that the FBI had opened a "counter-intelligence" investigation, a certain court reserved for investigating terrorists or spies could be used and, like the "HQ Special" investigation, it was a special court.

The FISA court was created by the Foreign Intelligence Surveillance Act of 1978 to grant warrants—normally to the NSA or the FBI—to find, identify, and apprehend spies or terrorists operating in the United States. It is a secret court. Within the court sits a single judge who is petitioned by whatever government representative is seeking a warrant. Any attorneys appearing in the court have to be licensed by the U.S. government to do so. The proceedings within the chamber are *ex parte*, meaning no defendants and no defendants' attorneys are allowed. Hearings held in the court are closed to the public. Records of the proceedings are not available to the public. In other words, the secretive FISA court was the perfect court to petition for a warrant to spy on a campaign in the middle of an election. And the odds were nearly certain a warrant would be granted. Between 1979 and 2004, the FISA court received 18,746 applications for warrants and 18,742 were granted.

The success rate to attain a warrant is based on the idea that federal officers will do the right thing—they will be truthful, they will act with integrity and in accordance with the Constitution. Unlike our normal legal system, there is no adversarial viewpoint presented to the FISA court to defend against misinformation in the application or to defend against bad actors within the government. Again, it was the perfect venue for a certain sort of warrant that no one would ever know about.

James Comey, Andrew McCabe, and Peter Stzrok signed for the FBI, and Rod Rosenstein signed for the Department of Justice, to apply for a warrant of surveillance on a some-time Trump campaign "advisor" Cater Page—who was actually an investment banker with some dealings in Russia. The application was almost entirely based on passages from the Steele Dossier concerning a meeting and understanding between Carter Page and Igor Sechin, a member of Putin's inner circle and the CEO of Rosneft, Russia's state oil company. There was something curious about the passages themselves. In the summary of the Steele Dossier dated July 2016 and numbered 94 is the following:

> "Trump advisor Carter PAGE holds secret meetings in Moscow with (Igor) SECHIN and senior Kremlin Internal Affairs official, DIVYEKIN.
>
> SECHIN raises issues of future bilateral US-Russia energy co-operation and associated lifting of sanctions against Russia over Ukraine. PAGE non-committal."

This passage is fine for a government leak and a sensational press story about a Trump advisor's secret meeting in Moscow. It is not evidence of a crime, or an act of treason. But this subsequent dossier report dated October 2016 (concurrent with the warrant application) and numbered 134 could be:

> "Close associate of SECHIN confirms his secret meeting in Moscow with Carter PAGE in July.
>
> Substance included offer of large stake in Rosneft in return of lifting sanctions on Russia. PAGE confirms this is TRUMP's intention."

If true, the changes in the second report make the interaction one of bribery, and connects Page directly to Trump—and Trump directly to the activity. For the FISA application, in order to corroborate the information from the dossier, the FBI and DOJ produced two media articles. The first was by Michael Isikoff of *Yahoo News*, written September 23, 2016: "U.S. intel officials probe ties between Trump adviser and Kremlin." The article itself was based on the dossier. The second was by Josh Rogan of the *Washington Post* and was based, in part, on the same research the dossier was based on—Nellie Ohr's research. The FISA application was based on circular reporting of false research, like so many of the multiplying media stories. The fact was, Carter Page never met with Igor Sechin. And Carter Page had never met Donald Trump in his life.

In American law, there is a wonderful rule based on the Supreme Court case *Brady v. Maryland,* which has since earned the name the "Brady Rule." It compels the prosecution in any judicial proceeding to show *any* evidence which may demonstrate a defendant's innocence to the defense and to the court. In a setting like the FISA court, where the defense doesn't appear, this rule is obviously most important.

When the FBI and the DOJ applied for the Page warrant, they had the following exculpatory evidence, helpful in proving the defendant's innocence, which they never presented to the court: they never factually corroborated the claims made in the dossier. The FBI claimed that Steele was "reliable" and "credible" when they knew he was not. The FBI also knew that the Clinton campaign had paid for the dossier and had fed Steele some of the information in the dossier. They did not inform the court about that either.

And there was more exculpatory evidence at the FBI's door. After Isikoff's article appeared on September 23 2016, the media erupted with breaking coverage of the fatal link between Trump and Russia—Carter Page. Seeing all the news pouring out of every media outlet, news which Carter Page himself knew to be untrue, he authored a letter to the FBI offering to go to their offices immediately and clear the matter up with the truth. The FBI refused the offered interview. They did not want Carter Page—they wanted the FISA warrant, and they got it on October 21. A warrant that provided all of Carter Page's future and *past* communications to the FBI's prying ear. The FBI thought they would find a gold mine. But after running spies after Trump campaign members and planting conversations to trap them—there was nothing. After months of reporters going to and from Moscow trying to verify the dossier and discover ties between Trump and the Kremlin—there was nothing. After searching Page's communications as far back as the FBI could find—there was nothing. Since the FBI had opened the "Crossfire Hurricane" investigation in July—there was nothing.

That was the true October 2016 "Election Surprise": despite hundreds in the government and the media trying to find *anything* on Trump, there was nothing. There was only the evidence of a shaft. And despite the maelstrom of media stories about investigations and treason, Trump won the presidency with 306 Electoral College votes to Hillary Clinton's 227. The Democratic Party, the administrative state, and the media failed to stop a perfectly legal, historic victory by an outsider who pledged to serve the American people by taking on Washington DC.

The Democratic Party, the administrative state, and the media did not take kindly to someone they did not approve of entering into the all-powerful American office of the presidency. When a seat of power becomes so central, when it becomes so overgrown that it is as omni-potent as an absolute throne, it is a power which persons "in power" think they should own—no matter how people vote. It is the greatest historical failure of our human nature when, in the centrifugal force of the allure of power, even otherwise good people commit bad acts. Even people who should know better believe they *do* know better—and should rule themselves, rather than an "other," no matter how the people vote. This failure of human nature is why we have a constitution.

The shock of the election loss lasted exactly twenty-four hours until the Democrats claimed Trump did not win...Trump had stolen the election and the Russians had helped him. They said it knowing there was utterly no evidence. The office that the American Left claimed the Russians and Donald Trump had stolen, they then set about themselves to steal with all the ensnaring mechanics and ferocity of those administrative state agencies which were built to be retaliatory.

— Shadow —

Leviathan's Retaliation

The mission to invalidate the people's vote got off to a poor start when an Intelligence Community Assessment brief was produced by the CIA and FBI for Congress around Thanksgiving 2016. It related that the Russians may have been up to their normal dirty tricks—much as they had for the last hundred years—to spread propaganda. Nevertheless, there was *no* evidence that Russia influenced the election in a substantive way affecting the results. This despite the fact that these agencies had been laser focused for months searching for just such evidence.

So, on December 6, under an atmosphere of great urgency, President Obama ordered CIA Director John Brennan to conduct a new "full review" of intelligence relating to the 2016 election. He wanted the review on his desk *before* Trump took power. Brennan took the lead, but rather than requisition information from the seventeen intelligence community agencies, he confined the "review" to the FBI, CIA, NSA, and the DNI alone and kept the other eleven intel agencies at a distance outside the review. And he handpicked the analysts who would work on the assessment. It was a confinement of the investigation to a distinct few—reminiscent of the "HQ Special" that was ongoing at the FBI.

Some members of the media did not wait for the new assessment. The *Washington Post* reported on December 9: "The CIA has concluded in a 'secret' assessment that Russia intervened in the 2016 election to help Trump win the presidency, rather than just undermine confidence in the US electoral system." The groundwork was laid for another media maelstrom, while Crossfire Hurricane was ongoing.

On December 29, the Obama Administration took action as though Russia had affected the election. Obama announced sweeping new sanctions against Russia, including the expulsion of thirty-five diplomats, the sanctioning of members of the GRU (the Russian equivalent to the CIA) and three companies affiliated with that organization, as well as the closure of two Russian-owned compounds in Maryland and New York. The sanctions put the incoming Trump Administration in a trap. If anything were done to ease the sanctions or recall the diplomats, however slight the response, there would be an uproar that it was positive proof of Russia's effect on the election, and it could be made to appear that Trump was doing Russia's will.

Another trap was laid by the directors of the select agencies reviewing Russia's role in the elections: Brennan of the CIA, Comey of the FBI, James Clapper of the DNI, and Michael Rogers of the NSA. On January 6, this select group briefed President elect Trump on the intelligence community assessment, which was suddenly completed at warp speed. After the meeting, James Comey also informed Trump about the existence of the Steele dossier and its "report" of Trump's escapades during a stay at the Moscow Ritz-Carlton—escapades which never happened.

On January 7, the unclassified portions of the ICA were released. On January 10, like clockwork, classified portions and information about the "confidential briefing" were leaked to the media and made the news, about the "confidential briefing. CNN's Evan Perez, Jake Tapper, Jim Sciutto, and Watergate hero Carl Bernstein reported, "Intel chiefs presented Trump with claims of Russian efforts to compromise him." And the reporting team released the dossier's following claim: "Allegations that there was a continuing exchange of information during the campaign between Trump surrogates and intermediaries for the Russian government." The report put the Steele Dossier front and center in the media's maelstrom.

Meanwhile, on the same day back at "HQ Special" where "Crossfire Hurricane" was ongoing, lead FBI investigator Peter Strzok sent a hopeful text to his lover, FBI Counsel Lisa Page: "We are discussing whether now this is out, we use it as a pretext to go interview people."

The media took leaks of a confidential briefing from agency insiders and reported it as news, even though the "news" was never verified. Then the FBI used the release of the "news" as a pretext for interviews in furtherance of its ongoing investigations. Then those interviews created more leaks and more "news." This became a widening pattern of action against the incoming Trump administration.

Two vital individuals within the incoming administration were caught in the webs of this pattern. There was a vital reason why.

Retaliation On Flynn

General Michael Flynn was a battlefield legend. For over thirty years of service he had been a valuable maverick. He personally revolutionized how intelligence was used on the battlefields of Afghanistan during the 2007 surge, which turned the tide of the war at that time. Previous to his service in Afghanistan, Flynn was the intelligence chief at the U.S. Central Command. After his service in Afghanistan, Flynn became head of the Defense Intelligence Agency. In all respects, it may be said Michael Flynn served his country with full faith, honor, and valor—until he threatened the castle.

General Flynn differed with the Obama Administration in some key areas. He considered the nuclear deal with Iran a security threat. He thought the U.S. and Russia should sync their intelligence to defeat ISIS in Syria. And he thought the corruption of the Clintons posed a threat to the country. Finally, he wanted to reorganize the intelligence community of Washington DC, just as he had reorganized intelligence on the battlefield. And he posed another threat....

General Flynn was Donald Trump's choice to be National Security Advisor, with all of the access to national intelligence the post entailed. That position entails being in touch with counterparts in foreign countries to ensure transitions between administrations are smooth without causing any firestorms. During the transition period, incoming Vice President Pence noted that Flynn had "been in touch with diplomatic leaders (and) security leaders in some thirty countries. That's exactly what the incoming national security advisor is supposed to do." There was only one contact that the outgoing administration was interested in.

The Obama Administration was involved in unmasking many incoming members of the Trump Team. Susan Rice—Obama's security advisor—admitted as much. She was not the only one. A phone call that General Flynn made to his Russian counterpart, Ambassador Sergei Kislyak, was then "unmasked," recorded, and leaked to the press by any of a number of possible Obama officials. It might have been Sally Yates, acting director of the Department of Justice, or FBI Director James Comey, or DNI Director James Clapper. There was so much unmasking and leaking going on in the transition period, it is hard to know who it was. The FBI had the recording.

Like clockwork, on January 11, Donald Trump was asked a question about whether there were any contacts with Russian officials before the election or during the campaign. Trump said no. Then, like clockwork, on January 12, an article by David Ignatius appeared in the *Washington Post* titled, "Why did Obama Dawdle on Russia's Hacking?" Ignatius writes: "General Michael

Flynn, Trumps choice for National Security Advisor, cultivates close Russian contacts. He has appeared on Russia Today…the Kremlin's principal international propaganda outlet." Flynn had appeared on the network once in December 2015. The article went on, "According to a senior U.S. government official, Flynn phoned Russian Ambassador Sergei Kislyak several times on December 29, the day the Obama Administration announced (the sanctions)…. What did Flynn say, and did it undercut the U.S. sanctions?" The reporter even brought up the Logan Act of 1799—a law no one had ever been prosecuted for in the history of the country. How did David Ignatius even know there was a Logan Act? Of course, the Ignatius article stirred the media maelstrom again, as it became the source of more stories and more fury.

General Flynn, in his phone conversations with Kislyak, did note the sanctions. On December 29, in the following context, he asked Kislyak not to escalate the situation:

> "What I would ask you guys to do—and make sure you, make sure that you convey this, okay? Do not, do not uh, allow this administration to box us in, right now, okay…?
>
> I know you have to have some sort of action—to, to only make it *reciprocal*….
>
> We don't need to, we don't need that (escalation) right now, we need to—we need cool heads to prevail….
>
> And then, what we can do is, when we come in, we can then have a better conversation about where, where we're gonna go, uh, regarding uh, regarding our relationship."

General Flynn did not discuss the content or extent of the sanctions. And he properly said they should not discuss it until after the transfer of power.

When Flynn was asked by Vice President Mike Pence if he had discussed the sanctions, Flynn said no. He did not clarify, however, that he did ask Kislyak not to allow the sanctions issue to escalate. Mike Pence then appeared on "Face the Nation" and stated, "They (Flynn and Kislyak) did not discuss anything having to do with the United States' decision to expel diplomats or impose censure against Russia." The persons who had tapped the Kislyak-Flynn conversation knew there was a semantics opportunity. The DOJ and FBI decided to take advantage of the discrepancy.

Normally, if an outgoing administration were going to send FBI agents to "interview" an incoming administration member, the incoming White House counsel would be notified of the matter, there would be a formal request, and there would be an explanation as to why the interview was being sought. In General Flynn's case, that did not happen. Sally Yates of the DOJ directed James Comey to ask his deputy, Andrew McCabe, to phone Flynn and ask directly for an interview. McCabe called and told Flynn that "some people were curious about his conversations with Kislyak." Flynn was so sure of his own innocence that he joked, "You know what I said because you guys were probably listening."

On January 21, McCabe sent lead "Crossfire Hurricane" agent Peter Strzok along with Joe Pientka to visit Flynn and conduct the interview. After the interview, the two FBI agents came away convinced that Flynn was truthful, and neither did the interview produce any "derogatory" information. The assessment by the agents should have ended the matter. Instead, a few days after the very interview she engineered, Sally Yates—then the acting attorney general—went over to White House counsel Don McGahn's office to tell him that Flynn could be subject to blackmail because he had been "deceptive" about his conversations with Kislyak, in a statement that was at odds with her own investigators' conclusions.

On February 9, 2017, the media axe dropped. The *Washington Post* printed an article based on more "leaked" classified material. Greg Miller, Adam Entous, and Ellen Nakashima wrote:

> National security adviser Michael Flynn privately discussed U.S. Sanctions against Russia with that country's ambassador, during the month before Trump took office, contrary to public assertions by Trump officials....
>
> Flynn's conversations...were interpreted by some senior U.S officials (nine *anonymous* "senior agency officials") as an inappropriate and potentially illegal signal to the

> Kremlin.... The emerging details contradict public statements by incoming senior administration officials, including Mike Pence. Another Senior U.S official (speaking on condition of *anonymity*) put it more bluntly, saying that "either Flynn had misled Pence or that Pence misspoke."

The fury of the media maelstrom escalated to a boil.

Donald Trump had to ask General Flynn for his resignation, which he received on February 13, 2017. Michael Pence said he was "disappointed" to learn the retired general had withheld information from him, and supported Trump's decision to ask for his resignation.

The outgoing administration, the administrative state, the media, and the Democratic Party got their man. A man the enemies of the United States couldn't defeat during thirty years of service to his country. It begs the question: why the elaborate set up? Why were so many agencies so interested that General Michael Flynn not be national security advisor? The author believes the answer is simple: If General Flynn had assumed the role, with his expertise in intelligence and with access to the Crossfire Hurricane work ups, he would have known immediately that the whole investigation was based on *no intelligence;* he would have found it was based on *no evidence;* he would have found that the investigation wasn't based on a crime. He would have found, as lead investigator Peter Strzok admitted to Lisa Page, "There's no big there there."

It would have been the end of the plan to get Trump out of the office he won by the people's vote, an office that some persons in those agencies felt that they owned.

Retaliation On Sessions

Having ridded the new administration of the greatest threat it posed, the next design was to take out Jeff Sessions, Alabama Senator and leading member of the Senate Foreign Relations Committee. As such, in 2016 alone, Sessions met with over twenty-five ambassadors from countries as varied as Poland, Japan, Korea and Canada—as well as the ambassador of Russia, Sergei Kislyak. It was an important part of Senator Sessions' job for the American people. Jeff Sessions was also tapped to be the new attorney general of the United States and head of the Department of Justice.

During Sessions' January 2017 confirmation hearing, Democrat Al Franken set a semantic trap when he asked Sessions: "What would you do if you learned of any evidence that anyone affiliated with the Trump campaign communicated with the Russian government in the course of the 2016 campaign?" Sessions answered, "I'm not aware of any of those activities. I have been called a surrogate at a time or two in that campaign and I did not have any communications with the Russians."

Democratic Senator Leahy followed: "Have you been in contact with anyone connected to any part of the Russian Government about the 2016 election either before or after election day?" Sessions answered: "No." The semantic trap was tripped. Sessions had met Kislyak as a Senate Foreign Relations Committee member on September 8 in his office. Sessions had also seen Kislyak, among a multitude of other ambassadors, at a Republican National Convention event. That was all that was necessary for the next maelstrom...

On March 1, 2017, the same *Washington Post* team of reporters who had singled out Flynn did the same for Sessions, when the article by Entous, Nakashima, and Miller led with "Sessions met with Russian envoy twice last year, encounters he did not disclose." Sessions met with Kislyak as a senator from Alabama, not as a part of the campaign, but that is not how the article read. That was all that was needed.

Nancy Pelosi, House Minority Leader, demanded: "After lying under oath to Congress about his own communications with the Russians, the attorney general must resign," she said, "Sessions is not fit to serve as the top law enforcement officer of our country." Chuck Schumer, Minority Leader in the Senate, demanded Sessions resign as well as part of a general Democratic Party chorus that Sessions had to go—despite the fact that all of them knew, and many of them had met with, Ambassador Kislyak as their Senate postings required. In 2016 alone, Ambassador Kislyak had visited President Obama twenty-two times in the White House.

Unsurprisingly, there were many useful Republicans who called for Sessions to recuse himself from any present or future Russia investigation, among them Jason Chaffetz of the House and Lindsey Graham of the Senate. The only senior Republican to hold firm was Leader of the House, Paul Ryan.

Rather than stand against the maelstrom, Sessions conceded and recused himself from the central investigation his office was involved in. On March 2, Sessions held a news conference to announce: "I have now decided to recuse myself from any existing or future investigations of any matter relating in any way to the campaigns for president of the United States."

The reason for the Sessions set up was like Flynn's. If Sessions reviewed the material that Crossfire Hurricane was based on, he would find there was no basis for it whatsoever. So, Sessions took the head post at the Department of Justice, but precluded himself from establishing justice—just what the Democratic Party wanted.

Rod Rosenstein would fill the role of acting attorney general for all matters related to Russia. The two people who posed a threat to the ongoing investigation were gone, the two who might have found out what everyone involved in the investigation already knew—that there was nothing criminal. They also knew that the nature of the Trump investigation had to change.

Rod Rosenstein, James Comey, and Robert Mueller had been colleagues and friends for many years as they encountered each other during various stints in the Department of Justice and the Federal Bureau of Investigation. They were a tight group, reminiscent of the tight group that worked on the HQ Special "Crossfire Hurricane," and reminiscent of the tight group of hand-picked analysts and intelligence agencies that produced the January 2017 ICA report. This tight group would be working together again to change the nature of the investigation.

Devin Nunes, a House representative from California, was one of the only Republicans to be working against the tide of public opinion that the media had so furiously moved against Trump. Nunes was chairman of the House Permanent Select Committee on Intelligence, and vowed in March, after the Flynn firing and the Sessions recusal, to find out exactly what evidence there was that began the Russia investigation: when the investigation started, who authorized it, what agencies and personnel were committed to the investigation, and just how many spies were used to "encounter" Trump campaign personnel. In other words, Nunes was going after information that Flynn and Sessions would have found had they not been stopped. James Comey was called to appear before the HPSCI committee on March 20, 2017. He came with a surprise.

The committee barely began its hearing when FBI Director Comey issued the following statement:

> "I've been authorized by the Department of Justice (by his friend, acting AG Rosenstein) to confirm that the FBI, as part of our counterintelligence mission, is investigating the Russian government's efforts to interfere in the 2016 presidential election and that includes investigating the nature of any links between individuals associated with the Trump campaign and the Russian government and whether there was any coordination between the campaign and Russia's efforts. As with any counterintelligence investigation, this will also include an assessment of whether any crimes were committed."

It was a bombshell. It was designed to be. The statement inferred the DOJ and FBI had enough evidence to assess whether uncovered activities were criminal. The statement also further insulated the investigation because it was ongoing. It also made the investigation about more than a campaign—it was about criminality on the part of Trump associates.

It was based on nothing. And the persons who designed the bombshell knew it. It was the beginning of a design to move away from Crossfire Hurricane, which had produced nothing, to an entrapment campaign designed to yield an obstruction case against the president. A few steps remained.

After Rod Rosenstein took his post as deputy attorney general, he almost immediately wrote a memo to Donald Trump recommending he fire James Comey for breaching agency ethics in the Hillary Clinton server incident, which amounted to a get out of jail free card. Jeff Sessions agreed with the recommendation. Armed with those recommendations and tired of Comey's duplicitous statements about the investigation, Trump sent a letter terminating Comey on May 9, 2017.

The firing led to yet another media maelstrom. The incident was compared to Richard Nixon's efforts to end the Watergate investigation. Demands for impeachment based on obstruction of justice and interference in the Russia investigation were heard across Washington from every prominent Democrat and over every media outlet. Trump countered that it was the recommendation of two of Washington's own, Rosenstein and Sessions. It made no difference.

Comey sprang another trap. By his own account, he had written a memo to himself about a meeting following Flynn's resignation on February 14 with Jeff Sessions, Mike Pence, Comey, and President Trump. When the meeting broke, Trump (per the memo) asked Comey to stay, and according to Comey, "The president then returned to the topic of Mike Flynn saying, 'He is a good guy and has been through a lot, I hope you can let this go.'"

Comey leaked the memo to a friend, Daniel Richman, to secure direct delivery to the *New York Times*, where in a May 16 article by Michael Schmidt, the "memo" story took on the following form: "President Trump asked the FBI Director…to shut down the federal investigation into Mr. Trump's former NSA Michael T. Flynn…. The president has tried to directly influence the Justice Department and FBI investigation." That is an accusation of obstruction based a one person's recollection of a conversation between two persons—an account taken as gospel by the press.

It was a sufficient cue for longtime Comey colleague and friend Rod Rosenstein to appoint longtime colleague and friend Robert Mueller as Special Counsel of a new investigation into Donald Trump. The irony was not lost on Trump, who noted, "I am being investigated for firing the FBI director by the man who told me to fire the FBI director!" Rosenstein's various roles in the investigation were bizarre, as well. He was to direct the investigation, be a witness in the investigation, and be the ultimate judge in whether a case would be brought against a president.

From Mueller's appointment on, the investigation was impenetrable. Any attempt by President Trump to defend himself would be viewed as an obstruction of justice. Trump's defense of himself, in other words, would make the prosecution's case. It was like one of those trick knots that are woven so that the more one struggles to get free, the tighter the knot becomes. And it was a brilliant maneuver—it made the Crossfire Hurricane investigation obsolete. Even if Devin Nunes' committee later came with a finding that there was "no big there there," the investigation from that point forward was about obstruction, and it was quite a trap.

So was the scope of the new investigation. It was upside down. For a Special Counsel investigation to be started, it has to be based on a crime. This one wasn't. Following is the order:

> The Special Counsel is authorized to conduct the investigation confirmed by then-FBI director James B. Comey in testimony before the House Permanent Select Committee on Intelligence on March 20, 2017, including any links and/or coordination between the Russian government and individuals associated with the campaign of President Donald Trump.

Such links or coordination do not constitute a crime.

The second part of the order was meant to widen the investigation's scope and directed Mueller: "...and any matters that arose or may arise directly from the investigation." The third part of the order is a series of perjury and obstruction traps, which reads, "the jurisdiction of a Special Counsel shall also include authority to investigate and prosecute federal crimes committed in the course of, and with intent to interfere with, the Special Counsel's investigation, such as perjury, obstruction of justice, destruction of evidence, and intimidation of witnesses."

Later in August, a "classified" memo, which further expanded the scope of Mueller's investigation, was withheld from the congressional oversight committee yet hung there like a sword of Damocles ready to drop. On the whole, the order looks like a license to find or create a criminal act and attach it to Trump. It is the inverse of our legal system's provisions: a man's name was given to the Special Counsel and Counsel was asked to find or manufacture a crime. Normally, a crime is committed and investigated by a prosecutor who sets about to find the person who committed a crime. Here, a name was given for an investigation to find a crime.

The members Mueller assembled for his team were of a certain kind. Of the attorneys hired for the investigation, many had personal relationships with the Clintons or business relationships with the Clinton Foundation. Of sixteen attorneys, thirteen were registered Democrats. The Special Counsel's office became a fountain of leaks that never ran dry…intimating bombshells would drop at any moment for the press to feed on and on and on.

Meanwhile, there was a substantive investigation going on at Devin Nunes' House Permanent Select Committee on Intelligence. Nunes' investigative team was led by a common-sense former military man and prosecutor Kash Patel, who had experience tracking illicit funding of terrorist groups. Patel's credo was simple: follow the money. It came to mind for Patel that Fusion GPS did not do all of its work for free, nor had the Steele report been pro bono. Patel worked to get access, via the courts, to Fusion GPS' finances, and he succeeded. He found the silver bullet—the indisputable truth that the Clintons had funded the Steele dossier and all of the pseudo research used to surround the Trump campaign with a web of lies.

And the committee was active in its approach at eliciting simple truths, which would add up to unwinding the web of lies, to discover a single indisputable truth. Patel called it the "three

C's" and applied it to integral individuals who were involved in different areas of the "Crossfire Hurricane" investigation. Nunes' team members asked:

> To former Attorney General Loretta Lynch: "Do you have any evidence of collusion or conspiracy or coordination between the Trump campaign and Russia?"
>
> Lynch: "No, I don't."
>
> To former acting Attorney General Sally Yates: "Do you have any evidence of collusion or conspiracy or coordination between the Trump campaign and Russia?"
>
> Yates: "No."
>
> To former FBI Director James Comey: "Do you have any evidence of collusion or conspiracy or coordination between the Trump campaign and Russia?"
>
> Comey: "No."
>
> To former Assistant FBI Director Andrew McCabe: "Do you have any evidence of collusion or conspiracy or coordination between the Trump campaign and Russia?"
>
> McCabe: "No."
>
> To Glenn Simpson, Partner at Fusion GPS: "Do you have any evidence of collusion or conspiracy or coordination between the Trump campaign and Russia?"
>
> Simpson: "No."
>
> To John Podesta, Clinton Campaign Chair: "Do you have any evidence of collusion or conspiracy or coordination between the Trump campaign and Russia?"
>
> Podesta: "No."

Case closed. It was that simple. The Clintons had funded a web of lies and the committee found, in February 2018, that there was "no evidence of collusion." Such was the finding of a team of heroes who refused to believe the lie.

The Mueller Investigation went on for another year before it finally admitted that it could not argue with the HPSCI's findings. But it added a stipulation, a last bit of news for the media:

their investigation did not find that Donald Trump was innocent. That, of course, is another instance of the inverse of American juris prudence being applied in this case. Every citizen, even President Donald Trump, is to be presumed innocent—by law.

The only factual evidence which ever existed is of a conspiracy to remove a lawfully elected President from office, carried out by critical agencies of the administrative state. Senior officials of the CIA, the DOJ, the FBI and the DNI, at a minimum, conspired within the administrative state to remove a duly elected President. They were not alone. The entirety of the Democratic Party, from its leadership down to its volunteers, were animated to remove a duly elected President from office. If I were to produce a list of the newspapers, television stations, websites of the media which in aggregate conspired in a design to destroy the Trump Presidency, it would blind the eyes with reading. It was a conspiracy built on lies, on fixed investigations and secret courts – it was a modern version of a medieval witch trial with Bills of Attainder and a Court of the Star Chamber.

When it was finally over, after the lie was exposed, and the investigation ended...when there should have been contrition for such anti-democratic and unlawful actions on the part of all involved, instead the administrative state, the Democratic Party and the media, moved to impeach Donald Trump for making a telephone call, about which there was *nothing,* whatsoever, illegal or impeachable.

The conspirators who were unsuccessful at removing Trump because he was obviously not guilty of conspiring with the Russians, moved the *next day* to launch a new conspiracy. Again, there were leaks of classified information, again Democrats accused Trump of treason. Again, the media went into a panic, churning out a fountain of lies, and filling our society with political poison. Again and again and again. Why?

Shadows of the Acropolis

Conclusion

The answer is in this text. The answer is in the birth, the growth, the invulnerability, the intolerance, and now, the presumed indomitability of the administrative state. The answer runs as deep into our system of government as our DNA or, in reality - our opposed DNA.

In Volume I, The DNA of Democracy, the critical DNA necessary to any democracy was chronicled, in depth, from history's first democracy to our own. Volume II, Shadows of the Acropolis, has chronicled the critical DNA demonstrated by our administrative state and how it has worked as an adversary to our original, constitutional DNA, since the administrative state's birth. In fact, our founding DNA and the DNA of our administrative state are opposites, and our nation is a hybrid.

Constitutional Democratic DNA

Founded on John Locke's philosophy..
Natural Rights of the Individual v. State ....
Limited Government ....
Constitutional Law ....
Rule by the Many ....
Sovereignty of the Individual ....
Explicit Will of the Many by Vote ....
System of Diffused Powers ....
Original Powers, Local and State rule ....
Checks & Balances between Branches ....
Legislation through Representation ....
Temporal Elective Offices ....
Laws written by Congress ....
The Constitution's Bill of Rights ....
Property Rights ....
Free Enterprise Markets ....
Capital Control of 10 x 10 miles of Land ....
State Levy of Taxation...
Sanctity of Original Powers ....
Individual Self-Reliance..
Freedom of Industry..
Faithfull Execution of Law ....
Respect for the states ....
Freedom of the Press ....
Freedom of Association ....
Freedom of Faith ....
Establishment of Justice ....
Belief in Free Elections ....

Administrative State Tyrannical DNA

Founded on Fredrich Hegel's philosophy
Rights of the State v. the Individual
Unlimited Government
Circumstantial Constitutional Law
Rule of the Whole
Sovereignty of the State
Implicit will of the "One" and "Few" by rule
Centralization of Power
Centralized Federal Rule
Executive Branch Supremacy
Legislation by Administration
Perpetual Appointed Offices
Rules written by Agencies
The State's Bill of Rights
Eminent Domain
State Controlled Markets
Control of a Continent's Land, Water and Air
Federal Progressive Taxation
Invasion of Original Powers
Reliance on the State
State Ownership of Industry
Arbitrary Execution of Law
Persecution of the states
Surveillance/Control of the Press
Persecution of Association
Persecution of Faith
Manipulation of Justice
Belief that only Democrats should be elected

I propose the relation is not just of opposites, but of diametric opposites, as the powers taken and lost are proportionate. Thus, the powers taken from the states by the federal government inverted their relative powers - in favor of the federal government, whereby we have lost our system of federalism. Thus, the powers the administrative state has assumed from Congress and folded into the executive branch has come at the direct cost of losing our system of representation and checks and balances, where all impactful decisions are now made – at the federal level.

This inversion of power applies to our rights. The more power Washington has to claim private land, the less right we have to our own property. The greater power that the FDA has to rule how our land is used, the less right we have to the use of our own property; and the less right our own enterprises have to make their own decisions. And it becomes personal: the more power the central government has over the education of our children, the less right you have to determine the content of your children's education.

The more power administrative agencies like the IRS have, to persecute a people's assembly, the less right you have to assemble. The more power the DOJ and FBI have to surveil and persecute the press, the less right to a free press you have. The more power intel agencies have to invade your privacy, the less right to privacy you have. The more power an agency, like the HHS, has to pass rules which invade the province of your faith, the less right you have to exercise that faith. The more the State invades your God given Natural Rights, as were supposed to be protected by the constitution, the more we have lost our constitution.

The more power the CIA, DOJ and FBI have to ensnare and persecute associates of a political candidate, the less right we have to choose our own candidates. The more power a State has to persecute its opponents, as the DOJ and FBI persecuted General Flynn, the less ability General Flynn, or anyone else has to defend themselves. The more power the State has to unlawfully remove a duly elected president from office, the less power we have to defend ourselves from tyranny.

The truth which the Trump episode illuminated is that the power of the office of the presidency has grown to be so great, its possessor must be approved by the administrative state... that is tyranny.

This text is a chronicle of how many virtuous diffused powers have been fused into the single power of the administrative state. This text is a chronicle as to the danger that concentrated single power now poses, as the State works concertedly and strategically to invade our God given Natural Rights and persecutes its political opponents...that is tyranny.

This chronicle has proven the assumptions made in part of our introduction, "The Inherent Problem of Government," that governments are living things; that governments feed on as much as they can take; they grow and seek to develop strength; they develop their own identity; they assume a territoriality and if challenged - they will retaliate. And governments possess the negative characteristics of human nature: governments are jealous, envious, covetous and ferocious in temper. Governments seek, as with our human nature, to be controlling and what a government cannot control or own, it injures. Such are the characteristics or DNA of the State.

And this chronicle has answered why you feel you are no longer represented, why half the nation is incensed no matter who the president is, why the nation feels so divided, why enmity is on the rise, why the media speaks many tongues, why decisions of governance are made in back rooms and why we no longer rely on democratic processes but resort to violence. Our representative government as it was established and our administrative state government, as it has grown, are opposites.

Something else has occurred, the State is no longer the creature of the Democratic Party. The Democratic Party has become the creature of the State. The Democratic Party has been overtaken by the DNA of its own creation. In fact and in the chronicle of their deeds, the Democratic Party's actions are very often contrary to the democratic ideals it professes to believe in. In truth, the very name the "Democratic" Party has become a falsehood.

AGENCIES
DEPENDS
LOBBY"S
DD
RD

CONSTITUTI ON
HISTORY
HEROES
ETHOS
LIBERTY TREE

As Americans, we are at another "Y" in the road between two kinds of government that are opposed. We might ask, as Socrates did, the most basic question as to which type of government to choose, by simply asking: "Who rules who?" If we live by our democratic DNA, the individual is the sovereign and the government is the servant. If we live by the State DNA of tyranny, the sovereign is the state, and we are its subjects. Every politician who runs for office should be asked which government they choose - based on this opposed DNA. The choice is that simple.

If you wish to know what the State thinks of our founding constitutional DNA, view what is happening with the rise of cancel culture, of social media banning and the extinction of freedom of expression on our university campuses. Why are we being pressured to accept Project 1692 and critical race theory, which upend the unique, historical sacrifices and advancements our society has made from the Civil War to the present? Why are we witnessing vandalism nationwide directed at statues of many of our national hero's? Do you wonder why all of this is occurring at the same time? Answer: The State is no longer tolerant of our national DNA of Democracy. It is no longer content to cut down limbs or crack the trunk of our common history, the State seeks to dissever us from the very roots of this nation's creation. The State seeks to amputate the DNA contained in our history, in our founding ethos and separate us from the heroes who made America a free and independent democracy devoted to the rights of humanity.

The Last Word

What is in a word? Everything, if it is the truth. Nothing, if it is falsehood. The truth is that the hardest obstacle to getting to "know yourself," is to overcome the falsehoods you tell yourself. It goes back as far as humanity, Oedipus refused to believe he murdered his father at a crossroads... He was blind while he had his sight and could only fully see the truth after he blinded himself from his falsehoods. A thoughtful study of our opposed DNA, may tell us about ourselves, about what we truly believe in.

The truth is we are all part of a national fellowship and in that fellowship, we are equals under a common constitution, which protects everyone's rights equally and insures everyone is equally represented, if that constitution is observed, defended and faithfully executed. But we have strayed by way of the empowerment of the administrative state for over a century from our original light, into the shadows... into being a shadow of ourselves.

The truth is that a vote for those who would further extend the powers of our administrative state is a vote to expand a tyranny that already exists in America. A tyranny that is diametrically opposed to the virtues of our nation's foundations. We are at the point when it must be proven whether our representative government controls the State or whether the State controls our representative government?

So, ends this chronicle, we end where the last century of our common history has placed us. We are at the precipice where the State has pushed us. We are opposites. So, what's to do now?

If, I may venture an author's opinion as a fellow citizen.

We must have faith in and fight for the five great systems of societal reconciliation upon which this nation was founded. Systems which created our society's prosperity, peace and freedoms:

Federalism, which allows local and state autonomy.

Representative Democracy, which gives to everyone the right of equal representation.

Constitutional Law, under which individuals are equally protected against government's ambitions.

Free Enterprise, which affords to each an opportunity for upward mobility.

And Christianity, whose virtues demand humility, understanding and peace with our political opposites.

One more truth to know: each of these are systems which many in the Democratic Party and in their administrative state seek to annihilate and replace with a single, central, socialist state.

In Volume One's section on "America" I began with the Native American's belief in, and system of, freedom as practiced by the Iroquois of the Six Nations. I leave the reader with the wisdom of one of the Civilized Tribes, the Cherokee:

"There is a battle of two wolves inside of us…

One is evil: It is anger, jealousy, greed, resentment, lies and ego.

The other is good: It is joy, peace, love, hope, humility, kindness, empathy and truth.

So, which wolf wins?

The one that you feed."

Acknowledgements

I would like to acknowledge my wife Erika who has shown great patience with me, while I have behaved like a mad sculptor consumed by his creation. My thanks for her patience is boundless.

The Author also wishes to acknowledge and thank,
Designer: Audria Wooster of Indigo Design
Illustrator: Robert Venables
The Edit Team: Books Fluent
and Printer: Michael Mueller

And Cocoa Bean Lyons, who faithfully sat at my feet through much of this writing...

Bibliography

Reader's Note: Some references made within Volume II of this series are related to the bibliography of Volume I

A

Affordable Care Act, "IN" Wikipedia.org, n.d., https://en.wikipedia.org/wiki/Affordable_Care_Act

Alman, Daniel, *IRS Scandal, How Barack Obama and Lois Lerner Used the IRS to Illegally Target and Harass Tea Party and Other Conservative Organizations,* Orlando, FL, October 31, 2018, Print.

Ambinder, Marc J., Inside the Council for National Policy, Abcnews, January 6, 2006, https://abcnews.go.com/Politics/story?id=121170&page=1

American Federation of Government Employees, https://www.afge.org/about-us/afge-at-a-glance/

American Federation of Labor and Congress of Industrial Organizations (AFL-CIO), Francis Perkins, https://aflcio.org/about/history/labor-history-people/frances-perkins

American Federation of Teachers, https://www.aft.org/about

American Postal Workers Union, https://apwu.org/our-union

American Presidency Project, The, Signing Statements, https://www.presidency.ucsb.edu/documents/app-categories/presidential/statements/signing-statements

Anagnos, John G., *Decline of the U.S. Presidency: William Jefferson Clinton's Legacy of Corruption*, Ocean View, DE, Songana Publishing, Inc., 2018, Print.

Anonymous, Trump Journal Blog, March 2, 2017, https://trumpjournalblog.wordpress.com/2017/03/03/march-2-2017/

Arrouas, Michelle, The View from The Pink Houses, The Brooklyn Ink, December 18, 2014, http://brooklynink.org/2014/12/18/54284-the-view-from-the-pink-houses/

Association of Centers for the Study of Congress, Demonstration Cities and Metropolitan Development Act, http://acsc.lib.udel.edu/exhibits/show/legislation/demonstration

Attkisson, Sharyl, "IN" Wikipedia.org, n.d., https://en.wikipedia.org/wiki/Sharyl_Attkisson

Attkisson, Sharyl, Attkisson v. DOJ and FBI for the Government Computer Intrusions: The Definitive Summary, Sharyl Attkisson, Untouchable Subjects, Fearless, NonPartisan Reporting, December 27, 2021, https://sharylattkisson.com/2021/12/attkisson-v-doj-and-fbi-for-the-government-computer-intrusions-the-definitive-summary-2/

Attkisson, Sharyl, *STONEWALLED: My Fight for Truth Against the Forces of Obstruction, Intimidation, and Harassment in Obama's Washington,* Harper Collins, New York, NY, 2015, pg. 325, Print.

Attkisson, Sharyl, *The Smear: How Shady Political Operatives and Fake News CONTROL What you See, What you Think, and HOW YOU VOTE,* Harper Collins, New York, NY, 2017, pg. 15, Print.

B

Balaam, David N./ Veseth, Michael, "Lenin's Critique of Global Capitalism," "IN"

Introduction to International Political Economy, 2nd ed. New Jersey, Prentice Hall, 2001, pgs. 76-78, https://www.pbs.org/wgbh/commandingheights/shared/minitext/ess_leninscritique.html

BalancingEverything.com, Welfare Statistics, https://balancingeverything.com/welfare-statistics/

Bandow, Doug, Why Does President Obama Dislike Freedom of Conscience?, Cato Institute, February 6, 2012, https://cato.org/commentary/why-does-president-obama-dislike-freedom-conscience

Barclay, William, *The Gospel of Mark*, Westminster, John Knox Press, 1975, Print.

Barnes, James Strachey, *The Universal Aspects of Fascism*, London, Williams and Norgate, 1928, Print.

Bauman, John F., "Row Housing as Public Housing: The Philadelphia Story, 1957–2013," *The Pennsylvania Magazine of History and Biography* 138, no. 4 (2014): 425–456.

BBC, Profile: Billionaire Philanthropist George Soros, May 31, 2018 https://www.bbc.com/news/world-44301342

Bhattacharya, Nandini, "Marx, Engels and Lenin on Socialism and Nationalism," *Jadavpur Journal of International Relations* 7, no. 1 (2003): 165-186.

Binder, Sarah A., The Federal Reserve as a Political "Institution," American Academy of Arts & Sciences, 2016, https://www.amacad.org/news/federal-reserve-political-institution

Blunt, Senator Roy, Blunt, Entire Senate Republican Conference Fight to Stop Resurrection of Biden-Obama WOTUS Overreach, February 8, 2022, https://www.blunt.senate.gov/news/press-releases/blunt-entire-senate-republican-conference-fight-to-stop-resurrection-of-biden-obama-wotus-overreach

Bomboy, Scott, How We Wound Up With The Income Tax, https://constitutioncenter.org/blog/yes-it-was-100-years-ago-that-we-wound-up-with-a-national-income-tax

Bradley Jr., Robert L./ Donway, Roger, "Capitalism, Socialism and the 'Middle Way': A Taxonomy," *The Independent Review* 15, no 1 (2010): 71-87.

Buchholz, Todd G., *New Ideas From Dead Economists: An Introduction to Modern Economic Thought*, New York, NY, Plume, 2007, Print.

Bur, Jessie, Feds Receive 1 Percent Pay Raise For 2021, Federal Times, January 4, 2021, https://www.federaltimes.com/management/pay-benefits/2021/01/04/feds-receive-one-percent-pay-raise-for-2021/

Bybee, Jay S., Ulysses at the Mast: Democracy, Federalism, and the Sirens' Song of the Seventeenth Amendment, Scholarly Works, 1997, https://scholars.law.unlv.edu/cgi/viewcontent.cgi?article=1365&context=facpub

C

California Teachers Association, https://www.cta.org/about-us

Carpenter, Ted Galen, Barack Obama's War on a Free Press, Cato Institute, February 11, 2021, https://www.cato.org/commentary/barack-obamas-war-free-press

Center For Applied Research in The Apostolate, Frequently Requested Church Statistics, https://cara.georgetown.edu/frequently-requested-church-statistics/

Chernow, Ron, *Alexander Hamilton*, New York, NY, Penguin Books, 2004, Print.

Chicago Teacher's Union, "IN" Wikipedia, n.d., https://en.wikipedia.org/wiki/Chicago_Teachers_Union

Clopton, Zachary D. /Art, Steven E., "The Meaning of the 17th Amendment and A Century of State Defiance," *Northwestern University Law Review* 107, no. 3 (2015): 1181-1242.

Cohn, Samuel, Race, Gender, And Discrimination At Work, New York: Routledge, 2018, Ebook.

Compass Media Networks, "IN" Wikipedia, n.d., https://en.wikipedia.org/wiki/Compass_Media_Networks

Congressional Research Service, U.S. Health Care Coverage and Spending, April 1, 2022, https://fas.org/sgp/crs/misc/IF10830.pdf

Constitutional Rights Foundation, How Welfare Began in the United States, https://www.crf-usa.org/bill-of-rights-in-action/bria-14-3-a-how-welfare-began-in-the-united-states.html

Cooke, Jacob E., "The Compromise of 1790," *The William and Mary Quarterly* 27, no. 4 (1970): 523-545.

Cullison, Alan/Viswanatha, Aruna, The Surprising Backstory of How the Steele Dossier Was Created, Wall Street Journal, May 9, 2022, https://www.wsj.com/articles/the-surprising-backstory-of-how-the-steele-dossier-was-created-11652103582.

D

Deloach, Ryan/DeRose, Jenn, Decoding the City: Urban Renewal and Mill Creek Valley, http://www.decodingstl.org/urban-renewal-and-mill-creek-valley/

Department of Taxation and Finance, Fiscal Year Tax Collections 2019-2020 report, https://www.tax.ny.gov/research/collections/fy_collections_stat_report/2019_2020_annual_statistical_report_of_ny_state_tax_collections.htm

Detroit Historical Society, Encyclopedia of Detroit: Black Bottom Neighborhood, https://detroithistorical.org/learn/encyclopedia-of-detroit/black-bottom-neighborhood

Detroit Historical Society, Encyclopedia of Detroit: Paradise Valley, https://detroithistorical.org/learn/encyclopedia-of-detroit/paradise-valley

Detroit Historical Society, Encyclopedia of Detroit, Uprising of 1967, https://detroithistorical.org/learn/encyclopedia-of-detroit/uprising-1967

Digital First Media, "IN" Wikipedia, n.d., https://en.wikipedia.org/wiki/Digital_First_Media

DiSalvo, Daniel, The Trouble with Public Sector Unions, National Affairs, Fall 2010, https://www.nationalaffairs.com/publications/detail/the-trouble-with-public-sector-unions

Dwyer, Philip, *Citizen Emperor: Napoleon in Power 1799-1815*, New York, NY, Bloomsbury, 2013, Print.

E

Eddlem, Thomas R., Before the Income Tax, The New American, January 18, 2013, https://www.thenewamerican.com/culture/history/item/14268-before-the-income-tax

Editors of Encyclopaedia Brittanica, The, Cabrini-Green, "IN" Encyclopaedia Brittanica, Inc., May 24, 2016, https://www.britannica.com/topic/Cabrini-Green

Editors of Encyclopaedia Brittanica, The, Nazi Germany, "IN" Encyclopaedia Brittanica Inc., 2020, https://www.britannica.com/topic/education/Nazi-Germany

Editors of Encyclopaedia Brittanica, The, Tennessee Valley Authority, "IN" Encyclopaedia Brittanica Inc., May 2, 2022, https://www.britannica.com/topic/Tennessee-Valley-Authority

Editors of Encyclopaedia Brittanica, The, Wagner Act, "IN" Encyclopaedia Brittanica Inc., June 5, 2020, https://www.britannica.com/topic/Wagner-Act

Education Minnesota, "IN" Wikipedia, n.d., https://en.wikipedia.org/wiki/Education_Minnesota

Edward Snowden, "IN" Wikipedia.org, n.d., https://en.wikipedia.org/wiki/Edward_Snowden

Eisenhower, Susan, *How Ike Led: The Principles Behind Eisenhower's Biggest Decisions*, New York, Thomas Dunn Books, 2020, Print.

Entous, Adam/Nakashima, Elle/Miller, Greg, National Security: Sessions Met with Russian Envoy Twice Last Year, Encounters He Later Did Not Disclose, The Washington Post, March 1, 2017, https://www.washingtonpost.com/world/national-security/sessions-spoke-twice-with-russian-ambassador-during-trumps-presidential-campaign-justice-officials-say/2017/03/01/77205eda-feac-11e6-99b4-9e613afeb09f_story.html.

Executive Order 13535, "IN" Wikipedia.org, n.d., https://en.wikipedia.org/wiki/Executive_Order_13535

Exploring Off the Beaten Path, Little Bighorn Battlefield-Custer's Last Battle, http://exploringoffthebeatenpath.com/Battlefields/LittleBighorn/

F

Fairweather, Nicolas, Hitler and Hitlerism: Germany Under the Nazis, The Atlantic, April 1932, https://www.theatlantic.com/magazine/archive/1932/04/hitler-and-hitlerism-germany-under-the-nazis/308961/

Federal Maritime Commission, Shipping Act of 1916 Centennial—Legislation Established Forerunner of FMC, September 7, 2016, https://www.fmc.gov/shipping-act-of-1916-centennial-legislation-established-forerunner-of-fmc/

Federal Register, Agencies, https://www.federalregister.gov/agencies

Federal Register, A Guide to the Rulemaking Process, n.d., https://www.federalregister.gov/uploads/2011/01/the_rulemaking_process.pdf

FederalReserveEducation.org The Structure and Functions of the Federal Reserve System, https://www.federalreserveeducation.org/about-the-fed/structure-and-functions

Federal Trade Commission, Federal Trade Commission Act, https://www.ftc.gov/enforcement/statutes/federal-trade-commission-act

Feldstein, Martin, "What Powers for the Federal Reserve?" *Journal of Economic Literature* 48, no. 1 (2010): 134-145.

Fitzgerald, Sandy, Wash Post's Ignatius: Flynn's Calls To Russian Ambassador Could Be 'Improper,' NewsMax, January 13, 2017, https://www.newsmax.com/newsfront/michael-flynn-russia-sanctions/2017/01/13/id/768476/

Florida Education Association, https://feaweb.org/about-fea/

Flynn, John T., *As We Go Marching*, New York, Doubleday and Company, Inc., 1944, Print.

Forbes, George Soros, https://www.forbes.com/profile/george-soros/#607b65012024

Forrest, Alan, "Propaganda and the Legitimation of Power in Napoleonic France," *French History* 18, no. 4 (2004): 426-445.

Friedman, Joanna, When Can the Federal Government Lawfully Terminate Employees? Federal News Network, March 13, 2020, https://federalnewsnetwork.com/commentary/2020/03/when-can-the-federal-government-lawfully-terminate-employees/

Frohnen, Bruce, Conscience & Property Rights: Obama vs. Little Sisters of the Poor, The Imaginative Conservative, September 6, 2015, https://theimaginativeconservative.org/2015/09/conscience-and-property-rights-obama-vs-little-sisters-of-the-poor.html

G

Gaetan, Victor, Macedonia to George Soros and USAID: Go Away, The American Spectator, March 24, 2017, https://spectator.org/macedonia-to-george-soros-and-usaid-go-away/

Gambino, Lauren/Siddiqui, Sabrina/Walker, Shaun, Obama Expels 35 Russian Diplomats in Retaliation for US Election Hacking, The Guardian, December 30, 2016, https://www.theguardian.com/us-news/2016/dec/29/barack-obama-sanctions-russia-election-hack

Garvey, John, ObamaCare vs. Little Sisters of the Poor, Wall Street Journal, March 20, 2016, https://www.wsj.com/articles/obamacare-vs-little-sisters-of-the-poor-1458504604

Gaspar, Vitor/Amaglobeli, David, "Fiscal Politics," *Finance & Development* 55, no. 1 (2018): https://www.imf.org/external/pubs/ft/fandd/2018/03/gaspar.htm

Genesis Communications Network, "IN" Wikipedia, n.d., https://en.wikipedia.org/wiki/Genesis_Communications_Network

GeorgeSoros.com, Open Society Foundations, https://www.georgesoros.com/philanthropy/

Global March Against Child Labour, Child Labour & Trafficking, https://globalmarch.org/about-us/our-focus-areas/child-labour-slavery/

Global Slavery Index, 2018 Global Findings, https://www.globalslaveryindex.org/2018/findings/global-findings/

Godechot, Jacques, Napoleon 1 Emperor of France, "IN" Encyclopaedia Brittanica, May 1, 2022, https://www.britannica.com/biography/Napoleon-I

Godfrey, Lieutenant Edward Settle, *The Godfrey Diary of the Battle of the Little Bighorn: (Annotated)*, Big Byte Books, 2014, Print.

Goldberg, Chad Alan, "Contesting the Status of Relief Workers During the New Deal: The Workers Alliance of America and The Works Progress Administration, 1935-1941," *Social Science History,* 29, no. 3 (2005): 337-371.

Goodman, John C., Why is Obamacare Such a Mess? There was No Adult in The Room When It Passed, Forbes.com, January 29, 2015, https://www.forbes.com/sites/johngoodman/2015/01/29/why-is-obamacare-such-a-mess-there-was-no-adult-in-the-room-when-it-passed/?sh=93c056578069

Gordon, David, Three New Deals: Why the Nazis and Fascists Loved FDR, Mises Institute, September 13, 2018, https://mises.org/library/three-new-deals-why-nazis-and-fascists-loved-fdr

Govtrack.us, HR 7839, Aid in the Provision and Improvement of Housing, And the Elimination and Prevention of Slums, And The Conservation and Development of Urban Communities, Adoption of Conference Report, July 28, 1954, https://www.govtrack.us/congress/votes/83-1954/s207

Govtrack.us, To Pass H.R. 7984, The Housing and Urban Development Act of 1965, July 15, 1965, https://www.govtrack.us/congress/votes/89-1965/s162

Govtrack.us, To Pass S. 3708, The Demonstration Cities and Metropolitan Development Act of 1966, August 19, 1966, https://www.govtrack.us/congress/votes/89-1966/s425#studyguide

Govtrack.us, To Pass H.R. 2516, A Bill To Prohibit Discrimination In Sale Or Rental Of Housing, And To Prohibit Racially Motivated Interference With A Person Exercising His Civil Rights, And For Other Purposes, March 11, 1968, https://www.govtrack.us/congress/votes/90-1968/s346

Grab, Alexander, *Napoleon and the Transformation of Europe*, New York, NY, Palgrave Macmillan, 2003, Print.

Green, Lloyd, The Age of Obama, A Strong Government and A Weak America, The Daily Beast, June 30, 2013, https://www.thedailybeast.com/the-age-of-obama-a-strong-government-and-a-weak-america?ref=scroll

Greene, John Robert, *The Presidency of George W. Bush*, Lawrence, Kansas, University Press of Kansas, 2021, Print.

Greenhouse Gas, "IN" Wikipedia.org, n.d., https://en.wikipedia.org/wiki/Greehouse_gas

Greenhouse, Steven, *The Big Squeeze: Tough Times for the American Worker*, New York, Alfred Knopf, 2008, Print.

Gregor, James A., *Italian Fascism and Developmental Dictatorship*, Princeton, NJ, Princeton University Press, 1979, Print.

Gregory, Paul Roderick, The Timeline of IRS Targeting of Conservative Groups, Forbes, June 25, 2013, https://www.forbes.com/sites/paulroderickgregory/2013/06/25/the-timeline-of-irs-targeting-of-conservative-groups/?sh=300ad8303572

Grossman, Jonathan, The Coal Strike of 1902: Turning Point in U.S. Policy, U.S. Department of Labor, https://www.dol.gov/general/aboutdol/history/coalstrike#*

H

Hawranek, Joseph P., *Clinton Scandals 1977-2016: 39 Years of Clinton Scandals and Corruptions 1997-2016 (Volume I of III),* Bloomington, IN, Trafford Publishing, 2019, Print.

Hayek, F.A., *The Road to Serfdom, Text and Documents, The Definitive Edition, Vol II*, edited by Bruce Caldwell, Chicago, The University of Chicago Press, 2007, Print.

Heideman, Paul, The Rise and Fall of the Socialist Party, Jacobin, February 20, 2017, https://www.jacobinmag.com/2017/02/rise-and-fall-socialist-party-of-america

Herman, Arthur, *The Cave and the Light: Plato Versus Aristotle, and the Struggle for the Soul of Western Civilization*, New York: Random House, 2013, Print.

Hibbert, Christopher, *Benito Mussolini: A Biography*, Geneva, Switzerland, Heron Books, 1962, Print.

Hill, Joseph A., "The Civil War Income Tax," The *Quarterly Journal of Economics* 8, no. 4 (1894): 416-452, https://www.jstor.org/stable/1885003

Hillquit, Morris, *From Marx to Lenin*, Canton, OH, Hanford Press, 1921, Print.

History.com Editors, 1967 Detroit Riots, March 23, 2021, https://www.history.com/topics/1960s/1967-detroit-riots

History.com Editors, Fair Housing Act, January 28, 2021, https://www.history.com/topics/black-history/fair-housing-act

History.com Editors, The 2016 U.S. Presidential Election, August 5, 2019, https://www.history.com/topics/us-presidents/us-presidential-election-2016

Hitler, Adolf, Volume One - A Reckoning Chapter XII: The First Period of Development of the National Socialist German Workers' Party, "IN" *Mein Kampf*, 1925, http://www.hitler.org/writings/Mein_Kampf/mkv1ch12.html

Hitler, Adolf, Volume Two - The National Socialist Movement

Chapter II: The State, "IN" *Mein Kampf*, 1925, http://www.hitler.org/writings/Mein_Kampf/mkv2ch02.html

Hodson, William Alan/Carfora, John M., Stuart Chase: Brief Life of a Public Thinker: 1888-1985, Harvard Magazine, September--October 2004, https://harvardmagazine.com/2004/09/stuart-chase-html

Housing and Urban Development Act. Pub.L. 89–174, 79 Stat. 667.

Hunt, Lynn/Lansky, David/Hanson, Paul, "The Failure of the Liberal Republic in France, 1795-1799: The Road to Brumaire," *The Journal of Modern History* 51, no. 4 (1979): 734-759.

Hurd, Richard W., New Deal Labor Policy and the Containment of Radical Union Activity, October 1, 1976, https://ecommons.cornell.edu/handle/1813/75883

I

Ignatius, David, Michael Flynn's Star Burns Out, The Washington Post, February 14, 2017, https://www.washingtonpost.com/opinions/michael-flynns-star-burns-out/2017/02/14/64814e48-f302-11e6-a9b0-ecee7ce475fc_story.html

Ignatius, David, Why Did Obama Dawdle on Russia's Hacking? The Washington Post, January 12, 2017, https://www.washingtonpost.com/opinions/why-did-obama-dawdle-on-russias-hacking/2017/01/12/75f878a0-d90c-11e6-9a36-1d296534b31e_story.html

iHeart Media, "IN" Wikipedia, n.d., https://en.wikipedia.org/wiki/IHeartMedia

Indian Termination Policy, "IN" Wikipedia, n.d., https://en.wikipedia.org/wiki/Indian_termination_policy

International Association of Firefighters, https://www.natca.org/2021/05/11/union-members-feature-international-association-of-fire-fighters/

International Labour Office, Global Estimates of Modern Slavery: Forced Labour and Forced Marriage, Geneva, 2017, https://www.ilo.org/wcmsp5/groups/public/@dgreports/@dcomm/documents/publication/wcms_575479.pdf

I.R.S., Table 1.1. All Returns: Selected Income and Tax Items, by Size and Accumulated. (Size of Adjusted Gross Income, Tax Year 2018 (Filing Year 2019), https://www.irs.gov/statistics/soi-tax-stats-individual-statistical-tables-by-size-of-adjusted-gross-income

Issa, Darrell/Camp, Dave, Darrell Issa and Dave Camp: The IRS scandal's inconsistencies, The Washington Post, August 6, 2013, https://www.washingtonpost.com/opinions/darrell-issa-and-dave-camp-the-irs-scandals-inconsistencies/2013/08/06/d70d2b6a-fbc8-11e2-9bde-7ddaa186b751_story.html

J

Jacobs, Jane, *The Death and Life of American Cities*, New York City, Knopf Doubleday Publishing Group, 1992, Print.

Jarrett, Gregg, *The Russia Hoax: The Illicit Scheme to Clear Hillary Clinton and Frame Donald Trump,* Broadside Books/Harper Collins, New York, NY, 2018, pgs. 127, 150, 156, 223, Print.

JudicialWatch.org, Judicial Watch Obtains IRS Documents Revealing McCain's Subcommittee Staff Director Urged IRS to Engage In 'Financially Ruinous' Targeting, June 21, 2018, https://www.judicialwatch.org/judicial-watch-obtains-irs-documents-revealing-mccains-subcommittee-staff-director-urged-irs-to-engage-in-financially-ruinous-targeting/

K

Kara, Siddharth, *Modern Slavery: A Global Perspective*, New York, Columbia University Press, 2017, Print.

Kaufman, Michael T., *Soros: The Life and Times of a Messianic Billionaire*, New York, First Vintage Books Edition, 2003, Print.

Kennedy, David M., "What the New Deal Did," *Political Science Quarterly* 124, no. 2, (2009): 251-268.

Keyes, Allison, A New Show About Neighborhoods Facing Gentrification Offers a Cautionary Tale, Smithsonian Magazine Online, May 9, 2018, https://www.smithsonianmag.com/smithsonian-institution/new-show-about-neighborhoods-facing-gentrification-offers-cautionary-tale-180969032/

Kirkpatrick, David D., The 2004 Campaign: The Conservatives; Club of the Most Powerful Gathers in Strictest Privacy, The New York Times, August 28, 2004, https://www.nytimes.com/2004/08/28/us/2004-campaign-conservatives-club-most-powerful-gathers-strictest-privacy.html

Knueven, Liz, The Average Amount Americans Pay in Federal Income Taxes, By Income Level, Business Insider, September 28, 2020, https://www.businessinsider.com/personal-finance/average-federal-income-tax-payment-by-income

Kratz, Jessie, The Compromise of 1790, Pieces of History: A blog of the National Archives, May 31, 2015, https://prologue.blogs.archives.gov/2015/05/31/the-compromise-of-1790/

Krebs, Albin, Adolfe A. Berle Jr. Dies At Age of 76, The New York Times, February 19, 1971, https://www.nytimes.com/1971/02/19/archives/adolf-a-berle-jr-dies-at-age-of-76-lawyer-economist-liberal-leader.html

Kuepper, Justin, Black Wednesday: George Soros' Bet Against Britain, The Balance, January 21, 2022, https://www.thebalance.com/black-wednesday-george-soros-bet-against-britain-1978944

L

Latzer, Barry, "Subculture of Violence and African American Crime Rates," *Journal of Criminal Justice* 54, (2018): 41-49, https://www.sciencedirect.com/science/article/abs/pii/S0047235217305214.

Laville, Sandra, Top Oil Firms Spending Millions Lobbying to Block Climate Change Policies, Says Report, The Guardian, March 21, 2019, https://www.theguardian.com/business/2019/mar/22/top-oil-firms-spending-millions-lobbying-to-block-climate-change-policies-says-report

Lawyer, Charity, Nonprofits and Political Activities, Charity Lawyer Blog, February 25, 2019, https://charitylawyerblog.com/2019/02/25/nonprofits-political-activities/

LBJ Presidential Library, http://www.lbjlibrary.org/mediakits/hud/

Leibiger, Stuart, *Foundling Friendship: George Washington, James Madison and the Creation of the American Republic*, Charlottesville, University Press of Virginia, 1999, Print.

Levin, Mark R., *Men In Black: How The Supreme Court Is Destroying America*, Washington, D.C., Regnery Publishing, 2005, Print.

Lewis, David Levering, *The Improbable Wendell Willkie: The Businessman Who Saved the Republican Party and His Country, And Conceived A New World Order*, New York, Liveright Publishing Corporation, 2018, Print.

Library of Congress, A Century of Lawmaking for A New Nation: U.S. Congressional Documents and Debates, 1774 – 1875, Statutes at Large, 1st Congress, 2nd Session, 1790, https://memory.loc.gov/cgi-bin/ampage?collId=llsl&fileName=001/llsl001.db&recNum=253

Library of Congress, History of the U.S. Income Tax, https://www.loc.gov/rr/business/hottopic/irs_history.html

Library of Congress, Native American Immigration, https://www.loc.gov/classroom-materials/immigration/native-american/

List of Advance Subsidiaries, "IN" Wikipedia, n.d., https://en.wikipedia.org/wiki/List_of_Advance_subsidiaries

List of Assets Owned by Gannett, "IN" Wikipedia, n.d., https://en.wikipedia.org/wiki/List_of_assets_owned_by_Gannett

List of Assets Owned by the Walt Disney Company, "IN" Wikipedia, n.d., https://en.wikipedia.org/wiki/List_of_assets_owned_by_The_Walt_Disney_Company

List of Public Housing Developments in the United States, "IN" Wikipedia, n.d., https://en.wikipedia.org/wiki/List_of_public_housing_developments_in_the_United_States

Little Sisters of the Poor Saints: Peter and Paul Home v. Pennsylvania, "IN" Wikipedia.org, n.d., https://en.wikipedia.org/wiki/Little_Sisters_of_the_Poor_Saints_Peter_and_Paul_Home_v._Pennsylvania

Living New Deal, The, National Labor Relations Act (Wagner Act) (1935), November 18, 2016, https://livingnewdeal.org/glossary/national-labor-relations-act-wagner-act-1935/

Living New Deal, The, New Dealers, https://livingnewdeal.org/what-was-the-new-deal/new-dealers/

Living New Deal, The, New Deal Programmes, https://livingnewdeal.org/what-was-the-new-deal/programs/

Lloyd, Annie, A History of West Adams Told Through Its Iconic Architecture, LAist, July 24,2017, https://laist.com/news/entertainment/west-adams-told-through-architecture

Lobingier, Charles Sumner, "Napoleon and his Code," *Harvard Law Review* 32, no. 2 (1918): 114-134.

Lowry, Rich, Obama vs. the Little Sisters, National Review, January 7, 2014, https://www.nationalreview.com/2014/01/obama-vs-little-sisters-rich-lowry

Lyman, Rick, After Trump Win, Anti-Soros Forces Are Emboldened in Eastern Europe, The New York Times, March 1 2017, https://www.nytimes.com/2017/03/01/world/europe/after-trump-win-anti-soros-forces-are-emboldened-in-eastern-europe.html

M

Marshall, Colin, Pruitt-Igoe: The Troubled High-rise That Came to Define Urban America – A History of Cities in 50 Buildings, Day 21, The Guardian, April 22, 2015, https://www.theguardian.com/cities/2015/apr/22/pruitt-igoe-high-rise-urban-america-history-cities

Martin, Emmie, Here's How Much Americans Pay In Taxes In Every U.S. State, CNBC, April 5, 2018, https://www.cnbc.com/2018/04/05/average-amount-americans-pay-in-taxes-in-every-state.html

Martin, Roscoe C., "The Tennessee Valley Authority: A Study of Federal Control," *Law and Contemporary Problems* 22, no. 3 (1957): 351-377.

Marxists Internet Archive, The Socialist Party of America (1897-1946): Party History:

Conventions of the Social Democracy in America, https://www.marxists.org/history/usa/eam/spa/socialistparty.html

Massachusetts Teachers Association, https://massteacher.org/about-the-mta/who-we-are

McBride, James/Siripurapu, Anshu, What Is the U.S. Federal Reserve? Council on Foreign Relations, January 27, 2022, https://www.cfr.org/backgrounder/what-us-federal-reserve

McCarthy, Andrew C. *Faithless Execution: Building the Political Case for Obama's Impeachment*, New York, Encounter Books, 2014, Print.

McGuire, Ashley, Obama's War on the Little Sisters of the Poor, RealClear Politics, November 11, 2015, https://www.realclearpolitics.com/articles/2015/11/11/obamas_war_on_the_little_sisters_of_the_poor_128691.html

McKenzie, Aimee, Catholic Hospitals in American Healthcare, Grand Valley State University, Honors Projects, May 12, 2017, https://scholarworks.gvsu.edu/cgi/viewcontent.cgi?article=1660&context=honorsprojects

Media Cross-ownership in the United States, "IN" Wikipedia, n.d., https://en.wikipedia.org/wiki/Media_cross-ownership_in_the_United_States

Medicaid.gov, January 2022 Medicaid & CHIP Enrollment Data Highlights, https://www.medicaid.gov/medicaid/program-information/medicaid-and-chip-enrollment-data/report-highlights/index.html/

Meenan, James, "Fascist Italy and Its Public Works," *Studies: An Irish Quarterly Review* 23, no. 92 (1934): 664-678.

Michigan Chronicle, Black Bottom and Paradise Valley: Center of Black Life in Detroit, February 2, 2017, https://michiganchronicle.com/2017/02/02/black-bottom-and-paradise-valley-center-of-black-life-in-detroit/

Michigan Education Association, "IN" Wikipedia, n.d., https://en.wikipedia.org/wiki/Michigan_Education_Association

Micozzi, Marc S., National Healthcare: Medicine in Germany, 1918-1945, Foundation for Economic Education, November 1, 1993, https://fee.org/articles/national-health-care-medicine-in-germany-1918-1945/

Mill, John Stuart, *On Liberty and Utilitarianism*, New York, Bantam Dell, 1993, Print.

Miller, Greg/Entous, Adam/Nakashima, Ellen, National Security Adviser Flynn Discussed Sanctions With Russian Ambassador, Despite Denials, Officials Say, The Washington Post, February 9, 2017, https://www.washingtonpost.com/world/national-security/national-security-adviser-flynn-discussed-sanctions-with-russian-ambassador-despite-denials-officials-say/2017/02/09/f85b29d6-ee11-11e6-b4ff-ac2cf509efe5_story.html.

Morse, Clarence G., A Study of American Merchant Marine Legislation, *Law and Contemporary Problems* 25, no. 1 (1960): 57-81. https://scholarship.law.duke.edu/cgi/viewcontent.cgi?article=2823&context=lcp

N

Napoleon.org, Timeline: Consulate/1st French Empire, https://www.napoleon.org/en/young-historians/napodoc/timeline-consulate1st-french-empire/

National Archives, 17th Amendment to the U.S. Constitution: Direct Election of U.S. Senators, https://www.archives.gov/legislative/features/17th-amendment

National Association of Postal Supervisors, https://naps.org/History-and-Mission

National Center for Education Statistics, U.S. Department of Education, Median Family Income https://nces.ed.gov/pubs98/yi/yi16.pdf

National Center for Education Statistics, U.S. Department of Education, Digest of Education Statistics, Table 205.70, Enrolment and Instructional Staff In Catholic Elementary and Secondary Schools, By Level: Selected Years, 1919-20 through 2016-17, https://nces.ed.gov/programs/digest/d17/tables/dt17_205.70.asp

National Center for Education Statistics, U.S. Department of Education, Digest of Education Statistics, Table 334 Current-fund Revenue Received From The Federal Government by the 120 Institutions of Higher Education Receiving the Largest Amounts, 1995-96 [in thousands], https://nces.ed.gov/programs/digest/d98/d98t334.asp

National Center for Education Statistics, U.S. Department of Education, Digest of Education Statistics, Table 370 Revenue Received From The Federal Government by the 120 Degree-granting Institutions Receiving the Largest Amounts, By Control and Rank Order: 2008-09, https://nces.ed.gov/programs/digest/d10/tables/dt10_370.asp

National Center for Health Statics, Health, United States, Hyattsville, MD: Public Health Service, 1989, Retrieved from Reed 1991, 13.

National Committee to Preserve Social Security & Medicare, Medicare, https://www.ncpssm.org/our-issues/medicare/medicare-fast-facts/

National Education Association, https://www.nea.org/

National Labor Relations Board, About NLRB: Our History: 1935 Passage of the Wagner Act, https://www.nlrb.gov/about-nlrb/who-we-are/our-history/1935-passage-of-the-wagner-act

National Nurses United, https://www.nationalnursesunited.org/press/rns-honor-nurses-week-with-lobby-days-for-federal-legislation

National Science Foundation, Rankings by Total R&D Expenditures, https://ncsesdata.nsf.gov/profiles/site?method=rankingBySource&ds=herd

National Treasury Employees Union, NTEU Endorses Legislation for 5.1 Pay Raise in 2023, January 13, 2022, https://www.nteu.org/media-center/news-releases/2022/01/13/fairact2023

National Union of Healthcare Workers, https://nuhw.org/about/

NBC News, Michael Flynn: Timeline of His Rise, Fall and Guilty Plea, February 14, 2017, https://www.nbcnews.com/news/us-news/mike-flynn-timeline-his-rise-fall-russia-call-n720671

New York City Department of Finance, New York State Sales and Use Tax, https://www1.nyc.gov/site/finance/taxes/business-nys-sales-tax.page

New York Post Editorial Board, Fresh Proof The Entire Russiagate Probe Was Nothing But A Political Smear, New York Post, September 25, 2020, https://nypost.com/2020/09/25/fresh-proof-russiagate-probe-was-nothing-but-a-political-smear/.

New York State Legislature, Assembly, *Proceedings of the Judiciary Committee of the Assembly, Vol. II.* Albany: J.B. Lyons Company, Printers, 1920, Print.

New York State United Teachers, "IN" Wikipedia, n.d., https://en.wikipedia.org/wiki/New_York_State_United_Teachers

New York Times Editorial Board, The, Spying on The Associated Press, The New York Times, May 14, 2013, https://www.nytimes.com/2013/05/15/opinion/spying-on-the-associated-press.html

Northern Kentucky Right To Life, "Big Brother" (President Obama) Vs. Little Sisters of the Poor, July 1, 2016, https://www.nkyrtl.org/uncategorized/big-brother-president-obama-vs-little-sisters-of-the-poor/

O

Ohio Education Association, https://www.ohea.org/about/

Open Secrets: Center for Responsive Politics, Foreign Lobby Watch, https://www.opensecrets.org/fara

Open Secrets: Center for Responsive Politics, Influence & Lobbying, American Federation of Government Employees, https://www.opensecrets.org/orgs/american-federation-of-government-employees/totals?id=D000000304

Open Secrets, Center for Responsive Politics, Influence & Lobbying, American Federation of State, County and Municipal Employees, https://www.opensecrets.org/orgs/american-fedn-of-state-county-municipal-employees/totals?id=D000000061

Open Secrets: Center for Responsive Politics, Influence & Lobbying, American Federation of Teachers, https://www.opensecrets.org/orgs/american-federation-of-teachers/totals?id=D000000083

Open Secrets: Center for Responsive Politics, Influence & Lobbying: Energy & Natural Resources sector, https://www.opensecrets.org/federal-lobbying/sectors/summary?id=E

Open Secrets: Center for Responsive Politics, Influence & Lobbying, Health sector, https://www.opensecrets.org/federal-lobbying/sectors/summary?id=H

Open Secrets: Center for Responsive Politics, Influence & Lobbying, International Association of Firefighters, https://www.opensecrets.org/orgs/international-assn-of-fire-fighters/totals?id=D000000135

Open Secrets: Center for Responsive Politics, Influence & Lobbying, National Active & Retired Federal Employees Association, https://www.opensecrets.org/orgs/natl-active-retired-fed-employees-assn/totals?id=D000021771

Open Secrets: Center for Responsive Politics, Influence & Lobbying, National Association of Postal Supervisors, https://www.opensecrets.org/political-action-committees-pacs/national-assn-of-postal-supervisors/C00092957/summary/2022

Open Secrets, Center for Responsive Politics, Influence & Lobbying, National Nurses United, https://www.opensecrets.org/orgs/national-nurses-united/totals?id=D000062602

Open Secrets, Center for Responsive Politics, Influence & Lobbying, National Treasury Employees Union, https://www.opensecrets.org/orgs/national-treasury-employees-union/totals?id=D000000346

Open Secrets, Center for Responsive Politics, Influence & Lobbying, National Union of Healthcare Workers, https://www.opensecrets.org/orgs/national-union-of-healthcare-workers/totals?id=D000070323

Open Secrets: Center for Responsive Politics, Influence & Lobbying, New York State United Teachers PAC Contributions to Federal Candidates, https://www.

opensecrets.org/political-action-committees-pacs/new-york-state-united-teachers/C00021121/summary/2020

Open Secrets: Center for Responsive Politics, Influence & Lobbying, United Postmasters & Managers of America, https://www.opensecrets.org/political-action-committees-pacs/united-postmasters-managers-of-america/C00100404/summary/2020

Open Society Foundations, George Soros, https://www.opensocietyfoundations.org/george-soros

Ourdocuments.gov, Keating-Owen Child Labor Act of 1916, https://www.archives.gov/milestone-documents/keating-owen-child-labor-act

P

Pauley, Bruce F., *Hitler, Stalin and Mussolini: Totalitarianism in the Twentieth Century,* 4th edition, Chichester, West Sussex, Wiley-Blackwell, 2014, Print.

PBS.org, Interstate Commerce Act, https://www.pbs.org/wgbh/americanexperience/features/streamliners-commerce/

PBS.org, The Black Church, https://www.pbs.org/wgbh/americanexperience/features/godinamerica-black-church/

PBS.org, The Dinner Table Bargain: June 1790, https://www.pbs.org/wgbh/americanexperience/features/hamilton-dinner-table-bargain-june-1790/

PD&R Edge, Why Did Pruitt-Igoe Fail?, U.S. Department of Housing and Urban Development, https://www.huduser.gov/portal/pdredge/pdr_edge_featd_article_110314.html/

Pennsylvania State Education Association, "IN" Wikipedia, n.d., https://en.wikipedia.org/wiki/Pennsylvania_State_Education_Association

Perry, Peter R., Theodore Roosevelt and the Labor Movement, Thesis, California State University, Hayward, June 1991, https://dspace.calstate.edu/bitstream/handle/10211.3/10211.5_40/Peter.R.PerryThesis.pdf?sequence=1.

Petshek, Kirk R., *The Challenge of Urban Reform: Policies and Programs in Philadelphia*, Philadelphia, Temple University Press, 1973, Print.

Pfeiffer, David A., Ike's Interstate at 50: Anniversary of the Highway System Recalls Eisenhower's Role as Catalyst, *Prologue Magazine* 38, no. 2 (2006): https://www.archives.gov/publications/prologue/2006/summer/interstates.html

Potok, Mark, Revealed: Conway, Bannon Members of Secretive Group, August 31, 2016, Montgomery, AL. Southern Poverty Law Center.

Powell, Jim, The Economic Leadership Secrets of Benito Mussolini, Cato Institute, February 22, 2012, https://www.cato.org/publications/commentary/economic-leadership-secrets-benito-mussolini

Premiere Networks, "IN" Wikipedia, n.d., https://en.wikipedia.org/wiki/Premiere_Networks

Presidency of Richard Nixon, "IN" Wikipedia, n.d., https://en.wikipedia.org/wiki/Presidency_of_Richard_Nixon

Q

Quigley, John M., A Decent Home: Housing Policy in Perspective, *Brookings-Wharton Papers on Urban Affairs*, 2000, p. 53-99, http://urbanpolicy.berkeley.edu/pdf/Q_BW00PB.pdf

R

Rahe, Paul A., *Soft Despotism, Democracy's Drift: Montesquieu, Rosseau, Tocqueville, and the Modern Prospect,* New Haven, Yale University Press, 2009, Print.

Reed, Wornie L., "Trends in Homicide Among African-Americans," *Trotter Institute Review* 5, no. 3. (1991): 11-17, https://scholarworks.umb.edu/cgi/viewcontent.cgi?article=1219&context=trotter_review

Rhode Island Federation of Teachers and Healthcare Professionals, https://www.rifthp.org

Robinson III, Charles M, *The Diaries of John Gregory Bourke, vol. 1 November 20, 1872-July 28, 1876,* ed. by Charles M. Robinson III, Denton, TX, University of North Texas Press, 2003, Print.

Rogers, Taylor Nicole, What George Soros' Life Is Really Like: How The Former Hedge-fund Manager Built His $8.3 Billion Fortune, Purchased A Sprawling Network of New York Homes, and Became the Topic of International Conspiracy Theories, BusinessInsider.com, June 28, 2019, https://www.businessinsider.com/george-soros-net-worth-wife-sons-news-house-career-2019-6

Rosenberg, Bruce A., *Custer and the Epic of Defeat*, University Park, PA, Pennsylvania State University Press, 2010, Print.

Rosenberg, Leonard B., "The "Failure" of the Socialist Party of America," *The Review of Politics* 31, no. 3 (1969): 329-352.

Ross, Jack, *The Socialist Party of America-A Complete History*, Lincoln, University of Nebraska Press, 2015, Print.

Rothman, Lily, What We Still Get Wrong About What Happened in Detroit in 1967, Time Magazine Online, August 3, 2017, https://time.com/4879062/detroit-1967-real-history/

S

Salem Media Group, https://salemmedia.com/salem-radio-network/

Sanchez, Julian, We Need Independent Review of Government Spying on Reporters, Cato Institute, May 24, 2013, https://www.cato.org/blog/we-need-independent-review-government-spying-reporters

Sandefur, Gary D./Martin, Molly/Eggerling-Boeck, Jennifer/Mannon, Susan. E./ Meier, Ann M., "An Overview of Racial and Ethnic Demographic Trends, "IN" eds. Smelser, Neil J./Wilson, William Julius/Mitchell, Faith, *America Becoming: Racial Trends and Their Consequences, Vol.* I, Washington D.C., National Academy Press, p, 40-103, Ebook.

Sandilands, Roger J., Guilt by Association? Lauchlin Currie's Alleged Involvement with Washington Economists in Soviet Espionage, *History of Political Economy* 32, no. 3 (2000): 473-515.

Schmidt, Michael S., Comey Memo Says Trump Asked Him to End Flynn Investigation, They New York Times, May 16, 2017, https://www.nytimes.com/2017/05/16/us/politics/james-comey-trump-flynn-russia-investigation.html.

Schneider, Michael, The Development of State Work Creation Policy in Germany, 1930-1933, "IN" Stachura, Peter D. *Unemployment and the Great Depression in Weimar Germany*, London, Palgrave Macmillan, 1986.

Scutti, Susan, Big Pharma Spends Record Millions on Lobbying Amid Pressure to Lower Drug Prices, CNN, 24 January, 2019, https://www.cnn.com/2019/01/23/health/phrma-lobbying-costs-bn

SEIU 1199 United Healthcare Workers East, https://www.1199seiu.org/about

Sellers, Robert, *Hellraisers: The Life and Inebriated Times of Richard Burton, Richard Harris, Peter O'Toole, and Oliver Reed*, New York, St. Martin's Publishing Group, 2011, Print.

Senate RPC, Obama's War on Coal, May 15, 2012 https://www.rpc.senate.gov/policy-papers/obamas-war-on-coal

Service Employees International Union, https://www.seiu.org/about

Shapiro, Ilya, Why Obama Keeps Losing at The Supreme Court, Cato Institute, June 7, 2013, https://www.cato.org/commentary/why-obama-keeps-losing-supreme-court

Shideler, James H., "The La Follette Progressive Party Campaign of 1924," *The Wisconsin Magazine of History* 33, no. 4 (1950): 444-457.

Shlaes, Amity, *Great Society: A New History*, New York, NY, Harper Collins Publishers, 2019, Print.

Shlaes, Amity, *The Forgotten Man: A New History of the Great Depression*, New York: Harper Collins Publishers, 2007, Print.

Silverman, Dan P., "Fantasy and Reality in Nazi Work-Creation Programs, 1933-1936," *The Journal of Modern History* 65, no. 1 (1993): 113-151.

Singman, Brooke, Flynn-Kislyak call transcripts released, revealing fateful talks over Russia sanctions, Fox News, May 29, 2020, https://www.foxnews.com/politics/flynn-kislyak-transcripts-after-dni-declassification.

Smart Asset, New York Income Tax Calculator, https://smartasset.com/taxes/new-york-tax-calculator#BS5uBZuEg0

Smith, Lee, *The Plot Against the President: The True Story of How Congressman Devin Nunes Uncovered the Biggest Political Scandal in U.S. History*, Hachette Book Group, New York, NY, First Edition: October 2019, pgs. 123-128, 206, 277, Print.

Smith, Ralph R., Agencies With Most $100,000+ Federal Employees and Lowest Average Salaries, FedSmith.com, September 9, 2020, https://www.fedsmith.com/2020/09/09/agencies-with-most-100000-federal-employees-lowest-average-salaries/

Snyder, Thomas D./Hoffman, Charlene M., *Digest of Education Statistics 1990*, National Center for Education Statistics, U.S. Department of Education, 1990, https://nces.ed.gov/pubs91/91660.pdf

Snyder, Thomas D./Hoffman, Charlene M., *Digest of Education Statistics 1992*, National Center for Education Statistics, Institute of Education Sciences, U.S. Department of Education, 1992, https://nces.ed.gov/pubs92/92097.pdf

Snyder, Thomas D./Hoffman, Charlene M., *Digest of Education Statistics 1997* (NCES 98-0015), National Center for Education Statistics, Institute of Education Sciences, U.S. Department of Education, 1997, https://nces.ed.gov/pubs97/98015.pdf

Snyder, Thomas D., Tan, A.G./Hoffman, Charlene M., *Digest of Education Statistics 2005* (NCES 2006-030), National Center for Education Statistics, U.S. Department of Education, 2006, https://nces.ed.gov/pubs2006/2006030_5.pdf

Snyder, Thomas D./ Dillow, Sally A., *Digest of Education Statistics 2010* (NCES 2011-015), National Center for Education Statistics, Institute of Education Sciences, U.S. Department of Education, 2011, https://nces.ed.gov/pubs2011/2011015.pdf

Snyder, Thomas D./de Brey, C./Dillow, Sally A., *Digest of Education Statistics 2014* (NCES 2016-006), National Center for Education Statistics, Institute of Education Sciences, U.S. Department of Education, 2016, https://nces.ed.gov/pubs2016/2016006.pdf

Social Security Administration, https://www.ssa.gov/history/hfaq.html

Soskis, Benjamin, George Soros and the Demonization of Philanthropy, The Atlantic, December 5, 2017, https://www.theatlantic.com/business/archive/2017/12/soros-philanthropy/547247/

Spartacus Educational, American History-Roosevelt and the New Deal-Lauchlin Currie, https://spartacus-educational.com/USAcurrieL.htm

Stallworth, Philip/Berger, Daniel, Tax Vox: Federal Budget and Economy: The TCJA Is Increasing The Share of Households Paying No Federal Income Tax, Tax Policy Center, September 5, 2018, https://www.taxpolicycenter.org/taxvox/tcja-increasing-share-households-paying-no-federal-income-tax

Statista.com, 2016 Election Statistics & Facts, April 29, 2019, https://www.statista.com/topics/2722/2016-election/

Statista.com, Total Medicaid Enrollment From 1966 To 2019, https://www.statista.com/statistics/245347/total-medicaid-enrollment-since-1966

Steele, Christopher, Company Intelligence Report 2016/94: Russia: Secret Kremlin Meetings Attended By Trump Advisor, Carter Page In Moscow, July 19, 2016.

Steele, Christopher, Company Intelligence Report 2016/134: Russia/US Presidential Election: Further Details Of Kremlin Liaison With Trump Campaign, October 18, 2016, https://www.voltairenet.org/IMG/pdf/Christopher_Steele_Report_on_Donald_Trump.pdf

Stern, Scott W., How Powerful Is This Right-Wing Shadow Network? The New Republic, February 19, 2020, https://newrepublic.com/article/156431/how-powerful-council-national-policy-right-wing-shadow-network

Sussman Brian, How Obamacare Became Law, Brian Sussman Show Podcast, June 26, 2015, https://www.briansussman.com/politics/how-obamacare-became-law/

T

Talent.com, Income Tax Calculator New York, https://www.talent.com/tax-calculator

Tennessee Valley Authority, The, The Great Compromise, https://www.tva.com/about-tva/our-history/tva-heritage/the-great-compromise

Terbush, Jon, Why Did the Obama Administration Spy on the *Associated* Press?, The Week, January 8, 2015, https://theweek.com/articles/464430/why-did-obama-administration-spy-associated-press

Texas State Teachers Association, https://www.tsta.org/join-tsta/

The IRS'S Systematic Delay and Scrutiny of Tea Party Applications, Hearing before the Committee on Oversight and Government Reform House of Representatives, One Hundred Thirteenth Congress, First Session, July 18, 2013, Serial No. 113-51, http://www.fdsys.gove and http://www.house.gov/reform

Thorndike, Joseph J., The Power to Destroy? Child Labor and Taxation, September 3, 2009, http://www.taxhistory.org/thp/readings.nsf/ArtWeb/D4E9F3A2CF4B1F4D8525762D003B4D65?OpenDocument

Timperlake, Edward/Triplett II, William, C., *Year of the Rat: How Bill Clinton and Al Gore Compromised U.S. Security for Chinese Cash*, Washington, D.C., Regnery Publishing, 1998, Print.

Tony Awards, Winners, https://www.tonyawards.com/winners/

Tribune Publishing, "IN" Wikipedia, n.d., https://en.wikipedia.org/wiki/Tribune_Publishing

U

UnionFacts.com, 1199 SEIU United Healthcare Workers East, Political Action Committee, Donations by Party, https://www.unionfacts.com/pac/1199_SEIU_United_Healthcare_Workers_East

UnionFacts.com, American Postal Workers, Political Spending, Federal Election Donations, By Party, https://www.unionfacts.com/union/American_Postal_Workers#political-tab

UnionFacts.com, California Teachers Association, Political Action Committee, Donations by Party, https://www.unionfacts.com/pac/California_Teachers_Assn

UnionFacts.com, National Association of Letter Carriers, Political Spending, Federal Election Donations, By Party, https://www.unionfacts.com/union/National_Association_of_Letter_Carriers#political-tab

UnionFacts.com, National Education Association, Political Spending, Federal Election Donations, By Party, https://www.unionfacts.com/union/National_Education_Association#political-tab

UnionFacts.com, National Postal Mail Handlers Union, Political Action Committee, Donations by Party, https://www.unionfacts.com/pac/National_Postal_Mail_Handlers_Union

UnionFacts.com, Ohio Education Association, Political Action Committee, Donations by Party, https://www.unionfacts.com/pac/Ohio_Education_Assn

United Federation of Teachers, "IN" Wikipedia, n.d., https://en.wikipedia.org/wiki/United_Federation_of_Teachers

USA.gov, A-Z Index of U.S. Government Departments and Agencies, https://www.usa.gov

USA.gov, Pay and Benefits for Federal Employees, https://www.usa.gov/benefits-for-federal-employees

U.S. Bureau of Economic Analysis, National Income and Product Accounts, Table 6.6D, https://apps.bea.gov/iTable/iTable.cfm?ReqID=19&step=4&isuri=1&1921=flatfiles&3Place=N.

U.S. Census Bureau, Medicare Enrollment - National Trends 1966-2013, https://www.census.gov/history/pdf/medicare1966-2013.pdf

U.S. Census Bureau, Statistical Abstract of the United States, 1967, https://www2.census.gov/library/publications/1967/compendia/statab/88ed/1967-02.pdf

U.S. Census Bureau, Statistical Abstract of the United States, 1992, https://www.census.gov/library/publications/1992/compendia/statab/112ed.html

U.S. Conlawpedia Weblog, Keating-Owen Act, http://sites.gsu.edu/us-constipedia/child-labor-law/

U.S. Department of Housing and Urban Development, History of Fair Housing, https://www.hud.gov/program_offices/fair_housing_equal_opp/aboutfheo/history

U.S. Department of Housing and Urban Development, HUD's Historical Timeline: 1950,

https://www.huduser.gov/portal/hudtimeline_1950.html

U.S. Department of Housing and Urban Development, Major Legislation on Housing And Urban Development Enacted Since 1932, https://www.hud.gov/sites/documents/LEGS_CHRON_JUNE2014.PDF

U.S. Department of Justice, Antitrust Laws and You,

https://www.justice.gov/atr/antitrust-laws-and-you

U.S. Department of State, 2019 Trafficking in Persons Report: United States, https://www.state.gov/reports/2019-trafficking-in-persons-report-2/united-states/

U.S. Foreign Intelligence Surveillance Court, "IN" Wikipedia, n.d., https://en.wikipedia.org/wiki/United_States_Foreign_Intelligence_Surveillance_Court

U.S. Government, U.S. Government Manual: Interstate Commerce Commission, https://www.govinfo.gov/content/pkg/GOVMAN-1995-07-01/pdf/GOVMAN-1995-07-01-Pg596.pdf

U.S. House of Representatives, Historical Highlights: President Woodrow Wilson Addresses a Joint Session to Avert a National Railroad Strike, August 29, 1916, https://history.house.gov/Historical-Highlights/1901-1950/President-Woodrow-Wilson-s-Joint-Session-message-appealing-for-the-avoidance-of-a-national-railroad-strike/

U.S. Office of Personnel Management, Healthcare & Insurance, https://www.opm.gov/healthcare-insurance/healthcare/eligibility/

U.S. Office of Personnel Management, Policy, Data, Oversight: Pay & Leave, https://www.opm.gov/policy-data-oversight/pay-leave/pay-administration/fact-sheets/federal-employee-compensation-package/

United States Senate, Direct Election of Senators, https://www.senate.gov/artandhistory/history/common/briefing/Direct_Election_Senators.htm

United States Senate, Landmark Legislation: The Civil Rights Act of 1964, https://www.senate.gov/artandhistory/history/common/generic/CivilRightsAct1964.htm

V

Van Pelt, Lori, Eisenhower's 1919 Road Trip and the Interstate Highway System, January 4, 2018, https://www.wyohistory.org/encyclopedia/eisenhowers-1919-road-trip-and-interstate-highway-system

Vance, W. Grant/ Eiden, Leo J., Digest of Education Statistics 1980, National Center for Education Statistics, Institute of Education Sciences, U.S. Department of Education, 1980, https://babel.hathitrust.org/cgi/pt?id=uc1.31210008874784&view=1up&seq=9

Vanguard, Max, *Hillary Clinton: Truth and Lies*, Orlando, 2016, Print.

Vaughn, Jesse Wendell, *With Crook at the Rosebud*, Lincoln, Nebraska, University of Nebraska Press, 1987, Print.

Vincent, Carol Hardy/Bermejo, Lucas F./Hanson, Laura A., Federal Land Ownership: Overview and Data, February 21, 2020, https://fas.org/sgp/crs/misc/R42346.pdf

W

Wagner, Erich, Trump Finalizes Pay Raise for Feds in 2020, Government Executive, December 26, 2019, https://www.govexec.com/pay-benefits/2019/12/trump-finalizes-pay-raise-feds-2020/162114/

Wang, Tabitha, Detroit Race Riot (1967), Black Past, July 3, 2008, https://www.blackpast.org/african-american-history/detroit-race-riot-1967/

Warren, Frank A., *An Alternative Vision: The Socialist Party in the 1930s*, Bloomington, Indiana University Press, 1974, Print.

Watson, Thomas Edward, *The Story of France from the Earliest Times to the Consulate of Napoleon Bonaparte, Vol. II,* London, The Macmillan Company, 1902, Print.

Weisman, Johnathan, I.R.S. Chief Out After Protest Over Scrutiny of Groups, The New York Times, May 15, 2013, https://www.nytimes.com/2013/05/16/us/irs-says-counsel-didnt-tell-treasury-of-tea-party-scrutiny.html

Wemple, Erik, AP: Government Subpoenaed Journalists' Phone Records, The Washington Post, May 13, 2013, https://www.washingtonpost.com/blogs/erik-wemple/wp/2013/05/13/ap-government-subpoenaed-journalists-phone-records/

Westwood One, "IN" Wikipedia, n.d., https://en.wikipedia.org/wiki/Westwood_One

Whose Downtown? Wordpress blog, Urban Renewal: The Story of Southwest D.C., https://whosedowntown.wordpress.com/urban-renewal-the-story-of-southwest-d-c/#_ftn2

Wickman, John E., Ike and "The Great Truck Train"-1919, https://www.kshs.org/publicat/history/1990autumn_wickman.pdf

Winkler, Albert, "The Battle of The Rosebud," *Faculty Publications* 3229, 2014, https://scholarsarchive.byu.edu/facpub/3229

Woods, Randall B., *Prisoners of Hope: Lyndon B. Johnson, The Great Society, And The Limits of Liberalism*, New York: Basic Books, 2016, Print.

Woolner, D., Unions-Key to Prosperous Post-War Economy, https://rooseveltinstitute.org/fdrs-championing-labor-unions-key-prosperous-post-war-economy/

Wouters, Olivier J., "Lobbying Expenditures and Campaign Contributions by the Pharmaceutical and Health Product Industry in the United States, 1999-

2018," *JAMA Inter Med.* 180, no. 5 (2020): 1-10, https://www.ncbi.nlm.nih.gov/pmc/articles/PMC7054854/

Y

Yale Law Journal, The, "Management of Public Land Resources," *The Yale Law Journal* 60, no. 3 (1951): pp. 455–482.

Yelvington, Brenda, Excise Taxes in Historical Perspective, "IN" ed. Shughart II, William F., *Taxing Choice: The Predatory Politics of Fiscal Discrimination,* New Brunswick: Transaction Publishers, 1997.

Z

Zeitz, Joshua, *Building The Great Society: Inside Lyndon Johnson's White House*, New York, Penguin Books, 2019, Print.

Zubik v. Burwell, "IN" Wikipedia.org, n.d. https://en.Wikipedia.org/wiki/Zubik_v._Burwell

Praise for But by the Chance of War

"A monumental work...Staggering and impressive unlike anything of its kind in both scope and artistic achievement"

—*Literary Inklings*

"A profound examination of the phenomenon of war."

—*Clarion Book Review*

"Overall it's a work of great scholarship... A sometimes brilliant and often moving poetic explanation of humanity's warlike ways."

—*Kirkus Reviews*

"An Epic of this magnitude deserves a series of book club discussions, or an entire course for Poetics, Classical Literature, History or Philosophy, it deserves that kind of time, attention and scholarship."

—*U.S. Review of Books*

"But By The Chance of War is well worth considering for fans of quality poetry–highly recommended...Military and general lending libraries alike will find this a fine read."

—*Midwest Book Review*

Forward Magazine
"BOOK OF THE YEAR"
AWARD WINNER
War and Military Category

Nautilus Book Awards
"BETTER BOOKS
FOR A BETTER WORLD"
Award Winner, Poetry Category